IT'S A FUNNY LIFE

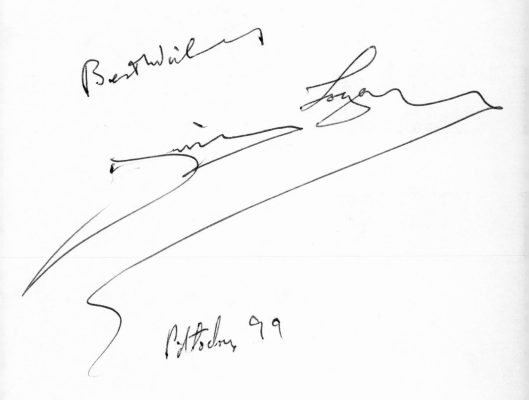

Jimmy
LOGAN

WITH BILLY ADAMS

It's a
FUNNY
LIFE

bw

First published 1998
by B&W Publishing Ltd, Edinburgh
ISBN 1 873631 87 1
Copyright © Jimmy Logan 1998
Introduction copyright © Billy Connolly 1998

British Library Cataloguing in Publication Data:
A catalogue record for this book is available
from the British Library.

Cover photographs courtesy of Erik Russell

Photo sections: pictures courtesy of BBC Scotland,
The Herald Picture Archive, Charles Green, Sean Hudson,
Renzo Mazzolini, Eric Thorburn, Douglas Robertson

Printed by Werner Söderström

CONTENTS

INTRODUCTION

I have always thought that I owed Jimmy Logan a very special thanks—the kind of thanks that people usually reserve for their fathers, for educating them or in some other way guiding the course of their lives in the direction of mellow fruitfulness. It was while watching Jimmy in the Alhambra Theatre in Glasgow when I was around twelve or thirteen years of age that I decided that, without doubt, a comedian was what I wanted to be. I have been brought up, like lots of people of my generation, listening to BBC Radio and early television. We were fed a diet of comedians who, while brilliant at their craft, were somewhat foreign to me. Jimmy Wheeler, Arthur Askey, Ted Ray, Billy Cotton, Max Bygraves; they were all very funny in their own right but tended to talk about things I knew little or nothing about. Being centred in the south or north of England, most of their references left me bewildered. There were amazing exceptions of course, like Max Wall in England and Chic Murray in Scotland, whose references were so abstract that everyone could identify with them.

On the fateful night at the Alhambra, among other hysterically funny things, Jimmy came on dressed as a Glasgow coalman, trousers tied nicky-tan style below the knee, with big leather back protector over his shoulders and sang in *my accent*—yes, *my Glasgow accent!*—a parody of Adam Faith's 'What Do You Want'. It was all about a coalman cheating housewives by including dross and slate in their bags of highly prized coal! The place was in uproar and somewhere in the darker recesses of my mind there came a sort of 'Eureka'! It was as dramatic as that.

Jimmy has of course achieved so much more than the average comedian. He has sung beautiful songs—my favourite is 'White Wings' about the pleasures of yachting on the Clyde. He has appeared in many films including several Carry-Ons. He has been an impresario and theatre owner to name but few. A legend in his own lifetime, the product of a legendary showbusiness family to whom must go the credit of keeping variety theatre alive for so much longer than anywhere else in the world, Jimmy has a talent that just seems to go on growing. The last time I saw him live was last year at the Pavilion Theatre in Glasgow where my dear friend, the late Danny Kyle, and I witnessed Jimmy in a hysterically funny impression of Madonna! At his age, he should know better, but to our benefit for years to come, I hope he never will.

With love and deepest respect,

Billy Connolly

DEDICATION

This story is my gift to the memory of my mother and father and to every 'pro' who ever walked on a stage. To Annie, Heather, Nick, Domenick, Leigh and all the family including many dear friends and relatives not mentioned but never forgotten. To all the theatres I have fallen in love with, and above all to my wife Angela for her understanding and loving heart and for giving life meaning. With it is a special love that will never end to R.J.L.S. and A.W.L.S.

1

NEW YORK, NEW YORK

I'm sitting in the back seat of a New York taxi. It's midnight and we're speeding past the skyscrapers of New York City. In the distance I can hear a police siren wailing—a picture you've all seen on television a million times.

On one side of me is Tony Bennett, and on the other, Liza Minnelli. And I'm thinking: "It's a funny life."

Three days ago I was in pantomime as Dame Lizzie Trotter, a traditional pantomime dame in *Jack and the Beanstalk* at the Eden Court Theatre in Inverness, Scotland, and now I'm driving through the most exciting city in the world flanked by two of the biggest stars in the world—another world.

It's all my sister's fault. Known as Annie Ross, she is one of the great international singers on both sides of the Atlantic, and great pals with Liza Minnelli. In fact, when I'm in America and say she is my sister, the jazz musicians don't believe me.

"Man, Annie Ross, your sister?" they say.

They don't get the Scottish connection.

Annie had opened that night at The Algonquin Hotel in cabaret. In the audience were Tony Bennett, Liza Minnelli, Carol Channing, Cy Coleman and a host of other stars.

It was a packed room but Annie had no idea I was there.

She received a standing ovation, and deserved it, and when she saw me, stopped the applause and said: "Ladies and gentleman, my brother's here from Scotland."

She threw her arms around me. And that made the 3,500 miles worthwhile.

The next minute Liza Minnelli says: "Let's go back to my apartment."

And so now we're on our way to Liza's penthouse apartment in Manhattan, the kind of place perched high up on the 50th floor, or is it the 60th, that Americans would call a very expensive piece of real estate.

Through a wonderful entrance we enter an enormous hallway painted all in white. I see a painting of Liza's mother Judy Garland. There's even an Oscar on a shelf.

In the centre of the main room stands a piano, and there are full length windows that provide a gateway to a stunning skyline. New York, when lit in the evening, is a wonderful scene, like looking down on the stars or a glittering carpet of diamonds.

Suddenly Cy Coleman is playing piano, Tony Bennett is singing, Liza Minnelli sings, Annie Ross sings, Cy Coleman sings—a million dollars worth of talent. And I can't believe I'm here.

Out of the blue, Annie says: "Come on, Jimmy, give us a song."

Tony is saying: "Yeah, come on, Jimmy." Liza is agreeing, everyone is joining in, Annie sits me at the piano and everything goes quiet.

At this point I'm in a panic. I can't even remember the words of 'God Save The Queen'.

What about 'Donald Where's Yer Troosers'? No, perhaps not the right choice for this occasion. Or 'These Are My Mountains'? On second thoughts, maybe not.

I'm a bag of nerves. I tickle the ivories and start singing the only song I can think of.

"The loveliness of Paris was somehow sadly gay . . ."

I am only singing the verse of Tony Bennett's international hit 'I Left My Heart in San Francisco', and the man himself is standing not three feet away. I can't look at Tony's face and although Annie is still smiling her eyes are saying: "I hope you know what you're doing."

I have no choice but to keep going until the end of the verse.

> "I'm going home to my city by the bay
> Cos . . .
> I belong to Glasgow, dear old Glasgow town,
> There's something the matter with Glasgow
> For it's going round and round."

Suddenly Tony starts laughing. They all join in the song, and I breathe a sigh of relief.

What a night that was. And I'm so glad I was there because I almost never made it.

When Annie invited me over for her opening cabaret at The Algonquin I said no.

"Don't be daft," I told her. "I'm on stage in pantomime in Inverness."

But, I was wrong. My run finished on the Saturday, and she opened the following Tuesday. I got on the next flight, and joined up with my brother Bert who lived in the States.

In Liza's apartment later that evening we sat round that piano singing for hours, and about four o'clock in the morning the only ones left were Liza, our friend Donny Spicehandler and his wife Louise, and my family—myself, Annie and Bertie.

Liza talked of the times she sang with Judy Garland the way we

3

had that night in her apartment. She lived alone in that big apartment with the only memories of her mother provided by the pictures on the walls, and as we left I felt she was sad after sharing time with a Scottish family who were obviously so close. In some ways I felt sorry for her—not as an artiste or entertainer because there is no doubt she is one of the unique entertainers—but as a woman whom I felt was missing out on something vital at that point in her life; a close family.

She and Annie were great friends yet I could see the difference between their two temperaments. In Annie I saw someone whose life was now built on a concrete base, not shifting sands; her strong character born out of the everlasting support of a loving and warm family—my loving and warm family who, through often traumatic life experiences, helped form the content character that exists within both of us today.

The question I'm always asked is: "Jimmy, how did you get into showbusiness?"

And the answer is simple. My father and mother were in showbusiness, along with all my aunts, uncles and cousins too. I remember as a child our house was always filled with music and the sound of somebody singing. If dad got an idea for a song he picked up his accordian. As one neighbour reminded me: "We knew you were home when we heard your dad on the accordian at three o'clock in the morning."

Mum went out once to buy a three piece suite for the house, and came back with a set of drums for the kids. We were that kind of family.

My mother's sister Ella Logan was a star of Hollywood films and Broadway. There is one cousin who is a minister but we don't mention that. However, a fine minister he is, and although he's on a different stage, he's a star in his own right.

Some celebrities complain about not being able to go anywhere without people talking to them or asking for an autograph. Not me. After a lifetime of entertaining, people will always smile or say hello when I walk down the street, and I regard it as a great privilege to have touched so many lives.

It's wonderful to hear someone say: "You're not . . . are you?"

And I say: "Well, I was this morning."

To be honest, it would have been a travesty if I had ended up in any other line of work. My family were so entrenched in showbusiness that people said I was born in the theatre trunk. I started young too. At the age of five I would stand in front of a mirror, and say: "Ladies and Gentlemen, I give you the one and only Jim Short."

Looking back, among other things I've been married four times, and I suppose I've made a habit of falling in love with beautiful ladies. Recently, at a friend's wedding, the place fell about when I said: "It's lovely to be at a wedding that's not mine."

I wasn't joking.

Every time I hear the music 'Here Comes The Bride' I think I'm late for my cue.

But I do admit to a lifelong love affair with one beautiful lady, and that beautiful lady is the theatre, any theatre. I've never known a theatre I haven't fallen in love with. Whether it was the old Metropole in Glasgow whose audience was the finest I've known, or the *crème de la crème* of the London Palladium, the Albert Hall, or the Carnegie Hall in New York, all these magnificent auditoriums hold a special magic for me.

Very recently, in one of the BBC's 75th anniversary promotional trailers, Billy Connolly paid a great compliment by describing me as the inspiration behind his decision to become a comedian. He first heard my voice on the Fifties radio series *It's All Yours* with Stanley Baxter, then saw me on stage in *Five Past Eight* at The Alhambra Theatre in Glasgow, and was struck by how I made people laugh using a strong Glesca accent. In those days you

5

rarely heard anything other than the proper, clipped prose of the BBC in London, so someone on the radio who spoke the same way he did, and being funny at the same time, was a real novelty.

When you look at how brilliantly big the Big Yin has become, it's nice to think I might have played my own small part in his success. Most of the youngsters watching those BBC trailers would have said "Jimmy who?", but Billy was recognising how every entertainer involved in this great business of ours has written their own golden page in its history. Just as Billy was first struck by me, I have always been in awe of the immense talent of Sir Harry Lauder—in my opinion Scotland's finest ambassador, and a true megastar.

My father felt the same way, imitating this great entertainer and singing his songs when he was a boy in the Dennistoun Minstrels troupe who kept the working classes in that area entertained long before the arrival of radio or television.

He and I were very close; so close, in fact, that he once tried to sue me just to keep us together. I had signed my first contract with the big theatre owners Howard & Wyndham, and cleared it with my father, whom I had worked with for many years, just to make sure there would be no trouble. The next thing I knew a reporter from the *Daily Express* was on the phone explaining how my father was going to take me to court. He had said if I left the family show it would be bad for business.

So we were a close family.

Years later Eamon Andrews presented me with the Big Red Book on *This Is Your Life*. It was a great accolade, and I was so proud. But at the end of the night I found myself among all the guests—who were there to pay tribute to *me*—gathered around my father playing piano. Even in my finest moments he still managed to steal the show.

But what a man he was. Jack Short may have been my father, but he was also one of my heroes.

He was born in 1896 in Dennistoun, Glasgow, the son of James Short, a foreman in Blochairn Steelworks, but somehow the theatre and its background soon became my father's life. He joined the Dennistoun Minstrels when he was still in shorts, and at the tender age of 12 ran away to England, not quite to join the circus, but to a marionette theatre where he worked the puppets on strings—including one of Harry Lauder. When my grandfather finally tracked him down and brought him back, he said my father had stolen his suitcase. It was the only way he could get it back.

He duly ran off again, this time to Northern Ireland, where he helped the boss of the marionette theatre set up a handcranking cinema. While he was running one of the outdoor concert parties that were very popular at the time, two of his brothers who knew nothing about theatre made the sorry mistake of going on holiday to see him. The minute they got there he whipped them up on stage and told them to make up an act as they went along.

My father soon returned to Scotland to start up a repertory-style company in Falkirk and Bo'ness called The Jack Short Players. He did everything from appearing on stage to putting up bills for the show, handing out leaflets and even painting the scenery.

Then some way into the horrors of the 1914-18 War my father was called into action. A great lover of horses and the uniform, he joined the Duke of Atholl's Scottish Horse regiment at Dunkeld in 1917.

The glamour of the job was shortlived. Uniforms were in such short supply that soldiers either dressed in a civilian jacket with khaki trousers, or the other way round. The humiliation was soon complete, as the horses they loved were taken away, and replaced by bicycles.

On his first leave after getting the full uniform, my father went back to Dungannon in Ireland to see a girl he had met there during his marionette days. He thought he would impress her. And he told me: "I'll never forget it, son. I was to meet her in this leafy kind of lane and there I was in my uniform feeling very proud. Well, she came round the corner, took one look at me, turned on her heels and went back from where she had come. I realised it was because I was wearing the British army uniform. She was one of the Irish rebels and was anything but impressed."

His regiment was soon sent to France as a replacement for other Scottish regiments who were being decimated. It seemed that if a battalion of 800 men went over the top it was more or less guaranteed only 300 would come back. The other 500 were wiped out—either killed or wounded in No Man's Land. Replacements would be brought in to boost the numbers back up to 800, and again only 300 returned. Flicking through the regimental history books and diaries of soldiers years later, I noticed how this percentage of dead, wounded and missing in action never seemed to change throughout the War, a sad and shocking indictment of the futility of such a conflict.

The Germans dug trenches more than 40 feet deep, while our boys' dugouts were generally no more than a few feet below ground level. I don't know if it was the Germans' way of saying Happy New Year, but on January 1, 1918 they bombarded the Allies' trenches with heavy artillery. One of those pieces of shrapnel had my father's name on it, crashing through the roof of his shelter before embedding itself deep in his right leg. He told me the shrapnel was travelling at such a speed that the mark left on his skin was the size of the dot of a biro pen, yet the actual piece of lead stuck inside him was as big as an old half crown.

A nearby sergeant took one look at him, and said: "You've got a Blighty, Jack."

My father was taken behind the lines to a military hospital where gangrene set in, and the medical staff were forced to amputate his right leg. He was just 21.

He told me by that time the pain was so terrible he couldn't care less what they did. Each morning he heard soldiers marching out to dig the graves of those who had been killed, or big holes to bury all the amputated limbs.

It was in great pain that he was taken from the hospital to a merchant ship for his journey across the English Channel. Wooden levels had been built into the holds to accommodate the vast numbers of wounded men, and my father and hundreds of his fallen comrades were packed in like sardines.

As if that wasn't bad enough, the ships were often held up for days waiting for the Channel to be pronounced clear of German submarines. Those endless hours must have been terrible for the injured men—plenty of time to be attacked by the psychological nightmares that reminded them of what they had been through, and the numbing fears of what the future might hold.

My father, however, managed to alleviate the pain and boredom for the men on his ship by somehow arranging for a piano to be hoisted into the hold. Being the man he was, for three days he took the boys' minds off the horrors of the situation by entertaining them with songs and jokes. To this day, I still don't know how he did it.

When he finally arrived back in Britain, he was packed into a hospital train for the grim journey up to Scotland. It plodded north, lightening the load of the wounded at every station, until, pulling away from Newcastle, the Scottish boys let out their first cheer in anticipation of the next stop—home. Unfortunately, the train ground to a halt just outside the city, and my father was carted off to an asylum that had been turned into a makeshift hospital.

Years later I met Bert Weedon, the famous guitar player.

"Jimmy," he said. "I know all about you and your dad, Jack Short."

"How?" I asked.

"My father was wounded in the foot in the First World War and he always wanted to go into showbusiness, but never did.

Anyway, he found himself in this hospital outside Newcastle and in the next bed there was a fellow called 'Jock' Short whose leg had been amputated. He thought your dad was wonderful, and whenever 'Jock' played in London in subsequent years, my dad dragged our whole family across the city to see him."

God only knows how many operations my father underwent in Newcastle. He was stuck there for months, and by the time he was transferred to Erskine Hospital near Paisley later that year, his leg had been reduced to a very painful, short stump.

There, my father was given an artificial limb. It's amazing to think that when the War broke out no firms in Britain made such a thing. The authorities, who had no conception of the sheer numbers of wounded who would return from the Front, were suddenly forced to commandeer castles, private mansions, hotels and all sorts of buildings for use as makeshift hospitals.

That's how Erskine House came into being in 1916. The big private house and the 460-acre estate were gifted by Sir John Reid, and when the Lord Provost announced plans for a servicemen's hospital to be built, the people of Glasgow, realising that boys like my father badly needed their help, dug deep into their pockets and raised a remarkable £200,000.

The hospital was run by an incredible surgeon, Sir William Macewen, who had done pioneering brain operations in the 1890s. With the help of Harold Yarrow's top craftsmen at nine Clydeside shipyards, Sir William designed the "Erskine Leg", which was made from willow wood; some of that raw material came from two trees he cut down without permission at Glasgow University—because men like my father were in desperate need.

When peace broke out in November 1918 my father went AWOL for about three days. He took his pals up to my grandmother's in Glasgow, had a riotous time, and when he returned was confined to barracks, as it were, by a furious matron.

He was 21 when he left Erskine to start his life again. Having a wooden leg would have been bad enough for the best of us, but for someone who lived and breathed the theatre it was an absolute disaster. Surely the last thing a man of his age would have contemplated was a life in showbusiness. Such obstacles, however, were hardly enough to divert Jack Short from his goal. I always found that when he got his mind fixed on something there was absolutely no way he could be persuaded otherwise. This was perhaps the most acute example of that type of thinking as he set out to establish an outdoor concert party in Helensburgh. There was no stopping him. He went straight to my grandmother's in Glasgow, waited until she went on holiday, then whipped her piano out of the house to use in his show where he described himself as *The Man The Germans Couldn't Kill*.

It was in Helensburgh that my father met my mother, May Dalziel, a beautiful woman from Glasgow who had made a name for herself as Sweet Mary Argyle, the Street Singer.

That didn't mean she sang in the street, of course.

What it meant was that this fellow would go out in the Newcastle area where they were working and say: "Ladies and gentlemen, last week I was in Glasgow and after dinner I decided to take a stroll with my cigar."

He probably didn't have two pennies in his pocket.

"As I walked the streets I heard what I thought was a nightingale. But it wasn't. It was a beautiful young girl singing in the streets to support her orphaned brothers and sisters."

They were never orphaned. If my granny had heard what he was saying she would have murdered him.

However, my mother was billed as this poor orphaned street singer who had golden hair, wore a plain black dress with a tartan shawl, and whose beautiful voice made her a wonderful success.

When she was 17, she went on holiday with her family to Helensburgh, and as she cycled along the promenade my father caught sight of her for the first time.

11

"Oh, I like that," he thought.

So he called her over, and said: "Would you like to come into theatre, my dear? You could take the tickets at the box office."

My mother looked at him rather sceptically. "Oh, could I?"

She never let on she was an established artiste but he must have impressed her.

It wasn't long before my father discovered she could sing, so before she knew where she was, they were up singing together in his concert party. After just three weeks he took her to Glasgow to get married. Their parents were dead against it, but they hired a horse and carriage in Queen Street, drove up to a lawyer's office and paid him 30 shillings to arrange the wedding. Then all three of them went up to Glasgow Sheriff Court where a sheriff stopped a bigamy case to give them a special licence. It sounds strange, but apparently that's where people got married in those days. I can picture it now.

"Guilty, your honour."

"Right, two years in jail. Take him away. Next."

Into the dock step my mother and father.

"Right, do you take this woman to be your lawfully wedded wife?"

"I do . . . ahem . . . your honour."

It must have been hysterical. He was twenty-two, and she was just 17. They went straight back to Helensburgh for their wedding feast—a fish tea with the rest of the company on the front. And they did the show that night. Then they had to go home to my Granny Allan to face the music.

In those days, theatres were an integral part of working-class culture. At one time in Glasgow artistes boasted how they could work every day for a year, and travel to each date by tram. Some halls they played in, which varied greatly in size, were nicknamed "busts". When people arrived they would be given a paper bag with biscuits and perhaps an orange inside. If they didn't like the artiste, they would blow up their paper bag and bang it. The show had gone "bust".

That noise in the middle of a performance let you know you were a disaster.

All over the country there were also lots of bandstands that often had little bits added on to become summer variety theatres— the venue for an outdoor concert party. Rothesay's bandstand, for instance, eventually grew into the Winter Gardens.

People, of course, couldn't go to places like Spain or Greece for their holidays, so they went to Portobello or Millport instead. It was normal for seven packed trains a day to be steaming into Portobello for a trip to the coast, and on the Clyde thousands of people went Doon the Watter to gems of towns like Gourock, Dunoon, Helensburgh, Largs and Millport.

A typical family would rent a house in one of these places for the summer season and pack it with mum and the kids. Dad, on the other hand, would stay back in Glasgow working until Friday night when he would catch the steamer from the Broomielaw. And he would join them for the weekend before heading back up the Clyde on the Monday morning to be back in Glasgow in time for his work.

The concert parties would perform on tiny stages with a paraffin light making a "fizz" sound. At the back there were maybe two wee rooms where the artistes would get changed. But those concert parties were always packed because the entertainment was so good. Some artistes used to "bottle" the crowd, holding a long pole with a wooden box at the end under their noses until enough money was coughed up. Others put a fence all the way round and charged a nominal entrance fee, maybe 3d.

I cut my teeth in summer concert parties, and so did a great many of our great stars, including the wonderful comedian Dave Willis, who made his name at Portobello. On one occasion a bizarre letter arrived at the council offices on the Isle of Bute from two artistes who wanted to run a concert party. The elaborate headed notepaper announced that Madame Clarette and Señor Alfonso had performed before such notables as the Grand Prince and Princess of Liechtenstein, and the Duke and Duchess of Bavaria. Having entertained the Crown heads of Europe, they now wanted to run a concert party at Port Bannatyne. Of course anyone who knows Bute will know Port Bannatyne in those days was just a small collection of houses.

Another lovely guy, Jack Allison, who for years ran a concert party in Kinghorn, Fife, previously toured with his brother in England with Fred Karno's comedy troupe. When Jack returned to Kinghorn one of the other comics said to Fred: "My brother's very good. You should give him a chance."

The brother was Charlie Chaplin.

At Helensburgh, my mother, with her great looks and beautiful voice, became the star of the show. In those days open air concert parties were immensely popular but money was always tight. My father's concert party often ended the week in the red. No matter how hard he worked, money would only be made if absolutely everything went according to plan, and nothing ever went exactly to plan. In our business when it is very good you make a little money, but when it is bad, you lose a fortune. It's full of peaks and troughs, and unfortunately the troughs somehow always outweigh the peaks. One day everything is marvellous, the next it all disappears and suddenly you have no idea where you are. That's just the nature of the business.

And so it was with my parents when they went touring around Britain.

By that time my older brothers Buddy and Bertie were on the scene, and my father was supporting the family, and his theatre losses, with a Government pension of something like 28 shillings a week. On one occasion when they were performing in Newcastle, business was so bad that one of the cast had to pawn his watch to find the money to take the company to the next town.

At that point our wonderful Government repaid the loyalty of men like my father who had fought for their country in the 1914-18 War—by telling them they were costing the country too much. Each man's pension was cut by five shillings, then the Government proudly offered a £1,000 lump sum to those who were willing to give up their pensions.

At first glance the offer seemed wonderful because that kind of money was a fortune. Many men cashed in their pension only to pour their £1,000 down the drain on things like drink. Quickly their money ran out, along with the chance of a new artificial limb or medical help in the future. As the years went by their wounds would need attention, and their artificial limbs renewed, but they would get no more help.

My father wanted to take the money too, but Granny Short wouldn't let him. Armed with an older, wiser head, she laid down the law and took the whole family into her home until my father and mother got back on their own financial feet.

They still did shows, but my father would do anything to make money. Once he and my mother's brother, Wee Charlie, bought a car for 30 shillings, and Charlie, who was a great mechanic, did the car up and sold it for £5. A great profit, but hardly a regular one.

At one point in the 1930s he used to type letters for his pal, Johnny MacDonald, who ran the Standard Variety Agency. And all this for an extra shilling. Nowadays people think they've got it tough when the television goes on the blink.

Despite the hard times, there was never any question that my mother and father might separate. She absolutely loved him and was incredibly loyal. At one point she was offered a part in a big touring show.

"What about Jack?" she instantly asked.

"No, it's you we want, May. We're not interested in Jack."

"Well, I'm not interested either."

It was a big opportunity, but she turned it down because she and my father were a team, and that would never be up for negotiation.

Eager to find something a bit more permanent than the lottery of the tours, my father took over the running of the Roxy Cinema in Renton near Dumbarton. And with his pittance of a pension every little scam seemed acceptable.

For instance, there used to be an entertainment tax where artistes were obliged to buy stamps to stick on every ticket they sold. The taxman would come round and check the boxes, and if the butts of sold tickets weren't stamped it could have ended up costing a fortune. Entertainers like my father couldn't afford to buy the tickets in the first place so he used to keep two boxes—one with and one without the stamps. A guy down at the railway station used to run like hell up the road when one of the taxmen stepped off the train, giving my father time to switch the boxes. When the amount of money left at the end of the week was the difference between paying and not paying people, no-one questioned such an entrepreneurial practice.

At the cinema my father took a firm decision to only employ ex-servicemen. He was the manager with one leg; the man who showed the films was deaf and dumb; the chap who took the tickets up the stairs had one arm; the pianist was blind. It was that kind of place.

The pianist was helped by a wee lad, the reel boy, who would sit beside him during the silent movies and tell him the scene—a wedding, funeral or chase perhaps—so he could play the appropriate music. Well, a few years ago I met a silver-haired man who was once the reel boy at The Roxy.

"I used to sit beside the pianist," he said, "and through sheer devilment, if a funeral was on screen I would shout: 'It's a wedding', or if it was a wedding I would tell him: 'It's a chase'. The audience didn't know what was going on. They thought the pianist was rubbish."

Occasionally the film would break down and my father would get the screen rolled up, sit down at a piano behind it, and play away until the film was fixed. Just like before he went to the War, he still did everything when he came back. He might only have had one leg, but he was all over the place putting up the bills. He loved everything to do with the theatre, and that most definitely rubbed off on just about all of his family.

I was the middle child in a series of five; two older brothers and two younger sisters.

Buddy, real name John Short, came first in 1921. He was the good-looking one with a great voice. When he was old enough he toured with my parents; they were known as May, Jack and Buddy. Essentially, he was great at everything he did. So we hated him for a start.

Bertie—Herbert Lawton Short—followed three years later. He was named after our Uncle Bert, but struggled because he was always being compared with his older brother.

"You're not as good as Buddy," was a comment aimed in his direction all too often. He wore glasses, wasn't as good-looking and couldn't sing as well as Buddy, and looking back I always felt he was unfairly treated.

You could say Bertie was the rebel in the family. The burden of trying to match up to his older brother ultimately made him liable to get everything wrong. Bertie was the kind of boy who would fall off a ladder onto a crate of eggs when you couldn't get eggs. He once got a job in a greengrocer's shop which was going fine until he washed the scales with some terrible stuff that left the outside covering completely ruined. That was the end of that.

Then he became what was known as a Castlebank Boy—one of the lads who came and collected your laundry and dry-cleaning on his bicycle, then brought it back again. Now that was service, or it was except when Bertie was doing it. You see, Bertie was a real chat-up merchant who got marvellous orders, but those marvellous orders always seemed to get mixed up and no-one ever got the stuff back that they sent away.

When he was about 16, during the Second World War, he ran away from home for a life at sea as a cabin boy. He returned and announced: "I'm determined to be a wireless officer."

He took up morse code, became very talented at it and achieved his ambition. It was the first job where he had achieved success, rising in rank to become a chief radio officer at a time during the War when hundreds of ships were being sunk in the Atlantic.

Bert took me aboard his first ship, an ageing Greek tanker loaded with depth charges and smelling of old cooking oil. I was aghast but Bert thought it was beautiful.

A couple of years later the Navy decided they had too many wireless officers and started to throw them out. They discovered Bertie was colour-blind, and that was that.

When he returned he bought The Modern Cafe, a fish 'n' chip shop in Port Glasgow that had been owned by some lovely old Italians. A sad story lay behind it, as all the Italians in Scotland were shipped off to places like the Isle of Man, where there was a massive prison during the War. Others were put on the *Arandora Star* and sent to Canada, but the ship was torpedoed and all those lovely Scottish Italians died in the Atlantic.

Bertie used to pretend he was an Italian. The customers would come in and say: "Aye, we're fighting you lot", and he would reply: "Hey, whaddya talkin aboot?"

He always fought like hell with my dad. One night they had fallen out, and Bertie took his ice-cream van along to a Logan Family performance at the Paisley Theatre.

He was parked outside the main door, shouting: "Buy your ice-creams from one of the Logan family."

And my father stood at the stage door screaming back: "Get that out of there. You've got no permission to be there. Go on, get out of here."

What a loving, warm family we were.

I was born in 1928, the same year as Mickey Mouse, and in 1930 was followed by Annabelle Macauly McDougal Allan Short, undoubtedly the most creative member of our family. Last, but most certainly not least, came Heather Allan Short in 1933, another talented sister.

In today's world, Annie's early life circumstances seem bizarre and complicated, because, when Annie was four, she went to live in America with her aunt, my mother's sister Ella Logan. Ella had begun as Ina Allan but changed her name as a young performer to Daisy Mars. When that didn't work, she called herself Ella Logan. And that is where the name Logan first came into our family. Some people say she chose it after sticking a pin in a newspaper race sheet and coming up with a horse called 'Triumphant Logan' but I honestly don't know.

She was, however, truly amazing.

At the age of 16 she took part in the open air concert party at Portobello with a very young and raw Dave Willis. Within a year she was starring in a musical, *Darling I Love You*, at the Empire Theatre in Edinburgh—and telling everyone she was American. None of it was true, of course, but it didn't matter because they believed her.

She was discovered by Jack Hylton and sang with his famous orchestra in London. She went on to score big successes in the capital before becoming a film star in Holland, of all places. Then she crossed the pond to become one of the biggest stars of her time in American theatre and films; the original leading lady in the Broadway musical *Finian's Rainbow*.

When Annie was four, she went to America with my mother

and father. It's difficult to explain this but I think in Hollywood at that time it was trendy to have a child. Ella Logan had suddenly discovered all the big stars had children, and therefore wanted to be a mother too.

Annie was just wonderful. She could be on a bill with tap dancers and by the end of the week she would know all their steps. In America the talent spotters who were looking for a new Shirley Temple noticed Annie, and she was given a contract with Metro-Goldwyn-Mayer to star in the *Our Gang* children's TV series. She also appeared in *Presenting Lily Mars*, with Judy Garland as her sister.

Then World War Two intervened, and Annie was destined to stay on in America to be looked after by Ella Logan. My mother and father had come back to look after the rest of the family. My father would have looked on the situation as a once-in-a-lifetime chance for Annie to be a success. And that wasn't to be missed.

Not surprisingly, this arrangement proved to be very difficult for Annie to come to terms with. To be left at such a young age with your mother's sister was extremely confusing for a child who had been part of such a close family unit back in Scotland. And to be told, as Ella told her, that she had been abandoned made it all the more harrowing.

The first time I remember seeing Annie was years later when this 17-year-old girl with flaming red hair walked off an aircraft at Prestwick Airport. She had changed her name to the middle name of her grandmother and become Annie Ross, a talented young woman making her own way in her own life. From that moment we struck up a special relationship that has only grown stronger as the years have past.

For years I celebrated my birthday on the third of April, the day I always thought I came into the world at my parents' house in

Glasgow in 1928. Then, as a young man, I applied for a passport and looked closely at my birth certificate. It said James Allan Short, my full name, was born on April the fourth. I was shocked, and immediately sought an explanation from my mother.

"Och, that was yer dad," she said. "He only went and put down the wrong date."

From that day on I considered my birth date the fourth, but every year until she died, my mother insisted on giving me a present the previous day. I suppose she was in the best position to know who was right.

Whatever the real date, I arrived in the front room of my parents' small house at 3 Inglis Street, Dennistoun. The nature of my parents' business meant we stayed at a number of houses, with a number of people, when we were youngsters. I recall a house in Glasgow's Riddrie area, many happy experiences with my Granny and Grandad Short at their home down the road in Bluevale Street, and we spent a great deal of time in Gourock staying with my Aunt Jean and Uncle Bert, who were just like second parents. There was also a spell at a house somewhere in London when I was a very young boy, and later, during the War, we lived in a nice top floor flat in Walmer Crescent, Cessnock, then moved to nearby Ibrox Terrace.

Not surprisingly, I have recollections of a rich and happy childhood. Living with Granny Short in Bluevale Street, for instance, can only be described as a children's paradise. Just down the road was a big yard owned by an Italian family called the Morettis. They were fascinating because they kept horses in stables. Mrs Moretti would also give us a "piece" with margarine and sugar, or roast dripping and salt. I would usually eat them while wearing a hat, any hat. I loved hats, and was always walking around with some form of headgear perched on top. It could have been a top hat or a bunnet. I thought they were all great.

Granny Short's house had a kitchen with a "hole in the wa" bed, and a little scullery and bathroom. Most vividly, though, I remember the blinds in her front room were always drawn, and everything polished. I think that room was only used on special occasions. In fact, the whole house had an air of polish, so much so that when I smell polish these days I instinctively think of Granny Short's house.

Granny Short was an amazing woman who was Sarah Crawford when she met my grandfather Jimmy Short, whom I was named after. They both had steel in their veins. My granny had worked in a steel mill, and so had all her brothers and sisters; my grandfather was a foreman in a steel mill.

They told me with great pride how the first ever steam-driven hammer was used in a Glasgow steel mill—a revolutionary technique that was to herald the beginning of a magnificent new era in the industry. And Granny Short's brother Samuel was the privileged worker chosen to pull the lever that started it all up. In Dennistoun that day Samuel became a celebrity, and every street burst into life with flags flying from every window. The womenfolk prepared mountains of food, and set up rows of tables outside before everyone got tucked in. It was a great celebration.

Life, of course, was far from easy. In his job as the foreman, the buck really did stop at my grandfather. The steel company would say to him: "Right Jimmy, we need this job done. Give us an estimate."

"£200," said my grandfather.

"Done."

And then my grandfather booked the men he wanted for the job, and paid them out of his own pocket. It could be said there wasn't much continuity of employment. A lovely old pensioner called Bill, who years later did some work in my house, told me how he always got the sack at Christmas before being taken on again after New Year—all so his employers could avoid paying him over the festive holidays. And that kind of practice was commonplace. It only really changed when a rather enlightened Winston Churchill established the trades' week holidays, arguing that the workers had to have at least one week off in a year, otherwise they wouldn't perform as well.

One of my grandfather's brothers died building the Caledonian Canal. My grandfather went up there to bring his body back, but wasn't allowed to move it because it was a Sunday.

My great grandfather, John Short, lived life on the edge. A builder by trade, his pockets were always full of tools. He would build tenements from the ground up, borrowing money to fund each floor. By the time he got to the top he was sunk, and ended up in the Debtors' Prison, a bizarre place in Duke Street full of men in top hats and tails pacing around contemplating how they had gone bust. The idea was that a period of confinement would purge the sin. If their relatives didn't bring them food, they starved.

My grandfather and Granny Short were a real pair. He used to drive her mad by singing a song 'Sarah With The Crocodile Teeth'. But she was a wonderful, wonderful character. When we went up to see her I would always get a bun or a biscuit, and I always went up there for my "Saturday penny". Mind you, she was a woman who, when things went wrong, had a backbone that was made of and stamped: Stainless Steel.

On their 65th wedding anniversary my mother and father said to me: "Right Jimmy, we're going away. There's a cheque. Have a party in Buddy's house for your grandparents and make sure it goes well."

But before we could do anything my grandfather went out and booked a hall at Bridgeton Cross. We all gave cheques, enough to pay for everything, and everyone in the family—aunts, uncles, cousins and even the minister—turned up for the celebrations.

I was in charge of the proceedings, and had to put up with an inquisitive auntie who nose aye bothered her, but it was a truly wonderful evening. My grandfather was dressed in a dinner suit, with big black boots, a flower on his lapel and a checked bunnet on top of his snow-white hair. That's how he went to these things, and he looked a picture. He also made a great speech.

"There's only one time when this woman has worn the troosers," he told us, and Granny Short was saying: "Och, would somebody stop that man."

"It was for a guy," he went on, describing the night Granny Short donned a pair of trousers to go out collecting for Guy Fawkes Night.

"Och don't let him start that," she shouted.

Towards the end of the night, the hallkeeper came round looking for his £35 for the hire of the hall.

"Grandad, I need £35 for the hall," I said.

It was easy to tell he had a good dram inside him because his cheeks were rosy red. Pulling out a pile of money from one of his pockets that would have choked a horse, he looked up at me, took a £5 note off, and said: "Here, take that. That's all he's gettin'. Ah'll talk tae you about this tomorrow."

I would never have considered questioning him, and soon found myself going round all my pals trying to make up the rest of the £30. The next day I went up to my grandparents' house, and, as soon as I arrived, he sent Granny Short out the room.

"This is men's business," he said, before handing over the rest of the money.

When we got back to their wee house at the end of that wonderful evening he sat down in his chair, still dressed in his suit and bunnet, with the flower now reduced to a stalk. Scratching his forehead, he suddenly asked: "Aye, whit time is it?"

"It's twelve o'clock midnight, Grandad."

"Och, that's a pity. I was going to go out and get you all fish suppers."

And I could just see him standing there in a queue in a fish supper shop with his dinner suit on, and his bunnet, and his faded flower saying: "Gie me half a dozen fish suppers."

Whenever I smell Sloan's Liniment I think of my mother's mother Granny Allan. If you went to her house in Cardonald at night, a great whiff of liniment would come flowing out when she opened the door. She would appear dressed in a white nightgown with her hair plaited and stinking of Sloan's Liniment. She used to rub herself from head to toe in the stuff every night before she went to bed. She was a lovely woman, always happy, giggling and laughing, but what a smell that was. Her husband, whom I never met, died many years before I was born. He ran the General Wolfe Pub just a couple of minutes down the road from our house in Bluevale Street.

Apparently, a few days after I was born, I made my first stage appearance when the legendary music hall star Randolph Sutton carried me on stage to my first round of applause. One of my earliest recollections comes from the short period we moved to London with my parents in the early Thirties when I was just a wee boy. We were living in a house in Aristotle Road, which I remember only because I used to act in front of the garage wall. Even at that age, if I was next to a wall I would burst into an act.

Anyway, my parents entered me for a local talent competition where I can only recall that the footlights about six inches up from the stage seemed to be about three feet high. I was scared, but still managed to win and was rewarded with a prize of a shiny two shilling bit. My father said he would keep it for me, and he did. He kept it all his life. I'm sure it was for the sentimental value.

Annie was born when we were down in London. Just a few weeks before she arrived, my father burst into the house one night and announced to my mother: "Now listen, May, we've got to leave tomorrow morning because we need to be in Aberdeen to start on Monday morning."

My mother, who was obviously heavily pregnant, was at this

25

point up on a ladder whitewashing the ceiling. The next thing my father knew the bucket of whitewash was all over him.

Despite this, they ended up going to Aberdeen and, shortly after they returned, Annie was born. She was known as The Metropolitan Baby because my parents were performing that week in the Metropolitan Theatre in Edgware Road at the time.

My mother was wonderful because she starred in the show and appeared with my father in variety, yet we were never neglected. You hear stories about kids in those days going hungry and starving, but that was never us. True, our parents were away a lot of the time touring and we stayed with wonderful people like my Aunt Jean and Uncle Bert, and a woman we knew as Big Bella Fae Bo'ness sometimes came to look after us. She ran the house when my mother wasn't there, and she ran us too. She was a figure of authority who you would never have considered arguing with. But I liked her very much. She was very strong, and probably needed all that strength to keep five kids on the straight and narrow.

Those arrangements were part and parcel of the theatre business. My parents had no choice but to go where the money was, so they could do the best for their family. My mother brought up a good family. If I committed a murder, I would never be able to say: "My granny didn't like me, my mother and father neglected me, and nobody else cared."

Nothing could have been further from the truth.

2

DEFENDING GOUROCK

I think of Bangor in Northern Ireland when I reflect on my summers as a child. It's the only memory I have of those times because every year, without fail, my parents took their show across the water and we went with them—to work.

It was never a hardship for a bunch of kids who accepted those working months as an entirely normal way of life. Just as the sons of Italian families worked in their shops selling ice-cream, or as the Pakistani and Indian boys helped out in their family stores, we were brought up within our own unique business. It was our life, we were young, and we knew nothing else. It was taken for granted that this was how things worked. At the age of seven when I became part of the show, it would never have crossed my mind to question what was happening.

In the Thirties my father, with the help of a £100 loan from Granny Short, took the company to Bangor for the summer seasons. If he returned, gave my granny her money back and still had some left over, it was considered a successful season.

We were all given jobs because—unlike home—there were no laws in Ireland prohibiting children from working in the theatre. It was the summer of 1935 when I was first put to work selling programmes, chocolates and cigarettes, while Buddy was on stage and Bertie worked the lights. Then my father roped me into some more alternative pursuits.

I remember very clearly the Flying Standard saloon car we had. One of the main reasons for such a vivid recollection was that my father would open the sunroof and stick me through it with one of those giant paper mashy heads covering my whole body. He would drive through the town announcing his show in the hope my outfit would attract people to come and see the Jack Short Entertainers.

On another occasion he got me into a kilt, put a red nose on my face, a silly hat on my head and lifted me onto the back of a donkey. Then I was off for another glorious trip through the town as a mobile advert for the show. Just in case the punters didn't know who, or what I was, my father put a big sign on my front and back proclaiming: "I'm no ass. Tonight I'm going to the Jack Short Entertainers."

The donkey hardly helped matters. Every time it came to a junction that led back to the stables, it tried to bolt down that road. We ended up having to virtually drag this stubborn ass along the road. I may have been young, but I was old enough to realise the whole thing for me was just terribly embarrassing.

Another job my father particularly liked to land on me was that of delivering bundles of leaflets to every house in the town we were in. Of course, I hated this and, instead of putting one flyer through each letterbox, I stuffed dozens through instead. I would have done anything to get rid of them.

My father's imagination knew few bounds. He used to put on special Scottish theme nights, and would serve haggis in the little ice-cream tubs. I had the job of holding the tray while someone else handed them to the punters. And if we had too many cups I could always be found during the show finishing off the spares in a quiet spot behind the stage.

It's also difficult to forget our infamous lucky programme competitions. Each night someone would win 10 shillings if their programme number was picked from a hat, but that sum could also mean the difference between profit and loss on the night.

My father had a cunning ploy to make sure this never happened. As myself and Bertie sat quietly at the front during the first house, dad shouted out the lucky number.

"And our lucky programme today is number 23," he said.

Bertie ran up through the audience to find the man with programme number 23. Amazingly, it was a pal of dad's who was over from Scotland.

"What a stroke of luck," myself and Bertie said to each other.

"There's the 10 shillings sir. Congratulations. And so let's carry on with the show."

Then came the second house.

"Programme number 41," shouted my father. "Ah, the gentleman at the back."

Once again Bertie ran up through the stalls, but seconds later he appeared from the audience with a worried look on his face. "But dad . . . dad, it's the same man who won earlier."

"Ahem," said my dad, butting in, coughing and making as much noise as possible to drown out the protesting Bertie. "That's all right. Thank you very much. Congratulations. On with the show."

And staring over at Bertie, he spoke more quietly. "I'll see you in the dressing room."

It was a rich and rewarding experience but by my fourth season, at the age of ten, I was dying to get onto the stage. My older brothers had also tapped me about the amount of money my father was paying me.

"You're a mug," said Buddy, "Working for only 1/6d a week. That's virtually slave labour. You're worth at least two shillings. You're a waster."

Those were cutting words, and they hit home. Ego duly bruised, I immediately stomped up to my father and demanded a pay rise. He refused, so I was left with no choice. I went on strike.

Of course, as soon as I did that my brothers disappeared from the scene. Suddenly there was a Mexican standoff before my father attempted a subtle form of mediation.

"Tell you what, son," he said. "I'll give you more money if you learn this song about the Lakes of Killarney and perform it on stage."

It was an ideal settlement; a chance to perform for the punters and earn more money into the bargain. It couldn't be better. My father supplied the costume to go with the part which consisted of a pair of riding breeches that were meant to go down to my knees but in reality dragged around my ankles, a top hat, tail coat and a whip. When the curtain finally went up for my first big appearance I was sitting at the side of the stage ready to go. The only thing was I didn't realise I wasn't on till the finale.

Soon, though, I got the hang of it all and the first house always went fine. The second house, however, was a different story. Nine times out of ten I missed my cue because I had long since been overcome by tiredness and fallen asleep. No-one even bothered to wake me. It must have been way past my bedtime.

I may have got my chance to go on stage, but I don't think I benefited financially from the arrangement. While my father may have handed out more money with one hand, he always found ways of getting it back with the other. During one tour round the south of Ireland I spent five shillings hiring a pony and trap in an ambitious attempt to impress a girl I fancied. I was sure it was a good idea, and was feeling confident.

The only problem was I had never driven a pony and trap in my life. Before I knew where I was, the pony had stopped in the middle of the street and was stubbornly refusing to go anywhere. Then it started to rain and the whole date turned into a complete disaster. The girl I liked bolted before the horse, and when I finally did make it home soaked to the skin my father was waiting for me.

"I'll pay for this but I'm taking it off your wages," was all he said.

Presumably he made quite a profit, because it was another six weeks before I was paid again.

We were in Bangor when the Second World War broke out in 1939. I was only 11 years old, but I remember the episode very clearly. When the Prime Minister Neville Chamberlain broadcast his sombre message on the wireless to say we were at war with Germany my mother just wept.

Our family made to sail for home immediately. One of the first things I saw was a whole group of reservists in Bangor marching up to the railway station with their rifles and kit bags. As they went on their way, all the women in the town were united in their tears, crying their hearts out, praying their men would return safely.

For me the idea of War wasn't frightening, it was exciting. When we sailed back into the Clyde I saw a trawler with a wee gun at the front. "So that's the British Navy," I thought.

Soon, my parents were off round Britain with the Entertainments National Service Association (ENSA), doing their little bit for the war effort by bringing some light relief to the troops. All the big stars like Vera Lynn and Will Fyffe were part of it.

Whatever part of the world British troops were fighting in, you could always be sure someone in ENSA wasn't too far away. One of the more unusual contributions was at Scapa Flow, where supply ships sailed out into the North Sea to rendezvous with submarines that needed to be reloaded. As those subs were being repaired, refuelled and stocked up with fresh supplies, their crews went on board the supply ship where, among other things, they would be entertained by artistes from ENSA in a little theatre that seated about 350 people. Six shows a day was normal with one crew replacing another after each show.

But can you imagine the reality of the situation? Those entertainers were performing on a ship that was effectively a sitting duck. Given all the U-boats that were in that area during the War, it is truly remarkable that the ship was never attacked.

One of the comics who risked his life every day entertaining on that ship was my great friend Billy Crocket—The Mad Musician—now 76 years young and very much a part of our "family". In 1943 he was marooned at Scapa Flow for seven months because the artistes were only allowed seven days leave. It would have been pointless going back to Glasgow because by the time he got there it would have been time to go back up to Scapa Flow again.

The entertainers on the supply ship were led by Jack Radcliffe, his feed Dave Jackley, the well known piano-playing double-act Bob and Alf Pearson, the soprano Ina Harris, six dancing girls and, of course, the one and only Billy Crocket.

And they were an inventive bunch. The supply ship was stocked with the kind of wonderful things that money couldn't buy back on the mainland, so guys like Jack Radcliffe carried someone else's accordion case which was loaded with Duty Free booze.

Thank goodness my parents didn't have to travel so far away, although we didn't go with them into ENSA because we were too young. Instead, my memories of the war years are etched in the Gourock home of Uncle Bert Lawton and his wife Aunt Jean—my mother's sister—who, as I have said, were like second parents to us. When my brother Bertie was born my mother handed him straight to Aunt Jean. We had stayed with them for a short time some years before when my parents went on a successful tour of South Africa.

I sometimes got into trouble. When I was about eight my Aunt Jean caught me smoking. She was brushing my good coat down when she heard this rattling noise. There was a matchbox in one of the pockets, and inside was a pin and a fag end. I had bought these cigarettes—SOS, three for a halfpenny—and she had found them. I got quite a row for that, quite a row. I thought I was being grown up.

By the second period we went to stay with them, of course, the circumstances had become somewhat different in a stretch of the Clyde that was being bombed to bits by the Luftwaffe.

Uncle Bert and Aunt Jean had no children of their own, but they were brilliant to us. He had been a chief petty officer in the Royal Navy in the Twenties and Thirties, posted in the Far East to what was called the China Station. He was from Portsmouth, a very smart man who often wore plus-fours. His trips to the pub at the end of the pier were a ritual, but he always had only one pint before coming back to Aunt Jean.

Bert came from a family with a proud naval tradition. His father was a naval tailor, and his brother joined up too. When he was in China he would send all his money home to Aunt Jean, and she would spend it all on her own family. He would come home on leave and find Aunt Jean without two pennies to rub together. Any other man would have murdered her for doing that, but Bert didn't care because he loved her more than anything in the world.

He would teach us to pronounce our T's and our S's and our R's, and that's why my diction has always been pretty good.

A tragic moment in his family's history centres around the Navy. His brother Jack was part of the Royal Naval Battalion that was cut off for months in the Siege of Kut during the 1914-18 War. By the time the city finally capitulated under the might of the Turkish Army, the thousands of men who had been holed up all that time with virtually no supplies were starving. The Turks may have treated the British commanding officer like a lord, but they marched his emaciated men across the desert with no concern for their needs of food and water. Those who fell by the wayside were bayoneted and left to die. Sadly, Jack was one of those. He was last seen collapsing before he was executed.

Aunt Jean was just lovely. She loved children and would do anything for us.

We all adored her, especially when she took us on picnics during the War. She made so many sacrifices that everything seemed to be for us. This, however, was the cause of worries like the Terror of Hastie's Bill, which only seemed to appear when a grocer called Hastie told Aunt Jean: "Take this hen, it will be good for the kids."

Of course if he said it was good for us, he could sell her anything. At the end of the month the invoice would come in, otherwise known as the Terror of Hastie's Bill.

One thing we wish she hadn't bought was a kind of gooey, yellow cod liver oil type emulsion. It was absolutely horrible, but every morning after a particularly good breakfast Aunt Jean would produce a tablespoon full of the stuff, make us queue up and force it down our throats before we walked out the door.

Then, as in all situations like that, she would add the immortal line: "Now that's good for you." She may well have been right, but oh dear, if something is good for you why is it always certain to taste bloody awful?

I've got a marvellous video of her 90th birthday in the big house I owned in Helensburgh. We cooked a wonderful meal, and I put her name on the salmon. She was up there singing, having a great time when I gave her a whisky and water. After a while someone said: "Would you like another drink, Aunt Jean?"

"Aye."

"What are you having?"

"Whisky—and don't put as much water in it as he did!"

She had arrived around midday, and was still going strong 10 hours later, well outlasting the rest of the contingent who had come up with her from Gourock. So much so, when they all decided to go home, Aunt Jean butted in: "Well I'm staying put. Ah'll see you all later."

About midnight there was a phone call. It was one of the folk from Gourock.

"Oh Jimmy, we're here in Gourock and we don't know how to tell you but Aunt Jean hasn't arrived back yet. There's no sign of her. We think there must have been a terrible accident."

I said: "There's no sign of her because she's still here enjoying herself."

Aunt Jean finally got home in the wee sma' hours . . . and kept the rest of them up until four o'clock in the morning.

She was some woman. One time when she was due to go in for an operation she hid her hands from the surgeon. He was speaking to her when he clapped eyes on them. "What's this, Mrs Lawton? Let me see your hands."

Grabbing her arms, he noticed Aunt Jean's hands were chalk white.

"My goodness. What is this?" he asked again.

"I've been whitewashing my ceiling, doctor," she said.

"You're in here for an operation and you've been whitewashing your ceiling?"

"Well, I was sitting back in my big chair at home looking up at the ceiling and I thought: 'If anything happens to me whoever takes this house will be saying she must be a dirty woman. On the other hand, if I whitewash it and the operation goes OK it'll be nice to come home to."

That story in itself is one thing. But what is truly remarkable is that when I tell the story at my one-man shows every woman in the audience nods in agreement.

I also vividly remember that Aunt Jean's favourite tune was 'Can't Help Loving That Man of Mine'. That was Aunt Jean's song. There was one occasion when we went to a big party and someone else sang it. She was far from happy.

35

Long after she was gone, I was driving back from Edinburgh and a choir was performing on Radio Scotland. Suddenly they started singing:

"Fish gotta swim,
Birds gotta fly,
I gotta love one man till I die,
Can't help loving that man of mine."

The thing was, it was a gay men's choir. I laughed so much I had to stop the car. I thought if Aunt Jean had been there and heard a gay men's choir singing her song she would have been so shocked. It was a wonderful moment.

My sister Heather flew home from America when she died.

At the funeral I said: "Some people have said my Aunt Jean had no children. That is far from true. She had my brother Bertie, my sister Heather and me. We were her children."

I felt that summed up how much she, and my Uncle Bert, meant to us all.

Their first floor flat at 75 Kempock Street was up a close lined by big wooden beams that were designed to stop the whole building collapsing if it was bombed during the War. There was a large wedge-shaped hall, and two bedrooms on either side of the kitchen where we ate all our meals. The lounge overlooked the Clyde.

From that window I often watched all the boats sailing up and down during the War. I was old enough to understand what was going on, and events like Dunkirk had a great effect on me at the time.

The only question people were asking after that was: "What are we going to do next?"

The answer was simple, coming from the lips of an incredible man on the wireless—Winston Churchill. When he told us that the British would fight to the last in trenches and all that stuff, everyone just said: "Right, that's what we'll do. It's going to be OK."

We knew what we had to do, and the people just got on with it. Everyone's attitude was amazing, although I reckon you probably had to be around at the time to appreciate just what it was like.

The odd bit of naivety was probably a good thing. Uncle Bert worked as a clerk in a local torpedo factory after he retired from the Navy, and was amazed to hear people saying: "Och, we'll be all right here. The hills are so high the Germans will never get over them."

It's worth remembering that the tallest peaks in our part of the world are about 2,000 feet, a small bump on the landscape. The Germans also had the ability to fly planes that dropped big bombs, and they did, right on top of every town up and down the Clyde.

I once stood on the pier head at Gourock during an air raid and watched Greenock in flames. It was a shuddering scene, and the town was only saved when the Royal Navy sent many men ashore to fight the fires. The following day there was a massive queue of women and children waiting for the ferries to Dunoon. It started at the pier and stretched right along Kempock Street. They were escaping because they knew Jerry would be back to unleash his horror again that night. I had a summer job at Ritchie's Ferries and that morning I helped evacuate hundreds of people. Those kids were told by their mothers they were going for a nice wee sail, and they loved it.

That night the men of the town went up into the hills overlooking Greenock, and set fire to the heather. When the Germans came back and spotted the flames, they thought the town was still burning and proceeded to drop their bombs on the hills. The town was saved.

It's an understatement to say these were hard times. Glasgow was almost blown to bits after a German bomber hit a warship which was sitting in the docks packed with ammunition. The Royal Navy fought the resulting enormous fire until they said they could fight it no longer, and the whole area was evidently evacuated. Eventually, Glasgow's own brave firefighters managed to put the fires out. The city had come within an inch of being devastated.

On another dreadful occasion a French destroyer, the *Maille Breze*, was anchored off the pier at Greenock Esplanade. She was being loaded with torpedoes when one suddenly went off. People ran for cover as the ship started blowing up, then slumped down into the water. Tragically, the French crew already on board were trapped with no way of getting out. Their comrades outside could do nothing, and were left with only one option, a terrible option. With water gushing in, they stuck their arms through the portholes and administered lethal injections to each one of the doomed sailors. They all knew their fate, and lined up to be killed off before they drowned.

Today, on the Lyle Hill above Gourock sits a giant anchor, and at the top of that anchor is the Cross of Lorraine, the sign of de Gaulle and the Free French, and a tribute from the people to the memory of these brave men—a poignant symbol that such great sacrifices must never be forgotten.

Everybody tried to do their bit for the war effort, including me. As a boy I was a member of the Army Cadet Force, the Boy Scouts, the Emergency Relief Organisation and I entertained the servicemen.

In the Army Cadet Force I dug slit trenches on a local golf course and a machine gun pit to cover the "boom" defences at the Cloch Lighthouse. And I remember the Gamble Institute—the Home Guard headquarters—delivered boxes of old American bayonets from the 1914-18 War that were covered with a horrible black grease. I was given the unenviable task of cleaning those damned things. It was a terrible job.

I also harboured great ambitions of joining up. Just like many boys my age, the attraction of the uniform was irresistible. A fighter pilot, for instance, was able to loosen the top button of his uniform, and I thought that girls would just fall at my feet if I was dressed like that. It was my dream to strut along the street in one of those uniforms, and hear people nudging each other saying: "I wonder which hero he is."

Alas, it was not to be. I had suffered a particularly bad bout of bronchial pneumonia which left me with a weak chest.

But as a boy I saw many sights on the Clyde during my time in Gourock. Just after Dunkirk there was the uplifting experience of witnessing a giant cruise ship sail up the Clyde with troops on board. They were Australians and New Zealanders. I was so proud of these men who had come halfway round the world to risk their lives at the worst time in our history.

Sometimes merchant ships sailed out of the Clyde with a plane, often a Spitfire, sitting on the bow. That signified they would be part of a convoy to Russia, and if the ship was attacked out at sea, these planes would quite literally be catapulted into the wind and the pilots would fight until they were shot or ran out of fuel—all too fully aware they had nowhere to land. Their only option was to crash into the sea, usually the freezing waters of the Arctic above Norway, and hope against hope that someone would pick them up within a few minutes. Otherwise, they just froze to death.

I once saw a tanker with a big SOS logo painted on it and a hole in the side that practically split the ship in two. You could have got two double decker buses through there. The crew of the ship, the San Demetrio, had taken to the boats after she was torpedoed in the Atlantic. When daylight came she was completely burnt out, but still floating. The men reboarded her, painted the huge distress signal and were picked up by a passing destroyer who towed her to safety, down past Gourock.

One grey morning in February 1940 I saw this enormous hulk

of a ship slipping out of the mist, and was struck by just how silent she was. I couldn't hear a thing. I was awestruck.

She was so big there was only one day in the year the tide was high enough for her to make it out to the open sea. It was the *Queen Elizabeth.*

Painted with camouflage stripes to disguise her shape, she sailed straight into the Atlantic and across to New York without any trial runs or anything. When the Americans saw her, it really made them sit up. They had never seen such a huge vessel, and reckoned if the British were up to building such a magnificent beast they certainly weren't finished in the War.

Perhaps the great impression she made played a small role in what I consider to be the most pivotal moment of the Second World War which occurred in Glasgow. President Roosevelt sent his personal envoy, the respected statesman Harry Hopkins, to Britain to find out if the Americans should help its old ally out. He arrived just as support was growing back home for the Yanks not to get involved, with such worthies as John F Kennedy's father Joseph claiming the British were finished, a stance for which he was declared *persona non grata* by the Court of St James.

In reality, Joseph Kennedy's assessment probably wasn't far from the truth. Although we never knew it at the time, Britain was on its knees at that point, only months away from almost certain defeat. A man who became a dear friend years later, Commander Sid Glover, said that after Dunkirk there was only one rifle for every 200 men. He was ordered to build heavy gun defences around the south coast, and told me how, every time one was finished, the Germans just sent the bombers over and blew them to bits.

Churchill was determined to paint a brighter picture when Hopkins arrived, and personally escorted him everywhere, knowing his report back to the President could ultimately mean the difference between victory and defeat for Britain. They went to

Salisbury Plain where the American was met by the impressive sight of a whole division of tanks. The minute he left, every flag and mark was taken off, and the tanks were shipped up to the Midlands. The following day Hopkins was impressed by another show of military might, completely unaware that the tanks rolling past him were the same ones he had seen the previous day.

At the end of his visit, before Hopkins sailed for home from the Clyde, Churchill gave a private dinner party at the Station Hotel next to Glasgow's Queen Street station. It was a tense affair, as Hopkins had declined to offer any opinions or hints of support throughout his trip, and was now only hours from leaving Britain to possibly fend for itself.

After the formalities of the meal, Hopkins was asked to speak. Everyone was on tenterhooks, desperate to know what he planned to tell Roosevelt. Thanking his hosts for their hospitality, he quoted from the Bible:

> "Where you go, I will go,
> And where you stay, I will stay.
> Your people will be my people,
> And your God, my God."

He had effectively told Churchill for the first time that he could rely on the support of America. It had been the only flicker of hope left in Churchill's mind, and apparently when Hopkins made this historic statement our greatest Prime Minister broke down in tears.

Winston Churchill was the rock on which Britain survived, of that there is no doubt. I met a lovely husband and wife, Guy and Barbara Agnew, who were in the Philippines working for Shell before the Japanese invaded and threw them in those appalling POW camps. On a wall in their cottage was a drawing of Winston Churchill, the kind you would see in the *Illustrated London News*.

"What's the story behind that?" I asked.

"We kept that in a biscuit tin buried under one of the huts in the POW camp," Barbara told me. "When things got to the stage we couldn't take it any more, we used to gather in the hut at night, dig it up, take out this drawing and pass it from one woman to the next. It was our only symbol of hope, all that could keep us going. When I returned to Britain after the War we went to a dinner and Churchill was also there. I longed to tell him about the drawing."

I only wish she had. It is what kept those women alive, and I believe had Churchill known he would have cried. If that seems like a strange statement to make about a character as strong as Churchill's, it is because I believe Churchill to have been a compassionate and emotional man.

On one occasion when I visited the House of Lords I saw the now famous painting of Churchill by Graham Sutherland. I thought it was a magnificent piece of work. His neck appeared old and jagged, almost like the white cliffs of Dover, his defiant head rising out of the stone, telling the Germans to back off.

The painting was done as a tribute. It was later handed over to the great man, but he absolutely hated it. When Churchill died his family destroyed the painting, a travesty in itself because works of art should never be destroyed, just as books should never be burned.

I never could understand why Churchill despised the painting, until one pleasant evening a few years ago I was having dinner at the home of Lady Maclean, the widow of one of Scotland's greatest heroes, Fitzroy Maclean. They had both known Churchill well, and a number of personal photographs were placed prominently on her piano. During the conversation I mentioned the Sutherland painting.

"Well Jimmy," she said, leaning forward to explain, "Winston Churchill hated war. He was in many ways a compassionate man. There was only one way to win the War, no sideways, and he had no option but to charge ahead. But when he looked at that painting he saw no compassion or pity in his eyes, and that is what he so hated about it."

From a woman who felt she knew him, I thought it was a remarkable and revealing statement. His hatred of the painting was well documented, but never before had I considered that a man such as Churchill had held armed conflict in such contempt.

In the War, shopkeepers used to put tape on their windows to limit the shattering of glass, and some had wires which ran from a central pressure point so that, if there was an explosion, the glass would push in, and not out. I particularly remember one sign in Gourock which read: "Please do not dunt the window."

In Greenock a double-act called Donoghue and Ramsay were in the middle of their show at the Empire Theatre when there was an air raid. In those situations the audience would be given the choice of staying where they were or going home. Whatever happened, the show went on.

Donoghue was the comic who wore the silly hat, but fed all the lines to the supposedly intelligent straight man, Ramsay. When the air raid was all over, Ramsay walked out and said: "Ladies and Gentlemen, the sireens have now went."

Like every other built-up place, a giant black blanket was thrown over Gourock every night during the War. The blackout made the nights long, dark and miserable. There were no street lights, and the general hardship of wartime existence brought little light relief in people's day-to-day lives.

The only news from the outside really came from the wireless, that big box in the middle of the room that every family in the country huddled around every day. Ours was no different. The wireless was powered by the accumulator—this big battery with acid in it that had to be humped down to the local electrician to be charged up. Then we got a modern wireless with a plug, and life became easier.

43

I listened to and loved programmes like *Workers' Play Time* or those featuring the likes of Tommy Handley. Of course, we always stopped in our tracks for the nine o'clock news from the BBC. I think the world stopped for the BBC because everybody believed every word the BBC said.

For a while that was about all the entertainment we got. Just after the start of hostilities, the Government ordered places where crowds might gather, and where casualties could be high, to close—with the exception of the churches. It was announced that there were to be no big sports events including football and racing, no dance halls, no theatres and no picture houses. Entertainment, and enjoying yourself, had effectively been banned, sparking a chorus of protest most eloquently summed up by George Bernard Shaw in a letter to *The Times*.

"It seems to me to be a masterstroke of unimaginative stupidity," he wrote. "During the last War we had 80,000 soldiers on leave to amuse every night. There were not enough theatres for them and theatre rents rose to fabulous figures. Are there to be no theatres for them this time? We have hundreds of thousands of evacuated children to be kept out of mischief and traffic dangers. Are there to be no pictures for them? The authorities, now all-powerful, should at once set to work to provide new theatre and picture houses where they are lacking. What agent of Chancellor Hitler is it who suggested that we should all cower in darkness and terror for the duration?"

Bernard Shaw understood the magnificent effect of a theatre or picture house, providing a glimmer of fantastic light in an otherwise hopeless existence. During the War, people would walk out of the blackout into these bright, fantastic places all over the country. It was just about their only form of escape, and what an escape; into a world so wonderful that it was enough for them to forget their troubles for a couple of hours.

Green's Playhouse in Glasgow was one of the country's biggest cinemas with a capacity of around 3,500. Above the cinema was a ballroom where the big orchestras would come to play, and in the cinema itself people could sit on these big two and three-seater divans; they were very comfortable and just like settees.

Silent movies heralded the arrival of the what would become the world's biggest entertainment business. It cost next to nothing to get in, but such was the success, Green's opened more big cinemas in places like Dundee and Ayr. In the Glasgow cinema, which later became the Apollo, and renowned for its wonderful rock concerts, the carpets all said: "If it's Green's, it's good."

When the time finally came to knock it down just a few years ago, they made an amazing discovery. Overalls hung up by men working for Green's were still hanging there in one of the back rooms, untouched after all those years.

It reminded me of the story behind one of my favourite turns of phrase. When someone's job is looking a bit dicey, that's where we get the saying: "His jacket is hanging on a shoogly nail."

It's a wonderful expression.

I was once in a restaurant where a poor fella couldn't pay his bill.

"Don't worry about that, Sir," said the manager. "We've had a lot of that lately."

"Is that right? How do you deal with it?"

"Oh, we just write your name on the wall, Sir."

"Oh no, I can't have that. I can't have my name on the wall. People will see it. The embarrassment would be too much."

"Don't worry Sir. They won't see it. I can assure you."

"Well, how's that then?"

"Because your coat will be hanging over it."

The first "movie" pictures were those machines down the coast where you put a penny in and saw a succession of pictures flicking past to give the impression everything was moving. When cinema arrived people couldn't believe what they were seeing, and some were scared out of their wits.

Watching a train being attacked by Indians in the American Wild West was truly staggering to your average Glesca punter. And when the train came rushing towards this massive screen, people actually jumped up and ran out screaming because they thought it was about to smash into the cinema.

In the 1914-18 War the public got a glimpse—just a glimpse—of what was going on in the Western Front. But they only saw the victory pictures. Even then, the Government was sharp enough to eliminate any news of the dead. By the time World War Two came around the technology involved in making motion pictures had developed enormously, and the authorities realised what a great propaganda tool they could be.

Occasionally Aunt Jean took us along to the Wee Gourock Picture House. It was just a normal wee picture house. If the lights had been turned on it would probably have been a disaster, but stepping out of the blackout with our little torches into this fantastic new world was just amazing. Big stars like Bing Crosby and Bob Hope would light up our lives, and films like *Mrs Miniver*, about the real-life heroics of people at Dunkirk, would give everyone a real lift. If we could do that, we could do anything. You left the cinema with a real spring in your step.

Another time I went up to the Bedford Cinema in Glasgow to hear a British sailor tell people about a dramatic rescue operation in Norway. The German U-boats had been torpedoing much of our merchant navy, and taking the captains and other vital men on board as prisoners. They were then transferred to a kind of depot ship, the *Altmark*. The Royal Navy finally tracked the *Altmark* down and chased her into a Norwegian fjord which was supposed to be in a neutral zone—and protected from any attacks.

This, however, was a priceless cargo and far more important than any international rules. The Navy went in and got their men out. It was a magnificent tale, and, told by one of the sailors who had been part of it, lifted the hearts and minds of the audience as they walked back into the grim Glasgow streets.

I went to Gourock Primary School, then Gourock High School, then Bellahouston Academy in Glasgow, but even then all I wanted to do was entertain people. I got a chance to do that in the First Gourock Sixth Renfrewshire Boy Scouts, known as Colonel Darroch's Own, which kept going throughout the War. We did our own bit to help the war effort by going to the big mansion house of Sir Guy Shaw at Inverkip to sing for the men who had been wounded, and were resting there. I also sold programmes outside the theatre in my Boy Scout uniform, and for the first time saw Will Fyffe rehearsing. I never got to see his act, and didn't have the courage to go up and say to him that my father and mother were in showbusiness.

Alongside our home in Kempock Street was the Continental Cafe run by a Scottish Italian called Toma, and above that cafe sat the Toc H Canteen, which was started in the 1914-18 War as a place where the men who had been on the Front could go, without drinking beer or other forms of alcohol. There was a piano, tea and coffee, and a small library where the boys could pick books to read. All in all it was a wee escape from their dreary barracks.

I played the piano in the Toc H Canteen. God knows how good or bad I was but I just did. I went up there every odd night or on a Sunday. I think it provided the boys with a little entertainment.

My little sister Heather and I also did shows at the Empire Theatre in Greenock for wastepaper and newspaper. Those who brought enough along got in free. Every little bit helped the war effort. People were told their frying-pans could be made into Spitfires.

Our biggest thrill, of course, was the occasion we were allowed on the same bill as the great Sir Harry Lauder at the King's Theatre in Greenock. It's difficult to describe just how big that was for a boy of twelve, but it ranked alongside a Royal Performance because Sir Harry was such an incredible man. If any of his orchestra were ever asked what they had done in their career, there was a stock answer: "Oh, I've played for Sir Harry Lauder."

Every second, and every minute and every hour of that day I can remember as clearly now as when I soaked it in all those years ago. The show had been organised primarily because there were a lot of Navy boys in town twiddling their thumbs. They had arrived when it was raining, surrounded by all these dark and drab buildings, and looking for something to do. Backstage, the place was full of Wrens who were given the job of making sure the girl singers had everything they needed. Every so often we would bump into an officer with his stiff upper lip and plum in his throat, commenting: "Mmmm yes, wonderful thing this theatre."

As we rehearsed our music, we heard a voice from the distance: "He's coming in the door."

The place froze. It was Sir Harry. He strolled in, and there was utter silence throughout a theatre that moments before had been a hive of activity. The stage that had been extraordinarily busy was, in seconds, totally empty. Everyone, including me, went into the wings waiting for a glimpse of the great man. He looked round and knew exactly the effect his presence was having.

Sir Harry made his way onto the stage where someone had placed a chair. He sat down and said: "Now ladies and gentleman, you've got my music so we'll start from the beginning." And he tapped out with his stick the tempo he wanted. I was spellbound.

That night the theatre was packed with all these Naval chaps who had nowhere else to go. When this little man wearing a kilt came on I'm sure they thought: "Oh, we'll send this fella up."

However, as I expected, Sir Harry had them eating out of his hands inside two minutes. And why not? He had been all over the world, and dealt successfully with a million audiences. A theatre full of bored sailors would have hardly presented his greatest challenge.

He may have been an elderly man, but Churchill had still asked him to go out and entertain the sons and grandsons of the men he had entertained in 1914. And Harry Lauder had gone back on the road again. I got the same awestruck feeling then as I got years later when I saw masters such as George Formby in pantomime at Liverpool, Jack Benny at the London Palladium or a very elderly Bob Hope at the Concert Hall in Glasgow. I was also bowled over by how wonderful Judy Garland was when I saw her at the Talk of the Town in London towards the end of her career. She may have been late on stage but when her 35-piece orchestra started playing that was it. Before she came on I just couldn't wait, and when I noticed that she wasn't her best I still thought she was wonderful. Watching a master or a giant of the theatre is a thrilling experience that you never forget.

We went back to live with my parents again in Ibrox, Glasgow towards the end of the War. There was a sign in the cupboard underneath the stairs that said: "To Hell With Hitler". That's where we were supposed to go during an air raid. When we slept there, it was in a cage; under an old iron table with wire all around it. If the house sustained a direct hit the thinking was that it could save your life.

Our home was one of a row of terraced houses, and always seemed to be busy with all kinds of people. The reason: soldiers were often billeted on us, and artistes came to stay too. It wasn't uncommon to come home to a party in full swing, and there was rarely a moment when someone wasn't sitting playing the piano or singing.

Not surprisingly, we played host to a fair few characters. A lovely fella called John Ralston was head steward on the *Queen Mary*, and was awarded the MBE purely for the number of trips he made across the Atlantic. Our home was his home when he came back from leave.

He was a giant of a man, so big and stout I often wondered how he kept his balance. He was also fond of a good dram, and had what we called a raspberry nose.

One night I got home and John had fallen asleep drunk at the side of his bed. We had the job of trying to get him up onto the bed, but it was useless. Nobody could lift him.

Another chap from the merchant navy told us how he got a job serving the captain's table on a wartime troop ship after telling the owners he had been a *maître d'* in a hotel. Even during the War the Captain expected and got the best of service, but this guy was so down to earth and without graces that when the Captain sat down at the top table he stood there, with pencil and notebook in hand, and shouted: "Hands up for soup."

The man I remember most who came to stay with us was Tom F. Moss, a stout artiste who wore a monocle, grew a little goatee beard and possessed a magnificent voice. He had enjoyed a certain degree of notoriety in Gourock before the War because he walked around with an animal on a leash—I'm sure it was a leopard—whose proper place should have been in the local zoo.

For a great dramatic finale to his act, he specialised in throwing his sword right into the stage at the end of his song 'And To Hell With Burgundy'. But sometimes he did it so well he was still standing there trying to get it back out when the curtain rose up again for the next act.

And the stage manager would shout: "Stop doing that, you're ruining my woodwork."

Tom was also fond of a good dram, and in a drunken attempt to come back to our home one night, he ended up going through the wrong gate, up the wrong path and ringing the doorbell to the wrong house. One of the neighbours, a spinster from the Highlands, who we saw little of, came to the door and said: "I'm terribly sorry, you're in the wrong house."

Rather than turning around and walking gingerly away, Tom did the next best thing. He took her hand and started singing 'Your Tiny Hand Is Frozen'. Of course she just happened to be an opera buff and joined in. Before anyone knew what was going on, the two of them were standing there belting out this wonderful aria for all the street to hear.

Many sad scenes are etched in my memory from my time living in Ibrox. For instance, the upper floor of the Thomson's Piano building at the Paisley Road Toll was occupied by a French Alpine regiment who had been rescued from Dunkirk. Now they were stuck hundreds of miles away from their countrymen in an essentially alien environment.

I also saw the Huns at Ibrox Park, but it had nothing to do with Rangers. Masses of German prisoners were brought to Scotland, and I saw a long line of POWs who had obviously been fighting in the desert. They all had suntans and their hair had been turned gold by the sun. As they were marched towards the football stadium, they all seemed over six feet high. Their guards, soldiers from a Polish parachute regiment, seemed half the size. I could feel the emotion of the occasion. At last, after all their country had gone through at the hands of the Nazis, these Polish men were in charge. You could sense they were willing the prisoners to make a run for it—so they could shoot them. The Germans, though, stayed in line, and the Poles practically had tears in their eyes.

A few years afterwards, when I had become relatively well known, I got a call from the Ministry of Pensions. They asked me if I would listen to a former POW who had been told by two guys at the BBC that they would help him make it as a professional singer if he cashed in his pension.

"Sure," I said. "Send him over."

He was a lovely man, but his story was astonishing.

Based in Singapore with the Argyll and Sutherland Highlanders, he was lying on the ground with his legs apart firing his rifle when a grenade exploded just behind him, and riddled the insides of those legs with shrapnel.

He was captured by the Japanese, and treated with a razor blade by a man called the Bamboo Doctor. Remarkably, still in extraordinary pain from his injuries, he escaped from jail with some other POWs and walked hundreds of miles north through the jungles until he got to Burma, where he was again captured by the Japs. Of course they had no idea he had escaped from Singapore, but he was taken back and, with a group of other men, tied to tree posts on a beach. Japanese soldiers then sprayed them with bullets, but amazingly he survived. He even showed me the bullet wounds on his legs to prove it.

Eventually, he was put on a ship full of POWs bound for Japan's slave labour camps. In the steaming hot, humid temperatures, he was stuck on a wooden plank with other prisoners all around him—on either side, six inches below him and another plank just above his nose. Lying there in the heat of the tropics they could only gasp for what little air there was.

Then, in keeping with this guy's luck, the ship was torpedoed, forcing them to break their way out of the hold into a shark-infested sea. When he was finally picked up, it was by a Japanese destroyer, and he soon found himself at work in some place near Hiroshima just before the Americans dropped the Big Bomb.

I listened to all this and honestly didn't believe it, but the man from the Ministry of Pensions said: "It's true, Mr Logan. Everything he has told you is true. A remarkable story, don't you think?"

It was indeed a remarkable story, but it was disgraceful that these two men at the BBC were trying to get him to cash in his pension. Sure, he was a pleasant guy with the kind of nice voice that would have had family members telling him he should be in showbusiness, but he was never going to be a star.

It reminded me of the situation my dad had been in when he was thinking of taking the £1,000 in exchange for his pension. His family had all chipped in to buy him an American "Harley" artificial leg, and it cost a fortune, but it didn't stop the pain in his stump. More than 20 years after being injured, during the Second World War, he was given special rations of methylated spirits to "freeze" the stump when it became too painful. It was just as well that pension was still there for him.

3

TREADING THE BOARDS

I walked out of school at the age of 14 without an academic qualification to my name. School holds no particular memories for me, good or bad. It just seemed to get in the way of an altogether more important reason for being alive, and I left to embark on a life for which I always knew I was destined.

Within a family who knew only one thing, showbusiness was everything to me from a very early age. Leaving school was merely the beginning of an incredible journey through the theatres of Scotland, learning new aspects of the trade in each and every one. Whether I was playing the accordion, taking the role of a juvenile lead or acting as the comedian's feed I always picked up little tips, and was able to develop my talents that little bit further.

Mind you, with a father like mine that was never going to be difficult. Not known at the best of times for his sensitivity, he came in one day when I was lying ill with measles in a "hole-in-the-wa" bed in the kitchen. He was holding a 48-bass miniature accordion.

"Here, take this," he said. "You might as well learn that while you're lying there."

And that's how I became an accordion player.

For years people have commented on me being left-handed

when I'm not at all. They would ask why I wore my watch on my right wrist, and until a few years ago I didn't have an answer.

Then someone asked me if I ever played accordion, and it clicked.

When playing accordion, the strap tends to catch on an artiste's wrist watch so they wear the watch on the right wrist.

My first job after school was as an assistant manager at the Victory Theatre in Paisley, working like a trojan and earning £2 a week. I got such an elevated position primarily because of the manpower shortage during World War Two.

And boy was it an experience. I would be at the box office from ten in the morning until two in the afternoon. Then I was off until five o'clock before returning to the box office for another hour. After that I got changed into my dinner suit for the night's performance and I never left the theatre before 10 o'clock at night.

It was the same routine six days a week, and the workload quickly took its toll. Even as a growing teenager full of energy I was waking up in the morning still absolutely knackered from the day before.

I lasted six months. I had asked for a raise and they said no.

From there I went back to my family, and a father who had expected a talented boy of 14 to be able to handle the kind of things an old pro would find tough. On one occasion he was preparing a programme for the Glasgow parks, and he said to me: "Right, there's the list of artistes and what they're being paid. Don't let anyone else know."

Suddenly I had to put the show on, pay the company out on a Friday and make sure nothing went wrong. I also played the accordion and helped to feed in any of the sketches. And all at the age of 14. That typified the kind of upbringing and training we had, and I was always taught that the most important thing was the audience.

My early years in the theatre consisted of working for, and later

55

with, my mother and father. Their comedy duo, Short and Dalziel, was relatively famous throughout Scotland. There was no drama school training for me. I was thrown in at the deep end and told to swim. I sat my degree on the stages of all our theatres, great and small.

Our family were all natural entertainers, and very good at what they did, but it was noticed at an early stage that I had the talent to go that extra mile, and maybe break into the big-time. Part of my apprenticeship was served on my own in some productions. For instance, when I was 16 I worked with two different directors at the Palladium in Edinburgh.

One said to me: "I don't like the way you walk on stage."

These guys were much older than me. I knew only too well I should be listening to them, soaking up the greater experience they had been kind enough to share. I learned things from everyone I worked with, even if it was how not to do something.

I was the juvenile lead in *Meet a Pal at the Pall*, a variety season of twice nightly performances with the programme changing every week over a 22-week run. Each week I had to come up with an act of about seven minutes that normally comprised three songs.

During the day we rehearsed our words and music for the following week's performance, then did two shows at night, so we rarely saw anything other than the inside of the theatre. When I left at night I headed for my digs in Fountainbridge where the landlady was lovely but the surroundings weren't. My room had a cold linoleum floor, and the fire was only turned on five minutes before I walked in the door. The next morning I would eat breakfast at a table set for one. For a 16-year-old boy the whole thing was utterly demanding, and never cheery.

About halfway through the run the first director left, and the second director, Fraser Neil, arrived. He was the owner of William Mutrie and Co., who at the time were the biggest suppliers of theatre costumes in Scotland.

Immediately he announced a change to the planned programme of the variety-style shows we were used to.

"We're going to do *Jeanie Deans*," he said, and suddenly the cast were confronted with the prospect of performing a complete show from beginning to end; in this case the story of how a woman called Jeanie Deans walked to London in the early 1800s to plead for the life of her sister who had been sentenced to death.

It proved to be quite literally a breath of fresh air for our wonderful accordion player, Elsie Kelly. Basically, she hated being the accordion player because the formula was always the same. At the start of the show the company came on, followed by the comedian who rattled off five minutes of gags, before saying: "Now let's have Elsie Kelly on the accordion."

Every time she came on and did a medley which always had to be in the same tempo. She also came on straight after the opening—possibly the worst spot of the night.

Elsie, bless her, had had a hard life. She was a lovely mother of two children who lived among massive unemployment in Greenock. Each day her husband cycled more than 20 miles to Glasgow to see if her agent had found her any work. And usually he cycled back again to tell her he hadn't.

Elsie was also fond of a wee dram, and during my time at the Palladium she sometimes played a completely different medley from the orchestra, although the audience never noticed.

In *Jeanie Deans*, I played the young minister in the first half, and the aged Duke of Argyll in the second half. I was old enough to be neither of them, and my make-up was so terrible I looked like I had a face full of tram lines.

Elsie pleaded for the part of Jeanie's mother, the old gypsy who did not enter until about nine little scenes in. Since she hated following the opening this was her big chance to get into something different.

"You can't play that part," said Fraser Neil.

"Oh please, Mr Neil."

"No."

"Why not, Mr Neil?"

"Because you'll take a drink and let me down."

"I won't take a drink. If I get this part I won't touch a drop. I give you my word. Please believe me."

Eventually Fraser backed down, and Elsie got the part.

On the first night she walked on stage as the old woman with a big stick.

"Ma man Wullie," she said in her old woman's voice. "He thinks ah don't know whits goin' on. But I understand better than anyone . . ."

And the audience who had been used to seeing her playing the accordion thought she was just wonderful.

At one point in the play she was holding a real knife with a broad eight-inch blade which she was supposed to stab into one of the actors' wooden hearts. In the end, Elsie got so carried away it was just as well he moved out the way.

The show was such a success it was held over for a second week. That was unprecedented, and even better for us because we didn't have to rehearse during the day.

Everything went swimmingly until the Thursday of the second week when Elsie arrived at the theatre "stotin'", as they would say in Glasgow. She stood at the side of the stage with a fair drink inside her, hanging on to her big stick as if her life depended on it. I looked over at Fraser Neil. His face was red and bursting, and he was frightened to speak in case he exploded.

Finally Elsie staggered onto the stage.

"Ma man Wullie," she said. But the pause seemed to last forever, until everyone thought she had forgotten her next line.

"He thinks ah don't know whit's goin' on." Then there was another long pause before she got the next line. Then an extraordinary pause, and then the next line.

The audience thought she was even more wonderful than before.

In the middle of the second half she was standing at the side of the stage. Fraser Neil did his nut.

"You've let me down," he shouted.

"Whit ye talkin' aboot?"

"You've let the show down."

"Whit ye talkin' aboot?"

"You promised me when you got this part you wouldn't take a drink."

Elsie paused, looked down, rubbed her brow and stared back at Fraser Neil.

"That's right, but how did ah know it was gonnae last for two weeks?"

It was 1945, and we officially beat the Germans in the middle of that season. Amidst the great celebrations, I was asked to play the accordion one night because Elsie had failed to turn up. She arrived the following evening with a doctor's note explaining that she had been very ill. Of course, everyone knew what had really happened.

Anyway, the comedians looked at the note and started laughing.

"Take it to the manager," they said, creasing up.

Then the manager looked at it and burst out laughing. "Take it to the producer," he said, and this continued until it had been round virtually everyone in the theatre. The whole place was falling about because the doctor had written: "Please excuse Miss Kelly from being absent last night as she was suffering from a severe gill."

After the Palladium in Edinburgh I went on to the summer season at the Hippodrome and Opera House in Dunfermline, a lovely old theatre in the town's Reform Street. It was built in 1900 but it's no longer there, the building long since knocked down. A few years ago, however, I went to Sarasota in the USA, and saw the interior of the Dunfermline Opera House in all its original glory. The auditorium had been dismantled, transported and beautifully restored thousands of miles away on the other side of the Atlantic. A lovely story.

The opening night of that season was interesting. In 1935 they had had a wonderful summer season in which the cast were dressed in the Pierrot costumes which were popular at open air concert parties. These consisted of big pointy hats with bobbles at the top and ruffles round the neck, and looked rather ridiculous. But before rehearsals started we were handed the costumes because it had become tradition to wear the bloomin' things on subsequent opening nights.

My existence was still a lonely one. Of the £8 I earned every week in Dunfermline, I sent £2 back to my parents in Glasgow. When I went home they always seemed to be having riotous parties in the house, and eventually I decided enough was enough. There was no way I was handing over my hard-earned £2 any longer just to keep their house in parties.

When I cut the money, they fell out with me. Nobody would speak to me.

A couple of weeks later I got word they were coming over to see the show, and I bought a half bottle of whisky so I could offer them a drink when they came backstage to my dressing room. I thought it would be a nice gesture, especially as I hated the stuff.

Well, they came to see the show all right but never came backstage. They met up with just about everyone else—including the managers and directors—but they never came to see me, even though they knew I was waiting in my dressing room for them.

It seemed that bottle of whisky had gone to waste until, some weeks later, the news came through that Japan had surrendered, and World War Two was finally, at long last, over. Everyone ran into the streets celebrating, but we had nothing to celebrate with. Just then I remembered the whisky in my dressing room.

Quick as a flash I ran over to the theatre only to find it all locked up. I looked around. There was only one option. Above the stage door was the toilet window. I climbed up a drainpipe, got the top half of the window down and before I knew what I was doing I was upside down in the darkness with my head over the bowl and my legs dangling over the ledge. Fortunately I avoided a terrible embarrassment and got clear. I ran up to my dressing room, got the whisky and resisted the temptation to climb back out, using the stage door instead.

Then we celebrated properly. I hated whisky but seem to remember we had a marvellous time that night anyway.

Peace also broke out in our own household around that time, because I agreed to start contributing again to the upkeep of the family. I did so just in time for a part in my first pantomime. My family were playing the Empire Theatre in Greenock, and my father said: "Right, you're going to be the Cat in *Dick Whittington*."

Now, if you ever get the chance to play the Cat . . . don't. It's a nightmare of a role. Whoever thought it up was taking the mick. Your legs are bent the whole time. And let me assure you that it is absolute agony.

Unfortunately matters weren't helped by the fact we were staying with my Aunt Jean. I say unfortunately because Aunt Jean was so clean it was unbelievable. If you had slept in a bed one night, the sheets and blankets would always be washed and dried before you got back.

The minute she saw the cat skin I was to wear in *Dick Whittington* she decided it needed a good clean. That in itself was wonderful, except it shrunk and was murder to work in.

That was 1945, but a funny thing happened almost 50 years later when I was playing at Pitlochry Festival Theatre. A very nice elderly couple came up to me, and the gentleman said: "Mr Logan, you won't know us."

He was right. I didn't.

"When our son was just a little boy we were at the Empire Theatre in Greenock in one of the boxes. You were the Cat in *Dick Whittington* and our wee boy started screaming in terror when he saw this cat. And your mother said: 'Don't cry son, it's just Jimmy,' and she lifted your head off to show him." So much for reality.

I believe when my mother took my head off revealing me underneath, the child cried even louder.

At another pantomime in the Edinburgh Palladium, I'll never forget that the principal boy was terribly, terribly upper class. She was Scottish, but came from England where she had been working with Jack Hylton, one of the great pantomime stars. She was terribly smart.

"Who's in the show?" my mother asked me when I was home during rehearsals.

"There's this marvellous, smart lady," I told her, explaining who she was.

"Och, I know her," said my mother. "Her family have got a milk shop in the Gallowgate."

I just laughed and said she must have been wrong. There was no way this terribly smart woman could be from the Gallowgate. But, sure enough, my mother was dead right. The following week a letter appeared for her on the notice board addressed c/o The Milk Shop, The Gallowgate.

After the War, when the family started the first of a number of 18-week summer seasons at the old Metropole Theatre in Glasgow, I was in for a couple of surprises. The first concerned our name. Up until then we had been known as individuals: Short and Dalziel, the comedy duo, myself, the rising star, Buddy, Bert and Heather. We didn't have a collective act, rather a mish-mash of people in a variety act who just happened to be in the same family. In fact, at one point there were nine relatives all playing in the same show.

As always, the programme was changed on a weekly basis, and it was a constant struggle to find new material or new ways to freshen things up a bit. One day I was looking at the programme for that week, and happened to glance on the back to see what was planned for the following week.

It said simply: "Come next week and meet the fabulous Logan Family."

It was the first I had heard of it.

"What's this?" I said.

"Och, that's us," said my father.

"Eh? What are we going to do?"

"Och, we'll think of something."

As strange as it may seem, that was the beginning of the family act that became famous throughout Scotland. My father was a very imaginative man, often doing things with rough plans to think about them later. This was one of those episodes, but a stroke of genius at the same time.

The Logan name had kind of gone full circle. My father's name was John Short, and he was known as Jack. My aunt began her life as Ina Allan and by seven years of age, deciding it wasn't glamorous enough, called herself Daisy Mars. That didn't make any impression on anyone so she apparently spotted that horse Triumphant Logan and changed her name again to Ella Logan. I, of course, was born James Allan Short but my father soon decided it wasn't a good idea to have the same name as him because the audience wouldn't think they were getting their money's worth. So he said I should be called Jim Logan, which eventually became Jimmy Logan as my popularity caught on with the public. And when that happened my father came up with the fabulous Logan Family.

Pity poor Ella Logan when she herself arrived at Prestwick Airport shortly afterwards.

And one guy said: "Are you Ella Logan?"

"Yes I am."

"Are you related to the famous Logan Family?"

That was a bit of a comedown.

"What do you mean related? They're related to me."

We took a lot of chances in those family shows. Few things were put together in advance. Instead we tended to make things up as we went along. I was on piano, my dad played the accordion, my mother, Buddy and Heather sang, and Bertie did other things including playing the xylophone.

We did all sorts of things. Buddy would be singing a nice melody and I would be screaming in the background: "Oh, dear God, take him away."

I picked up a trumpet for the first time on a Sunday, then went on stage on Monday night and played the Last Post. The only number I could play properly was 'In My Solitude'. I was absolutely terrible.

Then came the next surprise.

My father came up to me and said: "Right, listen to me. You're going to be a comic."

"Oh right. What do I do?"

It was another steep learning curve. I discovered I had a flair to play a schoolboy with a slight lisp that always got good laughs. Our secret was never down to good scripts because we didn't have any scripts. There were so many sketches you didn't have time to mess about on such trivial things as what was going to be in them. We took a lot of chances, and just made it up as we went along.

We did know the punchline, though, and stretched the sketches out to round off on that. Good comics know how to make bad jokes good, and if you got a big laugh at the end of a sketch like that you had succeeded.

It reminds me of a wonderful man Charlie Kemble, the father of the open air concert parties who taught so many guys like Jack Anthony and Alec Finlay to be good comics. They usually started out as smart juvenile leads, a bit like myself, but after benefiting from his wonderful training finished up as cracking comedians.

Jack Anthony once told me how he encountered that familiar feeling of being thrown head first into the deep end.

"Right son," said Charlie. "You're going to be in this sketch. Now you're the schoolboy and you've come in from school and want to go the pictures but your mother doesn't want you to go."

"Where's the script?"

"Oh, there's no script."

"So what dae ah say?"

"What would you say if you wanted to go to the pictures and your mother said no. Make it up."

"When dae ah come off?"

"When you get a big laugh."

So he went on with this woman, worked and worked the audience as best he could, and finally got a big laugh. The sweat was pouring off him as he rushed to the side of the stage but he knew it was all over, and let out a big sigh of relief.

The door next to the stage was locked.

"I got a big laugh," he said.

Charlie Kemble's voice came from behind the door. "It wasnae big enough."

That's how we all learned the business. Of course, there was always a shape to the sketch, and we certainly knew what the tag was going to be, but it was accepted that you would probably have to ad-lib your way towards it.

More experienced performers never let you stand still for a moment on stage. I once went on with Aly Wilson armed with just one gag, and we lasted about six minutes. When we were absolutely desperate we did this gag, got the big laugh, then launched into the finishing song. Young comics like me quickly learned to always keep going, and never to stand around looking like a dummy.

I remember rehearsing sketches as the audience were coming into the theatre.

I learned very quickly not to lose heart. If a sketch didn't go well in the first house we would all get together afterwards and make sure it was better by the second house. We were always told to keep plugging away.

"Remember the second house didn't see it in the first house, so it is completely new to them," we were told. "Audiences won't know it's a lousy sketch unless you tell them."

We had platforms on which to make our mistakes, then rectify them. I was told to react like a drunk, but I had no idea how a drunk reacted. The first time I got it wrong. "No, no," said the comic, bending his knees in all manner of directions. "Do it like this." I did, and it looked a whole lot better.

The comics nowadays have got it easy by comparison. If a guy tells a couple of good jokes today, and gets a laugh, he'll have his own TV series tomorrow. Ah well, if only it had been so easy in our day.

I may have known I was good, but one bad experience taught me to never, ever be complacent. Doing well and being noticed at the Metropole, I was asked to a charity concert at one of Glasgow's little Catholic halls. I agreed, and although I didn't have a lot of stand-up material because my acts consisted of characters being funny in sketches, I reckoned I could throw a few gags together. It was one of the biggest mistakes I ever made.

The people there gave me a lovely welcome, I went on brimming with confidence, said hello and told my first couple of stories. They got a laugh, but it was only half a laugh. Then I threw in the third one, trying to remember the fourth gag at the same time. I started off going downhill and slipped off the edge. It was a disaster, and taught me a very big lesson.

I've seen so many artistes who think they know it all. It's a statement I would never use, even when I'm on my death bed. Why? Because no-one ever knows everything about the theatre. Every production throws up something you had never realised before. That's part of the great thrill and buzz of being on stage.

The theatre is also a wonderful mistress. When you walk along the road and everyone is smiling, and you think everyone likes you, that is when she looks at you and says: "Sonny, you're getting too big for your boots." So she sticks her foot out, and you fall on your face. It's a racing certainty in life.

That was the start of the laughter at the old Metropole, and the beginning of my career as a funnyman. I did countless sketches with my mother, father and a great old comic called Mark Denison.

At that time in my life, I was also doing shows in what seemed to be every theatre in just about every town. There are many wonderful memories from these wonderful places. The Roxy in Falkirk, for instance, was just hysterical. It backed onto a graveyard and when we walked underneath the stage we could see they had used gravestones to pave the floor. We always said if you weren't dying up the stairs, you could be dying downstairs.

The chorus girls' dressing room was roughly halfway to the gallery, and directly above the boilers that in those days were fed by coke. On one occasion we raced upstairs after someone screamed for help, and dragged the unconscious girls out. They had been overcome by the fumes. There was a baby in a pram. We all feared the worst, but it was lying there bright as a button, the only one that hadn't been affected.

When I was playing the Roxy I got bronchial pneumonia, and I was holed up dreadfully ill in the Orchard Hotel for almost three weeks. Sweat poured off my body like water out of a burst drain, and they had to change the sheets on my bed twice a day. I never got taken into hospital. That only happened if you had double pneumonia.

Somehow my parents got me home. I was lying there in a pool of my own sweat when my mother announced that the Doctor was coming the next morning at ten o'clock. Given that this was in the days before the National Health Service, this was a major event in any household. So I was tossed out of the bed while all the sheets and pillow cases were taken away and replaced by fresh linen bedclothes. Believe me when I say they were crackling with the cold. Then I was told to keep my elbows off the bloomin' things so they would still look nice when the Doctor arrived. A fresh towel was also laid out. In fact the place would have been fit for a king.

Of course when the Doctor finally walked through the door, the house was full of "Yes, Doctor", "No, Doctor", "Three bags full, Doctor". I was the reason he was there, but the only concern in our house was for the welfare of the Doctor. The main thing was to make sure the Doctor was OK, his every need catered for. He must have died thinking how nice everyone he ever visited was to him. Meanwhile, no-one cared a jot about the sick ones like me.

In spite of all this I eventually made a full recovery, and went on to visit many more theatres that will always remain dear in my heart. The Empire Theatre in Greenock holds particularly fond memories, not least of my lifelong friendship with the Smith family. I used to dress under the stage, and the only way you could get down was via a ladder. On the left hand side was a white china sink which can only be described as being on stilts. If you wanted to wash yourself, you had to stand on a beer crate. It was another theatre where the dressing rooms were opposite the boilers, complete with coke fumes, and the stage was right above your head. It was indeed a heady cocktail when the fumes were flowing in at full blast and the dancers were battering the stage inches above you.

I went back to Paisley Theatre, another example of luxury. It was situated down at the River Cart, and the dressing rooms flooded when the river burst its banks. There were duck-boards in all the dressing rooms just waiting for the tide. And they had what I referred to as penicillin on the ceilings.

In Paisley, I got a vivid idea of what our business is really like. I had been down to do six minutes one night, and afterwards, the producer George Clarkson called me into his room.

"You did seven minutes Logan and I told you to do six," he said, sharply. "However, the act went very well and I'm not going to cut you. Just keep an eye on the time."

George, who was also director of shows at the Roxy in Falkirk, had formed a dancing act with four young girls, one of whom became Miss Bluebell, the founder of the world famous Bluebell Dancers at the Lido in Paris.

The Hippodrome Theatre in Hamilton was a lovely-sized theatre but the ceiling was made out of corrugated tin. Everything was fine as long as it was dry outside, but the minute the rain started you couldn't hear yourself think for all the rattling on the roof. I was the accordion player there in my father's show. I think I did nine weeks in the key of C. That was the only key I could play in.

The stage manger, George Ryan, was the father of about ten kids. Their home was a wonderful place to be, and I often stayed the night there. I think the mother just took in extra kids to fill the place up.

She told me how she and the kids arrived home one day to find most of the furniture missing. She was devastated because she thought she had been burgled. Then it became apparent that George was the culprit because he had needed the furniture for a show at the theatre.

I could sympathise with her predicament because people in the theatre always upheld the principle that there was nothing more important than the audience, and therefore the show. What had to be done, had to be done, and if that meant relieving the house of its furniture for a while then so be it.

If I had taken my father's furniture, as long as I told him first, he would have been fine about it. My brother-in-law Nick Capaldi was in charge of entertainment on a cruise liner and told me how women often complained that they never won any prizes at bingo. It wasn't a case of: "Well, Madam, that's what bingo is all about. Some you win, some you lose."

No, instead he took the attitude: "A fair point, Madam, I'm dreadfully sorry. Now can I offer you a bottle of perfume perhaps? I hope you accept our apologies. I'll try to make sure that never happens again."

Pleasing the customer is everything in our business. If you fail in that respect you've failed altogether.

Another theatre I have fond memories of is the Queen's Theatre in Glasgow. It was a lovely old place that always smelled of oranges. Wonderful people like Frank and Doris Droy worked there.

Doris was a magic lady. Some of the great critics from London came up and thought she was just unbelievable. She was a bit like my mother in a way, and Una McLean too, in that one minute she could look stunningly beautiful in an evening dress, and the next come back on again in big army boots and have you falling about with laughter.

They played the Queen's every winter in panto; Frank wrote the sketches and played the piano, whilst Doris would come on stage in a whole range of characters. They were loved, and always held the audience in the palms of their hands.

Doris was offered all sorts of deals but Frank wasn't part of them, so she always said no. Sadly they got into financial troubles and hit hard times. After Doris had a stroke, they ended up down in Manchester just trying to make ends meet. In the Sixties when I was touring down south with my play *Wedding Fever* we invited Frank and Doris along to see our performance.

That night Doris lit the theatre up all by herself.

She missed the opening but, as she was walking along the side of the stage on Frank's arm, I could see she was so excited.

"Listen to the Scottish voices," she said, pulling at Frank's arm. "Listen to the Scottish voices." She sat in the audience on the edge of her seat looking up with the biggest smile. She just stood out. It was a wonderful evening.

A comedian called Sammy Murray was also in their show at the Queen's Theatre. Typically Glasgow, he spoke like: "Hallo, are ye awright Chinas?"

I saw him in Paisley once when he appeared as a schoolboy who blew up a balloon whilst making the sound: "Whoossh, heh heh . . . whooosh, heh heh." And that's all he did. Before the balloon was half inflated, the audience were in hysterics.

One night at the Pavilion Theatre, Glasgow, a terribly sophisticated West End duo Layton and Johnstone were on the bill. They always turned out in full evening dress with a grand piano, a standard lamp and a settee on stage. They played in all the top places and were awfully smooth. At the Pavilion that night, it was also their last performance before Johnsone went to America to pursue his own career.

For this big occasion, Glasgow's upper classes turned out in force for their kind of artiste. The theatre was packed to the rafters.

At one point, someone had said: "This is all great, but we need someone to follow them. Who on earth is going to follow an act like that?"

They asked Sammy Murray.

So Layton and Johnstone did a classy show, and almost lifted the roof off the place. Then the music changed completely and on walked Sammy with a whip, and in his best Chinas accent started singing: "All the King's horses and all the King's men, weeeellll, marched up the Gallowgate and marched back again, weeeellll."

71

The effect was hysterical. It brought the audience crashing back to reality.

He was a wonderful comedian. When he died in the Gallowgate thousands lined the streets for one of the biggest funerals the city has seen. He lay in one of the undertaker's parlours just so hundreds of people could queue up and pay their last respects. "Oh, ma Chinas," I'm sure he would have said.

Before I hit radio or TV I was asked to do a Sunday concert at the Queen's Theatre. They even asked if I would finish the bill, and I thought that was just brilliant because it meant I must be the star. I wore a checked suit with a white shirt, red tie and "correspondent" shoes—those leather and white affairs that almost looked like golf shoes. I thought I looked so smart.

I was due to play a white grand piano but one of the legs was broken. When they propped it up with a beer crate it kind of spoiled the illusion. Then I discovered the foot pedals were on the wrong way so I couldn't use them either. To round things off I found out I was only the final act because they just wanted me to play 'God Save The Queen', and let the band get home early. Some star!

The summer season at the Winter Gardens in Rothesay was tough because there were supposed to be three programmes in one week. Twice nightly on Monday, Tuesday and Wednesday was programme number one, Thursday, Friday, and Saturday was programme number two, and Friday night was a midnight matinee which was supposed to be programme three. The following Monday programme four kicked in, and so on.

As you weren't supposed to repeat acts for something like 18 weeks, the artistes were imprisoned in the theatre. I spent my life trying to learn the words, and write sketches at the same time.

The most memorable moment of that summer, though, related to my first car, an Austin Seven I bought for £30 in Port Glasgow.

It had a canoe-style back which came to a point. It also had no brakes to speak of because the wires that worked them had, over the years, come very loose. I stopped it by changing down gears, which would have proved pretty useless in emergency stops.

Somehow I got over to Rothesay, and hit on an idea for a sketch. We moved all the seats into the stalls, pushed the car along two gang planks and up on to the tiny stage. The audience were stunned when they arrived. You could see them asking themselves: "How on earth did they get that thing up there?"

Things, though, had been getting particularly hairy in the car before we arrived so I finally got it into a garage. The day before we left Rothesay I got it back—still without any brakes. I drove down to the Pier at Rothesay, straight along the Pier, up the gang plank and onto the ship. I made sure everything was ready for me to do it in one movement because I'm sure it wouldn't have stopped otherwise.

The comedian Aly Wilson, who wanted me to leave to become his feed because we worked so well together, had been polishing his shiny car every day since we arrived in Rothesay. And he loved that car like a child.

Just before we were about to leave it broke down and he missed the boat!

When we got off at the other side my car wouldn't start. My brother Bert, who was driving a big Ford, brought out his tow rope and dragged me up the road. He was going over 40 mph and my wee car felt like the Space Shuttle coming back into the Earth's atmosphere. The kingpins were going, the wheels were shaking, and everything else, including me, was rattling. I thought the car was going to break up. I shouted: "Don't go so fast. Help." But he was completely oblivious to the panic behind him.

Either that or he was having an extremely cruel laugh at my expense.

*　　　*　　　*

As a growing boy I was genuinely more interested in theatre than the opposite sex. I was old enough to sell programmes and cigarettes at theatres, but I was never old enough to go out with girls for goodness sake.

My first girlfriend was Marion Dickie, whose sister married the great footballer Billy Steel. At school Marion was a soprano and a redhead. I thought she was great. I remember particularly how well she sang—in case we needed her for the show.

Our relationship didn't last that long because I used to get 10 shillings a week pocket money. I'd go up the town into Glasgow on a Saturday, and spend about 1/6d on my lunch at Woolworths. Then I went to see a film at the cinema opposite. By the time I came out half my pocket money had been blown on this weekly visit to a different life.

When Marion came along I blew all my pocket money. The next week the same happened, and I thought: "Nothing is worth that."

So I told her it wasn't working out. It was a bad financial arrangement.

I'm sure I kissed Marion but I certainly don't remember. Of course, there were the stories of couples winching in the back of cinemas. The only time I did that I was with Jack Milroy . . . and it wasn't the same.

There were other girls I was attracted to, like one of the Hunters who lived up the same close as us in Gourock, but I can't remember her first name. Another one was a bonnie lassie who, unfortunately, was six years my elder and the sister of my scout master. So that was the end of that.

At school there was one girl who I plucked up the courage to ask out.

"Would you like to go out on Sunday?" I said, nervously.

"Oh yes," she said. "Can I bring my brothers and sisters?"

"Oh fine," I said.

It wasn't the answer I had expected.

Well, Sunday duly arrived and I wore my best suit with a perfectly folded raincoat over one arm. I wore a leather glove on one hand while holding onto the second glove with my other hand. I thought I looked particularly dashing.

When I arrived to pick this lassie up I'm sure her father must have thought . . . well, I don't know what he thought, but I don't think the word "dashing" would have come into the equation.

Anyway, she brought two scrawly kids and we all went over to the Art Gallery. Then I took them back home again. And that was it.

"That was very nice, thanks," I said.

Another one I liked was a trapeze artiste, Patsy Silva. She and her parents lived in a real gypsy caravan at the foot of Govan Road in Glasgow. I used to go down there in my Boy Scout uniform carrying a big pole. Boy Scouts always had poles. I thought that would impress her.

I met Grace Pagan at my first show in Edinburgh where she was performing as a dancer in a double-act with her mother. Then a couple of years went past before we met up again when we were both playing at the Winter Gardens in Rothesay. We hit it off before she went away for a season in England, but friends of ours were all saying: "Why don't you get engaged? Why don't you get engaged?"

When she came back I asked her to marry me. She said yes. I was 19 and she was 18, and I still hadn't really had any proper girlfriends.

Our wedding was to be a lavish affair in Edinburgh with people like Martha Raye, a big American film star who was playing the Empire Theatre at the time, on the guest list. I bought a flash car and gave it to a mechanic pal to make sure it was perfect for the Big Day. But when I went to pick the car up it wasn't ready. He gave me an Austin, a really old Austin, as a replacement. I had no choice but to take it.

My brother Bertie and I planned to drive through to Edinburgh on the eve of the wedding after finishing our show at the Metropole. Before setting out we stopped at the home of our friend Jack Easy, the Wizard of the Concertina, for a cup of tea.

By the time we came back out to the car someone had nicked our hired morning suits.

Then on the way through to Edinburgh this really old Austin broke down, and we were finally towed into the capital at six o'clock the following morning. We were absolutely knackered.

I'm sure someone was trying to warn me.

However, we managed to hire another couple of suits, and sent for a taxi to take us to the wedding. When it rolled up I couldn't believe my eyes. I had never seen a taxi like it. It was like a cabriolet with a glass top, except it was a Rolls-Royce which must have sat 10 feet off the ground at the back. It looked like Cinderella's coach.

The wedding itself was wonderful, surprisingly free of the kind of disasters that had gone before it. Afterwards we travelled back to Glasgow to the excitement of the show at the Metropole which we still had to perform in. At the end Grace came on in her wedding gown, an idea of my father's. "It'll help the business," he said.

Eventually we got a flat in Glasgow, where the rent was £8 10s a quarter. I didn't have much money in those days, certainly not working for my father. And we only had £30 in the bank. He was good enough to buy us a bedroom suite, but forgot to mention that it didn't include the mattress and spring. We slept between the ends of the bed for a fortnight until we could afford to buy them ourselves.

4

SAUSAGES IS THE BOYS

The Logan Family were a fantastic success at the Metropole. Six tremendous summer seasons on the trot after the end of the War are testament to that.

We built up our own regular audience, an audience I probably loved more than any other. There was a real rapport with the punters, in fact it was so good they sometimes got carried away and started shouting out at us during an act. I loved it.

That, of course, was an especially good period for me. In 1947, when we were first billed as The Logan Family, my father was still billing Short and Dalziel alongside Jim and Buddy Logan. Soon, however, as I shot more into the limelight, they became Ma and Pa Logan, and my father decided Jimmy was a better first name for the rising comic. I was best known for my schoolboy character whose catchphrase was "It's smashin' Maw". That phrase became so well known we used it as the title for that show.

The Metropole is undoubtedly where I made my name. It was a launch pad for bigger and better things, though to this day I still find the whole thing rather surprising. Although we were extremely popular, the Metropole was probably on the fourth level of theatres in Scotland. The cream at the top were the Howard &

Wyndham theatres like the King's in Glasgow and Edinburgh, then came maybe the Moss Empires, followed by places like the Glasgow Pavilion. Below that there were a whole host of smaller, less prestigious theatres of which the Metropole was just one. We were probably Scotland's top music hall "family" team, and everyone from that part of Glasgow who came to see us undoubtedly thought we were stars, but had you asked your average punter anywhere else who Scotland's big stars were, they would never have mentioned The Logan Family, let alone me.

It's for this reason that I was utterly astounded when a telegram arrived in the late 1940s from America from the producers of *Top Banana* on Broadway. They wanted me, Jimmy Logan, this unknown comic from the other side of the world, to take Phil Silvers' place in the lead role. I couldn't believe it, and I thought it was a wind-up. None of which mattered anyway because I was contracted to my father who wanted me to stay at the Metropole, and continue going into Sunday concerts even though we were working our socks off during the week.

The press, though, had been good to me. In most of the write-ups I was declared one of the country's best young comics, and a couple of columnists even described me as the most promising since the great Tommy Lorne.

It was perhaps on the back of these accolades that, a short time later, my first big break really did arrive. Once again I couldn't believe my ears when I was asked if I would be interested in shooting a feature film in London with Gordon Jackson.

The question cropped up in a call from a friend of mine, Bill Tait, the cartoonist on the Glasgow *Evening Citizen*. I particularly remember his wonderful contribution to the stramash after another friend, Dr Tom Honeyman, bought Salvador Dali's wonderful 'Christ of St John of the Cross' painting for the Glasgow Art Gallery. The council got it for a song, something like £8,200 which included all the reproduction rights, but, as per usual, most people thought it was a complete waste of money. It seemed to dominate the letters pages of the papers for an age. 'Tait's Smile' on that occasion was just wonderful. He had a wee Glasgow punter standing looking up at the painting with the price tag of £8,200 stuck on it. And all the wee Glaswegian said was: "Jeesus Christ."

Anyway, Bill phoned me up and said: "Jimmy, The J. Arthur Rank Organisation in London is making a film called *Floodtide*."

"Oh right. Good for them," I said.

"Jimmy, they want you to be in it."

I almost dropped the phone. Bill explained that the J. Arthur Rank Organisation wanted me to go to London for a screen test. To this day I don't know how or why they came to choose me for the role. I had never uttered a straight word in my life, yet here I was being asked to star alongside a Big Name like Gordon Jackson in a Big Movie. Maybe they came to Glasgow looking for a funny young fellow, and someone said: "Have a look at Jimmy Logan." I honestly don't know.

However, it wasn't exactly a tough decision.

When I got to Pinewood Studios it was the first time I had been to a film studio. The minute I arrived someone handed me a full monologue, and said: "Look at that, then come back and do it."

I looked at all the words on the page and broke out in a sweat. I was used to making things up as I went along, and if ever there was a script, I never read it word for word. I can only say that I cottoned onto the gist of what was in front of me because there was a thread running through it. They put me in front of the camera and I did my best. I didn't have a clue.

Then they asked me to do one or two other wee things, which I did, and overall they seemed quite happy. This, of course, was a big boost to my confidence. I was now feeling pretty good about myself, and went for a walk into this giant old aircraft hangar. In the distance I could see a film set so I went over to watch. Of course, you weren't supposed to do that. But I didn't know.

The film was *The Blue Lagoon,* and Trevor Howard and Jean Simmons were getting ready to do a scene. I was gobsmacked. Here I was in this film studio watching two big stars, and I was part of it. What a feeling. Just then the air was filled by the sound of bells, and the whole place was sealed off for the scene. Standing out like a sore thumb, I suddenly realised I shouldn't have been there at all, and quietly slipped back into the darkness. When they finished their scene I realised what a ham bone I had been. They had performed beautifully. It occurred to me that any ideas I savoured of knowing what I was doing were utter rubbish.

On the journey home to Glasgow I was depressed and sure I wouldn't get the part, but when I got back I was told they had decided to take me on. By this time my father had become in-volved as well, and secured £100 a week compensation while I worked on the film.

There really was no stopping him. Before I disappeared from the show at the Metropole to start filming, he got me to record one of the songs I sang, Irving Berlin's 'When I Leave The World Behind'. When I was away, they put the spotlight on this empty box, and my father said disconsolately: "D'you remember when Jimmy stood there?" And the record played.

You would have thought I had died.

"Don't worry son," said my father. "It'll be good for business."

And he was right.

Filming *Floodtide* was a remarkable experience. Alongside con-summate professionals like Gordon Jackson, Rona Anderson, John Laurie, Elizabeth Sellars and Janet Brown, I quickly realised I had no idea what I was doing.

That was where Rona and Gordon, who were later married, met for the first time. Rona just took one look at him, and said: "He's mine." And Gordon had no chance.

When I first arrived in the studios, the director Freddie Wilson obviously noticed I was as nervous as hell. He spoke to Gordon, who took me for a coffee and asked me about The Logan Family. It was wonderful. Here was this big star who I had seen in films at the Capital Picture House in Ibrox showing a genuine interest in my family. I found out during that film what a lovely human being he was.

Overall, I was dead lucky to be surrounded by people like Gordon, Rona and John. When I wasn't doing stuff right, they were always there to offer advice, suggesting better ways to do things. There was no comparison with the stage. The mugging things that got laughs at the Metropole would have looked absolutely grotesque on camera.

Because Gordon had done so much radio and film, he was able to pick up a script and read it out loud the way he was going to do it. "Oh, it's a lovely day," he would say.

And I was supposed to answer: "Yeah, but I think the weather's going to change."

But when I said it, it came out: "Yes . . . it . . . is . . . but . . . I . . . think . . . the . . . weather . . . is . . . go . . . ing . . . to . . . change."

I was like a robot. The only way I could get round it was to learn every word off by heart, then say it over and over again until it sounded natural. It was hardly the most efficient way to go about things, but it worked for me.

In one scene I had to flip a coin. Not much to that I thought, but John Laurie pulled me up and said: "Do it this way. Do that, and that, then that. You see." I did, and he was right.

On another occasion Gordon Jackson got a hold of me, and moved me.

"Oi, what are you shoving me for?" I said.

"Don't stand there, stand here," he replied, moving me into position. "You're in better light now."

"Aw aye, that's just another way of saying the camera's on you."

It was a huge learning experience. When I first saw the rushes I thought: "Oh boy." Now that was a learning experience.

But we all had a great relationship and a wonderful rapport. One day Gordon Jackson happened to mention that he loved to play the piano, so I phoned up the property department and, using a disguised voice, said: "Can you send a piano to Mr Gordon Jackson's room?"

When we came off the set, I said: "Go and look in your room."

He was shocked. "Where did that come from?"

"We ordered it."

"You can't do that."

"No, it's done."

Then I switched around the name plates on the dressing room doors. It caused chaos.

I returned to Glasgow having learned a great deal, and utterly thrilled to have been involved in such a magnificent production. *Floodtide* came out in May 1949, and the response was just tremendous. People queued for hundreds of yards outside cinemas to see it, and it was an unqualified success.

The film broke down a lot of barriers, employing an all-Scots cast and using real Scottish accents, most notably my own, for virtually the first time. The story centred on an ambitious Scots farm boy, Jackson, who goes against his family's wishes to make a name for himself in the Glasgow shipyards. I played one of his workmates, the idle lad Tim Brogan.

I got rave reviews for *Floodtide*, and that role undoubtedly made me a "household name" in my own country. You can imagine what the reaction was like when I walked back on stage at the Metropole.

During the period *Floodtide* was made Rank gave people a seven-year contract if they could say "Dinner is served". Unfortunately, around that time, there was a big slump in the British film industry. Suddenly no-one was getting any work—including me. I had an agent in London, and thought the great reaction to the film would lead to more offers. I was quite content with the thought of becoming a film star. But there was nothing. The phone never rang.

In hindsight I believe it was a blessing. So I was great in *Floodtide*, and could have been big in films. But I wouldn't have been any good at anything else, and would never have achieved what I went on to achieve in the theatre. Looking back on my life on stage, that mattered to me more than any film.

Around that time I remember a write-up in one of the papers with photographs of big stars like Harry Lauder, Jack Radcliffe, Harry Gordon and Alec Finlay. The headline read: "Where are the men to replace these great stars?"

The article said Jimmy Logan was up and coming, but that was it. Of course, it was very flattering to be singled out like that, but I felt a number of other performers had been done a great injustice, especially my pal Jack Milroy.

I phoned up the newspaper, and said: "Have a look at Jack Milroy at the Queen's Theatre. I'm sure he will be great."

Jack and I are still great friends to this day. He's such a kind, funny and warm-hearted man. Recently, he came for dinner with his wife, Mary. "I love mince," he said, "because it's kind of half chewed before you get it."

The next time he came, we gave him salmon in a beautiful hollandaise sauce. "That was lovely," said Jack wiping the sauce from his lips. "It's the first time I've ever had salmon and custard."

Mary and Jack make a good team.

When I finished *Floodtide*, my marriage to Grace had barely begun. We didn't have enough money to furnish the flat in Ibrox and, in the post-war period, it was incredibly difficult to buy new furniture. We had curtains and a piano in the living room, and that was about it. There were no carpets anywhere in the house.

Instead, I painted the big hallway with Darkalene, a black shiny polished paint for floors, and Granny Allan gave me a maroon runner to put a stripe right up the centre. We thought it looked great at the time.

In the euphoria that surrounded the premiere of *Floodtide* in Glasgow, I invited everyone to a big party back at my house. Then I remembered I had no furniture. I rushed over to Paisley and asked the stage manager if I could borrow the giant carpet he used for plays. A friend also loaned me his new three-piece utility suite. The arms were about four inches wide and it was covered in Rexine, which meant you got stuck to it when you sat down, but it was new. My mother gave us chairs, glasses and a radio, and someone else gave us a standard lamp. For the guest room we borrowed a single bed that would have been impossible to sleep on because of a big bit of wood that ran up the middle of it. However, we had no intention of using it as a bed. That's where we put all the coats.

The party itself was marvellous, so full of people nobody would have noticed there were no carpets on the floors. The next morning a lorry arrived and took everything away. It would have been a disaster if anyone had forgotten their jacket and come back. We'd have had to tell them the house had been burgled.

My relationship with Grace, however, had started poorly, and things between us weren't going well. It may surprise people now, but in those days couples never dared ask what the other partner wanted out of life before getting married. People tended to get carried away with the emulsion of the moment, got hitched and that was that. Grace and I were no different.

It was only after we had made this enormous commitment that I realised we both wanted totally different things. She had no intention of staying in our new flat cooking and cleaning, nor had she any ambitions to be a mother. Instead, I found out she got married in the hope that we could become a double-act like her parents, the dancers Pagan and Ross. But I didn't want to do a double-act with anybody, let alone my wife.

To say the first few months of our marriage were difficult is an understatement. I would go to the theatre, while she would sit at home and weep.

We went through an extraordinarily tough time, which took its toll on my health. Finally I took my friends' advice and went to the doctor. He said my blood pressure was rocketing, and ordered me to take a week off. So my father, with my best interests at heart as usual, told me to do the first show of the new programme on the Monday night—the one the press came to.

"I don't want the press to know you are not in the show," he said. "It will be bad for business. So if you work the Monday night you can take the rest of the week off."

On the Tuesday myself and some friends went to the hills overlooking Largs where my mother and father had what can only be described as a Victorian wooden structure they affectionately called a "caravan". It had one big room, a bathroom, a wee cooking area, and a veranda with a beautiful view of the Clyde.

Each morning my pals put my bed out in the field, helped me into it, threw blankets over me and went into town to enjoy themselves. Meanwhile I tried to sleep in the fresh air. My friends insisted this was the best remedy for my condition, although I was somewhat suspicious.

One day they brought up one of the artistes from the entertainers at the front. His name was Chic Murray, and that was the first time I met a man who would soon become one of the greatest comics our country has produced. I wasn't really feeling well enough to enjoy his humour. In actual fact the audiences at that time didn't enjoy it either. The managers would tell his wife, Maidi, who was the mainstay of their double-act, to go it alone.

"No, no, no," she said repeatedly. "Chic's got magic in him. Just give him a chance."

But the audiences at that time weren't ready for Chic's unique brand of humour. He was way ahead of his time, so dry that people often wondered if he was being serious or not.

After a week of fresh air I went back to the doctor, who said: "You need another week off."

Once again my father told me to work the Monday night, then I went back to the hills overlooking the Clyde for another five days in a field in my bed. It drove me up the wall. When I returned the following week, my father told me he believed in the "no play, no pay" philosophy, which meant I only got money for the two Monday nights I had worked.

Gradually my blood pressure dropped, and the spirit of feeling between Grace and myself began to rise. Soon we were getting on fine, and Grace even came into the show at the Metropole, although not in a double-act with me.

There were some great stories from the Metropole.

You got bits of scenery in through the dock doors—giant doors round the back of the theatre where the base of the door was about seven feet off the ground.

I hit on an idea where I thought it would be wonderful if we could get a taxi onto the stage for one of our summer shows. And the best way to get the taxi into the theatre was through the dock doors.

A cabbie who wasn't working that week loaned me his taxi for £5. We made a run up to the doors using planks, kitchen tables and boxes, and tied a rope to the front of the taxi.

At two o'clock on the afternoon of the show the cabbie revved the taxi at the end of the lane, put his foot down and went straight up the gang plank. How it just didn't collapse I'll never know.

However, disaster struck. We hadn't reckoned on a wooden step behind the doors that covered the water pipes, and before we knew it the taxi had come to a halt with its chassis dangling on top of this step; the front wheels were dangling on the inside, and the back wheels were dangling on the outside. By this time the planks had collapsed.

We stood there analysing the situation. There was no way of getting the taxi in, and there was no way of getting the taxi out.

Suddenly it's six o'clock at night, I'm black and there's a queue of people waiting to get into the gallery. The police have arrived to keep people back in case the taxi falls.

And Alex Frutin, the owner, appears, shouting: "Get that out my theatre."

I couldn't get it in never mind get it out.

The show that night was hilarious because in a comedy item, someone would walk on and say: "It's still hanging there."

We finally got it in, and we did use it on stage.

On another occasion we got two swings, built a cut-out of the side of an aeroplane and painted it up. The idea was for myself and another comic Wee Dougie—who was about four feet nothing—to get into the swings and get pulled up into the scenery before the start of the show.

And he's saying to me: "You must be mad."

"Oh, don't worry, it's going to be all right."

There was no question of health and safety. We were hanging 30 feet above the stage but what an entrance it was going to be. As we started to be lowered onto the stage the audience would see the red and green lights on the wings of the plane, and us inside it. What an entrance.

However, it went disastrously wrong. As we were lowered in the stage was in complete blackout. The audience couldn't see a thing.

And when the lights finally came up, we had not only been lowered in, but we were standing there in the middle of the stage. We could have walked on.

Wee Dougie was a lovely man who came from Paisley. He was

selling newspapers at Paisley Cross when my father met him. The next minute he was a comedian touring with us.

I devised an act for him that we performed at the Empire Theatre in Edinburgh in a big charity concert.

He was wearing a beautiful top hat and tails, and his make-up was just marvellous.

I lifted him up, carried him on stage and balanced him on my knee with my foot on the chair. He was the ventriloquist's doll.

We did a double-act that went down very well before bursting into our final song. We went off stage, and I came back on to take the applause. Then Wee Dougie walked on. The audience gasped . . . because until that point they thought he was a genuine dummy.

More films may have failed to arrive after *Floodtide*, but the BBC in Glasgow certainly sat up and took notice. One of their top men, Howard M. Lockhart, had been sent on assignment to Australia, and in exchange, an Aussie called Trafford Whitelock came over to Scotland, where he decided to start a comedy series on the Scottish Home Service.

I was asked to be part of the show along with two other young actors, Eddie Fraser and Primrose Milligan, and a couple of more experienced folk from the Scottish Variety Orchestra. Until then these types of shows had never been successful, but Whitelock was sure *It's All Yours* would go against the grain and become a big success. To begin with, he couldn't have been more wrong. The first six shows were a disaster, and the script was so bad I was getting letters saying: "You stink," and "Get off the air ya big balloon." And that was just from my friends! My father told me: "Son, get out of that rubbish."

It was no wonder. The writers kept suggesting things like using the sound effect of a seagull when something funny happened. They would say: "Beeby the Seagull, do you understand? B B the C gull. Get it."

There would be guffaws in the studio. Meanwhile, I was about to commit suicide.

Never before had I been pilloried so much for something I was involved in. One of Scotland's top newspaper critics Gordon Irving, who became a dear friend, wrote an open letter to me in his column.

"Theatre enthusiasts in Scotland are watching your climb up the ladder with great interest," he wrote. "They're saying good things and bad things about you, Jimmy. In a nutshell, you're trying to do too many things at once . . . radio, films, stage. Don't, please, take on any more commitments if the scripts set you so much out of character as *It's All Yours* has done. Don't try to assume the phoney polite way of talking in your stage parts. It isn't Jimmy Logan . . . your fans don't like it. And don't overwork so much. You have a duty to a public which is hoping to see you emerge as a top-liner. Radio rehearsals in the morning, recordings in the afternoon, personal appearances, and two shows every night . . . it's too much for one who should be conserving his vitality."

He concluded: "Be natural. Be yourself. Don't hesitate to reject radio commissions if they look like harming your good, natural name."

The comment about the accent was unfair. I was using my own accent learned in a Glasgow school. It wasn't a Glesca patter you needed to be funny on the radio—it was good gags.

It was all very well telling me to cut down my workload, but in our business you took work when you got it. For a while, when our family show was in Aberdeen, I drove down to Glasgow early on the Sunday morning, recorded the radio show, then drove back up north for the stage show that night.

Gordon, however, had made a fair point on the quality of the scripts. Round the corner from the BBC at the top of Byres Road was a wee Italian cafe where Eddie Fraser and I sometimes went to drown our sorrows in coffee, and work out what on earth to do.

For a start, we knew there were some pretty serious technical problems that could be sorted out easily. For instance, there were microphones for the artistes but none for the audience. Those microphones would only pick up the laughter from the first few rows of the audience. So if people further back were laughing the microphones never picked it up. And we could hardly come back in in the middle of a laugh. The result was that the listener heard laughs, silence and then our dialogue eventually started again. Talk about making it difficult for ourselves.

By a stroke of luck, after about six awful broadcasts, Eddie Fraser got the job as the producer of the show, and brought in a young guy called Stanley Baxter who was doing exceptionally well at the Citizens' Theatre. Two new writers—Andrew McIntyre and Jack McLeod—were also hired. It made all the difference. Right away Stanley and I struck up a great rapport—giving the impression on the show that we couldn't stand each other—and the scripts improved immensely.

For instance, there would be a knock at the door.

"Does Mr Baxter live here?"

"Yes, bring him in."

I also said Stanley was the first comedian who was thrown at a custard pie.

The whole thing worked a treat. People were actually coming to Stanley or myself in the street and saying things like: "Hey Stanley. I'm a fan of Jimmy Logan's. You better watch it or you're going to get it."

Because it was radio our only image was our voices, and few people knew what we looked like. Apparently most folk thought I was a wee fat bloke, when in reality I was tall and slim.

It's All Yours also heralded the beginning of one of my catch-phrases—"sausages is the boys". Now, I've been asked through the years for an explanation of how this came about, or what it meant, but I honestly can't enlighten you.

The script writers came up with it one day, and said: "Try that. We think it might get a few laughs."

I thought: "What is this?"

They reckoned it would be perfect for one of my characters, the gormless youth Sammy Dreep, a kind of wee Glaswegian you could imagine wearing a bunnet and thick glasses, who always spat out phlegm when he was talking. He was the kind of boy who would say . . . "Aw yesh, Mishta Logan, don't worry about it Mishta Logan, no problem Mishta Logan."

So in one episode I suddenly said: "You can like eggs, you can like ham, but sausages is the boys."

The response was phenomenal, and before we knew where we were it had really taken on . . . "You can build your skyscrapers, you can build your palashes, you can take vasht areas of the deshert and give ush oil and water. But never forget . . . Sausages is the boys."

There's no intelligent explanation, but people everywhere were saying "sausages is the boys". A guy would be telling his pal about a great holiday down the coast, and his pal would say: "Aye, but sausages is the boys." Or a woman would be raving about her day at the shops, and her daughter would say: "Aye, but don't forget. Sausages is the boys."

It was amazing.

Another catchphrase which really took off was "Smashin' in't it". I had bought a Rolls-Replica—one of the original Rolls-Royces that were bought up by an enterprising company who put a new body on the back and renamed them. When I was doing *It's All Yours* I got a most beautiful coat of arms put on the door. It looked spectacular, and often drew curious glances from well-heeled businessmen in their bowler hats.

"I wonder what important person that is," they would think, walking over to see.

Of course, on closer inspection they saw a beautiful little royal blue shield with a white square in the middle to represent film, a pair of boots to represent my stage character, and a microphone. And the little gold band that usually said something in Latin proclaimed: "Smashin' in't it!"

At that point the bowler-hatted men would walk away decidedly red-faced.

We must have done around 180 broadcasts of *It's All Yours*. It was so successful I became known as Jimmy 'It's All Yours' Logan. The show went out on a Monday night, and I'm sure every woman stayed in ironing just to listen to us.

That's the show which originally inspired Billy Connolly to become a comedian. He heard Jimmy Logan on the radio being funny with a Glesca accent—something that was unheard of before then—and decided to follow the same road.

"Sausages is the boys" may have captured a nation's heart but my use of the Glesca slang didn't please everyone. During a debate on education in the House of Commons, Arthur Woodburn MP claimed the BBC was encouraging slovenly and ungrammatical speech—and that I was the chief perpetrator. Claiming "Sausages is the boys" was a terrible example of a country that had been providing the best education in the world for 50 years, this outspoken member for Clackmannan and East Stirling said: "I am not reflecting on the Scottish accent—a good Scottish tongue is a passport to anywhere in the English-speaking world—but it is distressing to hear raucous, ungrammatical and slovenly speech in some parts of Scotland. It is rather sad that the principal entertainment on the BBC is to hear our own people speaking. I need only point out 'The McFlannels' and the Jimmy Logan programme as examples of deplorable speech that passes for Scottish. I hope something can be done to get rid of this slovenly speech, bad articulation and bad grammar."

He went on to say that Scots girls, in particular, didn't want to be talking like that. "A nice voice is a great asset to a girl . . . the beauty of her face is greatly depreciated if she speaks with a raucous voice."

Comments like this seem absurd today, but it's a good example of the times we lived in then to see how much controversy was caused by simply celebrating the working man's way of speaking. As Cliff Hanley said in his column at the time: "Glaswegian's here to stay, and as far as I'm concerned, long life to it." Hear, hear Cliff.

It's All Yours made national stars of us all. Stanley was so popular he was snapped up by the theatre giants Howard & Wyndham to play pantomime in Scotland's best theatres. He was the really Big Name because he was playing the top theatres, while I was still with the Logan Family at the Metropole. That was a deliberate decision on my part. I still regarded myself as an apprentice who needed to master not just comedy, but my singing voice and the instruments I played as well. I wanted to be an all-rounder, and the best place to do that was in the music hall with my family where I learned every aspect of the trade—on stage and front of house.

Just after *Floodtide* a couple of years earlier, the big boss at Howard & Wyndham, A. Stewart Cruikshank, had sent for me, and as we sat in the circle of one of his great theatres, asked what my plans were.

"I'd love to do pantomime," I said to him. "I do this character who I think would make a great Buttons."

The character to whom I referred was a schoolboy I did in the family sketches at the Metropole. It always went down very well. Before *Floodtide* I had worn a big loose jersey, an old shirt and torn trousers. When I came back I bought a complete uniform of the posh Whitehill School with a blue blazer, grey shorts, white sand-shoes, blue and white socks, a nice white shirt and a blue tie.

My father hated it. "You're killing the character," he said. "They don't like you. They think you've gone snobby."

But I stuck to my guns because I thought if I ever got into the King's, Theatre Royal or any other great theatre, I couldn't go in with old dirty clothes. I was aiming higher—the gun was always pointed upwards, not at the ground.

So here I was sitting with the biggest boss in the biggest theatre company telling him about my nice clean-cut schoolboy who would be perfect for Buttons.

He listened intently, then asked if I would like to go into their summer show with the big comic Dave Willis. It wasn't an offer I was expecting but, after thinking about it, I asked for an awful lot of money—£35 a week. It was a big demand, but I reckoned if they paid me that amount they couldn't afford to have taken me off, even if Dave Willis had taken one look and said he didn't want me.

Not surprisingly, they knocked me back. I received a polite, diplomatically worded letter which said: "You are a young man asking for an amount we are paying to all-time stars, so we regret we cannot offer you a deal."

Even then, I was convinced I had done the right thing in standing my ground.

However, in 1952, his son Stewart Cruikshank, who had since stepped into his shoes as the big boss of Howard & Wyndham, asked me to go into their pantomime *Robinson Crusoe* at the King's Theatre in Edinburgh.

He was offering me much more money than the £18 a week I was getting from my father, and I was guaranteed to get paid if I was off sick. My father never gave me any wages when I was ill because he reckoned it made me come back quicker. More importantly, though, I felt I was ready to take the step up. I had served my apprenticeship, and the time was right to break away from the family to make it big on my own. So I talked it over with my father.

"Yeah, great. Fine, very good," he said. That was a typical answer from him.

I signed the five-year contract for summer and winter seasons with Howard & Wyndham before going out to the Malmaison Hotel with Grace for a celebratory meal. When we got in, there was a call from a journalist at the *Scottish Daily Express*.

"Jimmy, your father has said he will sue you if you leave the Logan Family. What comment do you have?"

"Oh listen, that's rubbish. I've talked this over with my father. He knows I'm going."

"No Jimmy, he says he'll sue you and it's going on the front page of the paper."

The following day it was indeed on the front page of the paper, under the headline "I'll Sue Jimmy Logan If He Quits, Says Pop". The family picture they used annoyed my brother Buddy because they had substituted my face for his, even though I was already in the photo at the other side.

In the story my father said: "Jimmy signed a two year contract with a two year option with me. And that means I have the option of his services for another two years. This isn't a family quarrel—it's a business quarrel. As far as we—Mum and I—are concerned this is going to law. It's a terrible thing, I suppose, for a father to sue his son but I have the rest of the family to consider."

He reckoned his business would suffer if he lost the "star of the show".

"But my boy Jim—he's still the best comic in the business," my father concluded. "No matter what happens over this contract business, his Mum and I wish him every success."

I had been tied to the family for some time but hadn't legally released myself because it was my family. However, I took legal advice from a lawyer and Queen's Counsel who both advised that my father could not hold me to his contract. It had been signed without any witnesses and, according to them, in Scotland a two year contract required witnesses.

Despite all this, I did a deal with my father where I would pay him £60 out of my wages every week when I was doing the pantomime for Howard & Wyndham. I even agreed to go back with the family for the following summer season at the Palace Theatre in Dundee.

My co-star in the pantomime at the King's was Douglas Byng, who played Robinson Crusoe. He was an artiste of class and experience who had a great reputation as a dame, and in smart cabaret and revue. I played his seaman pal, Will Atkins, resplendent in my Bounty-Mutiny hat, outsize boots and a paint-pot looking for a pillar box.

As I was "first top" on the bill, the stage manager said to me that I would be in the Number One dressing room, a great big L-shaped room, but I offered to let Dougie go in there because Number Two dressing room was up the stairs well away from the stage, and he had a lot of costume changes. I thought it would have made life easier for him.

"Put Mr Byng in Number One room. I'll go into Number Two," I told the stage manager.

However, it wasn't long before Dougie came storming in, and said to me: "How dare you! You must occupy your position in Number One room. If you are number one on the bill you should be number one."

I had only been trying to help, but that episode taught me a great lesson. As my mother and father had always occupied Number One I didn't think it mattered. But it did. If you are in the lead position you should lead.

Despite this, I still thought, from a purely practical point of view, that Dougie would be better off using Number One. A compromise was reached. We found a way of curtaining off Number One so that Dougie and the principal boy could use it for quick changes.

There are times in life when you feel very lonely, and waiting for your first entrance in a pantomime or play is most definitely one of them. Before the first performance of *Robinson Crusoe* I stood at the side of the stage and said a wee prayer. I knew if I did well in this panto, the door to the best theatres would open up for me. If not, it was back to the "Number Fours".

The responsibility for my success or failure rested solely on my shoulders because I had written all my own material. Dougie had also written some good stuff and, despite the dressing room misunderstanding, we worked well together.

That night Stewart Cruikshank came backstage, which was very unusual for him.

"Are you OK, Jimmy?" he said. "D'you need anything?"

"Thanks very much, Mr Cruikshank. I'm fine."

Everyone else kept well away because they could see I was concentrating on getting things just right. When I went on I was given a lovely welcome, and the whole night went very well. There were some lovely scenes, and some great comedy.

For instance, Dougie had written a scene, after the ship foundered, where two fishermen pulled in a whale which was about 16 feet long. When they cut the middle bit out, all the audience could see was Dougie and myself sitting inside its stomach having a cup of tea.

Of course, at the age of just 24, I thought this really was the life. I bought a second-hand Jaguar, a coat with a fur collar and had a big party on the opening night in my wife's family home. Every Thursday Dougie and I got dressed up in our dinner jackets, and went for a meal in the George Hotel.

"I hope you don't mind me saying this, Jimmy," remarked Dougie on one of those occasions, "but you really must go and get another dinner suit."

"Oh . . . ahem . . . I've got one ordered," I said, before rushing out to buy one.

I was spending money as if it was going out of fashion when I suddenly realised there were only a few weeks to go of the panto season, and I hadn't saved a penny. I immediately got an insurance policy for £10,000 from my dear friend Ernest Bromfield, the son of the Paisley baker Arthur Bromfield who had been a wonderful friend to our family. He once gave me a book on the life of Tommy Handley, and added his own inscription: "Success is backbone, not wishbone." Which I liked. He was a very fine man who I admired, and ultimately a great influence on my life.

The panto season lasted about 16 weeks and was tremendously successful. We got consistently great write-ups. One leading London writer's train got delayed so he came to see us, and we ended up getting nice press down there too. I was singled out for particular praise on many occasions, so by the time I left to go on a 22-week summer tour with my family, my reputation was sky-high.

And so was my head.

I got new scenery built, devised a whole new opening and even got the cast interested in *Slaughter on 10th Avenue*. When we went up to Aberdeen I had the audacity to go into the orchestra pit and conduct—even though I couldn't read music. This only served to annoy my father who felt I had become "too big for my boots". In his view I was encroaching on his territory as boss of the show. It would be the last show I starred in with the Logan Family, before I started out full-time on the next exciting stage of my career with Howard & Wyndham, almost a decade of pantomimes in the winter followed by the hugely successful *Five Past Eight* revue in the summer.

My long association with Howard & Wyndham started with the *Robinson Crusoe* panto in 1952, but a year later I was back in my home town in the starring role in one of the big theatres. It was a great moment. One of the newspapers even declared my official arrival at the top of the tree of Scottish comedy.

In *Puss in Boots* at the Theatre Royal in Glasgow I was Simple

Simon, and top of the bill alongside another great of the Scottish music hall, Harry Gordon. He was a big star before I was born, and if I may say so, more than a little suspicious of this young upstart whose name was before his on the billboard. As time went past, though, Harry felt less threatened by me, and realised we could be of great help to each other. I'm glad to say we ended up working so well that we became very close friends, teaming up for years afterwards in different shows.

Harry is another gentleman who wrote a wonderful page in the history of music hall. Being on stage with him in his home town of Aberdeen, where he was a legend, was an education in itself. I once accompanied him to the Braemar Games, and had I not known who he was, would have thought I was in the presence of royalty; such was the effect he had on people, constantly surrounded by a degree of love and affection I had never witnessed.

His story is incredible. Emerging from the Gordon Highlanders after the 1914-18 War, he used his nimble, brilliant mind and fine artistic qualities to start out in a double-act with his wife. They called themselves The Velmas, after a famous chocolate. Double-acts tended to have names like that—Guinness and Stout, and Knight and Day to name but two.

Harry was first known as a black-faced lightning cartoonist who drew quick sketches of members of the audience, and his wife was a champion Highland dancer. Soon, Harry left that behind and started running concert parties before taking over the Beach Pavilion, which he turned into the venue for some of Scotland's principal summer performances—magnificent productions that gained a reputation as the best seaside summer shows around, and which were often recorded for radio broadcasts.

Then he came down to Glasgow and did seventeen years of pantomime at the giant Alhambra Theatre with other big names like Will Fyffe and Alec Finlay, and eventually me. Harry was a brilliant comedian and wonderful pantomime dame.

Soon afterwards, though, he suffered a heart attack. He was off for quite a bit, and in the process lost his confidence because he hadn't been on the stage for a while, so I asked him to appear as a special guest on the *Five Past Eight* we were doing at the time. He agreed, and we managed to keep his appearance a secret.

We were doing one of our regular sketches featuring the McAuley family where I played the boy, and Jack Radcliffe and Helen Norman were my mum and dad. On this occasion I was holding an outrageous party in the house because the parents were on holiday. Harry, as a neighbour, was to barge in complaining about the noise.

When he entered there was a gasp from the audience. Then the roof almost came off its hinges. He had come in that night with his daughter, as nervous as anything. But when he saw the great reaction from the punters that settled him completely. It had brought him successfully back into the limelight in a protected way.

He walked in, sat down and sang 'Granny's Porridge', one of his big numbers. It got a great ovation. Then the police suddenly arrived back at my house with the parents, and we protested we were just having a party. They were having none of it, though, because someone was breaking the law by charging people to get in. That someone turned out to be Harry Gordon.

The great reception he got that night persuaded him he was well enough to come back into the business. He did another panto, did far too much work again and ended up having another heart attack. The day I went to see him I took some Cumberland sausages, which he loved, and administered a terrible row. He just sat there in his bed, staring straight ahead.

"You had to do this, you had to do that," I said, "and I know this is going in one bloody ear and out the other."

And he burst out laughing. He knew what I was saying.

Not long afterwards Harry took yet another heart attack, and was rushed into the Infirmary. His wife and daughter had no car, so I used to take them back and forward to the hospital. After the pantomime I would go to their house and sleep on a tiny two-seater settee, phoning the hospital every few hours during the night to check on his condition. He was at death's door.

One night, after a couple of weeks of this, I phoned and was pleasantly surprised to hear he was picking up. The medical staff were very happy with his progress.

I was delighted, and decided it was time to get a proper sleep in my own bed because I was absolutely exhausted. When I got up the following day I was told he had died.

Harry was cremated, and I registered his death. Then I took his wife and daughter in the car to the train station for their journey back up to Aberdeen. Beside me I had this little casket with Harry Gordon inside it.

"What should I put on the casket?" his wife asked me.

"I would put 'Harry Gordon—The Laird of Inversnecky'. He would like that."

Initially Harry had been suspicious of the young Jimmy Logan, but he became one of my closest and dearest friends. He was so full of life in the theatre that I almost thought of him as a bouncing tennis ball. When he died I bought all his dame's wigs and props, and his sketches and songs. He was an extraordinarily funny man, and I felt privileged to be alongside such a great artiste on the stage. There were things I learned by just watching him that I would never have otherwise thought of.

Harry Gordon joined me for the summer season of *Half Past Eight* that followed *Puss in Boots*. It was my first for Howard & Wyndham, and my first appearance in this great annual revue that had become such an integral and eagerly awaited fixture on the Scottish theatre calendar.

It all started way back in the Thirties when folk got their

summer entertainment at the open air concert parties in places like Portobello. In those days people only went to the theatre in dinner suits. But Howard & Wyndham realised there was a gap in the market to exploit—because all their big theatres were standing empty in the summer.

A. Stewart Cruikshank got some artistes together to start a summer revue called *Half Past Seven*. They played at the King's in Glasgow and Edinburgh, gradually building a name for themselves, until after the War when the Edinburgh show became known as *Half Past Eight*, even though it started at eight o'clock on the dot, and the Glasgow show was called *Five Past Eight*. Having worked in both, I asked Harry Gordon what the difference was, and he said: "Twenty-five minutes."

Fortunes were spent on beautiful costumes and wonderful scenery, and by the time I did my first one at Edinburgh in 1954 they had become the top shows around. They were magnificent, glamorous affairs full of great comedy, and lively singing and dancing. The 32-piece orchestra was conducted by the great Geraldo, and the dancers' hair and clothes were all styled and designed to suit their own individual personality. The cost of producing the shows was phenomenal but the standard was superb. People came from London to see what on earth this wonderful spectacle was about.

I did *Five Past Eight* every year until 1961, and I had a ball. I built up strong working relationships and friendships with people like Jack Radcliffe and Stanley Baxter. In the early days there would be about eight different programmes in the 22-week season, and we had a lot of gags and sketches to fill each one up. A lot of our time was taken up just thinking what the hell we were going to do next. But we also had great writers like Stan Mars, who would take our ideas and turn them into great comedy. Trying to find good writers was very difficult because they had to not only be able to write good comedy, but write comedy that suited your personality.

Often, we were working so hard we didn't realise just how wonderful it was to be a part of this great show.

No-one worked harder than the dancing girls, who were in the theatre six days a week from ten in the morning until one in the afternoon, then back at two o'clock right through until half past five in the evening before they started getting ready to look absolutely glamorous for that evening's performance.

Problems arose because these girls had no spare time, and no free moments to go shopping for food and other essentials. After six days in the theatre they were all white faced and tired, and at one point I told Stewart Cruikshank, on behalf of the girls, that this situation could not be allowed to continue. He called me the "Commissar of the Alhambra".

I particularly remember the girls were rehearsing one Saturday morning, dressed as usual in old clothes with their hair in curlers. They were rehearsing under working lights, and in a theatre under working lights all the glamour just disappears. It's dark and dull; like taking the pictures off your walls and realising you need to redecorate.

Suddenly, out of the darkness of the stalls and into this gloomy scene, stepped a tall, elegant gentleman, who said to the girls in his cultured accent: "I don't want to interrupt, ladies, but I used to work on this stage."

It was Cary Grant.

The girls almost collapsed. They couldn't believe their eyes.

Standing in front of them, and talking to them, was one of the most dashing, handsome and suave Hollywood film stars. He was there because, before he became famous in movies, Cary Grant was Archie Leach, one-time member of a touring unicycle act. And here he was dropping in on a theatre he had once played in years before.

The white-faced girls stood open mouthed in their curlers staring at the elegant gent before them.

"Would you like to join me for coffee in my hotel," said Cary Grant, noticing how tired and overworked the girls looked.

And they all went with him for an hour in their lives that none of them would ever forget.

I was once in a similar situation when I was touring with a show in San Francisco.

It was two-thirty in the morning, and I phoned up Tony Bennett in his hotel. I knew him because he's a great friend of Annie's, and I knew it would be OK to phone at that time because his show didn't finish until late on.

"Come on over, Jimmy," he said.

And there I was half an hour later in Tony Bennett's room listening to a recording of his latest songs which had still to be released. And I thought to myself: "Nobody's going to believe this."

Yet there I was sitting with Tony Bennett in the town where he lost his heart.

Interestingly, when he let me into this magnificent room in this magnificent hotel he had to remove towelling spread across the floor in front of the door. And when he closed the door again, he put the towelling back down.

He explained that hotels left a gap between the bottom of the door and the floor so they could slide newspapers into a room without disturbing the guest. However, around that time some unwanted visitors had been sliding gas cylinders under the door. The guest was knocked unconscious by the fumes before the un-wanted visitor would break in and steal all their belongings.

One opening night at *Five Past Eight* there was so much scenery up on what they called the Grid that halfway through the second half it all got tangled up. One jagged piece caught on another piece that caught on another piece. It was chaos, and as we came off from one act the stage manager said we would have to close the show.

And I just said: "I'm bloody sure we won't. I've never closed a show yet, and I'm not starting now."

Normally at the end of the show a big car came onto the stage, and when the chauffeur opened the back door two ragged looking street people stepped out. It was us—Jack with his violin, and me with the accordion.

So as they tried to release the scenery, Jack and I went on stage and performed this act that normally finished the show.

Meanwhile, they somehow managed to kick the scenery so hard that it all came free. I think the stage director Gordon Dickson applied the all important dunt—a brave act because he was 80 feet up and could easily have fallen down and killed himself.

Of course when it came to the end of the show that night we had already done the act, and the audience knew we had already done it, so we starting ad-libbing again. We played things like 'Side By Side', the orchestra joined in, and the audience joined in. That's what is great about theatre. The show had gone on, and you could say was better for it. It was a wonderful experience.

The pantomimes with Howard & Wyndham also marked a magnificent introduction to the type of act many people would later know me best for. As the years went on, they would also become the last vestige of the music hall.

I've done many in my career, starting with the role of the Cat in *Dick Whittington* when I was 17, long before *Robinson Crusoe* became my first Howard & Wyndham performance. In Glasgow the following year during *Puss in Boots* with Harry Gordon, I was approached by Stewart Cruikshank.

"What do you want to do next winter, Jimmy?" he said.

"I'd love to take this pantomime to Edinburgh."

"No, we can't do that," he told me.

"Why not?"

"Well, confidentially, we've just bought the Alhambra Theatre in Glasgow, and I want you to go in with our first pantomime."

So in the winter of 1955 I went into this giant and beautiful theatre with *Goldilocks and the Three Bears*. The principal girl was Betty Shaw. It was also my first experience with Duncan Macrae.

He was a great artiste and had a wonderful reputation but I discovered he could be a pain to work with at times. Duncan had built up a tremendous following at the Citizens' Theatre in Glasgow where the author James Bridie wrote plays specifically for him. You could tell because his performances were absolutely wonderful.

He was an intriguing individual, with a very angular posture and a personality people warmed to; a unique figure whom the public loved.

Duncan was a very, very good pantomime dame, but on one occasion when we were doing *Goldilocks* he showed another side to his personality. The scene was one I had written when the set represented a bus. I was the conductor, and there was a dummy as a passenger. Then Duncan tried to get onto the bus.

"You can't get on the bus," I said.

"Why not?"

"Because you haven't got a ticket."

"What about him?"

"He's a toon councillor."

That was the punchline, and normally it got a good laugh. But on this occasion, straight after the laugh line, Duncan suddenly whooped "oooohhhh" and killed the laugh. The following evening he did it again.

Afterwards I said to him: "Can I see you in my dressing room, Duncan?"

He came in, and I said: "You've done this for a couple of nights now. Why?"

106

"Oh, well," he said. "I'm expressing the bloody indignation of the ordinary people who can't get on a bus and this town councillor does get on."

"That's fine," I said. "But while you're expressing indignation you are also killing the laugh."

He wasn't a fool and knew bloody well what he was doing.

"Do you think so?" he said, feigning surprise.

"I think so, Duncan. Express it at another time."

Years later, when Duncan appeared in one of my plays, *Bachelors Are Bold*, he was at it again. Near the end of the opening scene Bill Tennent had a marvellous exit which, if done correctly, sparked a big round of applause from the audience. If he got that round of applause, the same happened when anyone else exited during the play. For the first four nights it worked like a treat, and was marvellous.

Then Duncan decided to make an impression. On the fifth night, just as Bill was going off and the audience were about to clap, Duncan jumped in and killed it. He thought he was being clever, but all he did was kill everyone else's chance of applause throughout the play.

I was boiling with anger. I stormed back to my office, stood in front of my desk and screamed: "I can't stand this man. What on earth is he doing? He's ruining the play."

Then I went round, sat behind the desk, and retorted: "Now listen, I'm the manager and from where I'm standing the business is good, the play is good and the audience love it. What are you complaining about? Just keep going. It will be all right."

And then I went in front of the desk again, and said: "It's all right for you. You're not on the stage."

And so I went on. You might think I was mad, and maybe I was, but I found it was a good way to relieve the tension. That's the effect Duncan tended to have on me sometimes.

What he did was wrong. I feel he could have been another

artiste who wrote a great page in our book of theatre history, but he lacked the generosity of spirit that, in the end, stopped him scaling the tremendous heights he could so easily have reached. That generosity of spirit that allows others to get laughs on the stage was missing. He wanted all the laughs, and that was to a certain degree his downfall.

When Andy Stewart came out of college he joined up with Duncan for a tour of Scotland. Andy told me how he got great laughs on the opening night, and was just thrilled. But Duncan was far from happy. He called the young pretender in, and said sharply: "I get the laughs round here, son. You just do your part."

Now that is a bad sign, and certainly doesn't reflect the way I've ever gone about my business. I think that if I'm presenting the bill, and paying everyone's wages, I want them to be as good as possible because it is costing a fortune. The better they are, the better everyone else does.

In London, I once saw Duncan share a stage with Alastair Sim. And once again Duncan tried to take over the stage. On this occasion it was a completely pointless exercise, because Sim just stood there until Duncan had done his bit, then took the whole thing over himself.

Few people realise that people like Duncan Macrae and myself were primarily responsible for the establishment of the actors' union Equity in Scotland. I remember clearly how Duncan at those early meetings would light a cigarette, then sit holding the match while it burned itself out. Suddenly, with a small pause, he would flick the match across the room, and no matter who was talking or what they were saying, everyone stopped dead until the offending match had burnt out.

It was hard to take your eyes off this fascinating character.

Duncan, as chairman, and an actor, Alex McCrindle, started the Equity ball rolling in Scotland, but for the first few months they struggled and weren't getting enough recognition. Then Alex suggested getting some people from *Five Past Eight* involved. I was approached, and agreed to become vice-chairman. Stanley Baxter also got involved.

We did a lot of good work. I laid out the formation of the first Equity committee to include the appropriate balances and counter balances. I took a lot of our decisions down to be passed at the head office in London.

In our first negotiations for Equity we met with the big theatre owners in Glasgow, including George Urie Scott and Alex Frutin, to get a better pay deal for the overworked chorus girls. They were being paid £2 a week and we fought for £4 10s. When we finally agreed on a raise one of these big theatre owners said: "This is the end. This will kill theatre in Scotland."

It was those negotiations that prompted Stewart Cruikshank to call me the "Commissar of the Alhambra".

And they just couldn't understand why Jimmy Logan, the son of Jack Short, who was in the profession and knew it backwards, would be on the side of the minion workers.

The hard work we put into getting Equity up and running remains the basis for how it operates today.

My involvement ceased after about six years when it was decided that people would be elected rather than appointed. That was fine, but a few years ago I was left bursting with anger when I appeared in an Equity show.

The history of Equity in Scotland was detailed in the programme, yet myself and Duncan Macrae didn't even merit a mention. Even though we had effectively put the whole thing into motion, and got it working successfully, the history started off from the point when people were elected. Our hard work was ignored, and usually is. That's why few people realise I was so heavily involved with the establishment of Equity.

It is recognised in the minutes of all the meetings that are still kept at the Equity office. And I think we deserve fair recognition for our efforts.

During my stint on *Five Past Eight*, the Moscow State Variety Theatre came to Scotland, and Stanley Baxter and I held a reception for them in my house. It was a quite hysterical evening.

In those days nobody was allowed out of the Soviet Union unless they agreed with the politics of the communist Government. So when we asked about the troubles in Hungary at the time they all stuck to the party line. They did so because they were afraid of the people in their company who were KGB members. It would have been distinctly unwise to offer alternative opinions.

"What are we spending on booze?" Stanley had asked me.

"Well, I've heard they don't drink very much," I said. "I've got £35 worth of booze."

Stanley was shocked.

I said: "Don't worry. It's on sale or return."

In those days that was masses of drink, but they drank everything in the house—including my private stock. The only word they knew was "visky". At the end of the night there was just one bottle left—the Glasgow vodka, Smirnoff.

In my big room downstairs they did wonderful puppet and juggling acts, and one guy played an instrument with three strings that I had never seen.

The amazing thing was that although we didn't speak Russian we were able somehow to have wonderful long conversations. I found out one of them had been a tank driver during the War.

Then there was the Glasgow Jewish comedian called Walter Jackson, whose mother and father were amongst the Russian immigrants who had arrived in Glasgow by accident years earlier. A whole group of immigrants were heading for New York when they stopped off at the Broomielaw, and someone said: "Right, this is it."

When I told Walter what I was doing he came over with the biggest bowl of borsch—a traditional Russian beetroot soup—you could possibly imagine. His mother had made it specially, and told him he had to keep stirring it. The poor soul stood in the kitchen all night with his ladle.

"Come for a drink, Walter?"

"Naw, ma mammy said I can't stop stirrin'."

It was a particularly cold night so we decided the Russians would get a nice, warm cup of borsch before they left.

I took two of the Russians up into the kitchen, pointed to Walter and the bowl, and said: "Borsch!"

"Niet borsch," they said.

Then they took a sip. "Ah borsch, borsch." They loved it.

And I said: "Walter: father, mother—Ruski."

And Walter took out these pictures of his father in the Imperial Russian Navy, and kept on stirring and stirring until the very last.

They invited me to Russia, but I didn't take them up on it. I wanted to go to America, mainly because I had relatives there, and a Russian stamp on my passport at that time could have caused big problems.

5

FIVE PAST EIGHT
TO THE LONDON PALLADIUM

When I was appearing in *Five Past Eight* at the Alhambra, Stewart Cruikshank invited me to supper at the Malmaison Hotel with Val Parnell, the Big Boss of the London Palladium.

Parnell was the English equivalent of Cruikshank. I was attending a meeting of two theatre giants, each one not wanting to say they were better than the other, but not willing to admit they weren't.

In the middle of the supper, Val said: "How would you like to play the Palladium, Jimmy?"

For a moment I was thunderstruck. The London Palladium was the top theatre in Britain—and the greatest variety theatre in the world. Trying not to choke on my food, I calmly replied: "That would be fine."

"Great," he said. "I'll fix it up." And that was it.

The moment of truth would soon be on me—just as the Palladium could propel someone towards international stardom, it had also been the graveyard for many an up-and-coming performer. I accepted the offer, but knew right away it was a big challenge.

A week before I was due to go in for a two week run, I went to the Palace Theatre in Leicester to get used to English audiences, and to see if my material was right. I was going to be the first Scottish comic at the Palladium for 16 years, but I decided to do my Scottish Teddy Boy act which had gone down very well on *Five Past Eight*. It was a big risk because no-one had really taken off a Teddy Boy at that time, and I certainly hadn't done it in England.

As soon as I got to Leicester, I bumped into one of the big English stars, Dave King, who was playing the same theatre.

"Hello, Jimmy, how are you?"

"Fine. How are you enjoying Leicester?"

He shook his head, and replied: "They don't like comics here, son."

That made me feel great.

The first thing I did was to go into the audience and watch King at work. It was a strange experience, because he did something I would never dream of doing on stage. He seemed to be of the opinion that if the audience weren't in hysterics after his first three gags they should be treated with disdain. If they weren't intelligent enough to understand his humour he just dismissed them.

But that's criminal because he was allowing them to drift away despite the fact they were enjoying themselves.

It reminded me of the difference between audiences in Glasgow and Edinburgh. In Glasgow it was Mum, Dad and the kids, and they just laughed their heads off. In Edinburgh it was Mum, Dad, the kids and Granny. Granny was very important because she owned shares in the Burmah Oil Company, and if Granny didn't laugh, nobody laughed. And Granny made sure they never came back. Therefore the laughter in Edinburgh was a bit quieter but that didn't mean they weren't enjoying the show as much.

Some crowds may only smile but they are still enjoying themselves. It's at times like that a comedian should work the audience to make them have a great time. They're paying good money to be entertained, and the last thing he should do is dismiss them. But that's how Dave King treated his audience that evening.

I worked in Leicester with Maggie Miles, who had been in *Five Past Eight* and pantomime with me, and the opening night was certainly an experience. First of all, the theatre was a quarter full. Then I was told the first couple of rows in the stalls were packed with London agents and representatives from the London Palladium. Finally, to round it all off, I found out Stanley Baxter was in the house. What an audience.

That night I did my Teddy Boy act which was fine, but we were also asked at the last minute to include another appearance in the second half of the show. The routine wasn't as good as it could have been because we basically threw it together, and afterwards a rather bitter double-act whom I had upstaged on the bill told Maggie: "He'll die a death at the London Palladium."

Thank goodness she never told me.

The following week I got ready to appear in the Palladium—a truly terrifying experience. Top of the bill was the big American star Johnnie Ray and a young, virtually unknown American called Joel Grey, who years later took the lead role in the film *Cabaret*. My wife Grace had come to London with me, and my mother and father flew down to see the performance.

When I got to my dressing room there were over 100 telegrams from friends and colleagues wishing me the best of luck. I had 12 minutes to make my mark on the biggest stage in the world, and as I sat there getting ready the enormity of the task was starting to sink in.

The theatre itself was just wonderful, a world away from the Palace in Leicester which had been flat and square.

When the Palladium orchestra had finished playing my music through for the first time they asked me if I wanted to hear it again.

"Yes," I said. "Not because there's anything wrong with it, but that is the first time I've heard it played quite like that. It's wonderful."

On the opening night I got word from the management that I had been promoted from an early slot of number four on the bill to number seven, the spot just before the finale of the first half—the top laughter spot, a truly great spot.

But my family had no idea this had happened, and when I failed to appear at my allotted time in the programme they slumped back in their seats, and feared the worst. "He's no well, he's run away—or both," said my frantic mother. "Maybe he's dead," added my father. "But they'll still have to pay him."

Backstage I may have been as nervous as hell as my big moment raced ever closer, but the people at the Palladium treated artistes differently. Regardless of who it was, they assumed we must be stars if we were playing the Palladium. I vividly remember a lovely fellow called George at the stage door who was just one of many who made me feel great before I walked on for the first time.

And what an experience that was. The Palladium wasn't number one for nothing. When you walked onto the stage, it was a giant stage, and when you looked out at the theatre, it was a giant theatre; its atmosphere was totally unique.

The programme said "Jimmy Logan from Scotland", but I opened with my back to the audience wearing my Teddy Boy suit and sporting long hair. As soon as I turned round there was a wild roar, and then when I showed off my loud waistcoat there was another big laugh.

It was an outfit built for laughter.

The whole time I was on stage I was a bag of nerves. It felt the way people sometimes feel when they have to make a speech in public for the first time. You can sense whether you've got the audience or if you've lost them. I knew at that point I had them, and I worked and worked to make sure they never drifted the way Dave King's audience did at Leicester.

When my act ended there was great applause but that didn't

mean a thing because all audiences—even the toughest of them—can be polite. For a time I sat alone in my dressing room until Grace arrived at the door.

"You were great, Jim," she said. "You went over big."

It was a nice gesture, but I didn't really believe it. Wives are always kind on occasions like that. Then my parents walked in, and my father said: "You went down well, son. And it was a good act."

At that point I breathed a huge sigh of relief. My father wasn't one for paying compliments, so when he said that I knew it had happened for me at the greatest music hall in the world. I felt great. Mum just said: "That was fine."

I played the Palladium for two weeks, during which time there were many fascinating experiences. There had been a lot of talk about Johnnie Ray being gay, so to dispel that speculation he turned up at the theatre with an absolutely beautiful girl who was said to be his fiancée.

On stage he was a sensation. The audience loved his songs, and girls were planted throughout the audience to rush on at the end and give him flowers.

But in the second week he announced he wasn't getting enough publicity, and decided to do something about it. Towards the end of his act he would usually be pouring with sweat, and as the curtain slowly descended during his last number he would finish off by slumping over the piano, supposedly exhausted. However, on this night in the second week, he collapsed completely.

Immediately his doctor, who just happened to be at the side of the stage, rushed on to administer first aid. Meanwhile, the lovely stage manager, a real Cockney, had to get the stage ready for the next performance.

He charged around, apologising each time he stepped over the prostrate star. "Charlie," he said, "take that over there and put that over here . . . oh sorry Johnnie . . . and Charlie do this . . . sorry Johnnie."

It was hysterical.

After my first night the management told me I had done 13 minutes instead of the 12 I was down for. "We know you haven't added any extra material," the stage manager said to me. "And we know it's the public reaction, but keep it as tight as you can."

I had started off not knowing if I was going to be any good, really sticking my neck out, but by the third night I was so confident I was ready to start doing some ad-libs.

When Joel Grey finished his act, he said: "Ladies and Gentlemen, my good friend Danny Kaye told me that when I was at the London Palladium I would meet the most wonderful audience in the world, and I want you to know that I agree with every word he said."

And I was just dying to say: "I was told in Scotland that when I came to the London Palladium I would meet the greatest audience in the world, and I want you to know it's the biggest load of rubbish I've ever heard."

I didn't because it would have been disrespectful to Joel, but as the Scottish Teddy Boy, it would undoubtedly have got a big laugh.

Overall, I loved my two weeks at the Palladium. The chemistry worked, and I can honestly say there were no bad nights. The audience were fascinating, reacting like no audience I had seen before. A comedian with ten gags could have them doubled up by number six, but if number seven wasn't so strong, it took him eight, nine and ten to get them back up to the level of number six.

Before I left, the management made a lovely gesture. Normally only the big star on the bill gets a plaque—a "Palladium Oscar"—recognising the fact he or she had played there. But the night I left Val Parnell walked up and gave me one. A lovely brass plaque for a dressing room door, it says simply: "Jimmy Logan, London

Palladium—Variety Season 1955." To this day, it's still one of my proudest possessions.

Around the time I appeared at the Palladium the country was submerged in a tuberculosis epidemic. Our hospitals were so packed that the NHS sent patients over to big skyscraper-style hospitals in a village near the millionaires' playground that was Lausanne, Switzerland.

Normally, these hospitals were frequented by the rich and famous. They were almost palatial. Just like a luxury hotel, patients would be met by a concierge at the front door and shown to a magnificent room overlooking the Alps. When patients were X-rayed they were given a postcard-size copy so they could check on the progress of their illness.

Now, courtesy of the NHS, four of these hospitals were full of ordinary working-class men and women from Britain. For me that made the NHS worthwhile.

The food these people were served was also the best Swiss cuisine had to offer; fine cheeses, steaks, cakes or virtually anything they wanted from that part of the world. But suddenly the papers in Scotland started carrying stories about the patients being so hungry they were cooking their own meals in the corridors. There were deep concerns that they weren't being fed properly.

Around that time I was asked by the Red Cross to go out and entertain these patients. I may have been offered the London Palladium, but I genuinely believed in the *Quid Pro Quo* concept—you get something, you give something back. So I went there to try and cheer up all these people with TB in this faraway place. I also thought it would be a good chance to find out if the "hunger" stories were true.

Of course, those were a million miles from the truth.

Being Scottish, some of the patients didn't like any of the "funny foreign food" they were being given. So one patient in one of the hospitals had said to the other: "I'd love a plate of mince." And at three o'clock in the morning they were caught cooking mince in one of the corridors.

I went round the hospitals speaking to the punters after I arrived, then did a three-hour show on my second night. I think I must have dragged out just about every joke I had ever heard. Then I spoke to everyone again, got photographs and notes from lots of people, and brought them back to Scotland to give to their families.

Stanley Baxter and I also got involved in a massive government campaign to raise awareness of the dangers of TB. I recorded Robert Wilson's 'A Gordon For Me', only with different lyrics under the title 'An X-ray For Me'. That song was played at football matches and other public events, and a film was shown in cinemas of Stanley and myself being X-rayed. The whole thing worked because people started going for X-rays, and that helped wipe out the disease.

There were some terrible diseases in those days. I once went to Carluke-Law Junction Hospital to entertain the kids, and the doctor introduced me to this adorable little girl with blonde hair who was wearing a nice dress. Then he drew back the covers on the bed to reveal two little sticks that were her legs. I was shocked.

And he said to me: "No-one ever comes to visit her."

The little girl was suffering from polio. In those days diseases like polio or TB suffered from the kind of stigma that was attached to something like AIDS a few years ago. People unfortunate enough to be struck down—even helpless young kids like that beautiful young girl—were treated like lepers. People wouldn't go near them because of their own ignorance. They were afraid of picking up the germ by being coughed on. Or in her case they just didn't care.

A lot of people think there must be an agenda when "personalities" go, for example, to visit those people in the Swiss hospitals or that little girl with polio. That may be true in some cases, but any voluntary or charity work I've done has always come about because I've wanted to do it.

I've been lucky in my life, and if I can use that status to pass on a little help to someone less fortunate than myself then great. It's not about getting something back, it's about giving something back.

The Stars Organisation For Spastics was the brainchild of a lawyer called Ian Martin in the Fifties. There had been a similar organisation in England to help spastics, but never one in Scotland.

I was one of many "stars" who were heavily involved from the beginning. We set up a working committee of which Mozart Allan was the chairman, and Larry Marshall and myself were vice-chairmen.

Then we started wondering what we were going to do.

"Well, I think we should take over the Alhambra Theatre for a week," I said.

This had never been done.

We also discussed what the show should be called. And I suggested *Stars For Spastics*.

One artiste immediately piped up: "Oh no, Jimmy, you can't call it that because that's like saying cancer. It will put people off."

When I look back at those times, calling that show *Stars For Spastics* was the best thing we could have done. It broke down barriers, making the word "spastic" acceptable for the first time. It became part of everyday language. Before that it was a word with a stigma attached. What we did was progressive.

Ironically, these days it has gone the other way. The word "spastic" is no longer politically correct.

I directed and produced our first performance—a week of shows at the giant Alhambra Theatre in Glasgow. All the artistes gave their services free.

The whole thing was a great success. Richard Hearne, known as

Mr Pastry, came up from London, taught us his act and we did the act with him on stage. The finish of the first half was my six-year-old nephew Nicky singing 'If You've Got Personality' with eight of Scotland's star comics, including myself, behind him dressed as schoolboys. It was a funny scene.

The finale was stunning, with magnificent costumes and scenery, and the wonderful music of Ivor Novello. And down the staircase came Olive Gilbert, the original star of all the great Novello musicals who worked with him all her life, singing 'We'll Gather Lilacs'.

We ran a canteen backstage without any alcohol, quite determined we weren't going to spend a penny, unlike some of these charity dos where people really go overboard on the hospitality.

But I felt we had to do something for our 250 performers who were giving up so much of their time for free. So we decided the most we would spend on them was five shillings each.

I phoned my friend Reo Stakis, the head of the big hotel and casino chain, and he said: "Of course I'll help Jimmy. You'll bring them to me after the show."

"All I can afford is five shillings a head."

"Don't worry about that, Jimmy."

Half an hour later Reo phoned back.

"I have a problem, Jimmy," he said. "I want to offer the company a drink but the licensing authorities will not accept these are all my personal friends."

In those days that was the only way he could provide a drink on licensed premises without charging.

I phoned the Lord Provost Sir Myer Galpern who was out, but I spoke to Lady Galpern and explained the situation.

It wasn't long before she phoned back, and said: "With the Chief Constable's compliments, Jimmy."

They knew what we were doing was for the good of Glasgow and beyond.

After the performance we all trooped up to Reo's restaurant where all 250 artistes were served a four-course meal, and a choice of any drink—fine wines, champagnes, liqueurs. And that was Reo Stakis's personal contribution. A wonderful gesture. So much for five shillings a head.

We got support from many areas. I was a member of the Glasgow Rotary Club alongside the former Rangers owner John Lawrence.

We wanted to improve the facilities where spastics got their assessments, and after one meeting I explained the spastics' situation to John outside the hotel. And standing on those steps, he said to me: "I'll tell you what I'll do, Jimmy. I'll give you six acres of land in Newton Mearns."

It was an unbelievable offer.

I consulted with the spastics' organisations who said it would be better to have a centre in the Paisley area.

And John said: "Right, you'll get a grant from the Government to help build something like that. What the grant doesn't cover, I will."

He also donated a beautiful bungalow on the Switchback Road in Glasgow which those organisations were able to use as a base for fundraising activities. The generosity of John Lawrence was breathtaking.

In order to get the backing of the City of Glasgow for such projects the Lord Provost arranged a meeting at the City Chambers between council officials, myself and representatives of the Scottish Council For Spastics in Edinburgh.

However, the Scottish Council told me they couldn't find anyone who was free to attend. My friend Hector MacLennan asked a friend of his, Dr Fraser, who was a representative of the Scottish Council, to travel down from his home in Inverness for the meeting. His son was a spastic attending Aberdeen University, who was on his way to becoming a lawyer.

It's just as well Dr Fraser went out of his way to come to that meeting because it laid the foundations for a fresh approach to solving the problems the spastics were encountering.

Throughout the years I've been associated with the children's charity Barnardo's—an association that got me into trouble with the Inland Revenue. I used to go to their home in Wishaw where I would see children in different situations with different kinds of handicaps. And when you see children in that situation your heart just goes out to them.

I discovered there were two places where they needed a piano. So I went to the Winter Gardens in Rothesay for two Sunday concerts, and used the proceeds to buy the two pianos.

Not long afterwards my accountant told me the Inland Revenue were refusing to finalise my end of year accounts. He said they were acting as though I was hiding some of my earnings.

"You have declared everything, Jimmy?" my accountant asked.

"Absolutely," I said. "I'm sure I have."

Finally a dreaded meeting was arranged with a tax inspector from the Inland Revenue.

It was a scary experience. He wasn't at all friendly.

"Are you sure you've declared everything?" he barked.

"Yes."

"Are you perfectly sure?"

"Yes."

"I'll ask one last time. Are you definitely sure?"

"Yes."

I felt like the book had already been thrown at me. I was a convicted felon.

He said to me: "You didn't declare your performances on Rothesay. Why not?"

And I told him the story of the pianos.

"Ah," he said. "You should fill in another form if you're doing that."

"I didn't know which forms to fill in," I said. "I just did the show because it was a worthwhile cause."

He then started asking me about my business and personal mileage. But by this time he had changed his tune. He actually gave me a very generous allowance.

I used to go down to the Bridge of Weir Homes to present prizes to the children, and I opened a big fête to raise money. I once took about ten of them to the circus, and they were all trying to sit on my lap or cuddle me because they wanted to be loved, wanted to be cared for.

In the Sixties I sponsored two lovely children in France through the Save The Children fund. I sent money to their mother every year and, when I went to Paris, used to see them and give them presents like bicycles or clothes from Marks and Spencer. When they grew up and no longer needed my help I sponsored another two French children.

I did it partly out of my love for children, and being able to give a couple of youngsters far less privileged than myself a better chance in life gave me a great thrill.

In Helensburgh I'm a patron of Childline, a wonderful organisation, and for 30 years I've been a member of the Glasgow branch of the Scottish Society For Mentally Handicapped, now known as Enable.

I can't remember all the things I have done for charity, and I certainly don't make a noise about it. I also don't like it when people say I'm well known for my charity work. It suggests I'm doing something to get something back. And that's not the case. What I'm trying to do is, when I can, support something that is worthwhile and help others less fortunate than myself. Simple as that. If I can help someone because my name is Jimmy Logan I will do my best to do that. I've been lucky in my life. I feel I should always do my utmost to give something back.

Now that hardly makes me a saint. Far from it, although I have been a member of the Saints And Sinners Club for the last 30 years.

A saint? The Lord would be waiting up at the gate with a shotgun to shoot me. "Is that him with the wings?" he would say.

Another worthy cause I've been involved with for many years is The Showbusiness Benevolent Fund, a wonderful organisation that has looked after old pros on a very personal one-to-one basis for more than a hundred years. I've been a President, a past President and I'm now a trustee of an organisation that watches out for these great pensioners all through the year, and organises all sorts of events for them. For instance, Helen Norman, who worked with Jack Radcliffe and myself on *Five Past Eight*, left her estate to the Fund when she died, and so we organised a week in Blackpool for the old pros. They went to see three shows, and stayed in the best hotels. But the most wonderful thing about trips like that is the fact that all these pros can sit and talk to each other about the business they know. The rest of the year they live in homes and houses surrounded by people who don't know anything about the history or the stories from the theatre. But for that week they all come alive again.

Theatre was the major form of entertainment when I came to prominence in the Fifties, but anyone with any sense knew television was going to play a major part in the future. When I was doing *It's All Yours* on the radio they had television down in England, but it hadn't yet arrived in Scotland. I knew, though, that it wouldn't be long before it did so I went to America to study commercial television. I wanted to witness this wonderful new medium in the land that was really pioneering its progress.

Many people were still sceptical. Before I went I met the owner of one advertising agency in a Glasgow hotel.

"Listen, Jimmy," he said, "I've told all my people not to put a penny into TV because it will not mean a thing in comparison to

125

newspapers. People get a newspaper that lies around the house all day and it's always there to look at. TV, on the other hand, is over in a few minutes."

I said to him: "I think you should re-think your position."

I knew he was talking out of his backside. It was so obvious how big TV was becoming in America. People like him thought another great Scot, John Logie Baird, was talking through a hole in his head when he predicted that a box in everyone's living room would soon be showing live colour pictures of the Prime Minister of Australia as he spoke in Australia.

In America, though, I saw enough to convince me that television would be a hugely important part of the entertainment business in the years to come. My first view of their television was an advert with a fellow who had a crying baby on his shoulder. Then the baby burped loudly into camera.

And the voice-over announced: "Buy a Zimmerman pen—it refuses to burp."

Hysterical, but other adverts convinced me of the importance of advertising on TV.

Grace and I travelled to America on board the *Queen Mary*. It was huge, just like the *Titanic*, but fortunately managed to avoid the icebergs. We were in third class where there were two distinct types of passenger; those who said: "We're going to America. Isn't it great?" and a little group of snobs who moaned: "We should have been booked first class but our travel agent made a mistake."

There were bars across the doors stopping people getting up to first class, but we found a way round and went to have a look. I entered a "Make A Hat" competition, and made one of a swimming pool because the one on the ship was only for customers in first class.

Anyway I did a wee show for the crew away down in the

bowels of the ship. Alongside me was a marvellous Jewish American comic, Henny Youngman, who was on his way home after a successful run at the London Palladium.

What a gentleman he was.

"Why don't you come to my house and have dinner?" he said that day. "Don't be like Tommy Trinder. He said he would come but he never came. I'll get a pal to pick you up."

When we were picked up in New York it was by a famous American comic called Red Buttons. He took us to Henny's house where we sat and ate at a massive table in an enormous dining room. There were doors off the dining room, and, such was the buzz of activity around us, I was sure there was a television blaring in every room.

Henny then kindly took me down to Jack Dempsey's place on Broadway. As he walked in, everyone turned to greet him, and he went out of his way to introduce me to as many people as possible.

"This is Jimmy Logan from Scotland," he repeatedly said. "He's a great comic."

It was a wonderful compliment he never had to pay, but he did so because he was a warm-hearted man, full of the generosity of spirit that puts the great above the good.

Years later when I was in my dressing room during *Five Past Eight* at the Alhambra, I was watching the wee portable TV that was always on when I was in there. And as I was getting made up, the announcer said: "Tonight at the London Palladium . . . Henny Youngman."

So I phoned the stage door at the Palladium, and asked them to pass on my best regards. When he came on TV a short time later he gave me a wee mention.

My stand-up material has never been my strongest point, but he was a genius.

These are some of my favourites:

—You have a ready wit. Let me know when it's ready.

—My wife will buy anything marked down. Last week she brought home two dresses and an escalator.

—I haven't talked to my wife in three weeks. I didn't want to interrupt her.

—I took my wife to a wife-swapping party. I had to throw in some cash.

—I miss my wife's cooking—as often as I can.

—That's a nice suit you're wearing. When did the clown die?

—Oh and I like your suit. Who shines it for you?

—He's frank and earnest with women. In Fresno he's Frank and in Chicago he's Ernest.

—What do you get for a man who has everything? Penicillin.

—A man can't find a lawyer. He picks up the Red Book, picks out a law firm—Schwartz, Schwartz, Schwartz & Schwartz. Calls up, he says:

"Is Mr Schwartz there?"

A guy says: "No, he's out playing golf."

He says: "Alright, then let me talk to Mr Schwartz."

"He's not with the firm any more. He's retired."

"Then let me talk to Mr Schwartz."

"He's away in Detroit, won't be back for a month."

"OK, then let me talk to Mr Schwartz."

He says: "Speaking!"

—Some people bring happiness wherever they go. You bring happiness whenever you go.

—I'd like to help you out. Which way did you come in?

—He willed his body to science. Science is contesting the will.

Unfortunately, Henny Youngman passed away in 1998, but I will remember him not only as one of the great all-time stand-up comics, but as a fine human being.

*　　　*　　　*

When I returned home from America, television was destined for Scotland. In 1953 I compèred the first cabaret show broadcast from Scotland at the Central Hotel in Glasgow. There were other appearances but I particularly remember the first television broadcast in 1957 from BBC's new Springfield Road studio at Parkhead Cross. It had been the Black Cat Cinema, and the BBC had turned it into a television studio. Why they chose that site I'll never know. It was on a main road, and every time tramcars went past the building, the needles on the studio's technical instruments virtually went off the scales.

Eddie Fraser—my producer on *It's All Yours*—was heavily involved in the show. Fay Lenore and I appeared in a wee sketch about a couple trying to get a crying baby back to sleep in the middle of the night. Every time I put the bairn back in its cot, it started crying again. Eventually when I sing 'You Can Come and See The Baby', a song I was well known for at the time, the baby goes to sleep. Then my morning alarm goes off.

By 1956 I had established a reputation as a top pantomime performer, who loved kids and was paid almost £500 a week by Howard & Wyndham to do those great 18-week winter seasons. It was because of this that Eddie Fraser asked me to do the first television programme for Scottish kids with Kathleen Garscadden, the voice of children's radio.

It was to be called *Loganberry Pie*. I thought that would be great, and immediately agreed.

When we got down to filming I suggested some ideas. For instance, I had an old gramophone record with the big horn and cylinder, and reckoned it would be a perfect prop for one of the songs.

I wanted to say to the children: "Now this is a gramophone record, believe it or not. And this is what they used to use when they listened to music." Showing them how it worked, I would

129

then say, "We put it on there, wound it up here, started it off and this is how it sounded."

At that point I wanted the camera to slowly zoom in on the bell of the gramophone while, in the next room an elderly man was being filmed singing 'After The Ball Was Over'. I hoped we could bleed his head into the bell of the gramophone so it gave the kids the impression that he was actually inside the gramophone, showing them where the music came from.

Unfortunately trying to explain this to Kathleen must have taken the best part of an hour and a half. She had spent her life on radio, never having to worry about how things worked visually, and judging by the expression on her face, I could just as well have been trying to explain Einstein's theory of relativity.

"Why don't we just put the man here, put a camera on him and he can stand and sing," she suggested.

I was almost tearing my hair out. "No Kathleen, we've got to have the connection."

"Yes, but he could just stand there."

The words "brick", "wall" and "talking to" sprung to mind as I went in to see Eddie Fraser, exasperated.

"Listen, Eddie," I said. "I don't think I can do this. It's taken me an hour and a half to explain a simple thought. It's driving me up the wall."

Eddie persuaded me to continue, and along with my dear writer friend John Law, we came up with a song called 'Loganberry Pie'. In fact, it later became the name of my first LP.

It went:

> "Try a slice of Loganberry Pie.
> Munch it, crunch it, you'll discover why
> Boys and girls enjoy it when they try
> A great big slice of Loganberry Pie."

The one-off show was recorded in a little theatre in Rutherglen in the south of Glasgow, which housed the local repertory company. Sometimes they put on a late evening show, a kind of revue, which the artistes from shows like *Five Past Eight* often came along to see.

When I was there I saw a young comedian called John Mulvaney who impressed me greatly, and I went backstage and said: "I enjoyed your work very much, Mr Mulvaney. If you ever want to come to *Five Past Eight* here's my card. We'd be delighted for you to be part of the show."

There was another one, Alice Dale, who turned out to be Stanley Baxter's sister.

I was very keen that *Five Past Eight* should give opportunities to Scottish talent. I was told there was a young straight actress at the Citizens' Theatre who had a wonderful sense of humour. Her name was Una McLean.

I saw her working, and she had, in my opinion, all the qualities that would work well in comedy. She had a wonderful personality and seemed to bubble inside with laughter, and I asked her if she would join us on *Five Past Eight*.

This was a big decision for Una to make as some of those surrounding her suggested it could destroy her reputation as a serious actress. But Una decided to join us and that was the beginning of an association that has lasted to this day.

When we were filming *Loganberry Pie* there were obviously a lot of children in the studio, including a number of handicapped kids. I asked some of them to come on stage for a trick I was about to do.

"Oh no, surely not?" said Kathleen Garscadden. "They're handicapped. You're not going to do one of these terrible Wilfred Pickles things."

In his show, Wilfred was infamous for saying things like: "He's

131

lovely, he's just lost his right leg and his left arm but you're all right now, aren't you, son?"

Kathleen thought I was trying to gain sympathy for the kids because they were handicapped. But she couldn't have been more wrong. As I've already explained, there was a far greater stigma attached to handicapped people in those days than there is now, and I wanted to do my little bit to get rid of that. If I saw a chance to do that, I jumped at it. On this television show I thought getting the children on stage—handicapped or not—was fine, because by the time I had finished no-one watching would be stopping to think if they were handicapped. It would emphasise that something like that shouldn't even come into consideration.

We didn't treat those kids in a different way or give them great concessions. They just got on with it like the rest of the children.

However, that old adage of never working with children admittedly rang true on a couple of occasions—none more hysterically than when I did a sketch that involved pulling a cloth clean away from a dinner table full of crockery, and without knocking any of the crockery off. Sometimes, if you did it fast enough, the crockery stayed upright.

Anyway, the idea on *Loganberry Pie* was to get one of the kids up on stage, put the plates and cups down on the cloth, then ask him to see if he could do it.

And just as he was about to whip away the cloth, I shouted: "Wait a minute." And, like the cruel man I am, I proceeded to put another bundle of dishes onto the table until it was absolutely packed.

"OK," I said, smiling. "On you go."

Of course now the joke was a cert to work. He would pull the cloth, the cups and plates would go all over the stage, and there would be hysterical laughter at his reaction and my face as I tried to pick up the broken pieces of crockery.

Perfect, you would think. Nope. That wee boy pulled the cloth away, and not one bit of crockery fell over. The children cheered, the TV crew fell about laughing and I had to stand there filling in time.

Around the same time I was also asked to appear on *Meet The Stars*, a popular variety show compèred by Tommy Trinder from the London Palladium. It was only shown south of the border, and they had decamped to Blackpool for a series of summer shows when I was invited on to do a "spot".

After doing *Five Past Eight* on the Saturday night, I travelled down to Blackpool on the overnight train with a promising young writer, Sam Cree. We tried to book into the same room in a hotel but that was a big problem. Two men booking into one room was not allowed. It was against the law.

The weather that day was absolutely awful with torrential rain and high winds. I got to the theatre and went through the music for my six-minute act, then returned to my dressing room. The show was being presented by George and Alfred Black, the sons of the great George Black who had created the brilliant Crazy Gang. Top of the bill was Jerry Colonna, a famous American comedian with a giant moustache who played the trombone and had made dozens of films.

As I sat in my dressing room, I got a message to go and see the Blacks in the stalls. They looked me up and down, then looked at each other.

"I think my suit will fit him," said George.

"No no, mine will be a better fit," said Alfred.

I was astonished. "Wait a minute, what's going on here?"

George piped up: "Dinner suits. Do you have one?

"Not with me."

"Jimmy," said George, looking suitably concerned. "The winds are so high at the moment that we're not sure if the show is even going to go out because the TV mast is blowing all over the place.

Also, we're very pessimistic about Tommy Trinder's chances of getting a flight up here to compère the show. So you're going to stand by as the compère."

I was a nervous wreck. I worried myself sick. I sweated blood. Sam and I racked our brains trying to think of material to get me through it. Sure enough, the mast was fine and Tommy Trinder didn't arrive.

I was going to be compère. Apart from the obvious problems of having to come up with all sorts of new material, I also had to learn the format of the show and all the games that were played on it. That was a complete nightmare. For a start, I had never seen the main game, Beat The Clock. Sometimes there would only be three little games within Beat The Clock, but the compère had to know at least twelve just in case it went the full hog.

By the time I was due to go on, my mind was so full it was close to shutting down. Trinder always wore a straw hat when he walked on stage so this time someone else was standing at the side of the stage with a straw hat—me.

"Yeah, I know you are expecting Tommy Trinder," I said when I walked out into the limelight. "Well it's going to be different tonight . . ."

These days I would do this sort of stuff in my sleep, but as a 28-year-old comic who was relatively inexperienced on TV, I was shaking in my shoes.

The show passed off without too much incident, and Beat The Clock went OK, although there were a couple of scary moments when I was living on my wits trying to remember how to work the game.

I introduced Jerry Colonna for the finale, stumbled back up the stairs to my dressing room and collapsed. I was genuinely sick with all the worry the show had caused.

Afterwards, everyone rushed to congratulate Jerry, which was entirely natural, because he was the big star. But no-one came near me. In the meantime I got changed. My friends the Moffats from Carlisle came in, and I just wanted to get out of the place.

We left and drove to Carlisle without having spoken to anyone since the moment I got off the stage. Even worse, no-one bothered to phone or write to my agent or me to express some gratitude for basically helping to save their show at the last minute. I was absolutely shattered that night—worse for wear from an experience that really took the guts out of me. I thought they would have at least written to say: "Thank you."

The side of the stage had been lined with an assortment of prizes—washing machines and things like that. I thought if they had even given me a hair-drier that would have been something. But there was nothing. It remains one of the most horrifying experiences of my career, and yet it was a success.

By that time, plans were well underway for a commercial TV station in Scotland. The Canadian media magnate Roy Thomson had bought *The Scotsman*, but wanted to get involved in this wonderful new medium.

So he went about raising funds to start up Scottish Television, and most famously said that running a television company was a licence to print money. That was a magnificent comment, but it was also a little unfortunate. At that same time television companies in the south of England were losing enormous amounts of money, so Scottish Television wasn't the guaranteed success that Roy Thomson was predicting.

Certainly, the vast majority of the Scottish worthies and moneymen he approached to buy shares in his new venture didn't share his enthusiasm. The list of those who refused reads like a roll-call of Scotland's rich and famous.

He came to *Five Past Eight* one night and took Jack Radcliffe and myself to supper.

Thomson said to us: "I'm starting up this TV company, Scottish

135

Television. If you've got any money you fellas should come in on this. It's gonna be really something."

We went our separate ways after the meeting, and when I arrived home Jack phoned me:

"What do you think?" he asked.

"You back the horse or you back the jockey," I said. "Why not?"

And so we became original shareholders in Scottish Television, each contributing £1,000. The list of people who refused to get involved seemed endless. We were just two of a few.

The opening night of STV in 1957 was an exciting evening for Scotland. We used our own set from *Five Past Eight*, and Roy Thomson did a hell of a job. He got a great guy over from Canada, Rai Purdy, who had some experience of TV. We had none. They put the whole thing together. It took a lot of guts and a big investment.

I appeared with Stanley Baxter who was doing *Five Past Eight* with me. We were ourselves at the opening, and later on came on as two babies, then appeared as two Teddy boys. James Robertson Justice held the thing together.

Difficulties arose, however, in other aspects of the evening. All the audience were there by invitation only, so they consisted mainly of official dignitaries from the different cities and towns. And because they were official, they weren't an easy lot to get laughter out of. That was just for starters.

The most frightening thing about that night was when I was waiting beforehand at the stage door to give my friend Hector MacLennan his tickets. Suddenly this young electrician collapsed in front of me. We got round him, and I could see his ears and his lips turning blue. I was massaging his heart—doing anything to keep him alive. He had had a heart attack.

Hector MacLennan, who was a doctor, came in amidst all this chaos. He took one look at the man, and grimly announced he was dead. They took him away like a sack of potatoes and put him in the stage manager's office. When I made my appearances on Scottish Television's opening broadcast that night, that boy's face was all I could see.

It suddenly hit me after I got home. I had performed this enormous event for Scotland, yet had watched helplessly as someone died in front of my eyes just minutes before it started. All through the programme I kept seeing this young man's face, and I thought: "Christ. I saw a man die tonight."

It was a horrible experience. I never forgot that.

6

FLYING HIGH WITH WHISKY CHARLIE

Everything I touched may not have turned to gold but it certainly seemed like it. In the latter half of the 1950s I was a star of television, radio, *Five Past Eight* and pantomime. In Scotland, I suppose, I was at the peak of my profession.

Everyone knew about my deep love for children, and I think it rubbed off in those wonderful winter performances. Luckily my paymasters at Howard & Wyndham seemed to be particularly fond of me as well, and paid me £500 every week for the privilege of appearing in those pantomimes at the Alhambra.

It was an enormous amount of money which allowed me to enjoy a lifestyle I could barely have imagined just a few years earlier. Shortly after joining Howard & Wyndham I paid £1,500 for a lovely 10-room house in Dowanhill in the West End of Glasgow. My father said I was an absolute fool as the rateable value was £400 a year. He said no-one in their right mind would pay such expensive rates, and dismissed my purchase as a complete waste of money.

In turn, I dismissed his sentiments. It was a beautiful big sandstone townhouse which I instantly fell in love with, and filled with lovely antiques.

My Rolls-Royce—with the registration plate JL10—was driven much of the time by my chauffeur Neil Galbraith. And although my life was the theatre, I did like to get away for some fishing or shooting.

This wonderful lifestyle also allowed me the opportunity to participate in pursuits I had never dreamed of. One of our friends at that time was a property developer Tony Provan—a man with a great imagination. His business ethics were such that I always felt he would end up in one of two places—as a millionaire or in Barlinnie.

In the end, I don't think he reached either but I particularly remember how he flew his own aircraft all over the country. One day he asked if I was interested in learning how to fly.

There were two reasons I said "no".

One—the tight changes of programme at *Five Past Eight* left little spare time.

Two—I wasn't remotely interested in learning how to fly.

Up until then my connections with flying had been pretty remote. In the early days of the jet aircraft I got an urgent call from a Scottish woman who was part of a civilian team taking part in a competition to see who could fly fastest from London to Paris. She told me they had been let down by a sponsor, and needed £500. In return for my help, she said we would get all the publicity.

"Could you come down right away to try and generate some extra publicity?" she asked.

I thought it was a worthy cause, and flew to London with a regular airline. They picked me up at the airport then took me to an airfield where this two-seater jet plane was waiting.

The pilot's arm was in a plaster cast. I thought: "That's a good start."

Then we took off, flew around for about 10 minutes, came back down again and had our photos taken. I rushed back to the airport, got in a plane and flew back to Scotland. In the competition itself they didn't win. To be more precise, I don't think they even took off. Apparently, the pilot got a bit too excited when his big moment arrived, put on too much power and dug the nose of the plane into the ground.

It was an inauspicious start to my involvement with planes. However Tony Provan possessed a fair command of the powers of persuasion, and kept at me to have a go myself until I finally agreed to accompany him to a big green field in Perthshire—otherwise known as Scone Aerodrome. Some of the stories there were legendary.

There was an instructor whose favourite trick was to tap a new student on the shoulder in mid-flight, signal everything was fine when the student turned round, then lift off his joy-stick and throw it out onto the airfield as they flew over.

It worked every time, leaving the poor student shaking like a jelly in front of the only control-stick in the aircraft. It was obviously a deliberate ploy, designed to bring a student back to earth if he thought they were getting too cocky.

This worked fine until one day the instructor tapped the student on the shoulder, gave the thumbs-up signal and threw the joy-stick out of the window. This time the student smiled back, gave the same thumbs-up signal and threw his joy-stick out.

This instructor almost had a heart attack, unaware the student had got a prop made after hearing about the instructor's prank.

My flying instructor on that first day was Tom Blyth, a man I can only describe as an officer and a gentleman. His exploits flying bombers in the War earned him the Air Force Cross and Distinguished Flying Cross. Like a great many of his peers he really missed flying when he came into civvy life so, just to stay in the air, he became an instructor.

He took me out to a Chipmunk single-engine two-seater aircraft. When we got into the cockpit with one seat behind the other he started going over what he called the "brief flight checks".

These appeared to consist of making sure we had two wings, a rudder at the back and wheels on the bottom. Everything, he decided, was in order.

Then he showed me the mass of dials inside the cockpit, and I thought: "I'll never learn this in a million years." I wasn't even particularly keen.

However, minutes later I was in the front seat as we taxied out to take off. Within seconds we were up in the air, then flew around for a while before Tom asked me to hold the joy-stick. I touched it a bit to the left to notice how the nose dipped a bit and the wing turned, and then to the right. We finally made our final approach and landed.

As I got out of the aircraft, Tom said: "When are you coming back for your first lesson?"

It was then that I had to make a stark choice. Either I decided it wasn't for me or I went through the rest of my life regretting not having tried it. So I made an appointment for my first lesson.

Despite the fact my schedule was packed because of *Five Past Eight*, I somehow made time to travel up to Scone for regular lessons. Usually I drove up during the day for my lesson, then sped back down to Glasgow for that night's show. Sometimes, however, I drove up after the show and stayed overnight in Scone. Within weeks I was hooked on something I hadn't been at all keen on to begin with.

Learning to fly was a tremendous experience. I conquered some of the great aviation mysteries—like plotting a course from A to B or taking the right steps to counteract wind and drift at 3,000 feet.

However, I really hated aerobatics. I would get myself up to 3,500 feet, check no-one had been stupid enough to cross my path or get underneath me, pull up the nose, put my left or right foot forward and let the aircraft turn over on its back before starting to go down in a spin.

Then, with the ground and certain death hurtling towards me at an incredible speed, I had to get out of that spin by myself. The trick was to do full opposite rudder while holding the stick in a central position, and the plane would clear itself.

Up until 1914 pilots had no idea how to do this, and a spin was indeed a precursor to almost certain death. Many young pilots were killed in that way until a mathematician came up with a solution in his classroom. Only when he bravely went up into the air and deliberately put a plane into a spin did he find out if his theory actually worked. Luckily for him, and many others since, it did.

I may have hated the aerobatics, but getting stuck in cloud was far more frightening. Pilots are quickly taught how to get out of a spin, or land safely if their engines fail, but suddenly becoming immersed in a big bank of cloud held far greater fears for me. The best way to explain what it is like is to imagine yourself sitting in a chair when suddenly your whole body slumps to the right. When that happens in cloud in a plane you automatically assume the wings have tipped to the right, and you are turning into a shallow dive. Instinctively you adjust. But that's a mistake.

The instruments in the cockpit still indicate that you are going straight. Your mind is playing tricks on you, and your body reacts in a very strange and dangerous way. It goes against everything your brain is telling you, but you have to put complete trust in your instruments no matter how wrong it feels.

That happened to me once when I was learning to fly and I hated every second of it. When I came out of the bottom of the cloud, I decided I would never allow myself to fly into cloud again.

My first fascination with flying was being able to do it properly. With an instructor in the rear seat, I always felt that if it went wrong then he was there to retrieve the situation. During each lesson I had the security of knowing that Tom Blyth was sitting behind me in the cockpit, but after a total of nine hours in the air with him, he announced I was ready to do my first solo flight. It

Pte. JACK SHORT, Late Scottish Horse, . . .
Att. Seaforth Highlanders,
Wounded in Action, 1st January, 1918, on the Cambrai Front.

MISS MARY ARGYLE,
THE SCOTTISH STREET SINGER.

Above: Harry Lauder's only son, Captain John Lauder, Argyll and Sutherland Highlanders, at Dunoon on his last leave with his fiancée Mildred Thomson. He was killed in action on 28th December 1916

Right: Myself on the roof of Aunt Jean's house in Gourock, about 1937

Opposite above left: My father, Jack Short, aged 12, as Harry Lauder with the Dennistoun Minstrels in 1908

Opposite above right: Myself aged 3, in London

Opposite below left: My father, minus his leg, determined to carry on in showbusiness

Opposite below right: My mother as Mary of Argyle. (She never sang in the street!)

First page: Private Jack Short, Scottish Horse, Dunkeld 1917

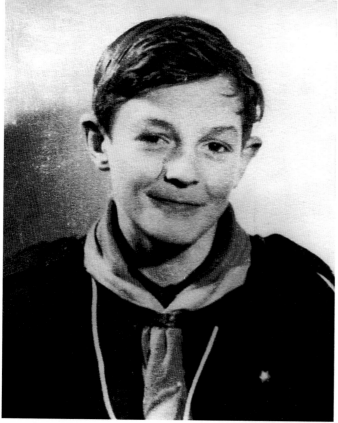

Above: My brother Bert (the tall one) and myself on a picnic at Aunt Jean's, Gourock, 1936

Left: In the Boy Scouts, defending Gourock in 1941!

Above: My brother Buddy

Above: Myself as a juvenile lead

Below: With Galbraith and the Rolls-Royce. Galbraith drove for the
Co-operative Society—mostly for funerals

Above: My aunt Ella Logan (front row) with the Portobello Concert Party in 1929. Dave Willis is in the back row, centre. Notice the dustbins in the background!

JACK SHORT STARLIGHTS STONEHAVEN 1924

ALEX ROSS STONEHAVEN.

Above: A young Ella Logan (front) as Daisy Mars, in Jack Short's Open Air Concert Party, 1924. Dad is on the far left, and Mum is behind Ella

Ella Logan in Hollywood. She was the original star in *Finian's Rainbow* on Broadway, while her films included *Woman Chases Man* and *The Goldwyn Follies*. Her hit song 'How are Things in Glocca Morra' was a world-wide success

Above: Our first show as the Logan Family

Opposite above: With my grandmother, after my first solo flight,
at Scone Aerodrome, Perthshire, in 1960

Opposite below: In G-AJWC ('Whisky Charlie'),
my twin-engined Miles Gemini

Above: Annie Ross, my sister (*left*). The two of us starred together on-screen for the first time in *The Ring of Truth*, 1996 (*right*)

Below: Family group, backstage at the old Metropole: from left—myself, Mum, Annie, Dad, Bert, Heather and Buddy. Annie had just flown in from the USA, and was in another world!

Above: The twins

Above: Angela and I on our wedding day
in Hove, 30th July, 1993

Below: With Aunt Jean in 1984, at Gourock
Primary School—I had been invited back
to my old school to speak to the pupils

Below: Heather with her husband Domenick
and their son Domenick Allen, in Florida

Above: On the occasion of my appointment as a Fellow of the Royal Scottish Academy of Music and Drama in 1988

Above: At Glasgow Caledonian University in 1994, where I was awarded the degree of Doctor of Letters. Someone said I looked like a walking accordian!

Below: Angela, JL, Annie and Heather at Buckingham Palace in 1996

Above: Harry Lauder in Melbourne, 1914. This was his 32nd performance, on Friday May 8th. The detail (*below left*) shows Lauder marching down the aisle with Sir Frank Tait, who brought him over from the USA after his American tour

Below right: Harry Lauder in 1917, with Charlie Chaplin. After his son's death, Lauder raised £1 million for the Harry Lauder Fund for Returning Disabled Ex-Servicemen. My father was among those who benefited

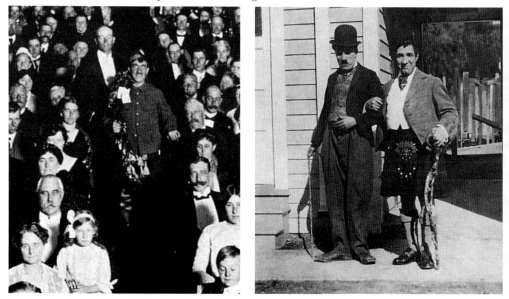

Right: My tribute—*Lauder*, directed by Clive Perry, which opened in 1976 with a Royal Performance before Princess Alexandra at the Lyceum Theatre, Edinburgh, before going on to South Africa, Australia and New Zealand

First page: Playing Archie Rice, *The Entertainer*, at the Byre Theatre, St. Andrews, in 1984, directed by Adrian Reynolds

Below left and right: My church shows, *Laughter in the Aisles*, 1997— talking about Chic Murray (*left*) and proving I'm still alive (*right*)!

Above: In a televised stage performance of *Babes in the Wood*, with Louie Ramsay, in 1958. The performance was interrupted by Eamon Andrews—Louie was the subject of *This is Your Life*. My turn came a few years later

Left: Five Past Eight—one of Scotland's great productions, with Jack Radcliffe and Eve Boswell, in 1959

Above: As Eddie Waters in *Comedians* at the Royal Lyceum Theatre, Edinburgh, in 1991

Right: As Lord Staynbyres in *Flouers o' Edinburgh*, directed by Clive Perry, at Pitlochry in 1996, with Ian Grieve.

Above: As Cardinal Gaetani in *Sunsets and Glories*, directed by Stuart Burge, at the West Yorkshire Playhouse in 1990, with Freddie Jones

Left: As *Uncle Vanya* in Basingstoke, 1991, directed by Adrian Reynolds

Above left and right: Dick Whittington at Kirkcaldy (*left*), and *Babes in the Wood* at the King's Theatre, Glasgow in 1995 (*right*)—in all I've appeared in more than forty pantomimes

Below: The Fabulous Fifties, which I produced and directed at the Edinburgh International Festival in 1993. This was also the year of my quadruple bypass operation, and look what it did to my hair!

Above: In *The Big Picnic*, written and directed by
Bill Bryden, at the Shed in Govan, Glasgow, 1994

Above: The Colour-Sergeant, in *The Big Picnic*

Above: In *A Month of Sundays*, at Pitlochry Festival Theatre in 1992, with Sarah Keyzor

Right: In *The Celtic Story*, directed by Dave MacLennan, at the Pavilion Theatre, Glasgow, in 1998

Opposite above: With Edith Macarthur in *On Golden Pond*, directed by Peter Farago, at Pitlochry Festival Theatre, 1996

Opposite below: As the Devil in *Mr Bolfry*, directed by Joan Knight, with Charles Youlten and Gail Watson, at Pitlochry in 1996

As Willy Loman in *Death of a Salesman*, directed by Clive Perry,
at Pitlochry Festival Theatre in 1992

was an extraordinary experience. I got up to about 2,000 feet, looked down on the city of Dundee below, and then behind me at the empty seat in the back. It suddenly struck me that I was up there flying this plane all on my own. If anything went wrong there would be no-one to save me. At this point in time it simply didn't matter if I was funny or could make people laugh. I had brought this aircraft up thousands of feet into the air, and now I had to get it back down again. On that occasion I succeeded. It provided me with a tremendous sense of achievement.

I had to sit tests as part of the process towards getting my pilot's licence where I would plot my course, and work out the speed and time of a given journey. On one occasion I opted to fly to an old wartime aerodrome at Silloth on the banks of the Solway near Carlisle. All the original RAF hangars were still there—some giant curved shapes, and others which went up to a point.

It was a Sunday, and as I approached Silloth the RAF controller, a girl, who was in sole charge, gave me landing instructions—plus the wind and weather at 30,000 feet, 20,000 feet, 15,000 feet and 10,000 feet. Given that I was flying at 2,000 feet, it wasn't very useful.

She was bringing me in like one of the fighter planes. All I wanted to know was what runway I was to use, and if I was clear to land. Eventually, I got the correct instructions, landed and requested taxi instructions.

In her terribly proper voice, she answered: "Taxi to the hangar with the twiddly top."

I said: "Roger . . . the hangar with the twiddly top."

She burst out laughing. She couldn't think of any other way to describe the hangars.

Eventually I received my pilot's licence at a big ceremony in the lounge of the Scottish Aero Club. It was a wonderful moment because I was now able to take people up to fly.

"Anyone want to fly with me?" I said.

Immediately a lady with a little daughter of about five put her hand up, and said: "Yes, I'll fly with you. Where are you going?"

I told her I was planning to take the Aero Club plane up the glen to Pitlochry, but after about five minutes in the air the little girl announced: "Mummy, I want the toilet. I want the toilet."

So the first time I took passengers up in a plane I had to turn back and do an emergency landing—just so this little girl could go to the bathroom.

Many years later I chose a marvellous actress, Sandy Imlach, to play the principal boy in pantomime at the Eden Court Theatre in Inverness. She was six feet tall with legs that went up to the sky. And she was a marvellous principal boy.

It was only during the run when I was talking to her that I realised I had met her before. She was the little girl who had needed the toilet.

By the time that little girl announced she needed the toilet I was hooked. I had trained in single-engined Chipmunks, and got my licence to fly Chipmunks, but soon afterwards I was told a pretty good twin-engined Miles Gemini aircraft was looking for a new owner.

It was a four-seater that had been built for the Royal Navy during the War as a communications aircraft. It cruised at about 120 mph, had a retractable undercarriage and no bad habits. Its call sign was GAJWC, which translated as Golf Alpha Juliet Whisky Charlie.

I thought to myself: "Whisky Charlie. What a wonderful title for a Scottish comedian."

That convinced me I had to have the plane. She was brought up to Abbotsinch Airport—now Glasgow Airport—and once a fee of around £2,000 had changed hands she was mine. After a couple of hours' flying and a brief exam, I would be licensed to fly her.

There were many wonderful experiences in Whisky Charlie.

On one occasion I flew my mother and father to Belfast—one of our favourite cities. We were up about 2,500 feet on a beautiful clear day looking over the Mull of Kintyre and Arran which were laid out like a map. I felt as though I could see for a thousand miles.

I turned round, and said to my mother: "Are you all right?"

"Aye," she said. "Just watch where you're going."

When we set down it was one of those landings that was so smooth she didn't realise we had touched the ground. I remember those landings so clearly—because they were so rare.

What a pilot really aims for is to cream the plane onto the runway in such a way he's not even sure if he's down himself.

"Did you come in with that?" said another pilot afterwards. "That was a nice landing."

And that made me feel great. It was the achievement of doing something right. It didn't matter whether I was a comic, a star, or someone who was liked by many. The important thing to me was that I was able to do something, and do it well.

Once a year I flew down to the Isle of Man for a concert with RAF band The Squadronaires and their conductor Ronnie Aldrich. He told me you could tell it was the Glasgow Fair holiday week because none of the taxis had windows.

I took my dad with me once, and when we were up in the air decided to let him have a go holding the joy-stick.

By the time we got to the Isle of Man I was saying: "No Dad, I'll take it."

"No son, it's all right."

"Leave it alone, I'll land it."

If I hadn't forced myself he would have tried to land it himself.

Mind you, my mother and father were dream passengers compared to my Aunt Mona who lived in Brighton. I invited her to dinner at a beautiful restaurant in Islay. When she realised we had to fly there and back she wasn't happy.

"Mona," I said. "You won't be frightened in my aircraft because it's more like being in a small car than a big jet plane. Don't worry, this will be really good. You'll love it."

After we got into the plane I did a few last minute checks and then started to move towards the runway at little more than jogging pace.

All I could hear behind me was Mona making a dull groaning sound.

"We're not even off the ground yet," I said to her. "In fact, we're hardly moving. We're just moving gently towards the runway."

"Ohhhhhhhh. Ohhhhhhhhh."

The noises were getting louder.

"Try not to worry, Mona. You'll be all right."

How wrong I was. When we finally did get into the air I thought poor Mona was going to have a heart attack. She was in an absolutely terrible state.

Planes are loud machines but, as we headed down the Clyde Valley, Mona's moans were so loud they were drowning out the engines. It was a brilliantly clear day, and there wasn't a cloud in the sky, but Mona was reacting as though we were headed straight for the eye of a hurricane.

I decided the only option was to divert to Prestwick Airport in Ayrshire, about 30 miles down the coast.

When we got there she evidently went straight to the ladies where she reproduced the contents of her breakfast. Amidst all this chaos a concerned stewardess rushed in, and asked: "Aw Madam, you look awful. Have you just flown from New York?"

"No . . . Glasgow."

I had to send for a car to come from Glasgow to take her back.

There were some magical experiences when I had members of my family up in the air. My mother's brother Jimmy Allan had fought with the Black Watch in the 1914-18 War and was a sergeant cook with the RAF in World War Two. After the War his furniture business in Aberdeen went belly-up so he emigrated to America, and settled in the deep south of Augusta, Georgia.

When he came over on holiday one year I showed him the City Chambers in Glasgow—an astoundingly beautiful building he had never seen—and took him up in the plane over the River Clyde. It was a wonderful moment because he had never been up in a little private plane before, and he had never realised just how close Loch Lomond was to Glasgow. I took him to places he knew well, like Arran and Largs, but when he saw them from the air the joy on his face was magnificent to behold. These places look so different from that perspective, and his enjoyment of the occasion gave me a great thrill.

When some of my American friends came over I offered to show them Scotland in a day. We flew over the magnificent views of Loch Lomond at 1,000 feet, then went over the mountains to Oban and up to Tobermory in Mull, where I used to fly round my pal Bobby McLeod's hotel, The Mish-Nish, until he came out and waved. We then came back along the Caledonian Canal, and flew over towards the RAF base at Lossiemouth, where I wanted to land.

At this point a problem developed. My radio was very old and didn't have a lot of power. The control tower knew someone was calling them up, but didn't know who I was or where I was.

Every time I pressed the button they just heard interference.

So the voice on the other end of the line told me to press the button once for yes, and twice for no. He then went through every detail he needed until he had established where I was and when I was due to land.

I was extremely nervous when I finally landed. I made a bit of a mess of it as well—one of those where the plane goes bump, bump, bump, settle.

When I got to the control tower I discovered the officer who had talked me through on the radio was a Polish Wing Commander resplendent in a uniform covered in medals. He looked absolutely wonderful.

"Well sir," he said. "For the record, you landed at 1.20, 1.21, 1.22 and 1.23."

It was a perfect description of my dreadful landing.

He then explained how he had used the same method of communicating with planes which had been shot up during the War.

We left Lossiemouth, flew over Aberdeen, stopped off at the appropriately named Scone for tea, and then went back to Glasgow. The whole trip had taken just a few hours—an American tourist's dream I suspect.

A few years later in London I used the Polish Wing Commander's excellent methods to talk to a friend who was completely paralysed in hospital. He had no way of communicating, but I noticed his eyes blinked.

I said: "If you can hear me close your eyes tight."

And he did.

"OK, close your eyes for 'no' and blink your eyes for 'yes'."

"Can you hear me all right?"

Blink. Yes.

"Do you want a glass of water?"

No.

We carried on this conversation for a long time. After I left the room a nurse ran after me.

"Mr Logan, excuse me," she said. "What happened? There seems to be something different about him."

I explained how we had communicated, and she seemed genuinely surprised. That way of communicating hadn't occurred to them. It seemed strange, but had I not had the experience of the Polish Wing Commander then perhaps it wouldn't have occurred to me either.

*   *   *

One Sunday I asked my friend, the great singer Calum Kennedy, if he fancied a day out somewhere by plane.

"Yes," he said. "Let's fly to Stornoway."

The airport was closed on a Sunday but I was licensed to land at any airfield at any time.

"All right," I said. "Stornoway it is. Let's go."

But at this point Calum's dear wife Anne arrived.

"What was that I was hearing?" she said to her husband, who was now looking despondent.

"We're going to fly up to Stornoway," he said. "It'll be lovely."

"No you're not."

"But why?"

Anne composed herself, looked Calum straight in the eye, and said: "Because if you fly up to Stornoway on a Sunday you will never play Stornoway or any of the islands again."

She had a fair point. The Sabbath was most sacred in places like Stornoway, so I suggested a place where there would be absolutely no religious problems concerned with landing on a Sunday.

"Why don't we go to Dublin?" I said.

To my utter astonishment, we were over the mouth of the Liffey two hours and five minutes after taking off—at exactly the time I had planned when I was plotting our flight back in Glasgow. I had secretly thought it would have been a miracle if I had even made it to Dublin.

As I parked the plane, Calum headed into the airport bar wearing the kilt. Evidently the second he entered a big hand came out, and said: "Welcome to Ireland."

By the time I arrived he was surrounded by hordes of Irishmen who were supplying him with copious amounts of the local beverages. It was typical of the type of wonderful reception people get in Ireland.

When we went into Dublin, however, I must say we came across the opposite end of the hospitality spectrum. Walking into the lobby of the city's top hotel, the Gresham, we were dealt with by two pretty girls behind reception. They were very smart and well-spoken, but they were off-hand and aloof. It was the first and only time I have ever encountered an Irish snob.

Looking down her nose, one of them eventually noticed us.

"Can we have a room, please?"

"It will cost you thirty pounds."

And she mentioned the price as though we would never have had that kind of money in a million years. It was a strange attitude because we were both very smartly turned out—Calum in the kilt and myself in an expensive tailored suit.

"We'll take it," I said.

The service got no better. That night we arranged to come down for dinner but a dance was in full swing when we arrived, and there were no free tables. We waited half an hour but nobody came near us. Then they started moving the tables away to make the dance floor bigger. One poor chap who was eating his meal quite rightly refused to move. So they started dancing round him.

We finally got a table, and they danced round us too. I was shocked at the level of service in what was supposedly the best hotel in Ireland. And after another long wait and no sign of food we walked out and proceeded to another well-known hotel, Jurys.

"We've just been insulted at the Gresham," I said. "Is there any chance of a meal?"

They couldn't have been more helpful and hospitable, and I'm glad to say I've still to meet another Irish snob.

Flying into Glasgow was a nerve-racking experience. Even then it was a large airport with a lot of activity. Visibility was often quite poor as well. At eight o'clock in the morning I can remember regularly being able to see five miles ahead of me after taking off, but two hours later that was down to just a couple of miles. The reason—the enormous amount of smoke coming up into the atmosphere as the city got going in the morning.

On one occasion the control tower asked me: "Where are you? Give us your exact position."

I had absolutely no idea where I was. It wasn't enough to tell them I was up in the air flying around. That really wouldn't have gone down too well, so I started frantically looking at the ground below for any familiar landmarks. There was a shed that covered the terracing of a football ground, and on the top it said: "Kilsyth."

So I called up and said: "Whisky Charlie, overhead Kilsyth Football Club."

It was done with panache, and no doubt they were impressed by the professionalism I showed in knowing my exact position, but it was a complete fluke.

There were some pretty frightening experiences during my time behind the controls of Whisky Charlie.

When I was doing my first comedy play in Aberdeen in 1961, I was asked to open a Spring Fair in Fraserburgh. Thinking it would generate some extra publicity if I flew up there, I invited some of the artistes in the play to join me for the flight.

Meanwhile, Angus Lennie, one of the actors in our production, told me he had a big publicity stunt arranged for the same day.

"I'm going out horse-riding," he said.

"I didn't know you could ride a horse."

"I can't but if I go and do an hour I should be OK. The press might be there."

"I've been on a horse. You'll kill yourself."

"Oh no, I'm sure it will be all right. Anything for publicity."

He was mad to even consider it. However, he proceeded, and so did I. The take-off from Aberdeen Airport went fine but suddenly I saw a warning light that meant one of the wheels hadn't gone up properly. This was a serious problem.

I radioed the tower.

"I think I've got a problem with one of my wheels," I said to the controller.

"Roger Whisky Charlie," came the reply. "One of your wheels is still down."

An emergency was declared, and the fire brigade and ambulance made their way quickly to the end of the runway. For the first time I had to pull an emergency lever I'd always been dying to pull to get the wheels down. I heard a thump, but I still didn't know if they were locked in position. I was going to have to land immediately, unsure if the wheels would buckle when the plane hit the ground.

Meanwhile, inside the plane, my passengers—Marillyn Gray, Norman Fraser and Mavis Main—were completely oblivious to the problem because they all had earphones on. I turned to them, gave a thumbs-up signal and announced I was returning to the airport. But I gave them no reason.

As we were coming into land, one of the actresses said: "Oh look, there's the ambulance and the fire engines."

But fortunately the penny hadn't dropped.

When we touched the ground I braced myself for the worst, but thank God the wheels worked a treat. We landed safely and taxied towards the hangar.

Of course, someone had phoned the newspapers, and by the time we got back to Aberdeen there were stories about Jimmy Logan's mid-air drama, and how the famous comedian battled bravely with the controls of his plane after his landing-wheels jammed.

The big story on page three of the *Daily Record* of Thursday, April 13, 1961, under the headline "Jimmy Logan In Air Scare—Drama after take-off" read:

> Rescue squads and passengers watched anxiously yesterday as Scots comedian Jimmy Logan played the leading role in a real-life drama over an airport.

They saw Jimmy's twin-engined Miles Gemini plane, "Whisky Charlie"—piloted by himself—fly a circuit of Aberdeen Airport with one leg of the undercarriage stuck.

It happened just after the Variety star had taken off for Fraserburgh with three friends WHO HAD NEVER FLOWN BEFORE.

Ambulance men and firemen were immediately called to action stations in case the other wheel would not come down again to allow the plane to land.

But it did.

And so the copy continued, describing in detail the drama as it unfolded, and my reaction to it all. It was a marvellous story played up to the full. But Angus Lennie wasn't so cheery the next time I saw him. He never got any press coverage on his horse, and returned to the play barely able to stand up because his legs were killing him.

Despite my promise never to get stuck in cloud, there were a couple of occasions when I did. And goodness me, they were scary. The first time I got into a cloud, I reckoned it wasn't very deep and climbed to get out above it. I was right; it wasn't very deep. But the minute I cleared that cloud I spotted another big, massive, giant cloud right ahead of me. There was absolutely no way I was going into that so I decided to get back down again.

I spotted a hole in the cloud I had just come out of and dived in. Of course, that was the worst thing I could have done because we were always told to descend gradually in situations like that. I pulled the power back and the next thing I knew I was in real cloud. It was like a meeting of the Clan McCloud—and I seemed to be right smack, bang in the middle of it. After what seemed like an eternity, I emerged from the clouds pouring with sweat and vowing—just like after a big drinking session—never to go near the stuff again.

153

That was before I took off from Glasgow one day just as the weather closed in at record speeds in the Clyde Valley. One minute it was totally clear, the next I could barely make anything out beyond my nose. On that occasion I'm not ashamed to admit that I panicked, called up the control tower and explained my predicament. At this point my instruments were spinning in all different directions, and so was my head. I was flying in the wrong direction and I had no idea where I was. Fortunately for me, these guys really knew their stuff and were able to use radar to guide me back to Glasgow. Had it not been for them, I would have been in real trouble.

Planes never held a fascination for me until I was actually up there in the sky, but boats and the sea have held a special place in my heart for as long as I can remember. I'm sure there are many explanations for my love of boats—my father owned a boat on Loch Lomond called the *Logan Belle,* and I spent a large amount of my childhood watching the hustle and bustle of the River Clyde from the streets of Gourock.

In Aberdeen I had a dear friend, Alex Morris. He was a lovely wee man who ran the Union Bar which sat directly behind the Tivoli Theatre. As the years and my appearances there passed, we became very close. Part of the reason for this bond was our shared affection and dream of a life on the ocean wave. We looked through all the magazines, and talked, and talked, and talked about what we would do should we ever buy a boat and set sail for exotic places.

But we were all talk. Neither of us truly believed in what we said until I went out and bought a brand new 22-foot Freeman cruiser—a truly marvellous vessel that was mounted on a trailer so big you could only just reach the deck if you stood on your tiptoes and stretched up as high as your hands would go.

I'll never forget the picture of pure joy etched on Alex's face when I went up to Aberdeen to tell him about my purchase. At that time he wasn't at all well with a bad heart condition, and relied on a cocktail of 18 pills each day with an emergency oxygen tank placed constantly at the side of his bed. He was confined to that bed for much of his time.

He genuinely couldn't believe I had actually gone out and done it.

I'll also always remember going down to Nuneaton in England where the cruisers were built to collect what would become my pride and joy. The night beforehand Grace and I booked into a posh hotel. The following morning a maid came into the room.

"Do you want breakfast, sir?" she asked.

"Oh yes," I said. "That would be great."

"Does your friend want breakfast too?"

I didn't know who she was talking about, then I noticed she was looking at my wife.

"My friend?" I said. And before she could answer I nodded. It was a wonderful moment—the only time I had ever heard my wife being described as my friend.

The boat I chose had a royal blue hull and a silver-grey deck top. It looked just beautiful on its own trailer.

After hauling her up to Glasgow, I asked Alex: "What's your great ambition?"

"Oh, I'd sail up the Caledonian Canal," he said. "But . . ."

"Right, no buts, you're going."

"But . . ."

"I said no buts. That's final."

Somehow Alex got himself dressed, stocked up on his pills, walked down to his car, put an emergency oxygen bottle in the back seat, and drove to Glasgow.

We towed the new boat up to Oban, stopping off at one point on a side road to get a cup of tea. But I couldn't get the water pump to work which meant we had no fresh drinking water.

However, I wanted a cup of tea and set out with my teapot and a torch to find a farmhouse—and some water.

As I walked away from the boat I suddenly heard a loud rushing noise from below. Shining my torch past my feet I noticed we had parked on a bridge right above a fast-moving river tumbling full of the freshest water. It was a godsend.

Our subsequent journey was magnificent. From Oban we sailed to Tobermory in Mull, then went back up to the entrance of the Caledonian Canal. At Banavie there were 19 locks to get us up to the right height—and we tackled every single one.

It would have been a tiring job for even the fittest of men, and I was deeply worried it would be too much for Alex. But I was utterly amazed when I saw him throwing the ropes, and running and jumping from the boat to open and close the locks. There was no sign of his oxygen bottle, and I never saw him taking any pills. He seemed to be living on the pure adrenaline and enjoyment of the occasion. Mind over matter can help at times. I think the regular drams we had helped too.

We sailed along the Canal to Inverness, and sailed back down the Canal, and down Loch Linnhe in a Force Eight gale to Oban.

A few months later Alex and I were off again. This time the boat wasn't the only thing in tow—the wives came too. We pulled the boat from Glasgow to the south of France, using the boat as a caravan on the way down, and loading her with duty-free booze so there were plenty of rations by the time we put her in the water.

On our first trip across to an idyllic little Mediterranean island a desert wind—the mistral—blew up. Two priests appeared as we prepared to return to the mainland, and asked us for a lift.

"Sure," I said, feeling a bit more confident about the stormy trip ahead.

It was a tricky sail. The seas were coming at the boat from every direction, and we just put our nose into them and hoped for the best. Eventually we got back to the main harbour and, as he was stepping off the boat, one of the priests commented in very broken English: "God Save the Queen. Very good capeetan."

We were very pleased with ourselves. We felt we had upheld the honour of the Union Jack.

Somehow, by the time we were ready to sail to Italy—which was just along the road as it were—all the duty-free booze had disappeared.

By the summer of 1959 I had reached the top in Scotland. It was said I could easily make £500 a week without setting foot outside Glasgow, and it was true. *Five Past Eight* was great, and the pantomimes at the Alhambra were magnificent.

Professionally, though, I was far from content. I may have been at the top in Scotland but I was determined to scale even greater heights. The wee box that was starting to appear in people's living rooms really fascinated me. I hadn't done a great deal of TV at that point, but I knew it would be vital if anyone was to be a success in our industry in the coming years. Even then, I realised its capacity to become such a powerful medium.

That winter I was down to do pantomime again, but one day a man called Eric Maschwitz, the BBC's head of light entertainment, asked me if I was interested in signing an exclusive contract for the BBC and going to London to present my own series for the network. The money wasn't as good as the Alhambra, but it was a wonderful opportunity I simply couldn't afford to miss. Great stars like Lauder and Fyffe had conquered many audiences outside their own country, and I wanted to do the same.

I appeared on the odd programme like the children's TV show *All Your Own* in March of that year, but everything was building to my first series scheduled to begin in November. *The Jimmy Logan Show* was a comedy variety show scheduled to run for six months every second Saturday night. I was delighted with my contract because my friend and colleague at the BBC in Glasgow,

Eddie Fraser, was coming to produce the show, and a lovely man George Inns—who went on to work with the Black and White Minstrels—agreed to direct.

I was happy with that arrangement as it is so important that the star works with the director and producer, and vice versa.

However, the BBC changed their minds and told Eddie he had to stay in Glasgow. Then George was forced to pull out, and I suddenly found myself in the daunting position of heading towards London with a distinct lack of new material. I had already used all the material I had for TV—which wasn't much anyway—in previous programmes.

The minute I met the new producer I knew there were going to be problems. He gave off an air of being completely *non simpatico*. And so it proved. I remember his name but I haven't mentioned it because I've spent so many years trying to forget it.

As soon as we clapped eyes on each other a few months before the first show I could tell he didn't like me. And by the time we started to work on the content of the show it had become an absolute nightmare.

Normally when a producer gets half a dozens sketches sent in, he will look each one over and say: "That's no good. That's a possible. That isn't." And so on. With this guy, though, he just sent me the sketches and said: "Choose what you want."

They wouldn't even be scripts. I would be given a choice between being a bus driver who has lost his way or a slave of the Roman Empire.

"How am I supposed to choose when I don't even know what's in the sketches? I can't tell which is good, and which is bad."

"Doesn't matter Jimmy," he said. "You've got to make your mind up now because our scenic chap needs to build the scenery."

That was typical of the way he worked. He didn't like me, so he had decided to do his best to make my show as bad as possible. I couldn't sleep at night, and often stayed up till all hours trying to make it work. But no matter how hard I tried, it was never going to work.

A couple of months before the first show I decided to go on holiday to Agadir in Morocco with Grace, Eve Boswell, my co-star in *Five Past Eight*, and her husband Trevor.

I was in a real sweat—not because of the hot weather, but because I had no decent material for the biggest break in my career, and a producer who seemed intent on destroying it. Whilst Grace, Eve and Trevor lapped up the sunshine, I lay back next to the pool thinking only of gags, gags and gags. I was a wreck.

When I was there this producer sent out about eight scripts. They made me sick because every single one was terrible, and obviously terrible. He had clearly decided to wash his hands of the debacle, and wanted me to sort everything out. A good comedian can make good comedy out of a bad situation, but these scripts were way beyond salvage. There was more chance of raising the *Titanic* than raising a laugh out of those.

There were of course some lighter moments while I was in Morocco that made me smile. One day we went to a village famous for its silverware where I bought the most beautiful old antique knife with an ivory handle that was all cracked and worn with age. It even had Arabic writing inscribed on it. I reckoned it was a real find.

I was intrigued to know what the writings were, so I asked the receptionist to get them translated when we returned to the hotel in Agadir.

"Certainly, sir," she said. "It will be ready for you here in the morning."

Sure enough they were able to translate it. Great, I thought, as I opened the envelope with the English translation inside. The beautiful Arabic writing on the blade said: "Property of the Hotel Sahid."

One night we were in a tiny little nightclub dancing to Eve's records which she had brought with her. Of course, Eve sang in about six languages but she didn't speak any of them. Even in French, which I had a smattering of, she could never have ordered a cup of tea.

Then she said: "Do you want me to sing, Jimmy?"

"Yeah, sure." And I went over to the piano.

In this nightclub every man was a Prince who had more than one camel. When Eve finished her first song, one of them said to me: "You are always the piano player for Miss Boswell?"

I'd just finished *Five Past Eight*.

"Yes," I said. "I always play the piano wherever we go."

However, we got talking, and he turned out to be a truly fascinating gentleman—the commandant of a camel regiment. He told us that a camel never sleeps when you go with it to the desert, staying awake all night to guard its owner. A camel, he said, will do anything once that owner has gained its full trust, love and affection. For example, if it sees you are dying of thirst, it will lie on its back and wait for you to cut it open to drink its stored water—even though it knows it will die.

Camels are also like elephants—they never forget. This gentleman told us how one of his fellow-officers once whipped a camel. Two years later it killed him.

Another evening we had a wonderful meal in a village on the side of a mountain near Agadir. A few months later it was devastated by a huge earthquake. When we were there it had been noticeable how everything went quiet in mid-afternoon—the wind, the wildlife, everything. Not a leaf stirred. Then they were struck by this massive earthquake.

Many years later I went back. The spot where we had eaten that lovely meal was just a flat bit of rock with the odd bit of stone lying around. The same could be said for the whole village.

*   *   *

The Jimmy Logan Show was an unqualified disaster. I kept fighting to make it better, but I was in a no-win situation. By the fifth show I finally conceded I was hitting my head against a brick wall, fighting a losing battle with the wrong producer.

My agent and I even went to him to see if we could sort things out.

"Of course I love Jimmy's work," he told my agent. "Don't be silly."

But nothing changed.

When we were rehearsing one Friday night—24 hours before the show was due to go out live—he was up in the sound box shouting: "Oh come on, get on with it, we've not got all night."

He was sarcastic and rude, and his voice was transmitted to the entire studio. Everyone could hear him.

"Excuse me," I said, and calmly went into my dressing room to take a breather. Inside, I was at the end of my tether. I couldn't believe I was being treated in such a shoddy manner.

It's at this point that I made my biggest mistake—I went back to continue the rehearsal. In hindsight I should have walked out, had a meal and gone to my bed. Then he would have been the one with the job of explaining to the BBC why I had left.

But at that point in time I didn't have the confidence to walk away, and I most certainly didn't feel I had the power. I also felt I would be letting so many other people down if I walked out on the show.

The shows themselves were poor, but I was in an impossible situation. I was expecting to be able to work with someone to come up with a great product but what I got was a man who was singing from an entirely different songsheet.

For instance, I stayed up until three o'clock in the morning trying to get the script for the bus driver sketch right. But it was an impossible task. When someone told the producer that sketch was terrible, his stock answer was: "Jimmy chose it."

He didn't say I had to choose it, that he had effectively forced me to choose it because they had to build some scenery.

The press reaction wasn't too complimentary either. In Scotland, where so much had been expected of me, there was a feeling of utter disappointment. One paper said my show failed because it was too Scottish. Another one said it failed because it wasn't Scottish enough. They did agree on one point, though. Both said it was rubbish.

By the time the series came to an end I was all too aware that my reputation had suffered. Television was becoming such an important medium, and as a result, I would say it took me at least two years to re-establish my credibility outside Scotland. That producer had succeeded in making me a failure, something which bothered me greatly at the time.

He didn't get it all his own way, though. At the end of a series like that it was normal for everyone involved to have a party. But he announced that there was going to be no end of series party for *The Jimmy Logan Show*.

There was also no way I was going to allow that to happen, and I immediately informed everyone we were having a party at the House of Lords. My friend Commander Sid Glover kindly agreed to allow us the use of his flat in the Palace of Westminster.

I thought if I was going to make an exit I would make it a good one.

A couple of days later the producer came into the office. Spotting the invitations, he barked: "We're not sending them out from here. It's nothing to do with us."

So I stamped them and sent every card out personally. There was even an invitation for him, and, like everyone else, a gift also. There was no way I was going to reduce myself to his pitiful level.

I licked my wounds, picked myself up and returned to the theatre. For the first time in my career I had taken a real knock, and judging by the looks on some people's faces, it was dead obvious. The most annoying thing about the whole situation was that it was so needless. I knew I had the ability to make a success of that TV series, yet factors I largely had no control over ensured that wasn't to be.

I returned to *Five Past Eight* for the summer season of 1960—a show still on a high from the most magnificently successful run ever the year before. With myself, Jack Radcliffe and Eve Boswell heading the cast, almost 400,000 people had come to the Alhambra during our 24-week season. That was almost 10 per cent of the Scottish population. Stewart Cruikshank immediately gave the go-ahead for the three of us to head the line-up again in 1960.

The secret of *Five Past Eight* was that it offered the glamour of what you might find in Paris or London alongside the unique Scottish humour you found nowhere else. It was so popular company bosses would send their secretaries down to stand in queues to make sure they got tickets for the next change of programme. There was tremendous pressure on the box office.

Those shows had style. There were a couple of years when our own dancers were replaced by the Bluebell Girls from Paris. They went down an absolute storm. When those internationally famous girls arrived on the stage of the Alhambra the audience just went daft. One night Jack and I came on for the opening, then I disappeared whilst Jack did his warm-up.

Then he said: "Now what about the Bluebell Girls, eh? Would you like to meet them again?"

And the audience screamed: "Yes".

The music played, then this long line of girls came on. They all wore black dresses down to their knees, diamond necklaces, had beautiful chignon hairstyles and a white fur draped over their arms. They looked absolutely wonderful.

"I'd like to introduce you first to Georgette," said Jack. "Hello Georgette. And here is Mimi. And what is your name?"

163

"Senzy," the dancer said in a broad Glaswegian accent.

"What?"

"I said Senzy. And you want tae know somethin' . . . ma feet are killin' me."

That was when the audience realised number seven in this startling line-up was me.

It was great comedy, and appreciated warmly by the Glesca punters. Trying to find the right material consistently, of course, was the greatest challenge. It was always our responsibility to judge whether it would go down well or not.

The drawback on *Five Past Eight* was that they kept changing the director, each one intent on stamping his own individual personality on the show. Usually it worked pretty well, but then we got a fellow called Dickie Hurran.

He was interested in the glitz and glamour, producing sets that cost a fortune. Which was fine. But he didn't appear to care about the importance of the comedy—the essential ingredient that made our show so unique, and popular. As a result he was always wanting to cut Jack and me back.

Our time on stage was perfectly reasonable. To the audience, a solid eight-minute production felt like eight minutes, but a good eight-minute sketch felt like three. So they felt we were never on enough anyway.

Dickie didn't realise this and wanted to cut us down even further. In the second half we would do the McAuley family scene, then Jack would do a sketch, and then an item or so later I would do a sketch and then we would do a double-act at the end. But Dickie Hurran cut that down to the family sketch, one sketch from Jack and my spot just before the finale. There was no double-act, and the audience left feeling rather short changed.

One evening we were going through a dress rehearsal for the big opening night. In this giant theatre there were only about half a dozen people in the stalls—Stewart Cruikshank, one of his assistants, a secretary, and so on, all around a table with drinks. Dickie Hurran was also there, as were the 22-piece orchestra, but that was it.

I was on stage doing an Aberdeen farmer's boy act. "Aye, fit like? Aye no bad. Foo's yer doos?"

It was the kind of act that drove Dickie up the wall because he had the whole stage decked out as an incredible white violin lying on its side. It was a wonderful spectacle that he envisaged with dancers in tails, and most definitely not to be followed by an Aberdeen lad in his farmer's clothes.

But here I was following the dancers in tails holding my shot-gun. It was all Chinese to Dickie.

Finally at three o'clock in the morning I walked on to the stage to do my final act. We had been there since eight o'clock the previous night, but we were professionals and we knew we had to get it done.

There was a message waiting for me when I walked off stage. Mr Cruikshank wanted to see me. I thought that was good—a nice wee whisky to finish up the evening.

"Can you change your act?" he said. "I don't think it will be right. Can Jack and you not do a double?"

Dickie Hurran had obviously been having a word in Stewart's ear. He was presenting caviar, yet we were coming on with mince. My feeling on that was very simple; if you've had 16 plates of caviar—no matter how good it is—you will eventually get fed up with it. You need the mince in between, and let's be honest here— has there ever been a sweeter smell than mince from a Maryhill tenement?

When I got home I phoned Jack—even though it was after four o'clock in the morning.

I said to him: "He doesn't like my act, Jack, and he says we should do a double-act but I've told him we can't do that because we haven't written anything or prepared anything."

I finally got to sleep at almost five o'clock, and at nine o'clock on the dot the phone rang.

"Hello, it's Mr Cruikshank," said the voice. "I've decided to take a chance on your act."

That night I was shaking like a leaf. Maybe he was right, and maybe the act would go down like a lead balloon. I stood at the side of the stage waiting for my turn thinking about him telling me it was going to be the kiss of death.

Finally I went on, and it was a smash. Each time I got a laugh I looked over to where he was sitting—not too obviously but enough for him to notice. He always held a big party after an opening night, and this occasion was no different. There was a big do at the Malmaison Hotel, and during the festivities he came up to me, and said: "All right, Jimmy. Here's a bottle of whisky. I was wrong."

Stewart Cruikshank was a great influence on my career. He gave me my first contract with Howard & Wyndham, and I considered him a real gentleman of the theatre.

Some years later I was at the BBC recording when I got a phone call. It was Mr Cruikshank. He sounded worried.

"Jimmy," he said. "I need some help."

"Sure, Mr Cruikshank, what is it?"

"Andy Stewart is on in *Five Past Eight* at the King's in Edinburgh, but he has taken very poorly, and can't open tomorrow night. I'm in an absolute jam."

"OK," I said. "Can you arrange the orchestra to be there at four o'clock for a band call."

"Of course."

Then I phoned my own stage manager at my own theatre and told him to get a load of things through to Edinburgh.

Meanwhile, I went on with my BBC rehearsal, then travelled through to the King's the following morning. The cast didn't know

Andy was off, and were genuinely shocked to see me. I told them that I could put in comedy acts where Andy would normally have done his stuff. After I explained this Andy's manager piped up: "Well, Andy does about 15 minutes at the end. If you could even do about eight that would help."

Cheeky bugger, I thought to myself. I'll do twenty.

All the other artistes stayed away from me as I stood at the side of the stage preparing for my act. None of them knew me. Then the director Freddie Carpenter tapped me on the shoulder, I walked on, and the curtain went up.

"I know what you're expecting," I said. "Well, he's not here. You're stuck with me. If you want your money back the answer is no."

I went right through the show and it worked like a dream.

When I was there someone mentioned that Stewart Cruikshank was deeply ill. He had cancer. Each day I travelled through to Glasgow to rehearse a play I was in, then shot back through to Edinburgh at night. On the Thursday, my last night, Stewart came through and took me for supper. During the meal he opened his chequebook, and laid it out in front of me.

"I'm going to send you a blank cheque," he said. "Fill it in with whatever amount you want."

It was a wonderful gesture, a measure of the gratitude he had for me stepping in at such short notice, but the following morning I left him a note. I told him how much I thought of him, and reminded him how he had opened the door to *Five Past Eight*, providing me with so many good times. I asked him to accept the last few days on me as a token of my gratitude for all he had done.

A few days later a letter arrived in the post. It was from Stewart, and it included a cheque. He said he appreciated what I had done but there was no way that, as the boss of the company, he was going to allow me to do all that work for no reward.

When he died shortly afterwards I arranged for all the front of house lights to be put out the minute the audience were in the theatre. For half an hour the illuminated signs and advertising lights were covered in darkness. That is how they pay tribute to the great stars on Broadway, and I considered Stewart one of the greats of Scottish theatre. I thought it was a fitting tribute to his memory.

To my surprise a letter arrived from Stewart's successor Peter Donald telling me the gesture had been noticed, and greatly appreciated.

Stewart was still boss when Jack and I did our final *Five Past Eight* in 1961. It was a dreadful finish to a wonderful run of almost ten years. In a sense we became victims of our own success. We had done so well that we got invited back every year, but people can't leave things that aren't broken alone. And Howard & Wyndham, spurred on by Dickie Hurran, were intent on attracting the big London stars up to Glasgow.

Normally *Five Past Eight* changed programme every four weeks but then Dickie Hurran had a brainwave which he thought could save money. He announced that in 1960—the season after my disastrous television series—there would only be three programmes. It was a lottery. The first programme was supposed to be five weeks, but ended up lasting eight. The next was supposed to be six, but it also lasted for eight weeks.

The following year Dickie announced there would only be two programmes of 13 weeks each. It was a move that took the pressure off the box office, but left the punters unhappy because the changes between programmes were limited. Some production scenes stayed the same, and although we changed the comedy, Dickie insisted on keeping the same opening, the same finish to the first half, and the same finale.

The public left feeling they had seen it all before.

Before the start of the season Dickie had also dropped the bombshell—without telling us—that the 1961 *Five Past Eight* would be the last featuring Jimmy Logan and Jack Radcliffe in the starring roles. In 1962, he told everyone, there would be new stars at the Alhambra.

To give Stewart Cruikshank his credit, he was on the phone immediately apologising.

However, after the debacle of the television series, it was to prove a bad omen for our last hurrah in front of the *Five Past Eight* punters. The whole thing was summed up perfectly on the final night when Dickie banned the usual spectacular array of gifts and flowers that were usually given to everyone at the theatre. He decided the women were to get one bunch of flowers, and the men one bottle.

The final show went like a fair, and the audience reacted like it was the greatest show they had ever seen. At the end Dickie Hurran came on and said something along the lines of: "There's people we don't often mention who we want to mention. Our stage manager, the assistant electrician, the man who takes the curtains up and down."

Myself, Jack Radcliffe and Eve Boswell were standing quietly at the back of the stage.

"Our lovely girls," continued Dickie. And he still hadn't said a word about us.

"Now next year as you know there will be different stars here but I hope you will still come back and enjoy another *Five Past Eight*."

And he walked off.

I walked forward and started to laugh in the way you do when you are laughing so hard you aren't able to tell anyone why, yet you don't know yourself.

"I should explain," I said. "Next year Miss Eve Boswell will not be here in *Five Past Eight*. However, as a little consolation prize she will be starring in the summer season at the London Palladium."

And Eve came forward to a wonderful round of applause.

Then Jack stepped up.

"Well," he said, "Howard and Wyndham have made a lot of money out of me and I've made a lot of money out of them."

And at that exact moment the theatre cat walked on. And Jack said: "And he's the only one who knows where he's going next year."

Three months later I came into the theatre and was told the theatre cat had been thrown out.

Dickie Hurran's reasons for being the way he was came down to the fact that he was a member of Wentworth Golf Club. His pals weren't impressed when he told them the stars of his show were Jimmy Logan and Jack Radcliffe.

"Scottish are they, Dickie?" they would say.

He hated that, so the following year he finally got his wish when he managed to get Max Bygraves, a massive star at the time, to star in *Five Past Eight*. They built a set called the Starlight Room that looked absolutely wonderful, and was brilliant for Max's material. But it was also no good for the Scottish comics. It had been difficult enough to play a farmer's boy in front of a big white violin, but this was impossible.

Max may have been a tremendous success but the production cost Howard & Wyndham about four times more than Jack Radcliffe and Jimmy Logan put together. And so their profit margins dropped considerably.

The following year Dickie got Dickie Henderson, but business wasn't so good. It was getting to the stage where the theatre would lose money if it wasn't full. A bit of rain could make the difference between profit and loss on any given night. The Scottishness was being drummed out of the show, and Dickie Hurran failed to realise that was the core of its success.

7

IRISH GENIUS AND A SCOTTISH FOOL

I left *Five Past Eight* and discovered I had lost my audience. It was a depressing experience.

I had been at *Five Past Eight* for so long that no-one would book me because they assumed I was with Howard & Wyndham. Sure, in Glasgow and Edinburgh I was well known, but suddenly I realised that theatre-goers elsewhere didn't really think too much of Jimmy Logan.

It only really hit home after I finished with *Five Past Eight*. I wasn't sure what to do but I thought Jimmy Logan was a well enough known name to carry a touring show round the country. So, after gathering an impressive supporting cast, that's exactly what I did.

The whole thing was a real eye-opener. I went up to Inverness, and we didn't do very well. In Kirkcaldy the business was terrible, and so it continued elsewhere in the same vein.

To begin with I couldn't understand what was happening. But then I sat down and thought about it. I didn't have a hit record, nor had I been on television for a while. What was there to draw these people to come and see me? The answer was obvious—not much at all.

Sometimes artistes disappear out of people's minds. They've still got talent. They're like a kettle full of lovely hot water but they're not on the boil.

Some people told me to chuck it, and on a few occasions I really felt like chucking it. From the adulation of packed houses in *Five Past Eight*, I was suddenly getting a lukewarm reception from a half-empty theatre in Kirkcaldy. It was terrible.

That tour was an unqualified disaster. It came about after a tour I had been offered abroad fell through, and I was left with about 20 empty weeks in my diary.

After I was offered the foreign tour, and before it fell through, I rented out my house in Glasgow to Dickie Henderson who was starring in the new season of *Five Past Eight*. Then the foreign tour was cancelled, and I had nowhere to live. I couldn't believe what was happening.

Our accommodation problems were solved when I rented 'Camult', a beautiful house in Fintry, north of Glasgow. At the same time Calum Kennedy's wife Anne took ill, and four of her five daughters came to live with me—Fiona, 12, Christine, 10, Morag, 8, and Morven, 3. The youngest, Deirdre, stayed with the nanny.

Each night the girls would lay out, for example, twigs on the dining room table, and the following morning would entertain me with a story about them. I was spoiled rotten watching them fight over who got the cereal, the milk, the bowl, the spoon, the cup and the saucer. They always had full breakfasts, and their plates were always cleared in record time.

The youngest girl, Morven, I called 'Tumshie', Scottish for turnip, a large round vegetable and a lovely warm nickname for a child.

I vividly remember we were all in the garden one day when the children started shouting to us.

"Quick, you better come because Morag has just eaten the dog's dinner."

It turned out that Morag had finished her full breakfast but had later decided she was still hungry. The dog was always given the best meat in the house so I wasn't too worried about Morag's health.

I watched her sitting beside the bowl looking quite pleased with herself. The dog wasn't looking so happy. And I tried to imagine how this wee girl who had polished off a huge breakfast could find the space for the dog's dinner.

Years later in 1998 I told this story at Morven's wedding. And Morag came up to me, and said: "Uncle Jimmy, you're dead, just dead. But I'll buy you a drink!"

When those girls came to stay with me there was no way I could look after them myself. I was too busy. So I told the students at the Royal Scottish Academy of Music and Drama, who were always looking for jobs, that I needed someone to help look after them. And a girl called Gay Hamilton, who went on to become a fine actress in her own right, arrived on our doorstep.

Gay was magic with the children. We had a cup of coffee one day, and Gay analysed the children. Her analysis was perfect.

It was obvious she had a fine gift of perception and observation, and I made the fatal mistake of asking what she thought of me. She paused for a moment, then said: "I think you are quite the loneliest man I have ever met."

I got quite a shock but said nothing because she was right.

At that time my life was in a bit of flux. My marriage to Grace wasn't going so well, and my career had come to a bit of a crossroads. Then I met Sam Cree.

Sam was a wonderful talent who came from the north of Ireland, and wrote for a great Irish comedian and actor James Young. Sam had met Jack Milroy in Ireland, and asked if he could write for him.

And Jack said: "I don't buy material, son, but contact Jimmy Logan."

173

To give Sam a feel for what I was like, I brought him and his wife over to Scotland.

The first thing she said was: "Where are the flegs?"

And I just looked at her.

"The what?"

"The flegs."

"Oh the flegs," I said, nodding. I had no idea what she was talking about.

Eventually we discovered that because it was coming up to the twelfth of July she expected the country to be bedecked in flegs. She was astounded to find this wasn't the way of things in Scotland. Certainly not with flegs anyway.

That was in 1961, and Sam and myself clicked. Well aware I was going to have to reinvent myself to keep up with the times, we formed a company called Star Scripts Limited with the aim of adapting and writing comedy plays to put on at theatres round the country. It was my chance to get into the lucrative management side of things, and with my name and Sam's writing ability, we thought we would make a good team.

I first saw Sam at work when he adapted the play, *The Love Match*. It was about football, and he put it into Belfast for James Young with great success. I thought it was a great idea, and later flew over to see the rehearsals which were excellent.

On the back of its success, James Young asked Sam to write a whole new play based on the same family. And Sam duly produced *Wedding Fever*. Once again I flew over to see the rehearsals, and once again it was excellent. It would undoubtedly be a hit, but I never realised just how explosive it was in laughter.

A few months earlier, when I was at the Opera House in Manchester doing Howard & Wyndham's winter revue with Tommy Cooper and Eve Boswell, I received a letter from the people at the Gateway Theatre in Edinburgh pleading for help.

They wanted me to do a play.

At first, I dismissed the idea. I was a comedian, not a stage actor, and my role in Star Scripts was strictly as a manager. But the more I thought about it, the more I warmed to the notion of acting on stage. Given what was happening in the theatre, I really needed to be able to adapt.

After speaking to Sam, I got back to the people at the Gateway and offered them the Scottish premiere of *Wedding Fever*, which had been a big hit in Belfast. I reckoned the subject matter was absolutely ideal for Scottish audiences, and it would be a perfect chance to establish myself as a comedy actor. A friend of mine, the director Denis Ramsden, was good enough to look at *Wedding Fever* for me, and declared that he thought I was good enough to do it.

Meanwhile, the plan to put it on at the Gateway fell through. First, they wrote back asking if the play contained anything that would upset the Church of Scotland—the owners of the theatre. I didn't think so, but we couldn't get our dates to marry anyway.

So, almost without thinking, I booked His Majesty's, Aberdeen and the Lyceum Theatre in Edinburgh to present *Wedding Fever*.

I certainly didn't do my sums beforehand. Before going up to Aberdeen I worked out that it would cost a fortune to get all the scenery and costumes made, and then some. At the same time I was only getting a £600 advance—half my normal amount—from the theatre.

Then the inevitable question marks about Jimmy Logan starring in a play started to emerge. The variety people were saying: "He wants to be Hamlet." And the rest of them were saying: "Him . . . an actor?"

The theatre people in Aberdeen seemed certain we had a huge turkey on our hands. During the dress rehearsal in the empty theatre, the manager passed me and said: "We've just had word from Edinburgh that the advance ticket sales are dreadful."

I said: "Are you trying to cheer me up or something?"

"No, but I just want you to know we have done our bit up here. You've got a full house on the opening night because we've been selling two tickets for the price of one."

Their attitude had me believing I was going to taste the ashes of disaster. I returned to my dressing room, looked in the mirror and convinced myself that no-one was going to notice this man in his make-up.

When the curtains went up on the first night the actresses walked out on stage. As I followed them their faces looked up at me, declaring: "Jimmy, this is murder." I was tempted to agree.

However, the most remarkable thing happened. The first laugh came, then the second and as each joke came, so the laughter built up above the level of the previous one. By the time we got to the interval the theatre was in absolute hysterics, and we walked off the stage holding hands, trembling.

The second half was twice as good again.

I can only describe the reaction to my first play as simply unbelievable. It gave me the greatest pleasure in the world. Word quickly spread, and every night we went down a storm. It was the same story in Edinburgh—we were a huge success.

The reasons, with the benefit of hindsight, were pretty obvious. *Wedding Fever* was a marvellous comedy play whose subject matter was ideal for Scottish audiences. For the first time on stage, it made everyone laugh at the Catholic/Protestant divide that is so predominant in parts of our country.

It was a wonderful play centring on the wedding of a daughter and son from two families who kick with different feet. There was one of those magnificent scenes when the in-laws meet each other for the first time after their children have announced they are going to get married. But they don't know each other's backgrounds.

I play the Rangers-supporting father who suddenly realises that my daughter's future father-in-law is called Patrick.

And I say to his wife: "Your name isnae Mary by any chance?"

"Oh no, I'm called Bernadette . . . after my mother."

After the great success in Edinburgh, I phoned Stewart Cruikshank to tell him we should bring it to Glasgow.

"Oh no," he said. "You're coming into Glasgow to do *Five Past Eight*, and if this doesn't do well it will affect *Five Past Eight*."

That was my last *Five Past Eight*, so the following year I brought *Wedding Fever* to the King's Theatre in Glasgow, at the same time *Five Past Eight* was on at The Alhambra. It worked like a dream again. We ended up playing to more people that year than *Five Past Eight*.

That annoyed Howard & Wyndham, and it wasn't long before Stewart Cruikshank was on the phone asking me to do *Five Past Eight* the following year with an English comedian, Al Read.

Wedding Fever had been a great success, but at that point I had nothing booked up in my diary. Times were still hard, and I needed as much work as I could get.

I said no. It was the only time I ever said no to Stewart Cruikshank.

My reasons were simple. Al Read was a pal of Dickie Hurran's. My name would get the punters into the theatre, then Al would get all the best spots during the show. His material was fresh, and I would have to find new stuff to compete with it.

"Sorry, Stewart," I said. "I'm not prepared to do it."

I felt a huge weight fall off my shoulders. I felt I was being used and I didn't like that.

In the end, things worked out fine the following year. I brought *Wedding Fever* back to the King's for another successful run, then followed it with a new play by Sam Cree—*Second Honeymoon*. It was the story of a couple who go back to a boarding house in Dunoon years after they first went there for their honeymoon.

There were two young juveniles in *Second Honeymoon* by the name of Tom Conti and Hannah Gordon. Hannah was a very beautiful girl who was told by my father: "You're wrong for the part because your voice is too deep." My father wasn't a great one for compliments.

At one point in the play she had to come on stage wearing a swimming costume and lots of body make-up. She had complained to us about this because there were no showers in the theatre.

The next day I went out and bought a galvanised tin bath. At the end of the performance we delayed her progress back to her room. When she got there she was met by the tin bath and half a dozen strapping lads standing in line—one carrying a sponge, another a towel, another soap and so on. She thought it was wonderful.

When visiting my friends Rosina and Ben in Paris some of the nightclub owners said that the French water tended to taint the Scottish whisky, and what could be better than water from Scotland? So in 1962 I founded the Scottish Water Company, and everybody laughed.

"You would have to be a comic to sell water," was a typical comment.

Of course, bottled water is now one of Britain's biggest exports so it seems I was a bit ahead of my time. I approached a small company to bottle the water, Barr's, who made a drink known only in Scotland called Irn Bru, now one of Britain's great national drinks.

The idea was right but to do it properly I would have had to give up the theatre to put in the time and resources required. That was something I couldn't afford to do. In 1969 I closed the company.

The winter show at Manchester Opera House with Tommy Cooper and Eve Boswell had not been at all to my satisfaction. Howard & Wyndham wanted to put a sophisticated revue like *Five Past Eight* in Manchester. But it didn't work—that wasn't the type of show punters wanted in the winter.

I had terrible rows with Stewart about it, and the following year tried to take control of my own destiny.

The Theatre Royal in Newcastle was due to be empty over the Christmas of 1961, and a circus had performed there the previous year. That meant Howard & Wyndham didn't have an attraction like a good pantomime to put in.

I pleaded with them to allow me to put a show in there. Stewart Cruikshank agreed.

An excellent director I had worked with before, Freddie Carpenter, was brought in, and he suggested doing a theatre adaptation of the *Loganberry Pie* children's television programme. It was a brilliant idea.

We had a quite magnificent opening of the cast in beautiful costumes representing all the ingredients that go into a Loganberry Pie. Then a giant pie was wheeled onto the stage, and a huge lid opened to reveal myself inside wearing a tartan dinner jacket.

The material was just the right mix so that the children and adults both loved it, and the whole thing went so well that Howard & Wyndham decided to take it to Aberdeen. There were still two weeks missing—so some bright spark at the head office booked us into Blackpool.

I say bright spark because Blackpool at the end of January is not always to be recommended. It's so quiet at that time of year that all the landladies go to Spain. You could fire a gun down the Golden Mile and be sure not to hit anybody.

Unsurprisingly the advance was terrible, and so was the size of the audiences. It was an unfortunate fortnight before we headed for a tremendously successful time in Aberdeen, and finally Edinburgh. The show was so good it even got a mention in Howard & Wyndham's annual report—no mean feat. But thank goodness they didn't mention Blackpool. I still have no idea how we ended up there. The bright spark in head office who booked us was probably asked to find somewhere that was free for those two weeks. Then he discovered Blackpool's theatres were empty. Pity no-one bothered to tell him why.

I recorded an LP of songs from *Loganberry Pie* at St Andrew's Hall in Glasgow. It went very well. I'm sure the Victoria and Albert Museum will have a copy.

In my time I also did five coast to coast tours of Canada and America, each one a magnificent and unique experience. Before departing on the first one my mother stuck a bit of white heather on my jacket for luck. When I got to Canada one of the stewardesses from the airline said: "Aw, white heather?"

"Would you like it?" I said, and she couldn't speak. She burst into tears.

The Canadian audiences were remarkable. We found that five minutes of material in Scotland would last ten minutes in Canada because of the amount of laughter, applause and sheer joy that it produced.

On our opening night in Montreal we were on stage for four hours. Neil Kirk, an American Scot who was running the tour, said it was too long. There was no way we could go on playing four hours every night. We would be burnt out by the weekend.

So we all got together to make some serious cuts. First we told the accordion player he would have to lose at least five minutes.

"I can't do that," he said. "They are wanting more."

It was a difficult process, but finally everyone agreed to cut back and we reckoned we had lost at least forty minutes. If we really worked at it, we could make it a really tight three hours.

At the end of the performance the next night, Neil Kirk was virtually doubled up on the floor in laughter. He was laughing so hard he couldn't speak.

"Well done guys, you cut the show," he said eventually, getting to his feet as he spoke for the first time in ages. We just stared at him—completely oblivious to what was so funny.

"Do you want to know by how much?" he added.

"How much?"

"Five minutes."

And with that he descended once again into uncontrollable fits of laughter.

Those tours were wonderful, and the audiences were always first class. In some ways, they gave me delusions of grandeur. The morning after each show we would go by bus to an airport and fly to our next gig.

That happened every day. The worst thing—quite seriously—was finding time to wash your socks or make sure you had a clean shirt for the next performance.

When we got to Vancouver it was sheer relief. We had finally got our show down to three hours, and we were there for a week. It gave us a chance to do the laundry.

After each show we were taken back to the hotel by the same bus driver. On the third night he suddenly made a big announcement.

"Ladies and Gentlemen," he said. "I owe you all an apology. I only saw your show for the first time this evening, and I now realise I could have brought my mother, my wife and my children too. Do you realise how rare that is in this country?"

On another occasion I played one night in a famous American golfing town, Pinehurst in North Carolina, with Moira Anderson and Peggy O'Keefe. The main course there had been designed in 1902 by the great James Braid, a world champion golfer who hailed from Elie in Fife.

On a bus to my hotel a lady who must have been in her sixties asked me what I did.

"Oh, I'm an entertainer," I said, smiling.

That put the shutters down. She went all frosty, and turned away.

"What do you do?" I asked.

"I do the public relations for the hotel you're playing tomorrow night, and I've done it for the last 40 years."

But it was very clear—she didn't want to talk.

The morning after the performance I arrived in the big hotel dining room for breakfast, and I was asked to share a table with this woman who had been so unpleasant on the bus.

After ordering my breakfast, she said: "Do you realise what you did last night?"

"No," I answered, racking my brain to remember what could possibly have upset her.

"You were on that stage for over an hour with not one bit of offensive material. Do you realise how rare that is in this country?"

"Eh, no, I did not."

"Believe you me, Mr Logan, it's extremely rare. I thought it was wonderful."

Another place I encountered this kind of reaction was at the Carnegie Hall in New York. At first the manager was very abrupt because the show had had very little publicity, and he thought no-one had heard of us. When thousands of Scots suddenly descended on the place, and the theatre was packed to the rafters, he looked more than a little surprised. By the end of the show we had won him over—again because he was impressed by the family nature of our performance.

He was expecting the usual rough show, and I found him initially very aggressive in his demeanour. It's a trait you see a lot of in the States and Canada, but never in Britain. I think my experiences on those coast to coast tours helped make me a little more aggressive in my own attitude, and more definite in my views.

For instance, I was once in a restaurant when I was told the guy who was in charge of the lights at the Carnegie Hall wanted to speak to me.

"Hello Mr Logan," he said. "I just want to check what kind of lighting you'd like."

Right away I was suspicious because it just wasn't the time or the place to be airing such a subject. I could sense he was just trying to throw his weight about. But despite my annoyance, I paid his question the respect it was due.

I explained the kind of lighting arrangements we were used to. "Well, our lighting is very simple because we are touring. You have full on, and you have the spotlight. Whenever you hear music, you fade the lighting down, leave the spot on, and bring it back up at the end of the song."

He wasn't happy with that.

"You can't have the spotlights on when it's full on," he snapped.

"No?"

"No sir, we don't do that at the Carnegie Hall. The spotlights don't mean anything when it's full on."

"Well," I said. "I've got news for you. I've appeared in every auditorium in Canada and America coast to coast, I'm just back from the Albert Hall in London, and they could all give me spotlights. So you're going to give me a spotlight in the Carnegie Hall. I know all about the Carnegie Hall. You don't impress me. I know what I want and that's what I'm going to get."

I had never spoken to anyone like that. Normally I would cajole and adopt the "c'mon lads" approach. But on this occasion the guy was treating me like a mug, and sometimes you have to react in those situations.

That, however, was but a small negative experience of a theatre that is without doubt one of the greatest auditoriums in the world. The times I played there it was always full of expatriate Scots—just like inviting a big crowd of friends back to your house, only a couple of thousand of them.

The old trusty jokes always worked the best to start those evenings.

"Anyone in here from Greenock?" I would ask, and a few people would yell out "Yes."

"I could tell by your webbed feet. It rains so much in Greenock that it's the only place in Scotland where the television sets have windscreen wipers."

On my last visit there my friend Tony Bennett and I went out every evening for a few drinks. One night he asked me to go to a big bar next to the theatre, The Carnegie Hall Tavern.

"Jimmy," he said, "There's a jazz pianist there and I think it would be good for him if we dropped in."

Inside the bar this black fellow was playing piano in a way I had never seen before. He only seemed to use the centre of the keyboard, but he was just magnificent. But I admired Tony for the fact he was helping the pianist out just by being there. That was such a nice gesture.

There were of course the cultural clashes across the pond, particularly, I found, in Canada. The first time I went over one of my goddaughter's cousins at the University of Toronto invited us for drinks. When we were there a young French Canadian started ranting off about Canada. It was a lot of stuff about the French Canadians being their own people, and their own nation and how he didn't want our Queen because she lived thousands of miles away. And he went on and on and on.

"We don't like the Queen," he concluded. "Why should we? We're more like the Americans. Why should we be tied in with Britain?"

My company had gone very quiet, and there was a stunned silence. How to give a polite reply in a foreign country, I wondered.

So I said: "Well, that's the best news I've heard since I landed in Canada because we don't really think of her as Queen of Canada. We think of her as our Queen, and to be honest, it's a bit of a shock to come here and realise she's also Queen of Canada. However, I understand your feelings. She's got beautiful homes in England and Scotland. If you don't want her all you have to do is say. There wouldn't be a problem. You're right—you are more like the Americans. You've got American money, and clothes, and cars. The sooner you're the next state in the Union the better."

Well the last thing they want, of course, is to be the next little star in the big flag. My God, that shut him up.

Another night we were in a beautiful cocktail lounge sitting quite a distance away from a group of French Canadians.

It wasn't long, though, before one of them called over.

"Hey, Angleterre?"

Using my smattering of the franglais, I answered: "Mais non, Ecossais."

"Aw, Ecossais, vous parlez français?"

"Oui, je parle français, mais très petit. Pardon."

Then this guy broke out into perfect English. "Hey, that is good. What do you think of Canada?"

"Canada's beautiful," I said. "I'd love to live here. I would love to try and build one of those wonderful French Canadian canoes which are works of art. Then when I had finished building it, I'd fill it with all the French Canadian friends I could find, sail it to France and say: 'What do you want to be like this country for? What's wrong with your own country? Some of the toilets you wouldn't like. They don't have a lot of Kleenex.'"

They didn't like that either.

I should point out that I love Canada and the Canadians, and France and the French. These are just a couple of small blips.

A few years ago on a train to London I met an old Canadian in his eighties who was quite crippled, and only able to walk with the aid of two sticks. It turned out to be the most fascinating journey I had ever had.

His name was Colonel Niven, and he was one of the most

remarkable human beings I have ever met. As a young man he took a buckboard and a horse, and rode right across Canada selling his goods. When he got to Vancouver he sold the buckboard and the horse, and travelled to California to make films.

In the 1914-18 War this old chap was an officer in a famous regiment called The Princess Patricia's Canadian Light Infantry. It was born when a millionaire called Hamilton Gault put up $6 million to train, outfit and send a regiment of men from universities on a chartered ship to Britain. He asked the Governor-General of Canada if it would be all right to call the regiment after his daughter Patricia.

The regiment was the youngest in the Canadian forces, but on the request of the Governor-General it was made the senior regiment of the line.

This old chap with me in the train was part of that regiment, and after the War became its commanding officer. He was the first Canadian Military Cross of the 1914-18 War. Years afterwards I visited their headquarters in Edmonton where a giant oil painting hung, depicting a terrible scene with, at its forefront, an officer and two men beside a machine-gun nest. Colonel Niven was that officer.

Unbeknown to him, all his letters from the Front during the War had been passed personally on to the King. He was invited to London to collect his Military Cross, and proceeded to have a riotous time.

He told me: "Jimmy, I had to hire a baton and a cap. I only had £2 in my pocket. The girlies had got the rest the night before."

He was so broke he sent for a black cab to take him to Buckingham Palace, but the staff in the hotel wouldn't allow such a move, and sent for the Daimler Hire Company to escort him to his Royal appointment.

Evidently the car that subsequently arrived had a bonnet eight feet long, pistons going like nobody's business, and a chauffeur weighed down by medals. Following the ceremony at the Palace, the young Lieutenant Niven was invited to tea with the King, who wanted to ask him about those letters.

He said: "I was sitting having tea with the Royal Family, and all I could see was those pistons going up and down outside. The car was waiting for me, the meter was ticking, I knew I couldn't afford it and I could just see the headlines—Canadian officer arrested for fraud at Palace."

"Well, Your Majesty, I guess I'll have to go."

That was brilliant. He was so worried about the fare he told the King he would have to leave. So he went out, got into the Daimler, and was driven back to the hotel.

"I put my hand in my pocket to the get the £2 I had," he said, "and asked the driver how much I owed. And he stood to attention, Jimmy, and said: 'Compliments of the Daimler Hire Company, sir.' I sent for a bottle of whisky. Whether he got back or not that night I don't know."

At 80 years of age Colonel Niven was part of the great history of Canada.

8

I LIKED IT SO MUCH
I BOUGHT THE THEATRE

There may never have been a theatre in the world I didn't fall in love with, but Glasgow's Metropole Theatre certainly influenced my life more than any other. My love affair with this wonderful old place began when my family established themselves there every summer for six years after the Second World War.

Long before that it had been called the Scotia Theatre in Stockwell Street, one of the oldest theatres in the country, dating back to 1862.

It was built by James Bayliss, who died eight years later, and the ownership passed over to his wife. Mrs Bayliss was the woman who, in the 1880s, actually auditioned a young boy called Harry Lauder, and told him to go home and practise.

In 1897 it was refurbished and reopened as The Metropole Theatre, and one of the first managers of that theatre was Arthur Jefferson, whose son Stanley collected tickets at the gallery box office. I still have a picture of that young man sitting in the box office. Stanley Jefferson, of course, became the one and only Stan Laurel of Laurel and Hardy.

One of the features of the original design that survived the refurbishment made it home to one of the most bizarre seating arrangements I have ever seen. Halfway up the stalls was a barrier that ran from one side to the other. In front of the barrier were plush red seats, and behind was 'The Pit'—rows and rows of wooden benches with wooden backs on them where people were usually crushed in.

When my family played there this odd seating arrangement was still very much in evidence.

But the Metropole had many good and bad points. On the good side, it was a working-class theatre which had an incredible foyer that stretched about 160 feet before opening into the old music hall. The foyer had a large old fireplace, and was lined with dark polished wood.

On the bad side, there were always rats scurrying about because the theatre sat right next to a place where chickens were slaughtered. This was a particular sore point for the chorus girls whose dressing room was in the lowest level under the stage. Each night they flicked on the light and chucked their shoes inside to make sure nothing nasty was waiting for them.

I vividly recall being in a sketch where I played a woman who had just discovered her husband was being unfaithful. I was carrying a blank revolver which I was to kill him with at the end. However, just as I was about to shoot, I noticed the orchestra had disappeared from the orchestra pit. And the only thing I could see was the biggest rat I had ever seen. It was slowly ambling along the edge of the stage—hidden from the audience by the footlights.

My heart was in my mouth because I couldn't work out what to do. If I fired the gun the rat might have jumped into the audience and caused mayhem. If I didn't, we couldn't finish the sketch.

Luckily it turned on its sizeable paws and waddled back down into its hole.

I knew the theatre after it became the Metropole. Never have I come across such a magnificent bunch of theatre-goers—they were an audience of the people, an audience of the music hall.

An excellent example of this was the way they once responded to Eadie Haley, a great star in the early Twenties of what is now known as the Citizens' Theatre. But life had been hard on her, and by the time my father brought her back to the music hall she was in her seventies and had gargled so many times her throat was well past its best.

She started to sing her famous song, 'Why Did You Make Me Care?', which all the audience knew. They quickly realised, however, that although she could do the verse well enough, she was really struggling by the time she got to the last few bars of the chorus.

And halfway through the song they joined in, instinctively helping out an artiste who they remembered had once been great. By the time they came to the end of the chorus everyone in the theatre was singing so hard it didn't matter what condition Eadie's voice was in. No-one could hear her.

The applause started about eight bars before the end, and then the whole theatre gave her their hearts. It was a wonderful example of what was so good about the old music hall, and the Glasgow audiences.

A wonderful critic at that time, Jack House, wrote many books on the Scottish theatre. He came to our show one change of programme, and I thought his resulting write-up was wonderful. Rather than say he liked this scene or that, Jack merely repeated the comments of the audience as the artistes appeared on stage. Our pianist Billie Wyner really hit the keys when she played. Often we would sit down at a piano, hit one chord and say: "Billie's been here already."

Jack House wrote how the lady next to him shouted: "She can fairly bash the ivories."

Then when my brother Buddy came on, someone else shouted: "Oh, you've got a lovely shirt on, Buddy."

They used to shout up to my mother. "Are you all right, May?"

"Yes."

"Ah, you've been doing too much shopping."

The great spirit of the old music hall was that the audience had no reservations. If they liked you, they didn't just like you, they loved you.

The Scotia was bought by a Jewish family called the Frutins. The father, Bernard Frutin, was one of the many Glasgow Jews who had originally come from Russia, and contributed greatly to the people and culture of their new home city.

Bernard Frutin had been a barber by trade but somehow got into theatre in a big, big way. He acquired the Scotia, and a number of cinemas, and enlisted the help of his three sons—Alex, Hyman and Louie. Alex, the most enterprising of the trio, ended up running the theatre while the other two looked after the bars and catering side of the business.

In 1961 the Metropole Theatre was engulfed by fire, and destroyed. The building might have gone, but my family's emotional attachment to the place always remained. The following year the phoenix rose from the ashes when Alex Frutin bought the Falcon Theatre, formerly the Empress Theatre, at St George's Cross. He paid £45,000, renamed it the New Metropole and spent another £25,000 refurbishing the 1,325 seat theatre.

In 1964 rumours started circulating that Alex Frutin wanted to sell up. I was immediately interested because the idea of actually owning a theatre had always appealed to me. The fact that it was the Metropole only served to strengthen that interest.

I was well off at that time—of that there is no doubt—but I didn't have the kind of money where I could buy a place like the Metropole, and not worry if it wasn't a success. It would take every penny I had, and then substantial loans from the bank to cover the rest of the cost. I knew it would be the biggest gamble of my life.

These thoughts, and many others, were whizzing around my head as I stood outside the theatre one night about 11 o'clock. Why was Alex Frutin selling? Was it in the wrong area? Would I be able to establish its reputation as a summer theatre? Was it the right time to buy a theatre when television was becoming such a powerful medium?

I stood there admiring this imposing black building. My heart told me it would be just wonderful to own a theatre. My head, on the other hand, knew it was a huge, huge gamble—one that was ultimately best left alone. Why risk all I had on something like this?

But that kind of thought process was the very opposite of the essence of Jimmy Logan. On most occasions my heart tended to rule my head, and this was no different. The thought of walking past the theatre again in five years' time thinking what might have been was not one I savoured. How would I have dealt with the fact that I had been a man who couldn't find the courage to fulfil a dream? I was sure that scenario would have proved far more destructive than any physical setbacks that could beset me as the actual owner of the place. I walked away from the Metropole that evening secure in the knowledge that I had to buy it, even if all the obvious pitfalls were still wedged firmly in my psyche.

My knowledge of the theatre soon became second to none. From top to bottom I went over every nut and bolt, and discovered all of its strengths and weaknesses. On a long holiday with Grace in Majorca I wrote up an extensive paper on the Metropole— and its prospects for the future. I believed the theatre would flourish if a restaurant and cocktail bars were built on the spare ground next to the Metropole. That way the theatre could close in the summer, yet still make a hefty profit from the large restaurant.

I showed my proposal to my accountant and lawyer. The positive feedback I received from both of them made my mind up once and for all—I was definitely going to buy it.

When negotiations started, Alex Frutin said he wanted £80,000 for the New Metropole. I couldn't believe my ears because I thought its true worth was closer to £60,000. My track record on estimating property values had always been sound when buying my own homes—and I saw no reason to go against my instincts this time. But Alex stuck to his guns, and my people advised me his value was spot-on. Listening to them was my first mistake.

When I was in Copenhagen visiting the famous Danish singers Nina and Frederick—who had guested on my ill-fated BBC TV series—I got the news that the New Metropole was mine.

I returned to sign the contracts, and pay Alex Frutin his £80,000. I was putting up half the money myself—just about everything I had—and the rest would be paid off to the bank over a period of a few years.

Never have I been so nervous as the moment I came to sign that personal cheque for £40,000. I may have signed thousands of autographs in my time, but my hands shook so much it took me six attempts to get it right.

I knew it was the right thing to do, though. The Logan Family had been stars of the original Metropole, and now Logan Theatres Ltd were the owners of the New Metropole.

As chairman of the board of directors, I renamed it Jimmy Logan's Metropole Theatre. My father was the managing director, and my mother and Grace the remaining directors. It was a proud moment for us all, not least when my father looked up at a sign outside the theatre that read in gold letters: Jack Short—Licensee. He was filled with joy, and so was I, although the most pleasurable moment of the whole episode was being able to grant my mother her wish of becoming a theatre director. My parents had done so much for me in my life that I felt I was doing a little something in return. It made me feel great.

My mission was simple: to provide Glasgow with a family theatre based on laughter—along the lines of the great tradition of

London's Whitehall Theatre. Many people at that time reckoned theatres were dying under the impact of rival attractions like television, but I firmly believed there was a place for a thriving theatre based on laughter in the city that was the best centre for entertainment after London.

I don't believe my confidence was misplaced. In *The Stage*, my friend Gordon Irving commented: "This is certainly the biggest news in Scottish showbusiness for years. It isn't every day that a performer buys a theatre and plans full-scale seasons of legit comedy and variety. The Logan Family's know-how is certain to give it a good impetus. With proper publicity the Metropole, catering for gala openings, plays and revues, and the possible addition, some time in the future, of a theatre restaurant where playgoers can dine before and after the show, presents every prospect of success."

After the buyout Alex Frutin agreed to stay on in an advisory capacity to help me get used to running the Metropole. For five months we basically ran the place together, both of us constantly in our own offices behind our own desks determined to make things work.

I liked the way he operated, arriving every morning at half-past nine and never leaving again until every single bit of paper on his desk was dealt with.

I enjoyed those moments when I would ask his advice: "What do you think I should negotiate this at?" He would say a certain price, and I would produce a wee smile because I had already done the deal for less.

Those were exceptionally enjoyable months, and I feel we worked very well together. But the time came when Alex decided to bow out, and handed the steering-wheel to the new driver.

My car, ironically, caused a fair bit of trouble with the staff. When I bought the Metropole I was driving my third Rolls-Royce— a beautiful Silver Cloud—but I thought I should give off a more business-like image and traded it in for a Vauxhall.

The staff, however, were horrified. Their faces dropped the first time I rolled up in that Vauxhall. They thought I had run into financial difficulties, and one particular person was spreading the rumour that I had overstretched myself to the extent I could no longer afford to run the Rolls.

This was all nonsense, of course, but in these situations rumours tend to get out of control. Intent on rectifying the confusion as quickly as possible, I got a friend to find me another Rolls. The first morning I drove up in my latest Rolls there was delight—and relief—etched all over the staff's faces. It gave them confidence in me, and lifted morale.

My father took a greater interest in the running of the theatre when Alex left the helm. My father had been everything in the business. All his life he had run his shows, and he had spent most of his life trying to run me as well. He was used to being the boss.

Now he was the licensee of a theatre, but in Jimmy Logan's Metropole I was the boss—a situation that obviously wasn't to his liking.

There were occasions when he would drive me up the wall. Once, while I was away on business, I asked him to order black leather stools for our cocktail bar, which was done in a very elegant mustard and black leather.

I returned a couple of weeks later to find the place looking like one of Richard Branson's jumpers. There were half a dozen stools all right—but each one seemed to be a different colour of the rainbow.

"I don't want these," I said, exasperated.

"Oh that's enough, Jimmy. They'll do fine."

"No. I would like the place to be tasteful."

I ditched the multi-coloured stools, and replaced them with black leather ones. But by doing so I had issued a direct challenge to his authority, and he was furious.

On another occasion I bought two beautiful bohemian chandeliers for the upstairs and downstairs foyers. By chance I had discovered a tube in the theatre walls that, with wires built in and attached to the chandeliers, would allow us to lower them to ground level, and clean them.

I asked our cleaner Mrs Smith to order the wires so she could do precisely that, but the next time I looked at the chandeliers they were still dirty.

"Mrs Smith, they need cleaning," I said.

"Oh but it's very difficult to do, Mr Logan."

"No, I told you just to lower them using the wires."

"No, Mr Logan, your father cancelled that. He said it was too expensive."

So I went against him again, and had the wires put in. This time he was really furious.

These disagreements were occasional, but when I came back from my next holiday, I presented him with a beautiful Omega watch so he knew there were no hard feelings.

"Look Dad," I said. "It's a nice watch."

Picking up the watch, he seemed quite delighted.

"Oh, that's lovely, son. Thanks very much."

"But look on the back," I said. "I got it inscribed for you."

He turned it round, and read the inscription aloud: "To Dad . . . from the boss."

I think he saw the funny side of it.

After a time, though, he became so unhappy with the working arrangement between us that he dictated a letter to our secretary Cath—who sat directly between our offices. His letter was to Calum Kennedy, who had just taken over the Tivoli Theatre in Aberdeen.

In that letter he said words to the effect of: "I have decided I'm going to leave the Metropole and go back to being an independent producer and director, and I think the talents I have might be of use to you, Calum. As you know I have lots of experience in theatre, and I'm sure you could do with someone beside you to help with all this very difficult work."

Meanwhile, Cath was standing there taking all this down. Not surprisingly she was horrified. "You're not signing that," she said. "You can't leave this theatre."

"Yes I am," he replied, stubbornly. "He can carry on without me. He's quite capable of doing it himself."

My father, of course, knew exactly what he was doing. He knew full well that the first thing Cath would do was to come blabbing to me. When she did, and explained what had happened, I picked up the phone, and asked to go and see him.

"Now listen, Dad," I said. "This is just nonsense. We've got a tremendous responsibility to keep this theatre running, and I need you to do what you are doing. You need me to do my thing. We need to work together. Otherwise the whole thing won't work."

I just kept talking and talking—which is exactly what he wanted me to do—and pleaded with him to change his mind. Eventually, he agreed.

Later that afternoon, Cath went in to see him about something else.

"Oh Cath," he said. "You'll be glad to hear that myself and Jim have sorted that wee problem out."

"Oh, that's good," said Cath.

"Now, about that letter I dictated to you earlier."

"The letter to Calum Kennedy."

"Yes, of course."

Cath stared straight at him, pulling her hand over her mouth.

"Oh, you've not posted it, have you?"

"Yes, Mr Short. You said it was urgent."

My father, of course, had no intention of ever sending the letter—it was merely a ploy to get me to plead with him to stay. But he hadn't counted on Cath being so efficient, and dropping it in the post box almost immediately. Which, of course, she didn't do either. She had sussed right away what he was up to, and put him through the hoop that day just to teach him a wee lesson.

The Calum Kennedy Show opened the Metropole, and it was a great success. But I never saw it. The same night I opened in *Second Honeymoon* at a rival theatre, The King's. I thought to myself: "Jings, Logan. You're competing against yourself."

Talk about making things difficult. But I had no choice. I had been committed to take my play into the King's before I bought the Metropole.

However, the initial productions at Jimmy Logan's Metropole were just great—a series of shows built for enjoyment and laughter. We followed Calum's variety show, an overwhelming success, with our gala opening performance on 1st September 1964 of *Wedding Fever*, followed by *Bachelors Are Bold* starring myself, Duncan Macrae and Bill Tennent.

Wedding Fever, directed by Eddie Fraser, had a great cast including Marillyn Gray, Paul Young and Stanley Baxter's sister Alice Dale. Our mainstay at the Metropole, Bob Temple, was also in *Wedding Fever*. When he wasn't on stage he was stage manager.

During the winter show he played many parts, and one night a fellow came to the stage door looking for some work, asking to see the stage manager. Bob duly arrived on the scene dressed as a woman covered in make-up.

"Hold on," he said, "and I'll get the other stage manager."

A few moments later our other stage manager, Sandy McFarlane, came down kitted out in full Highland dress and carrying the bagpipes, as he was appearing in the finale.

And the fellow who was looking for work said: "It's all right, I don't want to work here."

That's the kind of place the Metropole was.

An actress called Morag Hood also had a small part in *Wedding Fever*. During one rehearsal she arrived back from her lunch break half an hour late.

"Where have you been?" I said to her.

She had only gone to Partick to try and get a feel for the type of working-class family we were portraying in the play. When she got there she knocked on someone's door, explained who she was and what she was doing, and the woman of the house brought her inside where the family were having lunch.

I admired Morag for her attention to detail. Since then she has worked on stage, and in films, on both sides of the Atlantic, and was brilliant in the BBC's production of *War And Peace*.

Bachelors Are Bold was a brilliant Scottish comedy by T M Watson. The programme cover was designed by Emilio Coia, a dear friend and one of the great caricaturists. Duncan Macrae was the instinctive choice as the main character of the undertaker. He was very tall and thin with sucked-in jaws, and would make a perfect man to measure you when the time came. The joiner was Bill Tennent, who although he was an announcer in STV, had begun as an actor and knew what he was doing. He was somewhat round and rotund—the perfect physical appearance for a joiner. The only part left for me was that of old Uncle Willie who was supposed to be in his seventies, and getting on a bit. So I took it.

There was also a young actress called Jan Wilson who went on to work with me on many occasions over the years.

On stage I strongly believe artistes should not just learn to say lines, but must think and act as though they are the character they are playing. Sometimes I tested young actors and actresses out by throwing in lines that weren't in the script. On this occasion I decided to test Jan.

In the play she asked me: "What's a mortician." And my reply was: "It's American for an undertaker."

But on this particular night I said: "I've no idea." And I walked off stage.

So she was left with another actress on stage, and they had no choice but to fill in. A few minutes later I came back on, and said: "What was that you were asking me? Oh, it's American for an undertaker."

And I left that night thinking I had taught this young actress a lesson.

The following night she said: "What's a mortician?" And before I could open my mouth she added: "Wait a minute, I'll go and look it up in the library."

And she walked off stage.

So I had to ad-lib before she came back on and continued the play.

However, when Jan had walked off stage she was shaking. She had turned the tables on an older, more experienced actor, who was not only one of the stars but the theatre owner, and she was wondering how I would react. When the curtain came down she tried to slip quietly off stage but I went up to her and put my hand on her shoulder. "Well done," I said. I thought what she did was just brilliant.

Those comedy plays saved my career and exposed people to a Jimmy Logan they never knew existed. I never knew he existed either.

Much of that, of course, was down to the brilliant writing abilities of Sam Cree. In all I did 14 plays with Sam, and each one was a gem of a success.

They were all built for family laughter. *Wedding Fever*, the story of the daughter getting married, an event important in the life of every family; *Second Honeymoon*, a wonderful scenario where the husband and wife go back to the boarding house—owned by the same frosty-faced landlady—where they had spent their honeymoon 25 years earlier; *Widow's Paradise,* a play set in a caravan where a group of women go on holiday to get away from their men only to find their caravan belongs to a group of burly fishermen; *Don't Tell The Wife,* where the wife overhears the husband on the phone and thinks he's talking about another woman when he's actually discussing a dog. So she decides to get a young student lodger to make him jealous. Of course, when Jorge from France arrives, Jorge is a fantastically beautiful-looking girl who immediately makes eyes at the husband.

I refer to only a few of Sam's successes, but they all had one thing in common—and that was laughter. Some actors and actresses turned their noses up at these comedies and complained they weren't really plays. They said it was just a big sketch, and the characters were cardboard figures. That was only true if the artiste couldn't make people believe in what they were watching.

I learned in later years when I was performing in serious plays like *Death of a Salesman* that I had learned so many valuable lessons from appearing in the Sam Cree comedies. They were particularly hard work because the actor had to make a situation believable in order to make it extremely funny.

It's a little like a pantomime scene when the principal girl says: "Please don't take me to the dungeon."

I only believe in the pantomime if I believe in the way she is saying it. It's not just words. There's so much more to it than that. That's why I can't stand people who come out and say to the audience: "Every time I come on the stage, you shout 'Hello Tommy'."

Telling the audience you're on stage takes away from the magic story you're trying to portray. The object of a pantomime is to put stars in children's eyes, and to do that they have to believe. Little comments like "when I come on to the stage" destroy that belief.

The great thing about *Wedding Fever*—which was staggeringly successful—was when you looked along the front row there would be a solicitor and his wife next to a wee woman with sand shoes and a string bag, next to a football supporter; a complete cross-section of people, some of whom had never been to a theatre before.

They came in, the curtain went up, and the play, which was the first to send up the Rangers/Celtic, Catholic/Protestant divide in laughter, got into full swing. Within minutes the audience were in hysterics. We even had a woman who told me she was expecting a baby but insisted on going—even though the baby was due the next day. She laughed so much she went into labour. They whipped her out of the theatre to hospital, and the baby was born a few hours later.

Sam Cree was a unique talent, a wonderful writer who could tailor a play to the humour of the individuals lined up to star in it. He was brilliant at that.

For instance, I said to Sam that Grace Clark and Colin Murray would be great in a play—if he could write the right kind of play for them. They were two old pros who could always make me smile and roar with laughter. They had starred in the Metropole's first winter production, *Swing O' The Kilt*, a big tartan variety show, and, as usual, went down a storm with the Metropole punters who knew them so well. Gracie and Colin had never been in a play before but had the great quality of acting relationships founded on the gold of the music hall.

On my desk within three months was *Wedding Bliss*—the first play for Clark & Murray.

We opened it at Perth, before it came to the Metropole, and they were absolutely marvellous. You would have thought they had done plays all their lives. Business, however, wasn't so great because the punters associated this great double-act with dancing girls and music. But when I moved them into the Lyceum Theatre in Edinburgh they were a tremendous success. The critics thought Grace was magnificent, and Clark & Murray were essentially rediscovered.

I later did the same kind of thing for Rikki Fulton and Jack Milroy who had done Francie and Josie for so long. Their act was getting tired so I said: "What about a comedy play?"

When I was working at the London Palladium in pantomime I got a writer to come up with a play for Francie and Josie. He would write so much, send it down to me, and between my shows, I would sit and record my reaction to the script. Eventually we produced a finished article.

Jack wasn't too keen at first. "I don't want any of this play thing," he said. "It goes on all night. I'd rather do a wee bit, go off, come back on and go off."

But it was an outstanding success; so much so that they were soon whipped up to the Glasgow Pavilion, and began again a wonderful career.

I have wonderful memories of *Swing O' The Kilt* that featured great acts like the Alexander Brothers, Dagenham Girl Pipers and, to round it off, the Carl Heinz Chimpanzees. We put on a charity performance. That night my Granny Short came to the theatre to celebrate her 90th birthday.

The big sign outside the theatre said "90 Years". When the company were in line on stage the soprano stepped forward and sang 'As I Sat By My Spinning Wheel' which was one of Granny Short's favourite songs.

Afterwards she came on stage where all the tables had been set with food and drink for the company, and especially for her. As she was standing there one of the chimpanzees came forward and presented my grandmother with a bouquet of flowers.

At the end of the reception she was taken to the front of the theatre where a car was waiting to take her home. And as she walked through the foyer Granny Short kept repeating: "That's the first time I've met a monkey, the first time I've met a monkey."

*   *   *

Sam Cree was destined for greater things, and when he told me of his intention to leave to pursue other career opportunities, I didn't want to stand in his way. We had been a great team, but all good things come to an end and we both knew he could go on to earn an absolute fortune.

By that time all Sam's plays I had presented in Scotland were being presented in at least six different venues in England as summer season attractions, starring big names like Sid James.

Sam's personal life was difficult. He tried to help his older son David set up in a number of businesses that had one thing in common—they never worked out. One day Sam got a phone call to tell him his son had disappeared from his latest venture—a big entertainment complex in England—and left behind a string of unpaid bills.

Unfortunately Sam hadn't taken advice and organised everything under his company Star Scripts. He became liable for all his son's debts, and was subsequently wiped out. He lost his house, his car, all his money—everything. David disappeared, and Sam and the family never saw him again.

Sam, his wife and younger son Samuel ended up moving into a little cottage he had earlier bought for his mother and father. One night Sam came home to find his wife, who had been ill for some time, dead. She had swallowed some pills, fallen asleep and never woke up.

His younger son was away on a school trip aboard a ship when this tragedy happened. And when he returned, Sam and a minister were waiting at the dockside to break the terrible news that his mum was dead and buried.

Sam never really recovered from these tragic events and died after an illness.

I can't thank Sam Cree enough for the influence he had on my life and career. When I finished *Five Past Eight* I had no bookings in front of me. I was facing up to a very uncertain future.

I got involved with these wonderful plays of Sam's, and I never looked back. They were so good because they were solid family entertainment. You could go there with your parents and grand-parents and laugh, really laugh, without fear of hearing one objectionable line.

The first few years of Jimmy Logan's Metropole were a big suc-cess. We had a lot of hit shows, and we made a fair amount of money. We put on great comedy shows by Sam and many other writers; *The Love Match* by Glen Melvyn adapted by Sam Cree, *Cupid Wore Skirts* and *Married Bliss* by Sam Cree, *S for Sugar Candy* by Donald McLeod, *Friends and Neighbours* by Austin Steele, *Love Locked Out* by David Kirk and *Happy Landings* by Patrick Cargill to name just some of them. We did big business.

However, the day I bought the New Metropole I was all too aware that the theatre couldn't survive on the basis of those shows alone. It had never had a reputation as a summer theatre, and in those summer months there needed to be something else generating revenue.

Only then would its continued success over the long term be secured.

At that time theatres all over the country were really up against it. Outside factors like bingo, gambling, television and even bowl-ing alleys were hitting audience figures, and the doom and gloom merchants were even predicting that the end was nigh for variety and the music hall.

A lovely parish priest called Father Smith often dropped into the Metropole for a cup of coffee, or a wee dram, and a blether.

One day he said to me: "Y'know, Jimmy, when I came to this parish I had 10,000 parishioners and now I've got three thousand."

It was a telling statement. Redevelopment was the problem. Thousands of people who lived round about my theatre at St George's Cross were being uprooted from their city centre tenements into the new schemes miles away on the outskirts. If they wanted to come to the Metropole they were looking at a long and expensive journey—two buses each way, or a bus and the tube.

When men got home from their work at night they just wanted to sit and watch television—and that television was soon in colour, a wonderful novelty. Most families were short of money so if the wife—who had been bored to tears in the house all day—wanted to go out at night, she would invariably go to the bingo, a welcome replacement for the old-fashioned quiz nights. At the bingo the women could sit and natter with their pals—and maybe win a small fortune too.

Against this backdrop I risked everything on the Metropole. But I believed I could make a big success of the theatre, and for the first couple of years my plan worked a treat. Not wanting to take on too much at once, I concentrated on making the shows a success, and spent £30,000 improving and upgrading the theatre. We built lovely offices, a marvellous wardrobe and a canteen, and carpeted and decorated the whole place. The theatre looked just immaculate, particularly so for our two Royal performances.

Then, as things settled, I got cracking on the second stage of my grand scheme. I knew the Metropole wouldn't get a subsidy from the Arts Council or anywhere else for that matter, so we had to create our own way of generating money during the summer.

My plan was ambitious but simple; knock down the building next to the Metropole and erect a magnificent building housing restaurants and cocktail bars in its place. The money those establishments made would keep the theatre going when it was closed.

I thought we could run American-style showbars that had never been seen in Glasgow before. Artistes would perform while the punters ate and drank, and if those artistes were good enough they could go into the main theatre when it opened again in the winter. Those restaurants would have been popular in the winter too. We had dozens of bus parties coming to the shows, and those punters could have gone for a meal while the early show was on. There was so much that could have been done.

I stupidly thought getting a drinks licence for these places would be a formality, but the licensing authority turned me down without explanation.

To this day I still don't know why they came to that decision, but I suspect that the big Co-op Hall across the road had something to do with it. I would have been in opposition to an establishment with excellent eating and drinking facilities, especially popular with people who had been to funerals. And I don't think the Labour-controlled authority wanted to be seen sanctioning such a move.

That was the first of many downers.

I got a call one day from the chairman of the planning committee suggesting that the Metropole could be redeveloped to become the new home of the Citizens' Theatre. He said workshops and rehearsal rooms could be built on the ground at the side of my theatre.

I thought this was a marvellous idea, a solution to my problems, and agreed to allow a group of people representing the Citizens' to privately inspect the Metropole.

I was soon to find out I was merely being used as a pawn in their political game. They produced a damning confidential report claiming the Metropole was completely unsuitable. However, that confidential report quickly became very public, and before I knew what was happening, actors and others were appearing in newspapers branding the plan a complete disaster.

They said it would be a disaster because of the problems with my theatre. The fact that the problems they referred to were just nonsense didn't matter. When mud is thrown it tends to stick.

The actions of the people associated with the Citizens' were utterly disgraceful. They weren't interested in moving to another theatre. They wanted council funding to build a brand new theatre. And it seemed they would do anything to achieve that aim.

Having a go at Jimmy Logan's Metropole was just one tactic in their own selfish battle.

And I was thinking: "Wait a minute." What did I do to deserve such shoddy treatment? I dished out a generous portion of good-will by allowing them to inspect my theatre on a confidential basis. Then I became the victim in someone else's conflict.

So that was another downer.

Then I had another idea. Rangers had just built a big supporters' club, so I met a representative from Celtic to see if they were interested in turning the Metropole into a big Celtic Supporters' Club. I presented a scenario where the main auditoriums could be used for shows and functions. The supporters could drink at tables in the stalls, and come onto the stage to dance. The dressing rooms could be used for committee meetings.

It would be an excellent central focal point for the supporters.

The club greeted my scheme with great enthusiasm, and we got down to the nitty gritty of hammering out a deal. Two weeks before they were due to sign they changed their minds.

Yet another downer.

I even submitted plans to turn the Metropole into an American-style dinner theatre where customers could eat and drink at tables in the stalls, then go onto the stage and dance between acts. I showed Glasgow's Master of Works round the theatre explaining this concept.

And he just turned round, and said: "Glasgow's not ready for this yet."

My friend Reo Stakis, who owned a building in the area, was also at one point very interested in redeveloping St George's Cross, and told me he was willing to put £3 million into such a project.

He wanted to build a new headquarters for Stakis on the site where the Metropole stood, and offered to build a new theatre nearby.

It wasn't long, though, before Reo came back to me, and told me the planners at the council hadn't been in the least interested in his ideas.

I'm not sure how planning authorities come to their decisions. Reo told me how he had just returned from England where he had been at a council reception to celebrate the approval for a hotel Stakis were building.

At that reception Reo was approached by the Mayor of the town, who said that due to unforeseen problems, the site on which they planned to build the hotel was no longer available. Minutes later Reo, the Mayor and other council people were taken in cars to another site in the town. And the Mayor offered Reo this site to build his hotel.

Reo said: "It looks OK, but it has just taken us almost two years to get our plans through for the last site."

"Don't worry," the Mayor said. "Leave that with us."

The whole thing was passed and agreed within three months.

I have to say the planning authorities in Glasgow were consistent with me . . . consistently obstructive and unhelpful.

It seems that in 1964 the city fathers had taken a private decision to destroy St George's Cross as a traditional shopping area, and concentrate new shopping and entertainment developments in nearby Maryhill. I believe they had an agenda to move prospective developers into areas they wanted to develop. Because St George's Cross wasn't one of those areas, the Metropole was effectively hung out to dry.

That would go some way to explaining why all my plans to transform the Metropole—five in all—got nowhere fast.

One of my ideas had been to build a marvellous hotel and shopping complex around the theatre. The hotel would be similar to the Regent Palace Hotel in London, where the theatre was actually part of the hotel.

I approached a firm of architects, who took up the idea with a great deal of enthusiasm, and we went through my plans at great length. Not long afterwards a chap who was advising me said the plans had been presented to the Corporation—but my theatre wasn't mentioned as part of them. I arranged a Sunday meeting at the City Chambers with the Lord Provost and some of his top officials to find out what was going on. They assured me I would be informed of any further developments. But I never heard a thing.

The firm of architects with whom I discussed the proposals also had the brass neck to send me a bill for the work they had done. I was absolutely furious. After the third threatening letter I wrote back to tell them I would have no problem paying the bill as long as I could go before their official association first to explain how they had nicked my idea.

A few days later I received another letter saying they had decided to forget about my bill.

On one occasion I went up to the planning department myself, and said: "Unless you help me I'll go bankrupt."

"Don't worry, Jimmy," they said.

Again, I never heard another word.

The episode that takes the lovely biscuit in this whole sorry affair came when the chap from London who was advising me, said: "Jimmy, the planning department are guiding developers to ground up the road, and saying the Metropole Theatre hasn't got much going for it because it is a listed building."

I couldn't believe my ears. I was being told the building I owned was listed. It was the first I had heard of it.

I phoned up the planning department and spoke to a young lassie.

"I've been told the Metropole Theatre is a listed building."

"That's right, Mr Logan, the front is listed."

"But I'm the owner and I know nothing about this."

"Well, it used to be the duty of the Secretary of State to inform you, but he passed those duties onto the Corporation. You should have been told."

"I've never been told any such thing," I said. "How long has it been listed?"

"Two years."

"Why didn't I know about it?"

And she said: "The Corporation hasn't had time to tell you."

Two years! It put a different light on matters. If the building was listed, any chances of redevelopment were drastically reduced, to say the least.

The most annoying thing was that I had found this information out by complete accident.

What a downer.

In reality my great plans for the Metropole were dead in the water before they got off the ground. The night I came out of that licensing meeting after my first drinks application had been thrown out my father was boiling with anger.

I never said to him at the time, but—despite all my efforts in the subsequent years—I knew then in my heart of hearts that the theatre was finished. The only question was how long could it survive?

Just like in any crisis, the rain didn't just fall down on the Metropole, it really poured. Fighting for my professional life in the theatre was taking its toll on me away from it. My business commitments had long since forced me to sell my plane, and when the Metropole really started to struggle I gave up flying altogether. For similar reasons I also gave up my beloved boat, selling it to Eve Boswell.

At a time when my theatre was struggling to stay alive I could justify neither the time nor expense on such luxuries.

One benefit of nice living that didn't go was the wing I had

211

rented at Culzean Castle in Ayrshire. A year after buying the Metropole I returned from an American tour asking myself why I wasn't living in the country.

The only answer I could think of was that my wife didn't like the country. So when was I going to see the country? When they lower the box in, I concluded.

Coincidentally, at the same time there was an article in one of the papers on how the National Trust for Scotland were considering leasing a wing of Culzean Castle that had just been restored. I phoned them up on the off chance they would lease it to me, and they did—all 16 rooms and four bathrooms. It was absolutely magnificent.

It took 3,500 yards of carpet to fill my wing. I paid around £2,000 a year for the privilege, which was a lot of money then, and a friend Marjorie Bromfield, who owned Castle Antiques in Edinburgh, helped source the beautiful furnishings.

Like Mountstuart on the Isle of Bute, Culzean Castle is one of the jewels in the Scottish crown. The beauty of Adam's design and the location in Ayrshire on the edge of the cliffs provide a wonderful feel.

The battery of guns facing out to sea were built to deter the advances of the infamous Scottish pirate John Paul Jones, who later became an Admiral in the American and Russian navies.

In an effort to raise some money for the Red Cross, at their request I opened up my wing to the public for one weekend only. We finished up with 1,200 people trooping through the apartment. Thank goodness I wasn't in bed at the time.

Some members of my family were christened there, and a fair number of famous names including the Beach Boys appeared in the visitors' book.

When Tony Bennett was touring in Britain with Count Basie one summer I invited him to stay. I asked my housekeeper Mrs Duncan to put on all the "off peak" heaters to make sure Tony didn't get a cold. She was a touch confused because there were 35 such heaters, and it was June. Being Scottish, she would have told you: "If you're a bit cold just put on another jumper."

Evidently when Tony arrived, Mrs Duncan said: "Are you Mr Bennett the singer?"

"Yeah," he replied in his deep American accent.

"When I was told I had to put the heating on in June I thought there must have been either Africans or heathens on the way."

Tony wanted to take her back to America right away.

Showing Tony the wing, I introduced him to Diane who ran the restaurant with her husband Alec.

"Diane," I said. "This is Tony Bennett."

"Nice to meet you."

And she carried on.

The following day she screamed: "You didn't tell me it was Tony Bennett."

"I did."

"Yes, but not *the* Tony Bennett."

Meanwhile Mrs Duncan had become very blasé about her new guest, and was heard saying things like: "I saw Tony on TV last night with Sinatra. He was very good."

A dear friend, Hector MacLennan, who was later my neighbour in Glasgow for 10 years, came for a weekend in Culzean. I invited him down because he looked tired and overworked from his job as a gynaecologist, which involved commuting between Glasgow and London, and jetting all over the world on medical tours.

"Come down and relax at Culzean," I said to him. "It'll do you good."

We drove down from Glasgow on a cold winter's night with the torrential rain blown horizontal by the howling wind. All that was forgotten when we got inside the castle. The heating was on, the walls were three feet thick, the fire was roaring and we relaxed with two large whiskies.

213

Then the phone rang. It was Diane.

"Jimmy, my dog is having puppies and Alec is out. I'm very worried. I don't know what to do."

"Don't worry," I said. "I'll send someone round right away."

I wish I had a picture of Hector's face when I said to him: "There's a job for you."

He said: "Jimmy, I'm a gynaecologist. I know nothing about pups."

I insisted he didn't have to know anything. "Your presence will give the woman confidence," I said.

The next thing I knew poor Hector had his coat and hat on, had picked up his doctor's bag and was bent double against the wind and rain as he made his way over to Diane's apartment.

When he returned he said to me: "Thank goodness there was a woman there who has been to Edinburgh Zoo. She knew more about it than me."

The next day Diane phoned to ask me to thank my friend for his help.

"Diane," I said. "Just tell your dog that the man who delivered her pups was none other than Sir Hector MacLennan, the President of the Royal College of Obstetricians and Gynaecologists for Great Britain and the Commonwealth. She's lucky we're not sending a bill."

When I was at Culzean the National Trust decided extra funds must be raised to put the castle on a sounder financial footing. A committee was formed on which the Marquis of Bute and myself were installed as joint-chairmen. He was one of the nicest men you could hope to meet and we became great lifelong friends.

Another wing of Culzean was the Scottish home of President Eisenhower. It had been gifted to him, not because he had been Commander-in-Chief of the Allied Forces, but because he led Scottish troops during the Second World War. When it comes to Scottish soldiers, we Scots seldom suffer from humility.

I was talking to one of the workers on the estate one day when he mentioned "The General's Jeep" which had belonged to Eisenhower, and was now being used to haul logs. I was horrified.

Then I hit on the idea that a room should be created in the castle devoted to the life of the former President. Soon afterwards, I went on a tour of America and Canada, and somehow managed to arrange a meeting with the great man in the Waldorf Hotel in New York.

What an experience.

My Uncle Bill came with me, and we were met by young Secret Service agents dressed in pale grey suits wearing black shades who all looked the same. They were extremely polite, but wouldn't have missed a trick.

As we sat in a side room waiting for the big meeting I could hear the other members of Eisenhower's protection squad talking to each other on their radios. The only other things in the room apart from us were portable oxygen cylinders.

Then we were called in.

The former President, who was being assisted by a retired general, stood up over six feet tall to meet us. He looked as I had always remembered him from the newsreels and, when he smiled, 20 years just dropped off his age.

This was the "Ike" I remembered, and I kept calling him General even though he had since been in charge at the White House, and the most powerful man in the world. I should have called him Mr President.

He told me how he had visited Culzean three times, and when he was there that old Scottish castle became the White House of the United States. When I told him about my idea for the room he suggested that the British Government might donate some replicas of his many honours. He was very proud of the fact that he was the only man to hold the medals of the British Eighth

Army—The Desert Rats—and the American First Army. He also said he was immensely proud of his robes from St Andrews University.

We talked at some length until I knew it was time to leave. As I walked towards the door, and with a twinkle in his eye, he said: "Mr Logan, we've got to do something because after all I am an honorary member of the Maybole Pipe Band."

I laughed, and said: "Right General, we will."

Not many people know that Eisenhower was a pilot and, during the War when he felt frustrated by the actions of others, used to take a small plane up and throw it about the sky. On one occasion he landed badly and had to be taken to hospital.

The whole thing was kept secret because it would have a disaster had news got out that the Commander-in-Chief had been injured. My last memory of him was seeing his funeral on television after he died. They took him by train across America and at every little town and "halt" the men who had served under him stood with the American flag dipped in salute. For some this occurred during the day, but for others it could have been two or three in the morning. What mattered was that they were there to salute and say goodbye.

I never told Grace that I had rented the apartment at Culzean. We still had the big house in the West End of Glasgow and she hated the country—but she expressed an interest in going down to Ayrshire when she heard about it from someone else.

She seemed blissfully excited when she saw the castle.

Announcing plans to get two designers to do this and that and the next thing, I finally thought we had found something we both genuinely cared about.

That, in itself, was exceptional. Our relationship had been a largely happy one in all the years we were married, but at that point we were no longer pulling together. The best way to describe us was that if I wanted to go left, she went right. It happened continually.

I now feel though that Grace wasn't interested in the castle. She probably thought it would mean I would be spending more time away from the house, so it was better for her to be part of it even if she wasn't that interested.

My marriage to Grace had its ups and downs. At the beginning she made it clear she didn't want to have children, or just be a personality's wife. She had wanted us to be a double-act. It caused problems initially, but we worked things out and spent many happy years together. However in the Sixties, when my work really took over my life, we drifted away from each other.

It wasn't easy for her because I'm a very concentrated sort of person whose concentration only tends to be on what I am doing at that particular moment.

We may have had a lovely house, and many parties with lovely people, but Grace had formed her own distinct group of friends. Gradually she saw more of them, and less of me.

I wasn't happy. One night as I drove down to the castle in my Rolls-Royce I reflected on how I owned a wonderful theatre, had a lovely house in the West End, a beautiful wife, lots of friends and a caring family. And yet, looking at the hedges and trees lit up by my headlamps on this dark road I was travelling, I thought to myself: "Logan. You're the loneliest man in the world."

I was miserable, and a lot of that was down to the fact my marriage was going badly wrong.

It came to a head one night over a pot of mince.

After a long day in the TV studio I came home to find Grace and about eight friends having drinks and a lovely time. I excused myself before going down to the kitchen—which had a big window overlooking a small garden—to rustle up some food.

There was some mince in a pot, so I started heating it. I was exhausted and starving. Then Grace appeared at the door, sat down and started nattering away. I didn't say anything, just listened, until I eventually rose out of my chair to stir the mince. Unfortunately I made the fatal mistake of using a spoon on a non-stick pan.

"Don't be so stupid," said Grace, clearly irritated. "You should never use a spoon like that on a non-stick pan."

I turned to her, just to make sure I wasn't so tired I was hearing things. I wasn't, and I just couldn't believe what she had just said. Here I was, obviously exhausted from consistently trying to save my livelihood, and here she was having a go at me for using the wrong spoon in the wrong pan.

Instead of being angry, I suddenly became ice cold, and said: "If you had made the mince I wouldn't be using the spoon, would I?"

My comment only served to antagonise her, and drive the wedge further between us. That was when I made my big mistake.

What I should have done was pick up the pot of mince, said she was dead right, and thrown it through the big glass window.

Then I should have said: "Tell your friends to go. If you don't want to do that get a suitcase and go yourself."

It would have given her an almighty shock, and might have brought her round to the reality of the situation and saved our marriage. At that stage, it's certainly the only thing that could have pulled things together between us. The problems of the Metropole were piling enormous worries onto my shoulders, and I was also recording a television programme that in my heart of hearts I thought wasn't right. Never had I been under so much pressure and strain.

Giving Grace such an ultimatum would have been a signal that I had had enough, and that I didn't want her pulling to the left when I needed her to pull to the right.

Had the boot been on the other foot, and Grace had just returned home tired from a terrible day, I would have been the first person to tell her to sit down, make herself comfortable and ask what she wanted. What I expected had nothing to with being the man of the house, and everything to do with how people who love each other should react in certain situations.

As it was I merely left the kitchen, went to bed and fell asleep. The incident was never resolved, and relations between us kept on sliding downhill from that point onwards. It got to the stage where my life in my home didn't seem to be my own.

At Christmas, between performances in Aberdeen, I went to the best jeweller in the Granite City and bought a beautiful brooch which I had wrapped and put on the letter rack at the theatre with a note to say it was a present from a fan.

The first thing Grace said to me when she saw it was: "Did you choose it or did the man in the shop choose it?"

That statement really got to me. I had not only chosen it, but gone to the bother of picking it out specially when I was really tired between shows.

It was only a matter of time, I suppose, before Grace and I went our separate ways. I regard our time together as rich and happy in so many ways, but when the Metropole was really taking its strain on me Grace had her own friends.

She would probably say the same about me, which I can understand. I have every sympathy for the wife of one comedian who said a few years ago her life was too full of peaks and troughs. It was either up at the top or right down at the bottom—and that is not easy for anyone to take.

The marriage to Grace ended when I met a woman who showed genuine concern for my welfare. Gina Fratini was a fashion designer in London who was a friend of my sister Annie Ross. She had started out as Gina Butler, granddaughter of the Earl of Carrick, before marrying a very fine painter, Renato Fratini.

Once she had established her name in the world of fashion she sometimes went to Buckingham Palace to fit her gowns and other creations for the likes of Princess Anne, Princess Margaret and

Princess Alexandra. I met her a number of times on trips to the Big Smoke until one occasion when I suddenly realised she was such a caring person. And I reacted.

Gina was a wonderful woman who was concerned how I was coping under the strain of running a theatre that was struggling to survive. If I was tired, or weary or hungry or in need of some attention, Gina would be there for me.

For Grace and myself, our existence together had become pointless and stupid, and I decided it was no longer worthwhile continuing. I rented a flat, and one day when the house was empty, I cleared out all the things I needed and left that house for the last time. Unfortunately the whole thing became a public event when the press got hold of the story of my leaving.

Some time afterwards an altogether more bizarre affair rapidly grew arms and legs. I was between performances of a pantomime at the King's Theatre in Edinburgh when there was a knock on the door. It was a reporter from one of the newspapers.

"I'm sorry to trouble you Jimmy," he said, "but we have to ask you about the rumour going around of a romance between you and Moira Anderson."

My immediate reaction was one of raucous laughter because Moira, one of Scotland's best-loved singers, was a very happily married lady. I don't think we had even met more than a couple of times in the previous few years.

"Well," I said, "if you had said there was a romance between me and Andy Stewart I could understand, but most certainly not with Moira Anderson. That's absolutely ridiculous."

After the reporter left I wondered for a moment how on earth he had come up with such a preposterous story. Later I relayed this story laughing my head off to my dresser, John, at the King's. But he didn't laugh.

"I heard about the romance when I was in the supermarket this morning, Mr Logan," he said.

I couldn't believe my ears. "What? Me and Moira Anderson. Away ye go."

Most Saturday nights I drove back to Culzean Castle for the weekend, and that Saturday was no different. The following morning Mrs Duncan, who looked after the wing when I wasn't there, brought up a giant tray with my breakfast on it.

As was her wont, she planted herself on the end of the bed and filled me in with all the latest news from Culzean. When she finished I told her the story about Moira Anderson. And she didn't laugh either.

"Oh, Mr Logan, I didn't want to say but that's the talk of Maybole," she said.

She wasn't joking, and for the first time, I wasn't finding it so funny any more.

Even worse, Mrs Duncan then told me she had been watching Moira Anderson's TV programme the previous week with a group of women, when one suddenly piped up: "That Moira's pregnant to Jimmy Logan."

To which one of the older, wiser ladies replied: "There's no way she's pregnant."

"Oh no?" said another. "But that programme was recorded some time ago." A fine example of the technical knowledge of the modern-day granny.

The next day when I was in Glasgow more people told me about my supposed romance. Fiction had become fact. "Is it true, Jimmy?" they said.

The only time it was ever mentioned in the papers was a few weeks later when Moira, talking about herself, her husband and how happy they were together, said that if anyone repeated any rumours about her she would take them to court. And she was absolutely right to come out and do that—rather than let people sully her character with ridiculous stories about her personal life.

To this day I still don't know how that story originated, although I believe it may have something to do with the fact that Alyson Ritchie, my red-haired wardrobe mistress at the Metropole, who helped me move my stuff out of the house, could have been mistaken for Moira.

By the time those rumours were out of control I was deeply in love with Gina. Our relationship moved rapidly as I moved into another world—a world of fashion that I had never been exposed to before. When my divorce from Grace came through in 1967—19 years after we had married—I asked Gina to become my second wife.

She was very close to Lady Sassoon whose late husband Sir Victor Sassoon, four times winner of the Derby, had also been Gina's godfather. Lady Sassoon lived in the Bahamas—which is where Gina suggested we got married.

The day before the wedding I was sick with worry that everything which was going fantastically well would suddenly go tragically wrong if we made it official. That evening about 14 of us went to dinner but my nerves ensured I wasn't able to eat a single thing.

The following day we were married on a beach within the grounds of the Sassoons' lovely house in Nassau. For the ceremony itself, on a scorchingly hot Bahaman day, I was decked out in the kilt and full Highland regalia as a band played 'Here Comes The Bride' in the jazziest way imaginable. The whole thing was hysterical, and went some way to easing my butterflies.

One member of staff said: "M'lady, there's a man out there wearing a skirt."

My best man was my 16-year-old nephew Domenick—Heather's son—and the ceremony was conducted by Nassau's registrar general who was called, of all things, Clyde Roberts. We had a great meal afterwards with more than 20 guests.

The whole thing was a wonderful experience—which is more

than can be said for our journey back to Britain on the second voyage of the QE2. We arrived on the dockside at New York to be confronted by queues the length of a funeral procession. It seemed to me that we were already back in Britain before we even got on the boat. For some people this process took a full hour and a half, and when we finally got on I showed one of the stewards my ticket, and said: "I'm on A deck."

"No you're not," he snapped back.

I had just humped my case up the gangplank, and my temper was getting shorter by the second.

"Now, listen," I said. "I'm on A deck. It says so on my ticket."

"We've changed it," he said smugly. "It's now called Deck One."

His attitude was aloof—and astonishing.

"Do you realise what you're doing by making people wait for so long down there?" I said. "Is this what you call service?"

"Oh, they'll have forgotten about it tomorrow."

"Will they?" I said. "That will be interesting."

It didn't get any better. The only drink available on board was champagne. I couldn't even get a cup of tea. They didn't accept credit cards, and passengers were unable to bill drinks to their cabins, so I had to carry a pile of money wherever we went.

I said to a steward: "Where can we get something to eat, we're starving. We've had no time to get any lunch."

"Neither have we," he replied, and walked off. It was truly breathtaking.

Then, in the middle of the Atlantic, the ship broke down—and literally bobbed up and down for about two hours. It was just as well a storm wasn't brewing or an iceberg wasn't lurking, or God knows what would have happened.

A car had been sent to meet us at Southampton but, although the driver could see us, he wasn't allowed in to pick us up. We ended up in a packed train full of frustrated QE2 passengers, and it was far from a pleasant experience. For British Rail read cattle truck. One American woman said to us: "They call it the *QE2* because you queue from the moment you get on until the moment you get off."

In London we were herded into an area while our luggage was lifted onto the platform, then we engaged in a mad scramble to get there before everyone else. From start to finish the whole thing was a disaster. I think I was supposed to feel relaxed and stress-free after my luxury cruise. Instead I was ready to belt someone on the mouth.

In October that year my mum died. She had been ill for years, and spent the vast majority of the last few years of her life in Glasgow's Southern General Hospital. It would be wrong to say it was a relief when she finally passed away, but we were glad she no longer had to suffer any pain.

I was in Wales doing cabaret when I got the news, and I came back up to Scotland for the funeral service.

I won't dwell on my love and respect for my mother at the moment, that will come at a more appropriate point later, but needless to say her death greatly affected all of our family, not least my father.

She was a great, great woman.

Gina and I had moved into a flat in London, then sold up and moved to a bigger house. I spent my time flitting between Scotland and London, trying to keep my two businesses on their feet. The first one, obviously, was the Metropole, while the other business was Jimmy Logan, the artiste.

In a long period that was full of hard times professionally, there were some nice experiences. Whilst touring in Canada in 1968, I got a call from the agent Mike Sullivan asking me if I wanted to do pantomime at the London Palladium.

He flew over to Canada to sign me up for a certain amount of money, then probably went back and sold me to the Palladium for three times as much, but I couldn't have cared less. Just as it had always been my ambition to go to the Palladium as a comic, I would have given my right arm to do panto there. Now I was getting my chance.

The pantomime was *Robinson Crusoe*, with Engelbert Humperdinck in the lead role. I played his brother Billy, and Arthur Askey was our mother.

A few hours before our opening night we were rehearsing a scene where Arthur chucked himself onto what was called a dead trap—the kind of trap door where if you threw yourself on it you immediately disappeared underneath the stage.

But Arthur got a bit too excited, dived on the wrong spot, and a trap sprung up and belted him on the chest. Before we knew what was happening an ambulance had arrived and carted the poor man off to hospital with broken ribs.

The cast assembled in a dressing room where the general consensus of opinion was that the performance would have to be cancelled. That was the last thing I wanted so I suggested Arthur's understudy Billy Tasker should take his place. He was an old pro and would know the part. We agreed, split Billy's original part up between us, and the show was back on the road.

Later that day, when I was talking Billy through his part, a ghost-like figure appeared at the side of the stage. He had a pure white face and was wearing a tank-top. It was Arthur, returning to the theatre to collect his stuff. But Arthur, a wonderful pro who really knew the ropes, never came back during the 18 weeks we were there. He was simply in no condition to continue.

It's just as well. I was a fit man of 40, and I have to say two shows a day every day for 18 weeks amounted to the toughest and most draining piece of work I've ever done. The first week I was up, washed, dressed and having my breakfast by nine o'clock every morning. But gradually that became ten o'clock, then eleven, then noon, until I found myself so exhausted I was struggling to get into the theatre for the two o'clock matinee.

During that season I got a call from an advertising agency in Edinburgh asking me to do an advert for Simmers Biscuits. They sent down a fellow who had the format of the advert crystal-clear in his mind.

"My idea, Mr Logan," he said, "is that we film outside the London Palladium and then go into your dressing room where you're sitting relaxing with a cup of tea, and you say, 'Wherever I go in the world I always take Simmers Biscuits because I like them so much.' "

I had a quick think about that proposal, and decided it wasn't to my liking. "I'm not too happy about that because I don't want to say I like something that I've actually never tasted."

We discussed the pros and cons at some length before I remembered a recent TV show I had done with Bruce Forsyth. I had played a landlady with ill-fitting teeth who said things like: "Aw Mishter Forshyth. Yer a lovely man, a lovely man."

It was a very funny sketch.

So I came up with the idea where I would ask the landlady what she thought of Simmers Biscuits, and in a series of different ways she would repeatedly say: "Lovely biscuits, lovely biscuits." And that would be all she said.

After a little gentle persuasion the ad guy agreed, which in hindsight I'm sure he was delighted with. We put it together like that, and it became an absolutely stunning success when it went out on STV shortly afterwards. Once again I had produced a catchphrase that seemed to capture the heart of a nation. Just like "Sausages is the boys", people were saying "Lovely Biscuits" in response to just about anything. If they liked something—no matter what it was—they would say: "Aw lovely bicuits, lovely biscuits."

226

It was so well liked I became known as Jimmy 'Lovely Biscuits' Logan. In fact many people still know me better for Lovely Biscuits than anything else.

STV used the advert for about a year, and showed it to potential advertisers as an example of the best type of advertising.

The fellow from the ad agency was headhunted by another firm on the strength of Lovely Biscuits—and probably got a wage rise, company car and big expenses into the bargain. He did very well for himself as the man who created Lovely Biscuits. I thought that was rather amusing.

Years later Simmers brought Lovely Biscuits back for another advertising campaign—but in a completely different way. This time a very posh man with a proper accent was saying: "Try Simmers—they're lovely biscuits." But the advert didn't work. No-one related to it.

After hearing this a few times I decided to phone the company's managing director to tell him I thought they were doing it wrong. He thought I was on trying to get a job and became very defensive, arguing that it worked because the company were appealing to a younger audience.

The campaign went down the drain. It served him right. Given that I came up with the idea in the first place, he should have had the intelligence to listen.

At this point Jimmy Logan the business was going OK. In 1968 I was offered my own colour TV series on the BBC, and it was a good deal more successful than the debacle of almost a decade earlier. It was produced by John Street and John Hobbs, and the material this time was good because the writers were good.

I had learned from the previous experience. This time it was: "It's ma bat, it's ma baw, it's ma wickets."

I was the host of a variety show with songs, laughter and special guests. And it was a success.

227

The Metropole played host to another TV series. In 1965 a friend of mine, Francis Essex, the head of productions at STV, wrote to me asking if I had any ideas for new material.

I suggested taking the plays we had done at the Metropole, and tailoring them for television. *The Jimmy Logan Theatre Hour* was subsequently born, opening with me sitting behind my desk welcoming the TV audience on their visit to the theatre. The TV viewer was then led into the auditorium as though they were a special guest before things settled for the beginning of the performance.

The plays would be split over two different episodes, and went very well. But there was a complaint to the television authorities that this kind of programme broke commercial TV rules because it generated too much free publicity for the Metropole. After 16 weeks the shows were stopped.

Another consequence of *The Jimmy Logan Theatre Hour* was ultimately of far greater importance, although I didn't realise it at the time. The show *was* a great publicity platform for the Metropole but it also suggested to the viewers that instead of going to the theatre, if they waited the theatre would come to them. People would say: "Why should we bother going to all the trouble of getting to the theatre when we can watch the show from our front room?"

That would clearly be detrimental to the Metropole. In hindsight, one or two shows would have been good for us, but so many shows perhaps gave people the wrong impression that they just had to wait a little while before our productions appeared on television.

By the late Sixties and early Seventies the outlook for the Metropole was looking bleaker by the day.

I tried all sorts of things to tempt the punters in—all sorts of comedies, a lovely musical version of *The Wizard of Oz*, old-time music hall with Scottish and English artistes, summer shows with Eve Boswell and Johnny Victory. I even set up a mobile ticket office that went round the schemes.

I tried, and tried, and tried, but I felt as though as I was banging my head off a brick wall. Some shows made money, but never enough money. More often than not we ended up losing money.

One day I was told that Alex Frutin was offering to come in and help get the theatre back on a level footing. There was one condition, though; my father would have to leave.

It was an understandable requirement from Alex's point of view. He had been the owner of the Metropole at the time my father ran his summer shows. It was no surprise that he wouldn't be too keen on a situation where my father was shouting orders at him.

I got on very well with Alex, and loved every minute we worked together when I first bought the Metropole. I think we were a good team.

But there was no way I could accept his kind offer. I had to shave every morning, and look at myself in the mirror. Welcoming Alex back would have meant booting my own father out, and no matter how bad things were, I could never do that.

Through an intermediary Alex warned me I might lose the theatre. It was a lesser price to pay than losing my loyalty to my own family.

In 1970 I called a press conference at the theatre. The media, who had kept a close eye on my attempts to stop the Metropole going down the drain, came along fully expecting me to announce its closure. Instead I told them the Metropole would be playing host to *Hair*, the hottest and most controversial musical to hit London in years.

The journalists were stunned and, I'm happy to say, delighted for me. One of them shouted: "Oh, ya beauty." I remember one reporter wrote the story up that a congregation had gathered for the funeral, only to be told they were invited to the biggest party going.

Bringing *Hair* to Glasgow was a remarkable coup for myself, and the Metropole, and gave everyone an enormous lift. At that point the bank wasn't quite threatening to close us but the overdraft had been growing steadily for some time.

I knew it would take something special to avoid closure, and *Hair* seemed like the perfect remedy. It was a show that had caused quite a stir—primarily because of the on-stage nudity and its political stance against the war in Vietnam.

But *Hair*, a vibrant celebration of the hippie movement and flower power, was a wonderfully choreographed show with fantastic music that everyone was singing, even though they hadn't seen it. The producers didn't have to worry about attracting people. No matter where it was playing, people flocked from all over—and tickets were like gold-dust.

I knew it would be the same all over Scotland if I could persuade them to bring *Hair* to the Metropole.

So I went to see the producer James Verner and asked him to bring the musical to the Metropole, where it could stay for eight months instead of touring around all the time. I also offered to put in a new £6,000 lighting board in my theatre to ensure their advanced effects worked as well as possible, and offered them a bigger than normal cut of the ticket sales.

My sales pitch worked. I think the idea of not having to constantly move around theatres—an expensive operation on its own—appealed to them most. At the same time I was desperate. I was probably the only person who knew exactly how near the Metropole was to closing, and I needed to get something special and unique that would draw people from all over Scotland. That show was *Hair*. I was absolutely over the moon when they agreed to come.

It was a very exciting time. One day when I was standing in the foyer of the theatre watching some workers put up a big neon sign saying *Hair*, a taxi pulled up and a black girl about six feet tall stepped out onto the pavement. She was absolutely stunning.

Moments later she walked into the foyer with the taxi driver carrying her two cases.

And she said to me: "Can I leave my cases here?"

"No, dear," I said. "We've got dressing room number two set up for that because it is more secure."

Then she just looked at me, pointed to the cases, and I said: "Why of course."

I picked up the bags, and started showing her up the stairs.

"So what do you do here?" she asked.

"Well, actually I own the place."

And all I heard was: "Oh."

"But you're very welcome," I said.

She was one of a company of artistes who were young, fresh and full of enthusiasm. I had been slightly depressed when I saw *Hair* in Liverpool because the show seemed tired and complacent. The artistes looked as if they had been doing it for too long.

But I must have seen them on an off night, because when they arrived in Glasgow they were absolutely sensational. They ran around handing out flowers to everyone, promoting their message of peace, love and understanding that was all the rage at the time. The company manager for *Hair* was a young man with glasses. I didn't really notice him but I should have, because he became Sir Cameron Mackintosh, and our paths crossed again in future years.

My manager complained to me that they were using up all the lights during rehearsals every day. But I noticed that each of them could understudy about five different parts, and just to keep fresh they were performing different parts each night.

"As long as they are that enthusiastic," I told the manager, "I don't care how much electricity they use. It doesn't bother me because they are so good."

The content was considered outrageous and the language was often heavy, but it was a wonderful show that people came back to see four or five times. The audiences saw the gold within the content, and that was the most important thing.

The only person I knew who didn't come was my Granny Short. She came to all my shows, but she had heard *Hair* was a kind of dirty show and told me she was a "little" surprised I had brought it to Glasgow. Little was not the word she used, mind, but she didn't dwell on it. She just let me get on with it.

What she would probably have objected to was the scene at the end of the first half where everyone on stage took their clothes off, if you please, and waved big cloths up and down to symbolise the sea. The result was that the audience knew they were naked, but never quite got a glimpse to prove it. At the end all of the audience were invited to join in on stage as the strains of the song 'Age of Aquarius' blared out. A wonderful song.

In the ten marvellous months *Hair* was at the Metropole I can honestly say there was no trouble, apart from one minor incident involving a 16-year-old usherette who was the daughter of one of the cleaners.

One day I came into the theatre to be told that this girl had got carried away the previous evening, stripped off her uniform at the finale and danced naked around the stage with the rest of them.

The rest of the usherettes were all dying to tell her mother who was away on holiday in Australia at the time.

That morning I called the girl up to my office. She came in looking ever so slightly embarrassed. "Now why did you do that last night?" I asked her.

"Oh Mr Logan, I've watched every performance and I just believed in it when they told everyone to go up on stage and be one of them. I'm so sorry Mr Logan, I just couldn't help myself."

I said: "Well, I understand why you did what you did. But that's not what I am complaining about. What I am complaining about is the fact you are an usherette, and your duties here are quite specific. If there is a fire or a panic your job is to guide the audience out of the theatre and make sure everyone is OK. You can hardly do that if you are up on stage with no clothes on."

It would have been wrong to tear into her. What she did was a great example of the spellbinding effect *Hair* had on people.

Hair was also a great success in its ten months at the Metropole, and made a lot of money. It kept the theatre afloat, but unfortunately that was about it. Most of the money went to the people running *Hair*, and not the people running the Metropole.

I also made the mistake of taking out the planned winter show to keep *Hair* running. In hindsight I should have taken *Hair* off, run the winter show which was always successful, and brought *Hair* back.

There's no doubt, however, that the theatre would have closed if *Hair* hadn't come to the Metropole. But anyone who thought it would save the theatre was kidding themselves. It was merely a stay of execution.

9

HOW MUCH IS A FRYING PAN?

There are few greater accolades on British television than being presented with that Big Red Book, and hearing those immortal words: "This is your life." It was a sign that someone had made a decent enough contribution to the public good—in whatever way—to merit some sort of tribute in front of the watching millions.

When Eamon Andrews presented the programme, *This Is Your Life* really was a national institution. It's no exaggeration to state that many people particularly looked forward to his appearance on screen each week, and loved the mandatory few moments trying to anticipate on whom he was about to pounce.

The first time I was associated with the show many people thought I would be on the receiving end. It was in the days *This Is Your Life* was broadcast live, and Eamon Andrews opened proceedings standing outside the King's Theatre in Edinburgh. Inside I was bringing the first half of the pantomime to a conclusion—timing it exactly for Eamon's grand entrance in front of a startled audience and cast.

His target on this occasion was our principal girl, Louie Ramsay, a lovely girl from Stonehaven who suddenly became completely paralysed one night after a performance in a theatre in London. For months she was confined to bed unable to move, but slowly made a brave and full recovery.

When she came to do the pantomime I knew nothing about this, and I noticed her crying after rehearsing one scene where she had to be "flown" across stage.

"What the hell's up with you?" I said.

She replied: "Oh, I'm just in a bit of pain."

"Away, don't be daft. You'll get over that."

I only found out her situation when the *This Is Your Life* team told me they wanted to do Louie for one of their shows. The day of the surprise show I took Louie and her husband for a meal in Cramond, and a long walk along the banks of the Forth.

She told me one of her closest friends was Pat Hitchcock, the daughter of the famous film director Alfred.

"God knows if I'll ever see her again," Louie said. "She lives in California."

Of course I knew Pat was in Edinburgh, as was the television crew setting everything up for the live show from the theatre that night. I told the cast that the cameras were there to film the performance for prosperity—to get a fine example of pantomime on screen.

But during the first half I could sense that Louie thought something was up. The television people were giving me timings, so every time I was on stage I was adding or cutting bits to make sure we finished at exactly the right moment. As the comic, I was able to do that.

And Louie would be staring at me as if to say: "What on earth are you doing? Get off."

When the first half finally came to an end the curtain failed to come down, and Eamon Andrews stepped out from the back of the stage. The moment the audience spotted him they went absolutely daft.

"You've been on television for the past few minutes," Eamon said to the cast. "Well, tonight, one of the leads of this great pantomime is going to be the subject of this red book."

And, of course, everyone thought it was going to be me. But as the rest of the cast formed into a half circle, Eamon approached a somewhat shocked principal girl, and announced: "Louie Ramsay—This Is Your Life."

The show went out there and then, and the audience lapped up every minute of it. We were all drained when we came off—and then remembered we still had the second half of the pantomime to do.

The second *This Is Your Life* I was concerned with provided me with a great deal of pleasure because it couldn't have happened to a nicer chap, my great friend Chief Constable Willie Merrilees. His life story was utterly remarkable. At 5 feet 6 inches he was impossibly small for a policeman. On one hand he had only three fingers—that's what he was left with after his hand was caught in a machine.

He grew up among the masses of unemployed people in Leith, some of whom resorted to chucking themselves in the Water of Leith to relieve their problems. On no less than three occasions the public-spirited Willie dived in to pull those poor people out. And someone suggested his bravery should be rewarded with a job in the police force.

Given special dispensation by the Secretary of State for Scotland because of his height, Willie was signed up to answer the phones at a local police station. On the Saturday before he was officially due to start he went in to have a look around—and was called upon by detectives going on a raid.

"They'll never suspect you of being a polis," one said. "You're coming with us."

So Willie took part in a raid before he was sworn in. Then when he was sworn in, those same detectives said they wanted him as part of their unit. Willie sat all his exams and became a detective himself. During the Second World War, a stranger arrived at a train station in the north of Scotland with a suitcase and wet trousers. Not surprisingly the staff were suspicious he was a German spy, and alerted stations down the line. When this guy got to Edinburgh he deposited his bag in left luggage. Police went through it and found a transmitter so, when he returned to pick the case up, wee Willie was waiting dressed as a porter, and grabbed him before the spy could reach for his gun.

Willie's career took off from there until he eventually became the chief constable of Lothian and Peebles, one of the top jobs in the country.

Anyway, on this occasion, I met him on the train down to London.

"Hello Willie, how are you?" I said. "Where are you going?"

"Oh, I'm going down to London."

Of course I knew exactly why he was going to London even if he didn't. I was on my way down to be a guest on his appearance on *This Is Your Life*.

As he stepped off the train the camera crew and Eamon Andrews caught him. They reckoned if he was allowed to go into the city he would soon have smelled a rat, and their plans could have gone tragically wrong.

I was on *This Is Your Life* on other occasions. The great pantomime dame I had performed alongside, Douglas Byng, was honoured when he was 90. And I was one of about a thousand people who walked on at the end when Jimmy Shand got his Big Red Book.

My own turn to be presented with that Big Red Book came in 1973 when I was starring in a play called *The Mating Game* at the Apollo Theatre in London.

On my birthday, April 4, Gina told me the management had invited everyone to a big lunch in a hotel.

"Wear your kilt," she said. "Everyone will like that because they've never seen you wearing it."

Of course I thought nothing of it and went to the hotel for a marvellous meal. But after a while I was thinking that the whole thing seemed to be dragging on a bit. I even told Gina that it was time to leave.

"Wait a minute," she said. "There's a wee surprise for you."

Then I learned that some of the people from the Benevolent Fund in Scotland, who I had helped raise money for in the past, had come down with a small gift for me. My instant reaction was one of complete shock; surely if they were coming all that way they could have asked them to the lunch.

We all went down to a big room where a massive cake was waiting for me, and all the people from the Benevolent Fund sang 'Happy Birthday'. There were a couple of cameras and a spotlight. I thought the hotel were doing some kind of publicity stunt.

I smiled as they sang their hearts out, but I was very embarrassed. They really should have been invited to the meal. I couldn't get over the fact they hadn't been invited.

Then there was a small tap on my shoulder. I turned round, and there was Eamon Andrews.

"Oh hello Eamon," I said. "Nice to see you."

I just thought he had coincidentally been in the hotel.

"Well hello Jimmy . . ."

Looking down I noticed he was holding that Big Red Book of his, only this time my name was on the front of it.

"Jimmy Logan—This Is Your Life."

Now I had been involved with a number of his shows in the past but there was a completely different sensation when suddenly I was the subject of his attentions.

All I could say was: "You're joking, you're joking. You must be joking."

Of course he was anything but joking, and I was whisked off to a big suite in another hotel to prepare for the recording of the show in the BBC studios that afternoon.

It was just wonderful when I walked into that studio to be met by applause, music and Eamon Andrews. Gina was already there, and as the show progressed everyone I had ever known seemed to come in. My sister Heather had flown over from Florida with her husband and son, Buddy was there, and Annie and my brother Bertie had come from New York. My dear Aunt Jean had come all the way from Gourock. She just wouldn't stop talking when she was introduced.

"What was I like as a child, Aunt Jean?" I said to her, fully aware of the reply she would give.

And sure enough she turned to Eamon and said: "Beautiful child. Beautiful child."

The Toma family who owned the ice cream shop below our house in Gourock came into the studio, as did a number of stars including Barbara Windsor, Clive Francis, Gordon Jackson, Bruce Forsyth, Arthur Askey and Bill Simpson.

Of course my father was there as well, and did his usual take-over bit. Unbelievably the whole thing finished with him playing the piano, and everyone else in a crowd—including me—round the piano singing.

It was a wonderful experience, but absolutely shattering. It lasted 30 minutes but I felt as though I had been on stage for six hours. It's not every day that people you thought were on the other side of the world suddenly walk in from behind a door, and say: "Hello Jimmy, how are you?"

That night I had to rush back to the West End for the play, and when I got home all my friends were waiting. We stayed up until well after three o'clock in the morning.

The following day I arranged to meet some of those people for lunch, but I did a Rip Van Winkle, and ended up missing them. That's how shattering an experience it was.

*   *   *

Back in Glasgow the Metropole was on its last legs. I had tried my best to make that theatre work; even a 10-month run of *Hair* had failed to keep the wolves from the door. One morning in 1973 I was woken by the phone.

It was the bank with a stark, final message—my overdraft had reached £170,000. Don't come in here for any more money, they said. I pleaded for more time, but they had decided enough was enough.

I took money from other small companies I had to pay the company out on the Friday, then had the sorry task of closing the theatre I cared for so much. Not for nothing had I slaved away inside that great building at all hours of the night trying to think of ways to keep it going. It was a labour of love, and it was my life. Now, as I locked the door behind me for effectively the last time, it had gone.

Gone too was all my money. I had put all my eggs in one basket nine years earlier, and that basket was now empty, replaced by a heavy set of shackles in the form of £170,000 that I owed to the bank. I sold the costumes, anything in the theatre that was worth anything, to pay off the debt. But it was a pointless exercise, merely scraping at the surface of an enormous burden.

The year before I had gone to the bank and said: "I think I'll have to go bankrupt."

They refused.

The following year the theatre might have closed, but my responsibilities to the building and my debts were destined to crush me for another decade. In an area where so many tenements had been knocked down, the Metropole would become a blight on the landscape, stuck out on its own on the local skyline—a painful reminder of how the comic who owned it had fallen on hard times.

Many people have asked me why the Metropole failed. There are a number of reasons, not least the attitude of the local authority in blocking my attempts to turn the place into a thriving focal point for that part of Glasgow. Today I still firmly believe those plans would have worked had they been given a chance to breathe.

Unfortunately, however, they weren't, and in my heart of hearts I knew that was the beginning of the end. The music hall was under attack from many sides during my tenure at the Metropole, and while the gloomy predictions that theatre was dying were grossly exaggerated, it is fair to say that only the fittest outfits had any chance of surviving. That of course usually applied to the biggest theatres who had the resources, or the theatres under public ownership, who had stacks of taxpayers' money in the form of subsidies. The Metropole had neither.

Instead we were hit by not only the mass emigration of the local people to the outlying housing schemes, but things like bingo, TV and, most importantly, the Beatles.

Theatre had always relied on a family audience—everyone from the kids to granny came along to enjoy a night of clean, good fun entertainment. The children started off by going to pantomime and, by the time they were eight or nine, went with their dads to see a good variety show. As the great Sir Harry Lauder once said to me: "Keep it clean, son. The family audiences are the backbone of the theatre."

But in the early Sixties trouble arrived in the form of the Beatles. Up until then children had followed their parents for entertainment, but suddenly something new and exciting was on the horizon. They adored the Beatles, while the parents—who preferred the dulcet tones of Robert Wilson—looked on with disdain. You know the attitude: "Oh what a noise, and look at that—it could do wae a wash."

The fact that the adults couldn't stand what the youngsters loved only made them more determined. They had found their little bit of independence, and lost any association or interest in the family-orientated theatre.

241

If that was the sucker punch, the onset of television provided a near knockout blow.

Suddenly people had an option. Should they go to all the trouble and expense of going out to the theatre? Or should they stay in and lap up this marvellous new novelty dishing out free entertainment in the living room? It was hardly a difficult choice.

Those factors ensured the demise of Jimmy Logan's Metropole, but I always thought I had my other business—Jimmy Logan, the artiste—to fall back on. Until that is, around the same time, it became decidedly popular to slag off my type of act.

The problem was born out of Scotland's desire to be a thriving, modern nation, but somewhere along the line someone decided the best way to do that was to ditch our heritage. As a result wonderful parts of our culture like the kilt, tartan, heather and so on took an absolute hammering from just about every quarter— and Jimmy Logan, who more than anyone seemed to represent all these things, was top of the hit list. It felt like open season on Jimmy Logan.

Which was all so ridiculous, because the only people criticising the kilt were the Scots. I once watched a programme on BBC 2 filled with Scots who seemed intent on proving themselves to the English. "We're not like those people with all that heather and tartan rubbish," they said. "We're really terribly smart and we know what we're doing. We're as good as you and we're really terribly modern."

And the people in England—and everywhere else for that matter—wondered what was wrong with them. They loved the sound of the pipes and the beauty of the dancing. Whether people liked it or not, that was what symbolised Scotland abroad—and we were loved for it. It had, and deserved, its place within a culture that was respected and envied on the international playing field. It was one facet of a people who are genuinely held in special regard by other peoples around the world. Is the Military Tattoo at Edinburgh Castle packed out every night because it is so embarrassing? Would the Tartan Army be so popular abroad if they replaced their kilts with designer shorts? Of course not, but back in the Seventies people were determined to ridicule that image and all who represented it.

One head of STV apparently called all the heads of department to a meeting and said, in no uncertain terms: "If I see one person on that screen wearing a kilt then whoever puts them there will get sacked."

He epitomised the type of person who wanted to get rid of the traditional way television, for example, celebrated the New Year in Scotland. That in itself was utterly offensive to all people in the rest of Britain who consistently told me how much they enjoyed the distinctive Scottish themes of the Hogmanay TV shows, many of which I was involved with.

They loved things like Highland dancers—although not as it eventually became on programmes like *Thingummyjig* where the women wore dresses they washed the dishes in, and the men wore their kilts with sports jackets. No, they loved those occasions when the women wore white gowns with beautiful tartan sashes, and the men wore the kilt in full Highland regalia.

When you look back now at some of those New Year recordings, they really were marvellous programmes.

The first one I was part of was at Govan Town Hall in the 1950s. Given my television experience was still fairly limited at that point, I was as nervous as hell. It was a very intricate show where I had to do a big speech about what New Year meant to all of us. That was difficult enough on its own, but I had to finish right on the first dong of the bells—even though I had no clock to judge it by.

To make things worse a rather abrupt man came up to me in the middle of the show, and snapped: "Are you in charge here?"

"Well, I've got something to do with it."

"Right, will you announce now that the minute this programme finishes everyone has to go back to their buses because the drivers aren't going to hang around."

I said to him: "Well, I'm sorry but we're live at the moment, and our show is being shown all over Britain. I can't make that kind of announcement while we are on the air."

"I don't care what air you're on," he said. "These drivers are giving up their New Year to be here and I'm here to make sure they get home as soon as possible. That has to be announced."

I quickly realised it was pointless trying to get through to him.

After escaping his clutches I went back to concentrating on this speech which I really was nervous about. I genuinely thought I was going to make a meal of it. So a pal of mine who was a doctor gave me a pill, and told me to swallow it.

I was sceptical. "What is it?" I said.

"It's called Oblivon. It will calm your nerves."

A little later, as I contemplated whether or not to pop the pill, I bumped into this little fellow at the BBC who was very high up in terms of his job title, but about four feet nothing in terms of his height. A nice, intelligent man, he had been seconded to take part in one of the sketches.

Jack Anthony—playing a waiter—was to lift the lid off a silver tray to reveal this little man's head in the middle of a platter surrounded by salad. All he had to do was smile for the camera.

"Everything OK, Jimmy?" he said as we stopped to chat.

"Fine, thanks. Yourself?"

"Oh I was worried about that sketch I'm in tonight, Jimmy, but I'm not any more."

"Why's that?"

"I've got one of these."

And he opened his palm to produce one of the Oblivon tablets, and I thought: "Jees, all he has to do is smile."

As I expected, the night was filled with tension from start to finish but by the grace of God I finished my last line just as we heard the first bell and the sound of the hooters from the boats on the Clyde.

Afterwards I got back to my flat in Ibrox to be confronted by a man answering the door whom I had never seen before.

"Do you feel like a drink?" I said, trying to be hospitable.

"Oh, don't worry, pal. Logan's got plenty in here already."

"Has he?" I said. "That's very good of him."

The producers always wanted change. On another New Year show they thought it would be brilliant to broadcast live from Aviemore. In the main square a big saucer type thing was set up with four microphones lined up, and on the ice rink there was a big orchestra.

There was a lot of snow around, and a lot of local yobbos on motorcycles too. It was like Hell's Angels on Ice.

By the time we went live on air the whole place was in complete chaos. Motorbikes were thundering around all over the place, and snowballs filled with broken glass were flying around with our names on them.

I did my smooth, low-key, relaxing speech about New Year, along the lines of: "Tonight we've gathered in our own homes, and we'll think especially about those who are abroad or those who can't be there, or those we have lost. Remember the New Year is a time to reflect on the past and a chance to look forward to the future. So if you've had troubles bury the past because you are starting in a great place . . ." It really was very formal and sombre.

When the viewers saw this speech, all they could see was my head totally filling the screen, my mouth moving and nothing else.

The reason for this was simple: all around me everyone was going absolutely berserk. Some of the yobs had tried to grab me, and all of them were throwing anything they could get their hands on in our direction.

For the New Year speech I grabbed the four mikes, held them like a bunch of daffodils against my chest, and the cameraman zoomed in on the closest of close-ups so the viewers wouldn't see or hear the mayhem around us.

There was a flurry of missiles flying past my face. It was a miracle none of them scored a direct hit.

The whole place was in total chaos—gang fights had broken out. But somehow we managed to portray a serene, laid back and happy image for the watching millions.

Years later I did a one-off programme for STV called *Standing Room Only*. It was another example of why people were wrong to dismiss our proud heritage.

The programme's format worked very well. It followed me through a performance in pantomime, and as I changed costumes or got ready for my entrance I would describe our great theatre and music hall tradition. Then it cut to wonderful clips of stars like Harry Gordon's dancers tap-dancing. It was a silent film, but a sound tape of a tap dancer had been dubbed on and you could have sworn it was the real thing.

After the programme went out I got a phone call from one of the head honchos at STV.

"Marvellous reactions to your programme, Jimmy," he said. "I couldn't understand it. My boys are only about 11 years of age but they thought that clip of Will Fyffe singing was just marvellous.

"In fact they enjoyed the whole programme and I never expected them to."

He said all this with some amazement.

I said: "Wonderful. I've got some great ideas for a follow-up."

Needless to say I never heard from him again, even if he was staggered that his kids had loved it.

I can laugh now at those ridiculous scenes in Aviemore, or that chap's reaction to *Standing Room Only*, but it was difficult to see the funny side of the predicament I found myself in after the closure of the Metropole. At a time when I had debts the size of a mountain, I found work hard to get. For the reasons I've explained nothing was going right at all. But I'm not the type of character who sits back and dwells on my setbacks. I tend to have a large whisky, and then I get up on my feet and set about making the best of the situation.

That's how I looked on things at this point. Then I was offered a part in a *Carry On* movie.

Now I've gone through life doing all sorts of things. Some of those achievements I feel have been outstanding, and I am immensely proud of them. Then I find that lots of people seem only to remember me for my involvement with two *Carry On* films in 1972 and 1973.

They were a special breed of film, suggesting everything when the viewer knew exactly what was going to happen—nothing at all. It thrived on the type of humour that is seen today as sexist, outdated and Neanderthal—but people still love them.

I was fortunate to work alongside some great artistes on those films—Sid James, Charles Hawtrey and Barbara Windsor, to name just a few. Kenneth Williams was an interesting character—an artiste of absolute brilliance one minute, but a crude man the next.

The great thing about the *Carry On* regulars was that they all worked as a team. They were a well-oiled machine who knew each other backwards. For newcomers like myself it was very difficult to fit in. I remember we rehearsed one scene in *Carry On Abroad* where I was standing behind a very good artiste. It went swimmingly. The day we did the scene, though, he arrived wearing the biggest white hat I had ever set eyes on, and I was completely blocked out of the shot.

The following year I got a role in *Carry On Girls*—this time playing a gay director. I tried my best to master that part but it just didn't work. I guess there are limits to the kind of characters I can make people believe in.

Those films paid poorly but I was so desperate I needed the money. At that time I had less than £200 in my bank account.

My friends were very concerned about my situation, and always keen to know how I was coping. None more so than Reo Stakis, the businessman who ran the successful hotel and casino chain. He phoned me one day when I was in my dressing room taking a break from the filming of *Carry On Abroad*.

"Jimmy," he said. "I don't want to buy a theatre because I don't know anything about theatres but I realise you must be under a lot of personal pressure just now. In front of me I have a cheque which I will make out personally to you for anything between £5,000 and £10,000. How much should I put in?"

I was broke, pretty worn out and doing a film which was not a great pay day. That kind of money could also have provided me with a holiday that would help return me to battle—renewed and refreshed.

I said to Reo: "No, thanks." In fact, my pride said no, thanks.

"Reo," I went on. "I want you to know that is the kindest offer anyone has ever made me and I will never, ever forget it. But honestly, I am all right."

"Are you sure, Jimmy?"

"Yes Reo, I'm absolutely fine. Thank you so much for your concern."

Of course, I wasn't fine at all. I couldn't have been much worse.

The following Christmas Reo sent me a card reminding me he was there should I ever need help. What a magnificent gentleman who to this day remains a great friend.

They say when you are about to die your life flashes before you. That's not what happened to me. I was angry. I was angry because I still had so much to do in life.

It was while touring with Brian Rix in South Africa, with the play *A Bit Between The Teeth*, that I almost met my Maker. In Cape Town, myself and three other actors in the show—Donna Reading, Peter Bland and Vivienne Johnson—went to a beach at Liverpool Bay for a picnic. When we got there, Donna decided to go for a swim.

When we arrived we had noticed that the beach, and most certainly the water, was deserted, but thought nothing more of it. What we didn't know was that, two months previously, a fisherman was swept away to his death by the strong currents in Liverpool Bay, and ever since people had been warned not to risk swimming there.

At first Donna was fine, paddling away in the water to her heart's content. Then, suddenly, the Big Wave arrived and Donna was swept right out into the bay. She started screaming. I shouted to the others to get help and instinctively raced into the water to help her. I only do breast-stroke, but at a time like that it was just a case of "Let's get the show on the road."

I'd like to say I swam out to her, but in reality I was swept out to her. The moment I put my hand on her shoulder she stopped screaming. "Don't worry Donna," I said. "We will make it to the shore."

Then the currents took a grip again, and we were swept further out. Those currents were so strong there was just no way we could fight. At that point Donna looked at my face, and started screaming again.

We were repeatedly swept under the water, rising above the waves for just long enough to breathe in some air. And each time with the knowledge that this breath could be our last. I kept my hand under her chin as we were swept into another bay—smaller, but very rocky. We were being thrown against the rocks, and I had visions of dying on a remote beach on the other side of the world, stretched out on a rock in the same way a fish would be battered against a fishmonger's slab. You'll know what I mean when I say it wasn't really the way I wanted to bow out.

After what seemed an eternity, but in reality was probably closer to about 15 minutes, I let go of Donna, and Peter Bland, who had run round from Liverpool Bay on to the rocks, managed to get hold of her. Luckily, his foot was jammed under a rock, stopping him being swept away too. Eventually I managed to clamber out on to the rocks, absolutely exhausted.

I had lived to fight another day.

The battering my knees took on those rocks lived with me for substantially longer than that. Months later, I found that if I sat in one place for too long, my knees would seize up. I had to keep moving about.

Finally I went to a Harley Street doctor, who diagnosed bruised blood under the skin, and told me it would be a year before the pain disappeared. He was dead right.

Back home, all the strain on my professional life took its toll on my personal circumstances as well—not least with Gina.

It was very sad because I have so many fond memories of our time together. She was the type of woman who would laugh at my gags—even if she had heard them a million times before. We shared the same interests, and we made a good team. I helped her gain the confidence to be someone who became a tremendous success in the fashion world, while she made all my clothes for the summer shows at the Metropole, and designed costumes for the pantomimes.

In the first house we shared in St John's Wood, a very nice area of north London, Gina had a little showroom which was visited one day by a striking American woman. We talked for a while before she went on her way.

I said to Gina, "Who was that?"

"Raquel Welch."

I must be the only man in the world to meet the world's most beautiful woman and not know it. Even when Gina told me I still didn't know who she was talking about.

At that stage our marriage was wonderful, and I was desperately in love. We moved to a bigger house in Wandsworth—part of a converted mansion house—and for a long while our time together was happy and relaxing.

But as the Metropole went down the drain so did our relationship. Increasingly, when I arrived with my problems from Scotland, our lovely house would be filled with a grey face and a lot of worries. It was the last thing Gina needed; she had her own pressures trying to run a business at the forefront of the high-powered fashion world. What Gina needed was a husband to arrive on the doorstep, and say: "Right, you look tired. We're going on a holiday to relax."

Alas, with the world's problems sitting on my shoulders, I was not that husband.

Things came to a head in 1976 when I was in Bournemouth with *A Bit Between The Teeth*. During the day, I was writing my one-man show on the life of Sir Harry Lauder.

Gina came to see me at weekends, but it was so clear that we were drifting apart. From being a couple who had pulled out all the stops together there was now a distance between us. She had craved my advice to begin with, but now she didn't want to know what I thought. I suspected she was seeing someone else.

There was a great strain between us when she came up to Edinburgh for the opening night of *Lauder* at the Lyceum Theatre. She returned to London, and the following Sunday I reluctantly got in the car to go down too.

With two performances on the Saturday I had sung around 70 songs in total. As I drove south I was both exhausted and dreading the seemingly inevitable when I got to our house. At Stafford I stopped off for a meal with some friends.

It was very strange. I walked in, and they offered me the most wonderful food. I sat down, but I was in no condition to eat.

I said to them: "Would you mind if I just go to bed? I'm not feeling very good."

Something gave up. Three days later I was still in that bed. I got a bad fever and sweated so much my friends continually had to change the sheets. I was so ill I had no idea the doctor had been in to see me.

I think that my mind and body just said no. They weren't in the condition to be presented with yet more problems. When my friend's son drove me to London I put off going back to the house. Instead I stayed in a hotel for a couple of nights, then went to Poole where I achieved another ambition in life and sailed across the Channel to France.

On the way back I left most of my *café au lait* in the middle of the Channel. The seas were so big that the yacht seemed to be dwarfed by the crashing waves. It was quite an experience.

All along, though, I knew I was delaying the inevitable. And sure enough, when I got back to London it was just a disaster. Gina admitted that there was someone else, and she lasted two days in the house with me before disappearing.

I stayed for a week—a nightmarish week where I realised that the woman I loved so much had slipped away from me. I waited for her to come back but she never came back.

In a desperate attempt to see her, I went into her office—the base of a business I had helped build up. A new girl at reception said to me: "Gina's busy at the moment. What name will I give her?"

I was Gina's husband, and a director of the business, but at that point it hit home more than ever that I was no longer important, no longer part of Gina's life, no longer needed. I thought: "I'm getting out of here. This is not for me."

So I packed what I needed and set out on the journey back to

Scotland in my old RO 80 car. As I proceeded north I contemplated life on the road again. Here I was—at the age of 49—driving back to another life that had no home, no wife, no money, no theatre, no Rolls-Royce, no chauffeur, no castle, no plane, no boat and, most certainly, no laughs. Just two suitcases and a rusty old motor.

"How did it all go so wrong?" I continually asked myself.

When I returned to Glasgow I had few options. My beautiful house in Dowanhill had gone in the divorce from Grace, so I headed for my father's little one-bedroom flat in Ibrox. I slept on the settee in his front room and hung my clothes over the upright piano in the corner. It was to be my home for the next two years.

10

THE SCOTTISH MINSTREL

In times of crisis I have often got to the point where I wanted to just curl up in a quiet corner and ignore the rest of the world. But I'm not the type of character who would do that to hide from my problems. Rather, being alone afforded me the opportunity to focus my mind on dealing with the situation, and getting my energies back.

That's how I felt after the Metropole went down the tubes, and that's how I felt when I drove back to Scotland after leaving Gina. These were desperate times, but even in the most desperate of times I've never been one to dwell on my setbacks; to do that would be to inflict more damage on an already damaged psyche. Instead I've always resolved to try and move on—aware, even in my lowest moments, that things truly will get better in the long term.

Admittedly there were some nights sleeping on my father's settee with all my good suits hung over his piano when I seriously doubted those deepest instincts. Lying on his settee was like lying on a bed of rocks. It was very uncomfortable.

Being cooped up with my father in such a small flat sometimes stretched our patiences to the limit. As much as we held each other

Above: The first Royal show at Jimmy Logan's Metropole—HRH The Princess Alexandra, with her husband the Honourable Angus Ogilvie, attending a Royal Performance in aid of 'Stars for Spastics', on April 8th, 1965

First page: Princess Alexandra and her husband in the Royal Box at the Metropole. The beautiful flowers were arranged by Carole Wilson

Left: HRH The Princess Margaret at the Metropole's 'Night of Stars' for the centenary of Dr Barnardo's in 1966

Right: Façade of Jimmy Logan's Metropole Theatre, St George's Cross, Glasgow, in 1965

Below: The Metropole auditorium. The stalls would seat 690 and the main circle 445. The gallery originally seated 1000 but was destroyed by fire; when I opened it would hold 125

Above: With President Eisenhower, at the Waldorf Hotel in New York, in 1967

Opposite: Taking over the New Metropole—
Grace, Mum, Dad and I outside the building in 1964

Above: With Gordon Jackson, raising funds for the church organ at Largs after we had finished filming *Floodtide*

Left and opposite:
Filming *Carry On Abroad* in 1972, with Barbara Windsor and director Gerald Thomas (*left*), Kenneth Williams (*opposite above*) and Sid James (*opposite below*)

Above: At the top of Ben Lomond with the cast of *Take the High Road*, after my 'death'

Below: Talking to Lady Strathmore at Glamis Castle in 1985, where I was hosting a poetry reading by Dame Judy Dench and her husband Michael Williams, in aid of the Scottish Disability Foundation. The event was filmed by the BBC. The Queen Mother, patron of the charity, was guest of honour

Above: You've got plenty of pictures of me—take one of him instead! The Queen looks on, laughing, at Commander Edward Perkins, on his last day as her personal bodyguard

Below: At rehearsals for the 1983 Royal Scottish Variety Performance at the King's Theatre, Glasgow: George Barron, Gordon Jackson, Dougie Donnelly, JL and Jim McColl

Above and below left: Hosting the Royal Scottish Variety Performance at the King's, on October 2nd, 1983, in aid of the Prince and Princess of Wales Hospice. The hospice was Glasgow's wedding gift to Prince Charles and Princess Diana, who were guests of honour

Below: Una McLean, Hector Nicol and The Krankies are presented to His Royal Highness

Below: The Understudy! With Gregor Fisher—Rab C. Nesbitt, in 1997

Above: At the 1998 Royal Variety Performance of *Hey Mr Producer* at the Lyceum Theatre, London, with Mr Producer himself, Sir Cameron Mackintosh

Below: At the 1998 Royal Variety Performance, with Julie Andrews

Below: Filming *Captain Jack* with Bob Hoskins, in 1997

Above: With Billy Connolly during filming of *The Debt Collector* in 1998

Left: Helena McCarthy, at the age of 87, in Morocco filming a Lottery commercial in 1996. As we say in showbusiness—*follow that!*

in deep affection, our colourful relationship often produced drastic differences of opinion. In the Short household there was never a dull moment.

For a long time afterwards my thoughts centred on Gina, and I pestered myself with questions of what had gone wrong in our relationship. Perhaps only after we split up did I realise how much I loved her in the first place.

It was a terribly difficult time from which I genuinely took a long time to recover. One of the activities which diverted my attention from such destructive thoughts was the one-man show I had written on the life of my great hero Sir Harry Lauder. It was a project correctly labelled a labour of love that was produced out of anger, and possibly stands on its own as my proudest achievement.

I wrote *Lauder* at a point when my life was at an all-time low. Under the strain of the mountainous theatre debts my marriage to Gina was on its last throw. On a professional front, the traditional image of tartan and heather for which Scotland was rightly renowned was under furious attack from a group of people who didn't know what they were talking about.

I've already mentioned that this downer on our own fine traditions affected my professional standing, but possibly more infuriating was the fact that Harry Lauder was getting the blame for it all.

These critics were convinced that all of Scotland's ills were caused by people who wore this awful kilt, kept saying "Hoots Mon" and told terrible Scottish jokes. According to them, this meant that the ever so smart, intelligent modern brand of comedian couldn't get any work outside Scotland.

I don't think they entertained the possibility that they couldn't get work because they simply weren't good enough. The fact was that if you put Harry Lauder's coffin on the stage of New York's Carnegie Hall it would be filled a dozen times over. Stick all of those moaning-faced comedians on the one bill and the theatre would have been empty.

They were of course talking complete and utter nonsense, and quite frankly I couldn't have cared less about them. I was perceived at the time as "Son of Harry" but my reaction was to be proud of that tradition, and I stuck with it. Going abroad with the kilt representing Scotland is like possessing a passport inscribed in gold. Attempts to kill that culture should always be opposed.

More significantly, though, I was determined to make sure the name of Harry Lauder was dragged back out of the mud and reinstated with the respect it deserved. He was a legend of the music hall, and it was wrong for that to be taken away from him. His contribution was immense all over the world yet people were decrying him from all sides. And those people were all Scots. Outside Scotland Harry Lauder was still held in the highest regard.

These days younger folk naturally know nothing about Lauder. Had that trendy criticism been allowed to fester in people's minds his reputation might have been destroyed beyond repair. So, although he had been dead for more than 20 years, I was so angry I decided to write his life story for the stage.

Harry Lauder wrote one of the golden pages in the history of music hall—something that no-one had any right to try and take away from him.

Initially I considered commissioning someone else to do the work, but as I knew his history so well I thought I would make a decent enough job of it on my own.

During the long run of *A Bit Between The Teeth* in Bournemouth I put pen to paper. Each morning around half past nine I sat down to write. After writing for four hours I recorded those notes into a tape recorder. Then I lay in a bath listening to the recording and making mental notes. People work best in the strangest of situations, and that was how I worked most productively.

I sent the finished script to a friend of mine, the director Clive Perry, who was interested in putting the play on at the Royal Lyceum in Edinburgh. He liked what he saw and asked me to include more on Lauder's wife Nancy, which I did.

Lauder was a wonderful play telling a truly extraordinary story. Harry Lauder was the eldest of six children; the son of a potter and a mother who signed her name with a cross. When he was a boy his father took the family down to the Potteries in England to live, but tragically died just a few weeks later.

His widowed wife was left with a family to bring up on her own, and took them to Arbroath where she had relatives. The only way she could earn a living was to take in washing for the Big House.

Lauder's was a difficult childhood—much of it spent in the "half-timers" school where kids would spend half their day at school, and the other half working in the mill. His family later moved to Hamilton where Lauder, at the age of 13, went down mines looking after pit ponies. After becoming a miner he married the pit foreman's daughter Nancy Vallance, whom he met at a local singing competition.

Lauder's singing talent was first spotted at the Band of Hope concerts in Arbroath. Before marrying Nancy he made an unsuccessful attempt to make his way in the world of theatre. But after the couple produced their only son, John, he rose from the pits to try the theatre game again. He went on tour with a lifelong friend, Mackenzie Murdoch, and this time they were a success.

By 1891 Lauder was earning a handsome £4 10s a week, and his first hit song 'Calligan—Call Again' was written at the top of all his headed notepaper. He could have stayed in Scotland and lived comfortably on this healthy living, but Lauder's ambitions stretched far beyond the horizons of his own country.

He took a long time to become a success in London but when

it worked, it really worked. By the time he returned to star in the pantomime *Aladdin* at the Theatre Royal in Glasgow in 1905 he could command payment of £200 a week.

Lauder then did something which was quite unique. In an era when it was common for comedians to sing songs as well as tell jokes, Lauder wrote a love song—something that no comedian had ever tried. 'I Love A Lassie' swept through Glasgow quicker than the cold. It had a wonderful melody, and became the first of his really big singing successes.

He started to spend his time between Glasgow and London until, in 1910, one of the big American agents William Morris sailed to Britain to personally offer Lauder a contract worth $3,000 a week on the other side of the Atlantic. The only proviso was that Lauder was to wear the kilt wherever he went in America, and never be seen in trousers.

The tour was a big risk but Lauder agreed, and Morris went round every theatre the little Scot was scheduled to play in Britain buying out all of his contracts. In America he was an instant hit, first with the big Scots community and then, as his reputation spread, with theatre-goers in general. At one point he was so popular he had his own train, *The Harry Lauder Special*, ferrying him to dates across the country. In every town he was met by a pipe band. All this in the days when there was no television or radio; Lauder gained worldwide status through newspapers, magazines and word of mouth.

He was only a small man of around 5ft 3in with a barrel chest developed through his years down the pits. It helped give him a wonderful singing voice. But the interesting thing for me about Lauder's music was that, just like today's hits, people could dance to his songs. They always had a lovely melody and a nice feel of Victorian values about them. There was no-one better at writing a wee song that could really tug at the heart strings.

A fine gauge of just how big he had become is the story of

how a rival American theatre boss threatened to cancel one of Lauder's appearances. William Morris made a few telephone calls, the President was informed and the rival boss was threatened with action by the Attorney General. Lauder's show went ahead.

When the 1914-18 War broke out Lauder was in Australia on a world tour playing to packed houses. He returned in 1915, and on Hogmanay 1916 received the shattering news that his only son John had two days earlier been shot and killed by a sniper on the Western Front.

Lauder may have been devastated, and to a certain degree felt there was no longer any reason to continue himself. But after taking three days off—and returning to mourn with his wife in Scotland—Lauder came back to the show he was performing in at the time in London. His reasoning was that so many fathers had lost so many sons, and if he didn't go back to work then why should they?

In the finale of the show called *Three Cheers* he played a Scottish soldier surrounded by a team of Scots Guards singing the song 'The Laddies Who Fought And Won'. And the words are particularly poignant:

> "When the War is over and the fighting's done,
> And the flags are waving free,
> When the bells are ringing,
> And the boys are singing
> Songs of victory,
>
> As we all gather round the old fireside
> And each fond mother kisses her son,
> Aw the lassies will be lovin' all the laddies,
> The laddies who fought and won."

When he first walked on for that performance the audience

stood and cheered, and their applause went on and on. It was their way of saying they knew what he was going through. And they were with him.

In the finale the audience and the company sang 'The Laddies Who Fought And Won' for him. Harry Lauder stood centre stage, a father who had lost his son like thousands of fathers who had lost their sons, overcome with emotion. From that moment Harry Lauder wasn't just a kilted singer of songs, but part of the fabric of a nation. There can have been fewer more emotional moments in theatre's history.

Not long after that Lauder went across the Channel to entertain the Forces. But his trip had another purpose, and that was to see where his beloved son was buried. He arrived in France with a little portable piano, escorted only by an officer, a driver and a friend. Wherever he saw soldiers resting he would set up his piano and get them to sing with him.

The time came when he paid an emotional visit to John's grave, and he later wrote how he wished he could have reached down into that grave and put his father's arms around his son.

When Lauder returned he was one of the first to think of what was to become of the wounded soldiers, and shortly afterwards set up a fund for Returning Disabled Ex-Servicemen. He raised £1 million in Britain and America, and my own father was just one of the men who benefited from his actions.

Lauder returned to Australia at the end of the War, an artiste who was one of the best-known names in the world. It was there he received word that he was to be honoured for his services to the nation, and became Sir Harry Lauder—The First Knight of the Music Hall.

His song 'Keep Right On To The End Of The Road', written a few years later, became an inspiration for the millions of families who had been bereaved during the War.

In all he went on 22 world tours, many of them farewell tours, and was given the freedom of Edinburgh.

After Nancy died in 1928 his niece Greta accompanied him everywhere he went. On his tours Sir Harry suddenly became a target for women; he had a title, lots of money and was single. Greta was in her way a protection against that small but formidable army of matrons.

In 1931 he moved from his home in Dunoon and decided to return to Strathaven, the area near Hamilton where he had lived as a boy. He chose a piece of land before Greta negotiated with a local building company to erect what would become known as Lauder Ha'. It was bought in her name because Sir Harry reckoned the firm would have charged too much if his involvement had become known.

In fact one of Sir Harry's legacies is his apparent meanness. Many people believe he is the reason Scots are regarded as tight— when the real source of that myth lies in the bankrupting of the City of Aberdeen last century. However, Sir Harry's reputation was not entirely misplaced. He believed that, just like a commercial traveller, he could be "once seen and easy forgotten". So, determined to be remembered wherever he went, Sir Harry worked on the theme that people never remember your generosity but never forget your meanness. And he was determined to be remembered.

When anyone else gave a taxi driver a shilling, he gave him thrupence or a signed photograph. But he was remembered for it. Jack Benny had a similar reputation. When he played the London Palladium he gave all the people who worked with him a beautiful gift but asked them not to mention it until he had gone so as not to scupper his image.

Sir Harry played on the same instincts from a humorous point of view. Before the builders got to work on Lauder Ha' he went to their office, and said: "Right, when do you start?"

"Sir Harry, we'll be there on the first of May at eight o'clock in the morning to start building your house."

On the night of April 30 Sir Harry set up a caravan in the corner of the field that would house his new home. He did it through sheer devilment, and when they arrived the following morning he shouted over: "Hoi, you're five minutes late."

When I was an aspiring comedian with my family Sir Harry used to go round all the Scottish theatres in the summer. He sometimes came backstage to meet the performers, and give them some encouragement.

It was a big occasion when Sir Harry Lauder came to the theatre. He would arrive last and, as he walked down the aisle with Greta, the audience would always burst into a huge standing ovation. He knew his effect and he played it well. Artistes knew they were in the presence of a legend.

I had the privilege of being there when he came backstage at the Metropole. That was the first time I had actually met the great man. Then, some time later, I was introduced to him again after he watched our show at the Gaiety Theatre in Ayr.

On that occasion he invited me to Lauder Ha' for tea. It was one of those moments when someone could have knocked me over with a feather. I couldn't believe my ears.

For weeks I was so nervous about the prospect of going to Sir Harry's house, but I knew exactly how I would play the situation; I would shut my gob and listen. Speak only when spoken to.

I remember my visit there as if it was yesterday. I went up a big driveway to be confronted by a beautifully designed house made of grey granite.

The main hall was fascinating, two storeys high lighted by magnificent stained glass windows. Each window was surrounded by flowers and fauna from each country he had entertained in, and on the fireplace was chiselled an inscription:

Frae aw the airts the winds may blaw,
Yer welcome here tae Lauder Ha'

Staircases on either side of the hall stretched up to the top landing. Halfway up on one side was a beautiful oil painting of Lady Lauder, and on the opposite side was a portrait of Sir Harry. Taking pride of place at the top of the stairs on the landing was a magnificent painting of their son, John Lauder, in his Army uniform. It was one of those pictures where, no matter where you went, the eyes followed you.

Below the stained glass windows there was also a two-foot marble bust of Sir Harry.

On either side of the house were two fascinating rooms—his billiard room and another room that was filled with curios and mementos collected throughout his life. I saw a little piece of tartan picked off a barbed wire fence in No Man's Land from the 1914-18 War. There were dozens of silver cups signifying all the theatre box office records he broke. He also kept a wee old iron kettle that belonged to his mother.

That house also had so many lovely little touches. Every easy chair had a little wooden bar built in, so people could put their fingers under that bar to help lift themselves out of the chair. A special shelf was situated outside each bedroom so anyone carrying a breakfast tray could put it down while opening the door to the room.

There was a beautiful lounge and dining room, and upstairs were Sir Harry and Greta's bedrooms.

In a big room at the back of the house, above the garage, were all his theatrical costumes with things like pencils, rulers and pieces of string still in the pockets.

And there was another immaculate bedroom filled with furniture that was a little more old-fashioned. I never realised that although John Lauder had never lived at Lauder Ha', Sir Harry had recreated his son's bedroom from Laudervale in Dunoon. It was exactly as it was when John went off to war, and never returned.

I didn't know Sir Harry's life story at that point, and I was neither wise enough or mature enough, but I regret not having the presence of mind to ask Sir Harry what John meant to him, and how it felt to have lost a son the way he did. I wish I had asked how he managed to get through that performance of 'The Laddies Who Fought And Won'. Because I don't know how he got through that night.

When I was filming the movie *The Wild Affair*, I spoke to Bud Flanagan from The Crazy Gang about Sir Harry Lauder. He told me how he once made the great mistake of announcing during a show just after the Second World War that the great man himself was in the audience. And the audience went daft.

Bud said to me: "My mistake was saying: 'Would you like him to come up on stage?' 'Yes,' shouted the audience. And Harry Lauder came up on stage and did about 35 minutes singing his wee songs. It cost me a fortune in overtime."

During the Second World War, Sir Winston Churchill asked Sir Harry to entertain the sons and grandsons of the men he had entertained more than 20 years previously. He was an old man but he went round the army bases in an old Rolls-Royce. I have a picture of Sir Harry Lauder and Sir Winston Churchill sitting together. That was indeed the measure of the man. Our greatest entertainer's songs inspired our greatest Prime Minister. When Churchill was feeling tired or down, he used to put Sir Harry on the gramophone, and march up and down to the music.

At Sir Harry's funeral in 1950 there was a wreath from Churchill, which said: "To the Scottish minstrel." The minister at Sir

Harry's church told me it was the only funeral service he had conducted where tickets had to be printed—such was the demand from people to say their last goodbyes.

It was this magnificent life story that I felt compelled to tell. Sir Harry was pure music hall, pure theatre. He embodied the achievement that is possible in theatre. Most people who met him—including me—were simply in awe of the man. We aspired to be even half as good as he was—and that would have been a real achievement.

Those who ridiculed him years later did so more than 20 years after his death because they would never have dared when he was still alive. He was held in too much respect and admiration to be treated like that.

Sir Harry was an international superstar—a man whose big ideas took him way beyond the narrow-minded boundaries of the people who sought to criticise him. He looked marvellous in his kilt, and sang lovely songs which made him unique in the world.

Many, many people made a big impression on the music hall but if all those great stars became a pack of cards Sir Harry Lauder would be the Ace. The King was Will Fyffe, the Dundee-born star who first became famous when he sang 'I Belong To Glasgow'.

Harry Gordon was the Queen.

The Jack?

Take your pick from Jack Radcliffe, Alec Finlay, Tommy Morgan, Jack Anthony, Sammy Murray, Tommy Lorne or wonderful acts like Power and Bendon, Clark and Murray, or Frank and Doris Droy. After the War, it would be fair to include Chic Murray, Stanley Baxter, Rikki Fulton, Jack Milroy, Johnny Beattie, Mary Lee and Una McLean. More recently come Dorothy Paul, Billy Connolly and Robbie Coltrane. There may even be space for myself in there somewhere.

The Joker in the pack, of course, was always going to be Dave Willis—a natural clown who moved like a ballet dancer, and whose eyes "twinkled as bright as stars".

I've never seen a comedian like him.

Dave Willis was earning up to £300 a week in 1933. He would put £20 in his pocket, and the rest went to his accountant. He had a lovely house, but he never lived on his money. Occasionally the accountant would say something like: "Dave, you need another Rolls."

After the Second World War his heart took a wee flutter and he decided it was time to retire.

His accountant suggested he buy a hotel in which he would live on the top floor.

"Just pick up the phone for your breakfast, lunch, dinner, tea, whatever you want," the accountant said to him. "We'll get someone to run the hotel and you'll have no problems."

So Dave bought this hotel on the Island of Bute, and in his retirement became very plump.

One day two gentlemen from the brewers who supplied the hotel's beer came to see him.

"Mr Willis, we're sorry it hasn't worked out but you'll have to leave."

And Dave said: "Wait a minute, I own the hotel."

But it turned out he didn't. At that point the accountant was in court in Edinburgh for fiddling a woman out of most of her estate. And he'd done the same to Dave Willis.

The accountant committed suicide, and poor Dave was left with no money and no home. A man who thought he was worth a lot had to come out of retirement to get by. But he was no longer fit, and there was no longer the kind of work available that he used to be so good at.

When we did *A Funny Thing Happened on the Way to the Forum* at the Lyceum Theatre in Edinburgh, Dave was in the cast. Whenever he went on that stage all the young actors and actresses appeared at the side watching, learning. He still had his magic.

The opening night of *A Funny Thing Happened on the Way to the Forum* hardly impressed my mother.

"What did you think?" I asked her afterwards.

"Saw the forum," she replied. "Didnae see the funny thing."

Dave spent his final days in a small house near Peebles. He died in poverty.

His funeral was strange. It was some English form of Christian service where you don't mention the name of the deceased. We came out and someone said: "I've seen more people at the stage door waiting for his autograph."

And his son Denny, who was also a superb artiste, said he wished someone had said something about his father's life and what he had done.

And I said: "Denny, that's what I hoped to do but I didn't want to suggest it in case it was an intrusion. I thought the family had chosen it this way."

And Denny said: "Not at all."

Dave Willis was a fantastic comedian who knew what buttons to push to make people laugh. It's a difficult art. A good comic is someone who is very, very short of material and is able to get a huge roar of laughter out of a terrible gag.

Great comics can make bad gags good.

I only ever came across one comic who I thought wasn't getting as much laughter as he should. And I started thinking: "That's a good gag, so is that, and so is that."

I concluded that he was the only comic I knew who could take a good gag and make it sound terrible. It's not fair to say who he is.

There has in the past always been a shortage of women who understood comedy. Some did, but not many. Those who did, and who I worked with in my comedy plays, include Una McLean, Jan Wilson and Marillyn Gray.

Hard work is making a comedy funny. No work at all is a comedy that is funny.

In *Run For Your Wife* with Una and her husband Russell Hunter there was no work at all. That was primarily because they both instinctively know what makes people laugh.

Una has appeared with me in at least a dozen comedy plays and many pantomimes over the years. On the one hand she can play principal boy in those pantomimes, giving a wonderful performance without comedy. Then there is the total contrast of pantomime dame which she is just as good at.

Una has also rubbished the predictions of the doom merchants when she joined *Five Past Eight* by carrying on her excellent work in the serious theatre, and even appeared with Scottish Opera in *Fiddler On The Roof*. She and Russell make an impressive team.

Perhaps the most difficult place for comics to get a laugh was the Glasgow Empire. It had a fearsome reputation, especially if you were an English comedian.

I got to know one such comedian who came north with his wife to play the Glasgow Empire. His name was Des O'Connor. He came and stayed in my flat in Glasgow before his act, and I said: "What gags are you doing?"

He told me, and I advised him: "You can't tell that on stage. It won't go down well at the Empire."

Evidently that's what he got away with. I thought he had courage.

A couple of days later I picked up a newspaper which had a report on his second night. It said: "Des O'Connor faints on stage."

The theatre management said Des was such a perfectionist that he counted the exact number of steps it would take him to walk to the microphone. He got halfway there, and fainted. I thought someone must have moved the microphone to confuse him. But I must admit he did get a lot of publicity.

He left soon afterwards. I hate to remind him that he didn't pay his garage bill. That cost me another 10 shillings that week.

When Morecambe and Wise arrived at that theatre Sauchiehall Street was being dug up by the Corporation. Outside the stage door was a huge trench which Eric Morecambe spotted the moment he got out of the taxi.

He said: "They're digging our grave and we haven't even done the act."

On stage little Ernie usually appeared to sing his first big number and as the applause was ringing in his ears Eric walked on.

At the Empire Ernie belted out his opening number, rounded it off with a big finish and then . . . nothing. And on came Eric.

"Oh no," shouted a lone voice from the audience. "There's two of them."

Some of the Glasgow Empire stories are frightening, but a great many artistes went there and had marvellous successes. I think a lot of the non-Scottish artistes had been doing their act for so long it was as if they had switched on a tape recorder. At the Empire that was guaranteed to get them into trouble.

Another great hero of mine was the film star Jack Buchanan. My Uncle Bert once told me that if I could sing like Harry Lauder and look like Jack Buchanan I really had it made. Jack Buchanan was the kind of man women wanted to marry, and men wanted to be.

He was tall, dashing and possessed a very upper-class, slightly nasal English voice, but Jack Buchanan came from Helensburgh. He became a big theatre star in London and New York, then starred in dozens of movies. He even bought his own theatres and film studio.

After arriving in New York in the 1920s with a revue, Buchanan was so smart and sophisticated he sent his shirts back to Britain on the Cunard liner to be washed, ironed and pressed. People in the Big Apple used to say: "You're looking so Buchananish."

On his first visit to New York after the Second World War he was met by the Press at the bottom of the ship's gangplank. Unbeknown to them, Jack's Rolls-Royce with its British number plate was in the ship's hold. A few minutes later the Rolls, driven by Jack's chauffeur, drove alongside the assembled pack. They were all dumbfounded. And boy, was that impressive.

For a long time Jack Buchanan was considered to be one of the most eligible bachelors in the world.

To meet him in person was a thrill. The first time I was introduced was at the Malmaison Hotel in Glasgow around the same time my father had threatened to sue me.

"I see you're having some trouble, Jimmy," was all he said.

"Yes, I am, Mr Buchanan," I replied, wishing I looked like him.

I met him again at the opening night of STV in 1957. He was also on the bill, and as I was getting ready to do my Teddy Boy act I noticed his wife Susan was looking harassed.

"Jack's valet," she said to me, "has only packed three buttons for his evening dress waistcoat instead of four. I don't know what to do."

"Well, what do the buttons look like?" I said.

"To be honest, Jimmy, they're really like gents' fly buttons."

I pulled a fly button from my Teddy Boy trousers, handed it to her and said: "Will that do?"

"Absolutely perfect, Jimmy."

So Jack Buchanan, this immaculate man, appeared on that big opening night with the assistance of my Teddy Boy's fly button. How proud I felt.

I hardly spoke to him when he was rehearsing because I didn't want to disturb such a good professional. No-one—including me—knew Jack was very ill at that time. I later discovered he was dying from cancer.

He came off stage, and as he was leaning on the rails, asked when I was coming down to London.

"Well, Mr Buchanan," I said, "I'm in the middle of *Five Past*

Eight at the moment and it will be a few months. But I'll come down when that's finished."

"You must come to my theatre, the Garrick, and ask for me," he said. "We'll go out to dinner."

I couldn't believe I was going to be seen in London with Jack Buchanan.

Sadly, it wasn't to be as he died before I got there. The next time I was down his wife said to me: "Why don't we have that dinner Jack spoke about?"

So she invited me to their big apartment and showed me all his personal photos. She knew of my special interest in his career.

About two years later a parcel arrived for me at the Alhambra. Inside was Jack Buchanan's kilt, his Highland shoes and a note from Susan saying: "These belong to Jack and I think he would love them to be connected once again with the Scottish theatre."

Jack Buchanan enjoyed a close and warm friendship with another famous son of Helensburgh, John Logie Baird. They had known each other since school, and Buchanan went on to help finance Logie Baird's firm as he strove to develop the first television. A feat he achieved, admittedly with a different system to the one that was followed up, but the important thing to remember is that it worked—and he was first.

Few people realise that as long ago as 1928 Logie Baird was doing demonstrations of TV live from London—sending the signal via a ship in the Atlantic—to the United States. Buchanan's faith in his friend was such that he subsequently built a factory to make portable television sets. But, just as it was due to start, the Chancellor of the Exchequer introduced a giant tax on luxury items, and Buchanan lost a fortune. It didn't break him by any means, and I believe he still cleared up Logie Baird's debt when he died, and arranged for his wife to get a pension which she lived off until she passed away a few years ago.

The two of them were very close, and so closely connected to what has become one of the most important and powerful mediums in our lives today. Logie Baird was ridiculed when he announced that one day everyone in Britain would be able to watch the President of the United States broadcasting live from the White House. They thought he was crazy.

Mind you, he would have laughed if someone suggested that all the little boxes people watched these remarkable images on would be made in Japan. In those days Japan was a country where people cut each other's heads off for fun. They didn't make anything worth exporting anywhere else—the only thing of theirs that went into other countries was their army.

The opening night of *Lauder* was a Royal Performance in the presence of Princess Alexandra at the Royal Lyceum Theatre in Edinburgh on May 26, 1976. Against popular opinion at that time in Scotland, I believed it would be successful north and south of the border. My greatest commendation, I suppose, came from my sister Annie who was one of those people who couldn't stand Harry Lauder. Afterwards she approached me backstage, and said: "Jimmy, you performed a miracle tonight."

"What?" I said.

She smiled, and explained: "You managed to make me like Harry Lauder. That's a miracle."

I must have done something right. Annie thought Lauder was the end. In fact, if I was to be judged on one show in my life I wouldn't mind if it was *Lauder*. I had told few people I was writing it in the first place so when the announcement was made that it was opening in Edinburgh there was a decidedly mixed reaction. It gave the Son of Harry brigade plenty of opportunities to moan.

But at the end of that first evening there is no doubt that 100 per cent of the people who were there had been converted. The show subsequently got excellent crits in the press.

I think a lot of people who went along were surprised they enjoyed it, and surprised by the amount of information they didn't know about Harry Lauder. They all thought Harry Lauder was just this little guy who stood in the kilt and sang songs. When they realised what he achieved in life there was a change in their perception.

As a result of these things *Lauder* was a success north and south of the border. What did surprise me, though, was the interest theatres abroad were showing. Eventually I took the show to Australia, New Zealand and Australia. The audiences there loved the show too.

I particularly enjoyed Australia, partly I suppose because of the romantic feel for the place I had through such memories as the Anzac troops coming past Gourock up the Clyde during the Second World War.

I arrived in Sydney the day before Anzac Day and witnessed a huge parade of all these proud veterans in memory of their comrades who had fallen on the battlefields of both World Wars. Every Thursday an Army detachment marches to the war memorial to hold a ceremony remembering those men, and each night at nine o'clock everything stops in the ex-servicemen's clubs—again in their memory. Unlike in Britain where such things are rare, these former soldiers make sure the sacrifices of their comrades are never forgotten. And that is to be saluted and admired.

It was a real education going to Australia for the first time. I knew the country was shaped like a sheep with two legs but I had no idea how big the place was. I had flown from South Africa to Perth, and thought Sydney would be just a quick hop from there by plane. It took six hours—the equivalent of Glasgow to New York—and I was left flabbergasted. I had no idea the land mass was bigger than the United States.

At Australian customs I was asked by a snooty officer: "Anything to declare?"

"No."

"What about these walking sticks?"

I had some of Lauder's famous walking sticks with me for the show—all of them were the original antique sticks that Lauder had used in places like Australia sixty years earlier.

I said to the guy: "They are antique sticks—they belonged to Harry Lauder."

"I don't care who they belonged to, sir," he said. "You are not allowed to bring any kind of wood into Australia."

When I got to Sydney the Australian air pilots went on strike, and Douglas Fairbanks Jnr and Stanley Holloway—who I was due to follow at the Theatre Royal—were asked to stay an extra few weeks with their play. I was put up in a lovely hotel until the pilots got their dispute sorted out.

In Canberra—the Australian capital—I met one of my former neighbours in London who had been moved to the Embassy there. I asked him if he knew where I could throw a party in Sydney.

"No problem," he said. "I can get the use of the High Commissioner's residence."

My goodness. The High Commissioner was, of course, the Queen's representative in Australia who had the power to kick out the Prime Minister if he wished, and a few years earlier he had done exactly that. His residence was spectacular; we partied on a huge roof garden which overlooked Sydney Harbour. My friend also got hold of all the alcohol duty-free so I had this wonderful party in this amazing location, and it cost me less than £20.

New Zealand was also fantastic, a country full of wonderful old theatres that had been lying empty and closed for years. They had been part of the Tait circuit of theatres in which Sir Harry played in 1914 for £1,000 a week.

In Melbourne I met Lady Tait—a member of that family—who gave me a copy of a magnificent photo, taken from the stage, of Sir Harry walking down the aisle in the centre of a packed theatre in

Melbourne. There were perhaps 2,000 faces in that photo, and when you look closely you can make out just about every one, even those folk way up at the back of the gallery.

She gave me a copy of that photo which is now in a museum I helped create as a memorial to our greatest entertainer. It's based at Glasgow University, filled with mementos and souvenirs I took an active interest in collecting some time after he died.

I started collecting those treasures for a number of reasons, but primarily to ensure they were put in a place where they would be appreciated in the years to come by people who perhaps didn't know much about Lauder, but were keen to find out.

In 1966, when the sale of Lauder's effects was due to take place, I contacted the trustees, explained who I was and told them I had £5,000 to spend with the purpose of preserving Lauder's possessions for the nation. I asked if I could go to Lauder Ha' and point out the items I felt were most important.

They refused, and asked me to become just another gold-digger at the sale.

Their attitude, that profit was more important than preserving an important national heritage, caused me to almost burst with anger. I was so furious I decided to boycott the sale.

"They can take their greed and they can keep it," I told my staff at the Metropole.

The following Monday a woman who owned a cinema phoned the theatre to tell me how she had bought three giant oil paintings from Lauder Ha'—of Lauder, his wife Nancy and son John—for just £100 each. She was gloating at getting such a bargain.

When I told my friend Jack Radcliffe about this, he produced a Highland dirk and the small hunting knife called the sgian dubh. The dirk was inscribed: "To Jack Radcliffe from Sir Harry Lauder."

Jack said to me: "Here, son, you have these. You didn't get anything at the sale."

I swallowed my pride, and decided obtaining as many of

Lauder's possessions as possible for the country was more important than taking a principled stand against those greedy trustees. The sale was on for the best part of a week, so I asked two friends to go along the following day with just one instruction: "Buy, buy, buy."

"Buy what?" they said.

"Just buy."

And that's what they did. They returned the next evening with the upright piano he composed all his songs on, walking sticks, his make-up box, his mother's wee kettle that he had treasured. There was a cable to Sir Harry from King George V and Queen Mary, and I paid joint top price of £160 for a collection of orchestra music sheets and manuscripts by Sir Harry and his brother Alick. The boys bought a whole range of stuff; each one insignificant on its own perhaps but, together, a treasured insight into the life of a great man.

From that point on I collected as many of Lauder's possessions as I could, from wherever I could. Years later I was in a shop in Glasgow when I spotted the marble bust of Sir Harry that used to sit on a window ledge at Lauder Ha'. I remembered it from my visit there as a 17-year-old, and I bought it.

Another time a woman phoned to say she had seen a silver cigar box presented to Sir Harry in 1906 by a group of Manchester Scots.

"Great," I said. "Where did you see it?"

"In an antique shop in Eton," she said.

She had known of my interest and told the owner to write to me. I got a letter some time later addressed to Jimmy Logan, Glasgow.

I phoned him up, he described it and I bought it.

I collected Lauder's things from all sorts of places. The Boy Scouts even sent me an incredible secondhand book from South Africa documenting his tour there in 1922.

Over the years my collection got bigger and bigger until I

decided it really should be on public show somewhere for people to enjoy. In 1991 I contacted a friend, Lord Macfarlane, a man who has done a great deal for Scottish arts and culture, who arranged through the Macfarlane Charitable Trust for all 600 items to become part of a major display at Glasgow University.

If I had my way our memorial to Sir Harry would be far larger. It is, in my opinion, nothing short of a national scandal that there isn't a proper museum dedicated to his memory. In America they would put up a museum in George Washington's memory 200 miles from a spot where he once stopped to feed his horse. Here few people these days even know who Sir Harry was.

When Lauder Ha' came on the market I was fully committed at the Metropole, but I wanted to buy it and turn it into a national museum and hotel. I put my proposal to the bank who gave me an extraordinary answer:

"Look Mr Logan, you don't know this but very shortly there's a thing called the breathalyser coming out and when that happens there will be no more country hotels. They'll be finished because people won't be able to drink and drive."

I still have Sir Harry's piano in my front room, and I'm pleased many of his memories are there at Glasgow University for future generations to enjoy. History of anything is important, and a knowledge of the history of our theatre and the music hall is something that can only benefit people who bother to find out. A little insight into that teaches us a lot about the heritage of our country and people.

Harry Lauder and the music hall was entertainment of the punters. The majority of people never went to the theatre or the opera, relying instead on the great pleasure they derived from the music hall.

These days it is fair to say that pantomime is the last refuge of the music hall; all in one night you get song, dance, laughter, love, hatred, fear, good against evil. You can only talk properly about theatre today if you have already talked about theatre yesterday. And discussing the history of Scottish theatre would be pointless unless the history of the music hall was regarded as an integral part of it. The performances may have been fun and superficial but its effect on the society it existed within was significant.

Sir Harry Lauder was an integral part of that enjoyment. So were others like Will Fyffe, Harry Gordon and Dave Willis to name just a few. No man is immortal but each man I think is entitled to his place in history if he has occupied some place that is exceptional.

11

THE MAN THE GERMANS COULDN'T KILL

I was barraged with conflicting emotions when I toured abroad with *Lauder*. Visiting countries like South Africa, Australia and New Zealand was just wonderful. I met many interesting and exciting people, and stayed in magnificent hotels. There was no reason to complain.

On the flip side of the coin I was the loneliest man in the world. There were many good people around me but I felt alone. The people I really cared about weren't there; people like Gina.

In South Africa a friend told me if I was really in love with Gina it would take three years to get over her. At the time I thought he was a nut but three years later I realised he was dead right. Gina and I remained friends but it did take me an awfully long time to come to terms with the fact that we could no longer share the true bond that had once been so natural.

From months on that *Lauder* tour, used to staying in the nicest hotels, I had returned to Scotland and my settee bed in my father's front room. There's no getting away from the fact that life was miserable for a long period after that. The debts from the Metropole were still hanging over me, I was struggling to get over the loss of my wife and I had no home. Any work that came my way I tended to take because I had this seemingly never-ending string of bills to settle.

It's fair to say I was at my lowest ebb when a journalist from Scotland's biggest newspaper decided to stick the boot into me. For 99 per cent of my career I've had a great relationship with and great treatment from the press, but on the odd occasion they've given me a hard time.

The first time I suffered at the hand of lies was when I was a teenager playing the Metropole. I went to my first girlfriend Marion Dickie's house for a cup of tea but her mother was unusually edgy.

"Jimmy," she finally said. "How did you get home last Thursday night?"

And I said: "What do you mean?"

I wondered where this was going.

She said: "How did you get home from the Metropole?"

"I went home with my dad."

"In his car?"

"Yes, we go home every night in the car."

"You didn't take a tram?"

"No. That would be awkward. I would be quicker on the tube. Why do you ask?"

"Well, one of my friends was over the other day and told me she was so disappointed in Jimmy Logan."

"Why?"

"She said she saw you drunk on a tram last Thursday night with your make-up on and swearing like a trooper. I said there was no way that could be you, but she said she had known you and your family all her life and that the person she saw was definitely Jimmy Logan."

Marion's mother was visibly upset after accepting a blatant piece of fiction as fact. I was quite flabbergasted.

The worst example I've come across was a story in a newspaper throwing doubt on the circumstances surrounding the death of Sir Harry Lauder's son John during the 1914-18 War.

He was an officer in the Argyll and Sutherland Highlanders who was shot by a German sniper. Sir Harry received the terrible news on Hogmanay 1916.

Some time ago I was approached by a journalist on that newspaper who told me he wanted to do a general article about the Argyll and Sutherland Highlanders in which he would mention John Lauder. I spoke in great depth to the journalist about John's life before he returned to his office to write his story. When the paper came out I was absolutely disgusted.

His article painted a picture of John Lauder as some sort of barbarian or war criminal. It quoted two other soldiers who claimed he had been shot by his own men because they hated him. It said he had executed German prisoners whilst their hands were tied behind their backs, and had a habit of dancing a Highland Fling whenever a German trench was captured.

It is said you cannot malign the dead, and that is indeed the law. But there should be some rules in place to stop such scandalous rubbish as this being given credence in a reputable newspaper. Those who have knowledge of John Lauder, and how popular he was with his men, know that these claims are entirely bogus. There is a body of weighty evidence to back up the real story that he was killed by a sniper, yet that journalist and newspaper chose to destroy Lauder's name by printing the ridiculous claims of two men who possibly had some kind of agenda.

A short time later I was invited to dinner at the offices of the newspaper, and I used the occasion to take the editor to task. His excuse was that if he hadn't printed the story someone else would have. What kind of excuse was that?

I told him exactly what I thought: "It's obscene that we are sitting here at this lovely meal with this lovely hospitality and discussing whether a boy, who, to be very Victorian about it, laid down his life for his country, and whether someone who has been lying buried in France since 1916 was shot in the back, the arm, the neck, the leg is surely in the worst possible taste. I find it sad that we as Scots would ever dream of saying these things about John Lauder and, even worse, printing them."

I don't want to give the impression that my life has been spent having arguments or run-ins with the press because it hasn't. As I've said, most of my life consists of press reports I'm very proud of. One crit I particularly liked read: "There's one thing about Jimmy Logan—like it or not you'll always get your money's worth." I thought that was wonderful.

When I was at my lowest ebb in 1981 I did pantomime in Inverness, and we broke the box office record. I then went to do the wonderful play *Harvey*, at Perth Theatre, where the secret was always to get the audience to believe in the imaginary rabbit.

A pal came to see it with his wife and four kids. I saw him a few days later.

"How you getting on?" I said.

"How am I getting on?" he said, agitated. "We went to see your play with the kids the other night and they thought it was great. But every morning since when I've come down for breakfast there has been a place set for that bloody rabbit."

When I was appearing in *Harvey* I got a call from some people in London asking me to go to London as soon as I had finished to take up a role in a play *Gone With Hardy*, the story of Laurel and Hardy.

I was knackered, and didn't want to do it, but they phoned up every night pleading with me to accept. They were really desperate so I agreed.

There were obvious difficulties with agreeing to be in that play. Because it was the tiny Tricycle Theatre Company, they could only afford to pay £100 a week—a sum of money that just wasn't enough to keep anyone in London. So I depended on a couple of friends to put me up while I was there. Of course, the pay was poor but the play was great; we got excellent crits from all the London newspapers, and that's what counted. My earning capacity had obviously gone down in recent years but, believe it or not, I still gained great satisfaction from being part of a production that was good. No matter the circumstances, that always gives me a great buzz.

Then I got a call from Alex Scotland, a journalist on a big Scottish paper, who said he wanted to do a big feature on me. My feeling was that I was having a hard time in general, but business-wise things were looking up. After a very lean period, I had been in a wonderful pantomime that broke box office records in Inverness. That had been followed by two wonderful plays, and I had a few successes under my belt again. There would be no harm in doing an interview.

Alex arrived and we talked at great length in my dressing room. Then he came to Brighton where we had lunch. We talked and talked. Returning to London later in the day, we talked some more.

Unknown to me, however, Mr Scotland had another agenda. Behind my back he went to other artistes in the play, and said to them: "Jimmy Logan's done. That's why he is down here working for £100 a week. He can't get work in Scotland."

The following week his motives became clear. The newspaper ran a big article basically saying Jimmy Logan was finished. It left me spitting mad. Sure, I was having a difficult time but I had just had some great successes. Mr Scotland, however, set out to prove I was a disaster area. What annoyed me more than anything, though, was that I gather Mr Scotland didn't take the time to see the play.

I wrote to the organisation that dealt with complaints about the press before we toured Canada with *Gone With Hardy*. My secretary never sent the letter. I only wish she had.

That was one of the very rare occasions I had a run-in with the press.

After I lost the Metropole my secretary Heather Ewing and her husband Alex, who had shared all my ups and most of my downs, were absolutely fantastic. They stored bits and pieces of mine in their home in Glasgow, and another friend allowed me to put furniture from Culzean Castle into a big upstairs room at their house in Stirling. Such gestures of friendship provided the breathing space I needed to try and get myself sorted out.

Heather was part of the Campbell clan. When I took over the Metropole her grandmother Agnes was in charge of the box office, her mother Irene was the principal dancer in the show, and also co-producer and co-director. Her great grandmother had run the Campbell troupes of girls.

In Canada you can buy the famous MacDonald cigarettes. On the front of the packs is a beautiful Highland girl, and that Highland girl is Agnes Campbell when she was a world champion Highland dancer. It's ironic that a Campbell has been promoting those MacDonald cigarettes all these years.

Agnes would have been about 70 when I saw her dance at a New Year party. And it was truly mind-boggling. When a Highland dancer dances she jumps in the air and crosses one leg behind the other in a scissors movement. They usually jump, do two scissor cuts and land. I saw Agnes at 70 do three scissor cuts, and I had never seen that before. She danced as light as a feather. Irene danced, Heather danced and I had the privilege of seeing Agnes Campbell dance.

By 1978 the rut seemed deeper than ever. But I needed my own home. I had slept on my father's settee for two years, and it was driving me up the wall. Even though I had virtually no money because it was all going straight to the bank, I told Heather I really needed a house.

She was good enough to start looking around while I continued to work. One of the first houses she found that I went to look at just made me depressed. It was a part of a tenement in Glasgow, and no matter the time of day, always seemed to be cast in a shadow.

Then she told me to look at a house she had found in Hamilton Avenue in Pollokshields. It was a big house with three large bedrooms, a dining room, a beautiful big drawing room, a kitchen and another big room. It was truly beautiful.

But I don't know why she had asked me round because there was simply no way I could afford it.

"How much is it?" I asked her.

"£28,000."

"But Heather, you know I've not got that kind of money."

The previous owners had done what we in Glasgow refer to as a "moonlight flit", taking anything movable including the carpets. The kitchen had been ripped out, and even some of the fittings were missing. They had, however, been good enough to leave the underfelt behind.

Despite this dismal scene my curiosity got the better of me and we approached the bank that was selling.

A short time later I had done a deal to buy the house for £25,000. And I didn't have £25,000.

To be frank, given my financial position I was extremely lucky to get a mortgage. One of the reasons I stayed at my father's flat for so long was because, given my situation, no lender would have entertained me. But a few weeks earlier my lawyer had told me that one of his friends who authorised mortgages for that bank was just about to retire. And he had told my lawyer that if I could find a property quickly he would approve the mortgage before he left his job. Sometimes when people are in the kind of position I was in, a little bit of help goes a long way.

Without that kind of influence I would undoubtedly have got

nowhere, but when the house came up I got the mortgage by the skin of my teeth. My lawyer said we could borrow £5,000 from the bank as the deposit.

The night before he was due to complete the deal I went to my bed believing that finally, at long last, I was putting myself in a position to pull myself out of this terrible rut. But no sooner had I fallen asleep than I was awoken by a knock at the door.

My father appeared in the room with the lawyer.

I thought to myself: "If I just lie here with my eyes closed they'll just go into the kitchen."

But then the light went on, and suddenly I felt my father shaking me.

"Son, waken up, we've got a problem."

"What is it?"

"We've just got word that the bank is refusing to honour the £5,000 cheque for the deposit because they've found out who and what it is for."

I think the bank offering me the mortgage was a branch of the same bank I still owed stacks of money to for the theatre.

My dad then issued the ultimatum. No matter what, he said, the lawyer had to be at that bank the following morning at opening time with £5,000. I sat there hoping I would soon wake up—and it would all be a nightmare.

I said: "But I haven't got £5,000. If I was lucky and threw every penny I had in, without paying tax, I could maybe find £1,500."

My father looked at me for a second, rose to his feet and went to the upright piano. Lifting my clothes away, he removed the front from the underside of the keyboard and produced a tin box. Inside was a bundle of money.

He started putting notes onto the table. "Right, count that, and that, and that."

By the time we had finished counting there was £3,500 on the table. I wrote out a £1,500 cheque and the lawyer sat up all night finalising arrangements. When the doors of the bank opened the following morning he was standing there waiting with £5,000 in his briefcase.

From that moment I wasn't just paying back my debts on the Metropole, I was paying back my dad too.

But the important thing was that I once again had my own home. It had no furniture and no carpets but when I moved in I felt like I was back on my feet again. I used to have suites of glasses—and I mean suites—and now I had four wine glasses and two whisky glasses. I used my working desk as my dining table— with a nice white cloth and candlesticks on top it looked marvellous.

Gina sent up a big wagon with stuff from London but the house was so big it just disappeared when I moved everything in. For two years I lived with no carpets, just underfelt, until I sold a beautiful Steinway piano to buy new carpets. I eventually saved up enough money to get central heating installed and turned the extra big room into the kitchen. The original kitchen became a bathroom and I also built an office in another room.

Slowly but surely I was getting myself back on a level keel. But I was to find out again in the not too distant future that you can never be sure what's lurking round the next corner.

I owed a lot to my father on many occasions, not least when he dug into his life savings hidden away in that piano to get his middle-aged son out of a hole. We may have had our differences in life, our personalities may have clashed, but my relationship with my father, and my mother, was as close as any you will ever find between two parents and their child.

They were wonderful people who were always there for me when I needed them, and sometimes when I didn't. Like the occasion when my father decided to sue me.

Shortly after that episode, in 1955, when I was with Howard

& Wyndham in *Five Past Eight* and the pantomimes, my father and mother decided to hang up their showbusiness hats. They bought a hotel in Rhu outside Helensburgh, and called it Logan's Hotel.

In those days you couldn't drink late unless you had a late licence, and you had to have a good reason to get it. One year, out of the 365 possible days, my parents got 272 late licences. I think the local policeman was in a constant battle with my father trying to catch him out.

That hotel was full of many wonderful stories, some of them unrepeatable on these pages. One that can be told, however, concerned a pal of the family called Jimmy Bennett, who used to work in the Barras and had come down for a relaxing weekend at the hotel.

When he walked in on the Friday my dad took one look at him, and said: "Oh Jimmy. Am I glad to see you. I need some help in the bar."

Needless to say Jimmy ended up working Friday night, Saturday night and Sunday night. When I saw him late on Sunday evening he was leaning against a wall, his shirt soaked to the skin and sweat dripping onto the floor. He could hardly speak he was so out of breath.

"Jimmy," he said. "I'm *&?x!!!:;+!"

"What was that?" I said.

I think he said he was exhausted.

Jimmy wasn't too pleased on the Monday morning when my father gave him the bill for three nights' accommodation.

It was one of those hotels that was slightly mad, a Scottish Fawlty Towers shall we say. I'll never forget the faces on a young couple who had just seen a greyhound running through reception with a chicken in its mouth.

My brother Buddy was the manager. I got an urgent call from him one day asking me to come over. When I got there my father was crouched up in bed with massive pains in his chest. I got a heart specialist I knew to come and see him. He diagnosed an ulcer, and told my father he was bleeding internally.

They called an ambulance but it took all our efforts to get him in because he wanted to drive to hospital.

In the ambulance he said to me: "This is the first time I've been in one of these since 1919."

One day my mother took a heart attack. She was lying upstairs recovering in bed when she had one of those moments that said the ceiling needed done. And she got up and started painting the room.

I always go on about my father. My dad this and my dad that. But every now and again, some lady stops me and says: "Now wait a minute. What about your mother?"

My mother was lovely, in my eyes anyway. She may have dyed her hair blonde but when she was on stage she had that quality I'm sure all great comediennes would die for. In one sketch she could look absolutely stunning—as though she was going out for an evening at the Savoy Hotel—then the next sketch she would appear as a woman from the Steamie and have the audience in hysterics. Doris Droy had that same quality, and Una McLean still has it.

My memories of my mother centre round a Singer sewing-machine. She not only starred in all our family shows, she cooked the meals and made all the costumes for the girl dancers as well. That sewing-machine seemed to be on 24 hours a day.

She was the kind of woman for whom her family came first, with the theatre running a very close second. In the show if I cracked an ad-lib in the first house that got a big laugh, she would crack it in the second house and I was left trying to think of something else. She made sure our minds were going all the time, and wasn't above giving us a good thump if she thought we weren't doing things properly.

My mother had many other talents but one in particular stood out for me. She could make ribs like nobody else made ribs. When she made boiled ribs with carrots and onions the meat would just fall off the bone. One time I phoned her up when she couldn't walk very well, and said: "Ma, I'm having a party. I want to start off by giving them a taste of your special ribs."

"Oh away, rubbish."

"Yes I do."

A couple of hours later she came over with my father carrying two enormous plates of ribs. When I told her everyone thought they were wonderful she felt good. Once she cooked ribs in the theatre. The audience were all licking their lips throughout the show. Afterwards everyone was asking where they could get them.

She was the boss in the house but when we were touring with the family my father was most definitely the boss. If we asked Mum about something she would always say: "See yer father. He'll tell you what to do."

She always gave him his place and she always took his side. I will never forget one occasion when she came to me furious with all the bad and stupid things he had done. She was so angry she spent an age slagging him off.

I was so angry about her being so upset that the next time I saw my father, I said to him: "Hey, what did you say to my mother?"

And my mother, who was there, turned round and said: "Don't you dare talk to your father like that."

I couldn't believe it. I was only trying to help and I ended up getting a mouthful from both of them.

The thing about my mother was she could control my father, and he was virtually uncontrollable. She had an amazing ability to suddenly come out with vicious one-liners. Whenever my father started telling stories or gags my mother was brilliant. Her timing was perfect. She would keep topping his gags with one-liners until his side of the room went very quiet.

*   *   *

The chap who came to stay with us during the Second World War, Tom F. Moss, had a wife and daughter. She was a lovely little girl who at that time was about four years old. Recently Angela and I went to London to see my dear friend Lady Sassoon who was getting very old and frail.

"Meet me at Claridges," said Barnsey, the name we knew her by.

She had her favourite seat, and the staff there had known her for years. They always called her M'lady.

We arranged to meet at half past seven, but she didn't get there till nine o'clock.

"I'm running a little behind," she said.

By this time she had great difficulty walking but she was determined to maintain the same style she had enjoyed for years. Her favourite trick was to walk to the taxi holding her glass of champagne, and sometimes drive off still drinking it.

On this occasion I was starving, and wanted to eat at the hotel, but she wanted to go to her favourite club, Annabel's.

"Come on, finish this champagne, Barnsey, I'm starving," I said, when I was suddenly interrupted by an immaculate woman who had appeared beside me.

"Don't stop her drinking her champagne," said the lady.

"I'm not stopping her drinking her champagne. I want her to finish her champagne so I can take her for a meal and buy her more champagne."

"So how are you, Jimmy?" said this elegant lady changing tack.

"How do you know me?" I asked.

"Oh, I just do. And how are Buddy and Bertie?" She continued through my family.

I started to answer, then thought: "Wait a minute, I've never met you, yet you know all of my family. How?"

"Jimmy, I knew your mother and father very well. Your mother

291

was the most wonderful woman. I will never ever forget her. I first met her when I was four years old when my mother and I went to your house. Your mother put her arms round me and made me feel like one of the family. My father was Tom F. Moss."

I was quite stunned.

In the 1960s my mother's health deteriorated, and she spent much of the last few years of her life in hospital. One Hogmanay she was very ill but still managed to come downstairs in her dressing-gown. She checked that all the food was set on the table for anyone who came in to first foot. Then, using the stick she relied on to get around, she hobbled back up to her room, most likely to white-wash the ceiling.

I can remember another night when she was in her sixties she was waiting patiently for my father to come home from the thea-tre. At one point she went away quietly to put on lipstick, then came back into the living room and stood at the window for about half an hour waiting for him to appear. The moment he came in the door she shouted: "Where the hell have you been?"

I knew she was OK at that point. If she had been soft and gentle there would definitely have been something wrong.

My mother died in 1969, just a month after she celebrated her golden wedding anniversary with my father. By that time she had been in hospital for nearly three years. She had been confined to bed for much of that time.

My father managed to carry on after my mum passed away. I thought everything was all right with him until we opened our winter show at the Metropole. It went so well, and at the interval I found him in tears in his office.

When you see your father in that situation it gives you a real shake.

"What's wrong?" I said.

"This is the first show when she has not been here," he said.

And that brought the whole thing home to me. How much of a team they were, and how much he relied on her to succeed in his own life.

My father, though, was a strong man. He got on with his life for years afterwards but always remembered her fondly. He was always thinking of her. Whenever her name was mentioned you could see his eyes welling up, and when he saw a show, he often said: "Your mum would have been good in that."

I went round to my father's house one day.

He said: "Right, this is what I'm going to do. I'm going to sell the house, put the money in yours and come up and live with you."

I said: "Wait a minute."

As soon as I said that his eyes looked like a one-armed bandit spinning at full speed.

I said: "You've always been a man who has been independent. Do you not think it would be wise to close your house or rent it?"

"Rent it? I've never rented a house in my life."

"Well, if you closed your house you could come up to live with me, and if you didn't like it, you could go back down and live in your house. If I didn't like it, you could go back down. How can you be so sure you will like it?"

That was it. He wasn't going to come even if I pleaded with him.

Shortly afterwards he went off to join my sister Heather and her husband Nick Capaldi on a cruise ship where they were in charge of entertainment. They had a talent contest on the ship and my father did his act. Afterwards he collapsed with a heart attack. By all accounts he survived by the skin of his teeth.

I asked a friend of mine to meet him at the airport when he got back to London. She was told there was only one door from which he could emerge. Typically, my father found another door to come out of, missed my friend and made his own way back up to Scotland.

It was a tricky time for us. I got up at six o'clock one morning when he was staying with me to find him standing at the window in his bedroom looking out at rabbits in the garden.

He said to me: "Heather doesn't want me to live on my own."

That meant he wanted to come and live with me, but he didn't want to ask. I said that was fine.

"Can I have this room?" he said when he arrived.

"No, this is Annabelle's room," I said. "You can have the room next door."

"Can I have the same wallpaper?" he said when he got into the room next door.

"No, we'll find another wallpaper."

My father ended up living with me for four years. If I am brutally honest some of those times weren't easy. But that was the nature of our relationship.

For as long as he had been in the business he had always acted as front of house manager. Before the opening of one of my plays in Edinburgh, Heather Ewing managed to persuade him to come. The next day he complained the whole thing had taken too much out of him.

He said to me: "I can't do it any more."

I managed to persuade him to return to the fold when the tour arrived in Inverness. I had a little smile because the first thing he packed in his suitcase was his dinner suit, shirt, bow-tie, shoes and socks. After that he thought about what he would wear during the day.

Changing into that dinner suit, of course, had always been a big job for him. Lumping that artificial leg around all the time, he had to take the right leg, bend it back, get the shoe and sock off, and put another sock and shoe onto his artificial foot. Then he had to reposition the leg and make sure the belt round his waist, and strap over his shoulders, were firmly secured. It was a big job.

That night he stood at the front of house and never saw any of the three other theatre managers. He said to me later: "Jimmy, what kind of theatre is this?"

He thought if the other managers had known their job they would have been there.

That was his last night working in a theatre. He was a man in his eighties with one leg, who was very ill, yet he showed the lot of them up. He knew the business inside out, and they didn't know a thing about it.

Even at that stage he was determined to do the job as well as he always had done. The customer, the audience, was always of prime importance. He never forgot that, and he never let us forget it. The fact that there was no-one at the front of house that night to answer people's questions showed they had no idea of such a vital concept.

We had a good relationship, and it was a particularly warm and rich relationship during the last few years of his life. Of course we quarrelled; if we hadn't then something most definitely would have been wrong. I fought with my father, my family fought with my father, in fact come to think of it, everyone fought with my father. I'll always remember how he would give me hell when he thought something had gone wrong.

"Why didn't you tell me?" he would say.

"I didn't tell you because you could have done nothing about it and I didn't want to worry you," I would say.

"Well, next time tell me."

I always kept stocks of drink in a little open space in the lounge at the house in Hamilton Avenue. He swore he never touched those drinks, but if I was away on tour I would usually return to a house with not a drop of drink in it. Given he was the only one living there, I didn't have to be Inspector Clouseau to find my suspect.

"What's happened to all the drink?" I asked him on many occasions.

"I didn't touch it."

What he meant was that when he brought a crowd of friends to the house they got stuck in. But he always insisted he never touched it. However, I knew damn well he touched it. One night I rushed into the house with two bottles in a paper bag, put them down on the sideboard and rushed out to make it to Edinburgh in time for pantomime.

When I came back Aunt Jean, who was visiting, said to me: "Oh, your father has been through a terrible time while you were away."

"What happened?" I said.

"Oh, he took a drink and he almost poisoned himself. I had to give him jam for his throat."

"What drink did he take?"

Then my father, who was slumped on his chair looking decidedly poorly, looked up.

"I took a drink from the bottle in that paper bag on the sideboard," he said to me.

"But you told me you never drank anything I put out?"

"Don't give me that."

He didn't find that funny at all.

"Ah well," I said. "The beauty of what has happened, Dad, is that you took a drink of Goddard's Silver Dip so you'll now be shining inside as well as out."

He had drunk a glass of a substance used as a polish for silver, and this fact had me in hysterics for the rest of the night. It was a wonderful way for him to be finally caught red-handed.

A few months before he died, when he wasn't feeling at all well, he suddenly said to me: "Son, I'd love to have a bath."

Of course, he was unable to bathe himself so I got a bath ready, wheeled him into the bathroom on a chair and helped him into the water. Then I bathed him, helped him back out, dried him, put his pyjamas on and placed fresh sheets on his bed. Then I did the most nerve-racking thing I have ever done—I cut his hair.

When I got him into bed he said something I would never have expected, and something that will remain with me for as long as I live. He grabbed hold of me, and said: "Thanks for all you've done, son. You've given me another ten years on my life."

Being Scottish I instantly replied: "Och, away and don't be daft."

But he was deadly serious. "No, son, I want you to know. It's important."

It's a conversation I will always treasure. We told each other what we meant to each other, and I'm so glad we were able to do that. When he died a few weeks later I thought: "Thank the Lord we had that conversation."

A great friend of mine, Walter Carr, sadly died recently. Shortly beforehand I wrote him a letter expressing my appreciation for all the years we worked together and I told him I thought he possessed the generosity of nature that I believe is vital if anyone is going to make it in our business. I've known many big stars who didn't have that quality; the kind of people who would say: "I'm the one who gets the laughs here. You just stand at the back."

But Walter, and many others I have known, weren't like that. They possessed that generosity of spirit in spades.

He wrote back to me before he died expressing his gratitude for my letter. I think it meant a lot to him, and my experience with my father certainly taught me a very valuable lesson: that people should always come out with their feelings before it is too late.

Too often folk are unable to express their true feelings. It's in the Scottish nature to keep those feelings bottled up inside them until it's too late. And that is always a source of enormous regret for so many people.

Many people, I feel, don't treasure their parents enough. They drop in when it suits them when they should really be showing their gratitude in every possible way for what those parents have done to make their children what they are.

I may have been my father's third son but he would discuss things with me—in business particularly—before he would discuss it with the others. He didn't often ask for advice but on the rare occasions something worried him he would come to me and we would share the problem.

I think he did that because he knew my character best—a character, I suppose, which was like his in many ways. I believe, for instance, that I inherited a lot of his grit and determination— qualities that came to the fore at those times when I was down and feeling like hell. I think I also inherited some of the determination of a man who came out of that terrible War with one leg but still succeeded in the world of showbusiness. Through many difficult times he always picked himself up, dusted himself down and moved on.

I would never have said it to him when he was alive, but my father was without doubt one of my heroes. The more I thought about him after he had gone, the more I appreciated and admired the qualities of a man who was a true survivor in life.

One of the things he never achieved, though, was what I call inner contentment. My father when he was alive was never at peace with himself. Part of the reason for that was because it wasn't in his nature; he was a bit like me in the sense that he always wanted to achieve more than he already had done. He was never happy with his lot. Another reason was that in his life he never quite earned enough money to make him feel financially secure. Even if he finished one summer season with a decent profit he immediately started worrying about the prospects for the next show.

My father passed away in 1982, when I was in pantomime with Terry Scott at the King's Theatre in Edinburgh. It was a terrible time. I went to the theatre the next day, called in the stage director and said: "Now, I'll be all right as long as nobody comes up and says: 'I'm sorry.' If anyone says that I'm finished. Please let people know."

The resulting performance felt strange, and there were some moments I thought I wouldn't be able to continue. Little phrases made me think of him, and waves of grief kept flowing over me. At one point when I was singing a number with Una McLean I genuinely felt I was going to break down. All I can remember was holding on to her hand as tightly as I could.

Off stage I had the support of my friends like Noreen and David Kinnaird, and at the funeral the minister, Jimmy Currie from Dunlop, gave a beautiful service. We went to the crematorium, and it was so busy people had to stand in the aisles, including my dear friend Reo Stakis. My eyes welled up with pride when I looked at this scene. I thought to myself: "Yeah, it's standing room only. Dad would have been pleased."

Some people may be surprised that I continued to perform in pantomime at that time, and that's fair enough. However, in our business the show must go on. It may be a well worn, clichéd and somewhat sentimental phrase, but I believe in its every word.

To give some examples of what I mean, Annie wasn't at my father's funeral. When I told her he had died she was in an American airport about to board a plane for Los Angeles.

"I'll get the next flight to Scotland," she said.

"Wait a minute, Annie," I said. "Is your trip to LA for a possible job? Is it important?"

"Well, yes, Jimmy, but . . ."

"No buts," I said. "You get on that flight and go to LA because Dad would be angry if you missed out on that job just because of him."

In a family to whom the theatre was everything, that's how we proceeded. It was how we were brought up, and how we were expected to act. The important thing was that Annie was willing to fly back from America just to be there. And that is what would have mattered to my father.

My brother Buddy retired in his later years to live in England. When he died I was in a show at the King's Theatre in Edinburgh. I wanted desperately to go to the funeral but I just knew I couldn't. The show would have been cancelled, and that wasn't an option. I would have been letting down the rest of the people involved in the show, and most importantly I would have been letting down the people who had bought tickets to come and see it. I didn't go to the funeral, and I know Buddy would have understood.

In October 1969 I was down at Tito's Club in Cardiff touring in cabaret. I was doing it to find out if I was any good at cabaret, and took my friend Hector Nicol, a wonderful comedian, with me to see if he could write any stuff while I was there.

One afternoon I was sitting watching a film at a local cinema when I felt a tap on the shoulder.

It was one of the staff. "Mr Logan, you're wanted outside."

Hector was standing in the foyer. He looked as white as a sheet.

"Jimmy, your mother has died."

I almost collapsed, and again like all situations when someone so close dies, it was an absolutely horrendous time.

But I stayed in Cardiff because I had a responsibility to the show and the punters who had paid their money. I did the cabaret that night, and again the following night. Straight after that show I got a train to London, and then caught the first shuttle flight up to Glasgow.

I went to my mother's funeral, flew back to London straight afterwards and got the train to Cardiff just in time for the show that night.

Most people don't understand this "show must go on" idea. When I try to explain it people tend to think I'm on some sort of ego trip. That really couldn't be further from the truth.

In the old days your contract said: "No play, no pay." You just couldn't afford to be off for a few nights. If the show closed what was to happen to everyone else who was depending on the star of the show for their week's wages?

They make the show work just as much as the star. At the start of rehearsals there are only blank sheets of paper. Then everyone works their socks off to make sure the show is successful. It is essential to have that great team spirit.

Occasionally there will be one artiste who is only interested in himself or herself, but that is an exception to the rule. In theatre there is a contract between the punters, the owners, the managers and the artistes. If one of them pulls out it affects everyone. That is what is meant by "the show must go on".

My mother knew that as well as anyone—she would have told me to get back to Cardiff straight after her funeral. If coming to her funeral meant having to cancel the show, she would have told me not to come to the funeral.

Those were the principles of my parents, and those are my principles. Every performer has to make their own choice and live with it. I can understand why people would walk away from the show in terrible situations like that.

But the week my father died I actually played to the most people I ever played to in that theatre. I got the returns on the Saturday night, went home to the house, put all the returns with the figures on his bed, and said: "Go on, Dad. Have a good look at that." I left the lights on in his room that night.

That's what counted for my family. People will say it's senti-mental rubbish but I don't care.

I know my mother, father and Buddy would have understood. If they had been in my situation they would have acted in exactly the same way.

Perhaps the most extreme example of our family's attitude to-wards the theatre, and the importance in our lives it played, was with my younger sister Annie. She was only four when she was left by my parents in America to be brought up by her aunt Ella Logan.

The idea of a mum and dad leaving their oldest daughter in a foreign country is difficult for most people to understand. It was certainly difficult for Annie to understand, and undoubtedly contributed to the often traumatic life she has since led.

When Annie was left with Ella in the late 1930s people had different attitudes towards things. Hollywood was looking for a new Shirley Temple and Metro-Goldwyn-Mayer, who offered her the contract to appear in the *Our Gang* films, thought she was it. My father felt Annie was being handed the opportunity to become a big star of showbusiness, and in his view that shouldn't be missed for anything. My mother would have stayed with her in the States, but she was the star of the show back in Scotland. Without her there would be no way of feeding the family there. So my mother and father returned to Scotland minus a daughter who was directed into a new life in a new place. Then the Second World War intervened too.

Annie went to school with future stars like Elizabeth Taylor and Jack Jones, but my first memory of her is that of a 17-year-old girl with flaming red hair stepping off a plane at Prestwick Airport. Ever since that moment we have formed an extraordinarily close brother-sister relationship, and I'm sure our bond is partly due to the fact we were brought up so far apart.

As Annie grew older, so did her resentment of my father for the decision he made to leave her in America when she was such a small child. It's not hard to imagine why Annie would grow up thinking her real parents didn't love her, and we've spent many, many hours talking over all the issues. In those discussions I've tried to impress upon Annie that no matter how misguided my father's actions may have seemed, he was doing what he thought was best for her; he did it because he loved her as his daughter and wanted to do everything in his power to get what was best for her—and the best didn't come much better than an opportunity to get into American movies.

Coming to terms with or even understanding those motives was impossible for a youngster who grew up resenting her parents for what they had done. Consequently, her relationship with her "adopted" mother Ella Logan was also a tortured one—particularly as Ella was a big star who lived within the somewhat unreal world of American film and theatre.

During the Second World War, when I was a teenager playing the giant in *Jack and the Beanstalk* at the Gateway Theatre in Leith, Ella was flown to Britain to entertain the American Forces. She visited me, and announced: "I'm going to take you to London and introduce you to Val Parnell."

Now Val Parnell was one of the biggest theatre owners in Britain. If we weren't quite talking about God, we were certainly talking about God's assistant.

We went down to London on the overnight sleeper, and when we got to the Savoy Hotel the man behind reception said: "I'm sorry, madam, we don't have a room."

Ella was nonplussed. "Who is here who is American?" she asked.

"Senator Claude Pepper, madam."

Senator Claude Pepper, of course, was only President Roosevelt's personal envoy to Stalin in Moscow.

And so Ella phoned him up: "Come on up, Ella," he said, and immediately offered her the vast suite he was staying in that the British Government had provided.

We then sat down for breakfast—an experience, quite frankly, I couldn't possibly forget.

We were in the middle of a world war and Pepper was sitting there talking away about Stalin. As we ate, he got a phone call. It was Ernest Bevin.

Meanwhile, sitting at his table was this gangly 16-year-old eejit who was eating a kipper, and trying like nobody's business to get the bones out of his mouth. And the kipper was lovely. Of course, I was dying for another but I didn't have the courage to ask.

Then we went along to meet Val Parnell, this god of the theatre world. Ella had taken me along because she thought it would be good experience for me. I was wearing a borrowed suit, but I never uttered a word when I met him. I was too nervous.

All in all, it was a quite unbelievable day.

I admired Ella Logan enormously as an artiste. She reached the peak of her profession in America because she was brilliant. However, there was another side to her. And that other side was Ella Logan, the person.

On one occasion in the middle of an American tour I went to her beautiful big house off Sunset Boulevard in Los Angeles. It was enormous—it had an outside swimming pool and a big guest house past the trees to the rear of the grounds.

Ella started talking about Annie, who had run away from Ella's home when she was sixteen.

That day, as we sat in the garden, Ella was like an artist painting a very detailed, convincing picture. She told me she had been out with the police in a patrol car, a pursuit she regularly enjoyed.

She said to me: "Jimmy, they suddenly got a message from headquarters and said they were taking me back home. I said I wanted to go but they said I couldn't because they had just got a call concerning Annabelle. D'you know what they told me, Jimmy?"

"What did they say, Ella?"

"They said to me that I didn't want to go to this house because she was living there with another girl, and the house was full of drugs and alcohol."

"Oh, right," I said, but without looking shocked or surprised, and without offering any opinion.

Ella continued on, painting a picture that Annabelle had a very,

very bad reputation. And I could see she was waiting for a reaction.

She went on: "And lots of men go up to that house—sailors, blacks, latins, all kinds of horrible people."

The longer this tale went on, the sadder and sadder, and more lurid, it got.

I finally said: "I see. And it was Annie?"

"Yes. It was," Ella replied, looking sadly towards the ground.

"When did this happen, Ella?"

"Two months ago."

"You're sure of that?"

"Oh yes," she said.

I said: "Two months ago. That's very interesting. I haven't had a chance to tell you yet, but for the past six months Annie has been with me in Scotland."

Her face dropped. It was a lie that became all the more elaborate and dramatic as she told it.

It's funny how some people are. Ella Logan was brilliant in many ways but she was used to dominating the scene. She meddled as the years went past.

All of these strains took their effect on Annie. In the Sixties, when I rented my house out to Dickie Henderson during his stint on *Five Past Eight*, I got word that she had taken ill while touring with Count Basie in Berlin.

When she got back to Britain she looked absolutely terrible. She was exhausted from overwork, so we admitted her to an exclusive nursing home in London where she would get a chance to relax and recuperate.

At the time I was leading a bit of a nomadic existence myself. I had signed an agreement with Dickie on the basis I would be away touring for 20 weeks over the summer. But that was at the time I suddenly realised audiences outside Glasgow and Edinburgh weren't so keen on Jimmy Logan's show, and much of the tour fell through.

I found myself with nowhere to live, so I rented the beautiful house in Fintry, north of Glasgow, which is where I brought Annie to help her recover. Annie stayed with me for a substantial period of time and I helped her to find the road on which she travelled to get her life back.

In a family who were all talented, she has always been the most creative and unique member. Her reputation today is truly international, and I'm proud just to be her brother. We have a strong relationship which is based on a mixture of love and admiration for each other.

The same can be said of my relationship with my youngest sister Heather, who is very much like our mother.

Like my mother, Heather is very creative. When she was in the family show she was a wonderful singer with a good style, and she was really good at comedy. She met her husband Nick Capaldi in our show. He was a fantastic accordion player who got his eyes on Heather when she was about 17, and the next minute they were getting married.

I can't say my father or mother were very pleased, but Nick is a wonderful man who has been a wonderful husband.

Nick is a Scottish-Italian whose father owned a beautiful cafe called the Golden Arrow in the High Street in Ayr. He didn't want his son to leave the family business for the stage, but Nick was determined.

One week the local critic gave him a wonderful review for his rendition of 'Tea For Two' on the accordion, and Nick was so thrilled he showed that review to his dad.

"Look Dad," he said. "It says my rendition of 'Tea For Two' was brilliant."

His old Italian father was not impressed. "It should be 'Tea For Two and Coffee For Four' up at the High Street," he said.

Nick and Heather emigrated to America where they worked together for quite a time before sending for their young son

Domenick. I remember watching that wee lad at Prestwick, all four feet nothing of him, standing next to an air hostess who was about six feet tall. And she was taking him away to America to see the Cowboys and Indians.

The family settled down in Florida where Nick and Heather had a wonderful act in the showbars in the big hotels. By this time Heather was doing impressions, singing songs and playing all sorts of instruments. They could go on and do two full hours, have a break, do another two hours, have another break and do another two hours all of different material. They were quite incredible.

After their son joined them they went to entertain on cruise liners, and Nick became the director of entertainment on some of those big liners.

Heather is also tremendously talented on the creative side of things. What started for her as a pottery hobby blossomed into a thriving business making beautiful and unusual teapots. She turns her hand to everything.

Their son is a marvellous musician who can orchestrate for a 30-piece orchestra. He worked with his parents for many years before deciding to go off on his own. Soon afterwards Liberace's manager saw him some place and took him up to work for about three years with Liberace.

He married firstly Charlene Tilton, the actress from the TV series *Dallas*. We met her a few times, and she was very nice. Of course I wasn't married to her.

I was fascinated by the way her mood and body movements changed with her hairstyle. If she had a Spanish hairstyle she took on the persona of a latin. It was quite amazing. I saw her in *Who's Afraid of Virginia Woolf?* at Guildford. I must say I was not prepared to be impressed, but I was. She is a fine actress.

After Domenick and Charlene were divorced he carried on entertaining in various ways. On a ship where he was lead entertainer he met Leigh Zimmerman, a stunning girl who is six feet tall with legs that reach up to the stars. They fell in love, and she became his second wife.

Leigh was one of the leads in the *Will Rogers Follies*, a big musical that had been on Broadway and toured America. She is now back on Broadway in another great musical, *Chicago*.

Recently my wife Angela and I had the thrill of going with them to The Music Box Theatre, Irving Berlin's old theatre, to see Domenick as the narrator in *Blood Brothers*, and then we saw Leigh in *Chicago*.

Heather, Nick, Domenick and Leigh are a wonderful and talented family. And Heather is a kind, warm-hearted human being who reminds me more than anyone else of my mother.

Of all my brothers and sisters, I was least close to Buddy, primarily because he was away all the time. The oldest of the five, he appeared in an act with my mother and father, and they were called Jack, May and Buddy. When the Second World War broke out, he was sent by the RAF to train in Canada, but kept up his stage work and reappeared after his discharge to sing with the 22-piece orchestras of the time featuring such big names as Henry Hall, Geraldo and Lew Stone.

Eventually, Buddy joined up with us again in the Logan Family, then did all manner of things including a stint in charge of the sound at the Mitchell Theatre in Glasgow.

He had acquired an interest in photography, and built up a wonderful collection of his own photographs during those tours with my mother and father. Eventually he ran his own camera shop in Glasgow before retiring to England to be near his grandchildren. Of all things he even became a ringmaster with Roberts Brothers Circus and when I went down to visit I found my nieces getting up on trapeze and doing other tricks. I couldn't believe what I was seeing.

After surviving a couple of heart attacks Buddy died. He had a good life and made many friends where he lived . . . as a packed church for his memorial service showed.

I was a lot closer to Bert. He was always compared unfavourably to Buddy, who was better-looking and a better singer. Bert fought against that with humour. When he was in the family show he decided to learn to play the xylophone, and I don't think he'll mind me saying that I always thought he was the world's worst xylophone player.

One night, unknown to him, we tied string to that xylophone, and halfway through his act the xylophone mysteriously began to move off stage while a frantic Bertie continued to play. It was hysterical.

On another occasion Bert was talking to Mark Denison, the wonderful old comedian who appeared at the Metropole.

Bert said: "Last Wednesday I accidentally threw my right hand xylophone stick away but carried on playing with the left hand stick. You should have heard the applause."

And Mark said to him: "If you had thrown both sticks away you would have got double the applause."

At the Metropole we had what were called front of house gags. I, for instance, would appear in one of the theatre boxes and do a routine with my mother or father who were on stage. But Mark Denison was barred from any of those sketches because he tended, when the sketch was over, to drift off to the nearest pub.

My father attempted to get round this by telling the stage door keeper: "No artiste is allowed to leave this theatre during the performance without my permission." And the stage door keeper said to him: "The only one who leaves at the interval is the violinist."

My father was suspicious because he knew Mark would go to any lengths to get to the pub. Sure enough, when the violinist appeared at the interval it was Mark wearing a false moustache, a borrowed hat and carrying a violin case under his arm.

Bert was tremendously popular with people as an individual. He emigrated to New Jersey in America, got married and things went up and down for him. Eventually he was divorced.

He started selling advertising which he was good at because he had a sense of humour, and could chat people up.

Bert was also mad on golf, and always blamed the clubs for his bad play. So I went out and bought him a matching set of Auchterlonie golf clubs that should have been put on a wall as objects of beauty, and never let near a golf course.

The next time I saw Bert I asked him: "How's your golf?"

And I got the same answer. "It's terrible, it's rotten."

It didn't matter what clubs he played with.

Bert underwent heart surgery in the early Seventies, but even after the surgery he was never seen without a cigarette in his mouth. One Friday evening my sister Heather phoned from New Jersey.

She said: "I'm with Bert in hospital and he is not well. He is really not well."

I understood what she was saying, and spoke to Bert. I could tell by his shortage of breath and the weakness in his voice that it was serious. That night I couldn't sleep. At five o'clock the next morning I said to myself: "I can't say goodbye to my brother on a telephone."

I went down to Prestwick Airport and booked myself onto the first flight to New York. By seven o'clock that evening I was sitting at the side of his hospital bed.

Heather had been sleeping on a chair in his room for a week, and she was clearly exhausted. So I took over. Officially, we weren't supposed to be there sleeping overnight, but I said to one of the nurses: "I'm sorry but we're a bit like the Arabs in our family. If one is ill we arrive bringing everything but the sheep."

Not long afterwards Annie flew in from Los Angeles.

The nurse looked at me, and replied: "Mr Logan, so many people in this hospital die without relatives or friends near them, so it's a great pleasure for us to see a family who care."

Bert wasn't supposed to smoke in his room but there was a designated smoking area. At three o'clock one morning he woke up asking to have a cigarette. I helped him out to the smoking room. By that time it obviously made no difference to his health.

After he had managed just a few puffs, Bert said: "I don't know what's wrong with me."

And I looked at my lovely brother and burst out laughing.

I said: "You haven't the strength to smoke the cigarette and you don't know what's wrong with you?"

But Bert had a lovely sense of humour, and saw what I was getting at. We laughed together.

At the end of the week I had to come home so Heather took over again. Remarkably, after a time, Bert recovered to such an extent that Heather got him on a flight back to her home in Florida.

He collapsed with another heart attack before the plane touched down, and an ambulance was waiting on the tarmac to take him to hospital when they landed.

But in his inimitable stubborn style, Bert took one look at the emergency crew and announced: "I'm not going with them. I'm going home with Heather."

And he went home with Heather. Eventually after a week he was taken into intensive care in the hospital but fought through again, and with the care of Heather and Nick, built himself up to the extent that he was able to return to his home in New Jersey nine months later.

He had decided to spend the cold winter with our cousins in North Carolina, and was in the travel agent booking his ticket, with a cigarette in his mouth, when he collapsed and died.

Bert left his body to medical science. It was two years before I saw him again—when a parcel containing his ashes arrived while I was at Heather's home in Florida.

I took Bert home with me but somehow managed to lose him at Heathrow Airport. He finally turned up at the lost property office and I brought him back to Scotland.

Bert wanted his ashes scattered on Scottish waters, and I did say to someone at the time that I wanted to hire a boat to enable me to grant his last wish. But somehow life intervened. I just haven't got round to it yet. Perhaps it's a reluctance to say a final goodbye.

The best way to sum up my family is to say it was like having an audition; everybody else was hoping to get the job.

It's a tradition I'm confident will be continued. I have stood at the side of the stage of the London Palladium, a stage I first worked on in 1955, and watched my enormously talented nephew Domenick give a wonderful performance.

Buddy's son John has for the past few years been the manager of the Churchill Theatre in Bromley. And their love for the theatre will ensure that our family history is passed on to future generations.

12

THINGS AIN'T WHAT THEY
USED TO BE

My own family have always lived for the theatre, but it is through the theatre that I have developed an enormous affection for another bunch of relatives you may have heard of—the Royal Family. I believe they work damned hard at portraying a wonderful image for our nation at home and abroad.

In one TV programme on the BBC two "comedians", in one of their sketches, urinated on the Queen's head. To claim, as they did, that they were justified because the BBC had renewed their contract, and had given them a series in the first place, was unforgivable. In reality, their actions not only said everything about them and the sad state of the BBC in the Nineties, but also summed up what is wrong with people today.

Had they been told to urinate on their own mother's head they might have thought twice about it.

Whatever they thought of the Queen was unimportant. What was important was that they showed her no respect whatsoever. And that was utterly wrong.

I have great admiration for people who do their jobs well, whatever their jobs are. In this book I have spoken at varying lengths about people I admire, mainly in my own business, who

313

all have one thing in common; they do their jobs well.

The same can be said of the Queen, and for that reason I hold her in the highest regard. I realise that's an opinion that may not be so popular these days, but I will always hold it. And the reason I will always hold it is because I have been around long enough, and lived through enough experiences, to appreciate the value of the Royal Family in our nation.

Too many people complain they do absolutely nothing. Those people should get their eyes checked. I watch what they are doing a little more closely, and rarely a moment goes by when they are not working. I admire people who do any job, and do it well. Every time a member of the Royal Family walks into the public spotlight they are doing a job, and nobody does that job better than the Queen. Nobody.

There is a picture in this book of a great friend of mine, Commander Edward Perkins, who was the Queen's personal bodyguard for at least 15 years. He had been bodyguard to her father the King through the Second World War, and then when the King died, became the bodyguard to the young Queen. I struck up a great friendship with him after we were introduced by my friend Chief Constable Willie Merrilees.

The photograph was taken at the time of Commander Perkins' retirement when the Queen encouraged the assembled press corps to take a picture of the man they were normally supposed to steer well clear of, and most certainly not photograph.

Afterwards the Queen invited Commander Perkins to Buckingham Palace in order to say an official goodbye. He arrived in the car with his wife.

"Just wait here," he told her. "I'll be back in a minute."

The Queen's officials had advised her to award Commander Perkins the Queen's Police Medal—one of the highest decorations a policeman can receive. But when he went in to say goodbye to all the family, she said: "Kneel."

He had arrived at the Palace as Commander Edward Perkins, but left as Sir Edward Perkins.

When he returned to his car, his wife asked: "Well Edward, what did you get? A watch?"

"They dubbed me," he replied.

"Don't be so bloody stupid Edward," she said, thinking he was joking.

"I'm afraid it's true. You are now Lady Perkins."

From that point on, Sir Edward was a regular guest of the Queen and the Royal Family. In fact, his wife once said to me: "My husband has all his life been in love with two women. I just happened to be one of them. And the other one was the Queen."

I regard myself as an alternative comedian; an alternative to the comedians who thrive on the type of material you would expect to hear in a public lavatory, but not on the stage or television screen going into millions of family homes.

And I speak on behalf of a large majority of greyhairs who are not only sick and tired of the violence, the subjects and the language used in theatres and on television, but the so-called values in society today.

Some of us over 25 find some things hard to understand these days.

For instance, if the Royals are so unpopular why can we in the theatre raise so much more money for charity if it is announced that one of the Royal Family is attending? If marriage is as unpopular as people tell us why, if your daughter is getting married, is it so difficult to book a hotel? Why, at a time when elderly people are so sick and tired of violence in our society, does the law sometimes not seem to be harsh enough on those who perpetrate these appalling crimes? Why is it that when a 13-year-old girl has twins, newspapers seem to celebrate the fact with big colour spreads and quotes from her 13-year-old boyfriend telling everyone how

315

delighted he is, and how much he wants to raise the children? The girl is thrilled to see her picture in the papers while the boy won't have to pay out a penny in support. She will also be able to get a house and £1,000 to furnish it, and the taxpayer will pay the coal, gas and electricity.

We greyhairs are worried by the fact that Britain has the largest number of illegitimate babies born to under-age teenagers in Europe. When I visited Kiev in the Ukraine I asked how big the problems were with graffiti and the destruction of property, and the answer I was given was: "It's not so much of a problem, Mr Logan, because our prisons are so bad nobody wants to be caught."

When I asked about young girls getting pregnant, I was told: "There isn't really a problem because if she does get pregnant she gets no help from the State, no money and no free house."

Many politicians argue that girls don't get pregnant to get free houses and a government grant. Their answer, it seems to me, is to put more psychologists in the schools. They might say I'm naive but I don't think it will work. All I can say is that we live in a different world.

For me it's a wonderful world we live in, but these days it is also a crazy world. I'm old-fashioned in the sense that I preferred the gentler world we once had.

When I say I'm alternative, I mean that my alternative is for there to be more common sense, more justice and more understanding of the greyhairs who are finding life these days very difficult.

Through a number of Royal Performances I've organised or been involved with, I've seen at first hand the excellent work the Royals do. When I was married to Gina I organised a ball in Glasgow to be attended by Princess Margaret for the children's charity Barnardo's.

On the day itself, a woman who did a great deal of work for Barnardo's, Emma Cochrane, said to me with some embarrassment:

"Jimmy, I don't quite know what to say but you've not been put on the top table even though you organised it all. I'm terribly sorry."

"Don't worry," I said. "I've got quite a lot of friends coming and I'd rather be on their table so I can look after them."

After the meal, someone said to me: "For God's sake go to the Royal table, Jimmy, because if that guest on her right tells her once more about the new sewage works I think she'll explode."

So I went over to the head table, and I'm happy to say she looked quite delighted to see me. We had met before, and she tapped the seat beside her.

"How are you?" she said, gesturing for me to sit down.

I usually have a technique where I say: "Ma'am, would you care to dance or would you like another coffee?"

It gives them the choice. And she said: "Oh, I'd love to dance."

We had quite a conversation afterwards, and she showed a very knowledgeable and human side to her nature. At the end of the evening she said she was ready to leave. I asked if she could wait a moment while I organised some music.

We played 'Auld Lang Syne' and 'Will Ye No Come Back Again'.

"Oh, am I supposed to cry?" she asked.

I said to her: "Well, of course you are, even a wee bit would help."

We both laughed, and everyone bid her a fond farewell.

When I was married to Gina we were invited by our friend Lady Sassoon to her house in Dallas, Texas.

It was a place where the swimming pool started inside the house but, when a glass wall opened up, ran out into an open pond in the garden that could be crossed by a little bridge. A simple little house you might say.

Our visit was part of the export drive, and Neiman Marcus, one of the top stores in America, was holding a "British week" in which quality goods from across the Atlantic were being promoted, including The Gina Fratini Collection.

Neiman Marcus is the kind of store that sells "his and hers" submarines, and where you might see an item costing $55,000 sitting next to something at $12—the American version of Harrods.

On the opening night of "British week" Lord Mountbatten was guest of honour at a special dinner on the top floor of the store.

During the War Gina's father had been in charge of all the rice supplies to India, and this was known to Lord Mountbatten who came twice to see her fashion collection which was compèred by the Big Boss Mr Marcus himself. Rather like Al Fayed appearing at a microphone in Harrods to sell a special product, Mr Marcus and his son regarded it as a personal privilege to look after each customer.

Lady Sassoon also gave a party at her beautiful home for Lord Mountbatten.

In tribute to my Scottish heritage, I was played in by four pipers standing on the main staircase which rose up on either side of the hallway. Not a bad entrance, I must say.

When Lord Mountbatten spoke—both at the Neiman Marcus dinner and the party—there was a measured tone of authority and knowledge in his voice. We were aware that we were listening to a statesman who had great experience of life and was a major player on the world stage.

Lady Sassoon asked me to give him her late husband's best brandy and cigars.

I said to him: "Before you say no, the brandy is 1902 and the cigars are of the same quality." He was no fool, he took both.

Later, I sat at the piano and sang some old Scottish songs that went very well. After I finished an American lady sat down and sang sweetly, but Lord Mountbatten's famous designer son-in-law David Hicks drew me aside, and said: "Get her off the piano and go back there yourself. He's getting bored."

I said: "I can't do that because when we leave here she has to live here. It wouldn't be polite."

I wasn't going to be hassled by anyone. If you have dealt with a second house on a Saturday at the old Metropole then no-one is going to boss you around.

The husband of one American guest flew in on his private jet, and called up before he landed but his wife refused to speak to him. Nobody would speak to him. There was no way they were going to leave Lord Mountbatten's company for one minute.

When I heard of Lord Mountbatten's death I did not think of him as a world leader or the commander in Asia. I just saw the elderly grandfather with the kind eyes who, having done his best, should have been left to pass away his last few years watching his grandchildren growing up enjoying life. What a waste.

The most wonderful member of the Royal Family is the Queen Mother. She is at the heart of our nation, part of its very fabric. I saw the way she lifted people's hearts when she and her husband King George VI stayed in London while the bombs were going off during the Second World War.

In Copenhagen, the King of Denmark displayed similar loyalty when the Germans invaded his homeland. He could have scurried off elsewhere but chose to stay behind to give his people something to believe in. Every day he appeared from his palace on horseback, rode round the city, and gave his citizens hope. When the Nazis ordered all Jews to wear a yellow star he rode round the city the following day with a yellow star emblazoned on his jacket.

Like him, our King and his wife, who is now the Queen Mother, were also an inspiration in those difficult times. These days she's not appreciated the way she should be, but when I did my first Royal Performance in 1953 the whole nation loved her with its heart.

It was while I was touring in a show with my father and mother that I got an invitation to perform for the Queen Mother and Princess Margaret at Wemyss Castle in Fife—the castle where Mary Queen of Scots met Lord Darnley for the first time. The letter was from Captain Wemyss, the head of a distinguished family who were hereditary high admirals of the Scottish fleet. On the roof of the castle there was still a gun that would have been fired centuries before to warn of a Dutch attack.

Lady Victoria Wemyss, who lived to be 104, was a wonderful lady. I once commented on a set of beautiful chairs she had in her dining room.

She said to me: "Y'know, Mr Logan, they were in the original inventory of the castle. Some relatives of mine got married and took them away, and a few years ago my husband discovered them in a house in Fife. He offered to buy them but the lady wouldn't sell. Sadly, she died soon afterwards so we bought those chairs at auction and brought them back to the house again."

I said: "Oh, that's a wonderful story. How long were they away?"

"Three hundred and fifty years," she said.

She told the story as though they had been taken away yesterday.

The night I was due to perform for Royalty I was playing with my parents at the Opera House in Dunfermline. In typical fashion my father wouldn't even let me off the finale so afterwards we raced down along a windy road to this enormous castle.

I was barely through the entrance when someone said to me: "Mr Logan, come through. We would like you to meet the Queen Mother."

I was awash with nerves. I spotted her a mile off looking absolutely radiant in a beautiful dark green dress that flowed into a creamy green as it reached its centre. She walked towards me, then spoke.

"Oh hello, we've been so looking forward to you coming."

That was a nice thing to say, although I knew I was supposed to be a surprise act. So that was a good start.

When I started my act, I ad-libbed a bit about the paintings on the wall, then sang my first song 'I'll Never See Maggie Alone', which considering Princess Margaret was there, was not the best choice.

But it worked. There was a lot of laughter, and I stood there thinking of the old sink under the stage at the Empire Theatre in Greenock. And I was saying to myself: "Jings, Logan, you've come a long way."

Everything went well, and afterwards I had a wonderful conversation with the Queen Mother.

I enjoyed her company so much I had to stop myself saying: "Y'know Ma'am, I wish you could meet my mother. You two would get on terribly well."

I just knew if my mother had been there she and the Queen Mother, as two women with similar senses of humour, would have got on like a house on fire. Then she spoke to my musical director, George Thallon, and she said: "Do you always play for Mr Logan?"

"No, Ma'am, I'm a traveller for Youngers the Brewers."

"Oh," she said, "we're practically next door neighbours."

Holyrood Palace, of course, was right next to the Youngers brewery in Edinburgh.

Finally, the Queen Mother and the Princess made to leave. The Queen Mother said: "Lovely to meet you, Mr Logan. I shall follow your career with great interest."

And I thought: "Oh, I don't believe this is happening to me."

When I got home everyone was waiting in the house for a minute by minute description of the evening. They all sat open-mouthed, lapping up every word. That's the effect meeting someone from the Royal Family had in those days.

A few weeks later I was passing Bluevale Street in Dennistoun where my Granny Short still lived, and I thought it was an ideal opportunity to pop in and see how she was.

She had her mob-cap and apron on, and had clearly been doing some dusting.

"Oh, come in, son," she said. "This is lovely. Come in. Well, imagine seeing you."

"Sit down," she said firmly. "Sit down."

And my Granny Short started to tell me how a woman stopped her in the street and said: "I see yer grandson has been entertaining the Queen Mother and Princess Margaret."

This woman had read all about my experience in the papers, but Granny Short knew nothing about it. She then proceeded to tell me what it meant to her because she never dreamed that any of her children or grandchildren would entertain Royalty. I sat there listening to her, and my eyes just filled up. So did hers as she poured out her heart in the most wonderful way. It was a magical moment, and I suddenly realised how proud she and others were of me—and how privileged I was to be on the receiving end of those feelings.

Fortunately for me there were many other great experiences with Royalty, my favourite being a charity poetry reading at Glamis Castle attended again by the Queen Mother. It was being hosted by the Countess of Strathmore, but by chance her husband the Earl of Strathmore was abroad, and her son was with his regiment in Hong Kong. Because of my involvement with the Help The Disabled charity, Lady Strathmore asked me to be the host—and escort the Queen Mother that evening.

I had the responsibility of taking the Queen Mother through to the room where Dame Judy Dench and her husband Michael Williams were doing the reading.

As we were walking through, she spotted a big stuffed bear.

She said to me: "Oh, I remember that bear was there when I was a child. When it was put here in the corridor I used to be frightened of going past it."

I then presented her to various people before we went into

the dining room. I sat in the corner beside the grandfather clock.

The time came when I had to propose a vote of thanks to Judy and Michael. As I stood up the grandfather clock behind me started on its hourly chime.

The resulting speech was like the start of *News At Ten*.

"Your Majesty."

Bong!

"My Lords, my Ladies."

Bong!

"Ladies and gentlemen."

Bong!

By this point the whole room had collapsed in laughter, including the Queen Mother.

I then started to praise Judy and Michael, and added: "Thank you so much for giving your one day off to help the charity."

Then realising who was beside me, I quickly said: "And to be in the presence of Your Majesty."

The Queen Mother laughed, looked at me, and said: "You just managed to talk your way out of that, didn't you?"

Which was very true.

Later, Judy asked me when the Queen Mother would be retiring to her quarters. And I said: "Not until she says thank you to everybody."

And that is exactly what happened.

When the Queen Mother left the room just before eleven o'clock that night, she went down to the kitchens to thank all the staff and volunteers who had contributed to the evening on behalf of the charity.

Like her daughter, when the Queen Mother does a job, she does it so well.

The year after I bought the Metropole we were honoured when Princess Alexandra and her husband Angus Ogilvy agreed to attend a big Stars For Spastics charity evening. I went to a lot of expense to make sure everything was exactly right. I had my own private office done in the Ogilvy tartan, and had a special toilet built solely for her use.

I also had special Metropole Theatre matches made for the occasion. In fact, at one point I was keen on starting a company to make matchboxes for special occasions. Inside each one was a special welcome to HRH and her husband. I know she admired them because she filled her handbag with them. And Angus was asked to put a few in his pockets.

As she was being presented to everyone, one of my staff approached me in a panic. "There's a bomb scare," he said. "There's a bomb scare."

"Well," I said. "Don't go that way because you'll interrupt proceedings. Go round the other way."

I remained cool because I had been in the business long enough to know that crank callers did that kind of thing all the time. We weighed up the risk, and decided to carry on, which is how these things are usually dealt with.

The theatre that night looked absolutely beautiful. The band rail was a mass of freesias and the Royal Box was just spectacular—all done by my florist friend Carole Wilson.

The whole place was supposed to be cleared for a security sweep two hours before the Princess arrived, but the girls were still doing the flowers. I think the MI5 boys could see how splendid it was going to look, and let them get on with the job.

At the end of the show I went to my office, and said to the Princess: "Ma'am, when you are ready, the artistes are waiting to be presented."

And she said: "Just a minute. You must be exhausted. You've been working all night."

"Sit down," she added. "What are you going to have to drink? I insist."

I said: "I'd like a whisky and water."

"Right," she said.

She went over and poured the drink, and brought it to me. I couldn't believe I was being served a whisky by a Princess. What a moment.

"When I married I loved whisky and porridge," she said. "Then I discovered to my horror that my husband didn't eat porridge and didn't like whisky."

I said: "Well, you could get a divorce for that."

And she was absolutely wonderful. We went downstairs and I presented the cast. As we were leaving the theatre to go to a restaurant owned by Reo Stakis she spotted a man in a wheelchair tucked away against the outside wall. I never even saw him, but when I looked round she was over talking to him.

At the restaurant I left her alone. She was talking to all the artistes at the top table and I went to the side table. It gave the others a chance to be with her. When she got up to leave and everyone stood, she signalled me over, and said: "Would you escort me to my car?"

That was a lovely compliment—a kind gesture showing her appreciation for the night I had organised.

There are many Royal memories, but the biggest Royal Performance I organised was attended by Prince Charles and Princess Diana. It was the Royal Scottish Variety Performance at the King's Theatre in Glasgow, and all the money was going to the City of Glasgow Hospice which was the city's wedding gift to the couple.

I was determined to give Scottish artistes the pride of place instead of the usual scenario where big English and American names would take over, leaving the homegrown acts confined to a wee novelty box.

And so I got together every big name in Scotland I could think of; people like Gordon Jackson, Rikki Fulton, Johnny Beattie, Scotland The What, Kenneth McKellar, Bill McCue, Moira Anderson, and George Barron and Jim McColl from *The Beechgrove Garden*—to name just a few.

It was a very strong bill, and everyone seemed pretty pleased with the planned programme. Then I approached the TV companies with a view to getting it on the telly. STV weren't happy at all—they said they had to sell the programme in England to make it financially viable but the bill didn't have enough big names who were known south of the border.

One London paper phoned me and asked: "Who are your stars?"

And I went through the whole cast, and the reporter said: "Yes, but who are your stars?"

I said: "That's my stars."

The BBC weren't interested either. They claimed they couldn't afford it, but I suspected it was a bit too Scottish for their liking as well.

Now I had an option. I could ditch some of the Scottish acts, get big acts in from down south and get it on the telly. Or I could run with the spirit of the fact that it was the Royal Scottish Variety Performance and give Scottish acts their rightful place on the bill. So I stuck to my guns.

Then the people in London surrounding the Prince and Princess started to complain. The bill was too loose, they said. It would have to be changed. So I went to London for a meeting with a Major who had something to do with the Royal couple.

I walked in, and the first thing he said was: "Look, Mr Logan, I haven't got a lot of time."

I had come all the way from Glasgow, and he didn't have a lot of time. But I was polite.

He said to me: "Right, let me just ask one or two questions. How long does the first half last?"

"An hour and five minutes," I said.

The room was filled by wails of laughter. "Of course you're joking, Mr Logan?" he said.

"No." I remained deadpan.

"An hour and five minutes," he shouted, summoning his secretary to join the fun. "Oh Deirdre, he wants them to sit there for an hour and five minutes in the first half."

More wails of laughter, even longer this time.

"How long is the second half, Mr Logan?"

"Another hour and five minutes."

Now they were in hysterics. "Oh really," he said, turning away to laugh again.

I had had enough.

"Now wait a minute," I said. "I don't understand. What exactly do you envisage?"

He looked up. "Oh, I thought if they came in and had 35 minutes, say, and then they went round where the artistes were and had a drink and something to eat for maybe half an hour, and then back for another short bit."

And I said: "And what do the audience do, a full theatre, when they are going round having a little bite to eat for half an hour? I'm not asking them to do any more or any less than they do in London for the Royal Variety Performance. This is the Royal Scottish Variety Performance."

He changed his tune when he saw I wasn't for lying down. There were no more laughs, and eventually he made his excuses to leave before anything was sorted out.

The following week one of his lieutenants was sent up to Glasgow to thrash out the details with me. He was the kind of person who didn't impress me one little bit.

"All right," he said, "tell me about the show."

"Well," I said, "it's due to start around 7.30 and I just want you to know that if the Royal couple are a bit early we'll be ready to go."

"Oh, you mean you'll need more time."

"No, I'm just letting you know that one way or the other we will be ready to go."

They knew I had presented Royal Performances before, but those hadn't been with Princess Diana so, in their eyes, that didn't count.

He was argumentative. He moaned that the press would take the whole thing over, despite my assurances that that would never happen, and then claimed we would never get sixty people into the bar where the reception was being held.

At that point the head of the theatre Tom Malarkey could hold his tongue no longer.

"Excuse me," said Tom. "The last time Her Majesty The Queen was here there were ninety people in this bar and there was still plenty of room."

We planned to present the Royal couple to everyone on stage. He wanted us to pick six, and said the rest could watch. And I thought: "Oh yes, I'm going to pick six out of all the artistes in Scotland. I don't think so."

He said to me: "I'll tell you something. The show will finish at ten o'clock on the dot and at exactly five minutes past ten the door of the Royal car will close and they will leave, regardless of what part of the programme you have on. I have a helicopter waiting for them and that's what is going to happen."

They had an attitude of "what we say goes whether you like it or not". I thought the Prince and Princess were marvellous, but the people who surrounded them—their public relations if you like— were a disaster zone.

Despite all these veiled "threats", the show was a brilliant success. Even Hector Nicol, who had a reputation of being a rough comic, made a great impression. Before he went on I said to him: "Now listen, Hector, you've got seven minutes and I know you. I want seven minutes of clean material. I want you to show in seven minutes that basically you are a very funny man, and don't need any of the rough material. This isn't the audience for that. You don't need it. You'll be marvellous. I have great faith in you."

My decision to put him on the bill caused all sorts of problems. I had six letters complaining that a comic like him shouldn't be performing in front of Charles and Diana. He ended up going so well that he did nine minutes instead of seven, and the Prince thought he was great. Afterwards the Prince came back stage, and asked Hector to repeat some of the jokes.

When Peter Morrison started to sing his third song John Grieve and I appeared in the aisle as two window cleaners with our ladder and buckets. The idea was to cause chaos as we tried to find our seats in the third row—we did it well, getting in everyone's way and sticking the ladder in all directions.

And we said: "We've just come straight from our work. Sorry about that. There was no room for the ladder in the cloakroom."

Then we realised we were in the wrong place—we were supposed to be seated in a box. I took the ladder into the central aisle, started walking down and you could hear the audience saying: "Oh no, they're not going to go to the Royal Box. Oh no."

You could hear them gasp. Well, we went to the Royal Box, I went up the ladder and I looked up to Diana's face about 24 inches from mine, and it was looking radiant with the biggest smile in the world. What a beautiful woman she was. She was enjoying every moment.

And I said: "There's been a double booking."

And John said: "Oh no, he's hired a suit. It must be his . . . definitely."

"No, no, wait a minute," I said. "Sorry, but I think you're in the wrong seats."

We finally got down the ladder and went into the other box, and by that time the audience were in hysterics. The sketch worked an absolute treat.

Jack Milroy had a great series of gags. He said: "Is there anyone with a husband who never stops talking?"

And as he held up a mousetrap he looked up at the Royal Box, and got a huge laugh. Then he threw the mousetrap into the audience. Afterwards Princess Diana came up to him, and said: "Why didn't you throw that to me. I could have caught it. I was very good at catching things at school."

The Royal couple came backstage and talked to everyone. It was a great atmosphere and a marvellous night for Scottish theatre. The TV coverage, though, was very poor. ITV sent a camera crew from London to film them walking in the theatre, the BBC sent nothing and STV sent nothing. I thought that was rather sad. Even if they had treated the performance as a news item they could have come backstage and filmed the couple with the artistes—showing our stars in the same style their peers in London were used to. That would have been good for Scottish theatre and good for them, but the television bosses obviously didn't think so.

I gained a great deal of respect for Prince Charles that night when a frightened little girl of just seven froze as she was asked to do her curtsey. The Prince just took her hand, and said in a comforting voice: "Now, show me your curtsey." And she did it beautifully.

I thought that was a lovely human touch, and I really warmed to him.

Halfway through meeting the cast this equerry butted in, and said to me: "Time."

He was obviously banking on the fact that if he pressured me enough I would approach the Royal couple to tell them they had to go. And I thought: "You can tell them yourself, matey boy."

Everything was fine until the Princess just happened to glance round at me as I was looking at my watch. The Prince saw this, and announced it was time to leave. I wasn't at all worried as everything had gone perfectly. The car that had been definitely leaving at five past ten was still there at quarter to eleven when they finally decided to depart. Our show lasted the two hours and ten minutes I said it would.

*   *   *

One of my favourite stories about the Royal Family concerns an occasion when the Queen met Tommy Cooper.

"I suppose you will be going to the Cup Final on Saturday, Ma'am," he said.

"No, we're not going," she replied.

"Oh, can I have your tickets?"

The wedding of Charles and Diana was a true fairytale. He was a handsome man, and she was an incredibly beautiful woman who made even the most fantastic clothes look even better. It was very sad that their marriage was enveloped in sadness, and a tragedy that someone as special as Diana was taken from us in that car crash in Paris. I think most people will agree that a whole nation wept for her in a way it has wept for few others.

I believe, though, that the Queen took a lot of unfair stick in the aftermath of Diana's death. At a time when her grandchildren needed love and comfort she was there for them in Balmoral. Most people forget that. She had watched her son come through a particularly acrimonious divorce with Diana, so she was perfectly entitled to keep her feelings private at that time.

Perhaps she suffered from the growing unpopularity that seems to have beset the Royal Family in recent years. My view is that the senior Royals like the Queen, the Queen Mother, the Princess Royal, Princess Margaret, Princess Alexandra and so on have always been great ambassadors for our country. The problem seems to have been some of the younger Royals whose actions have sometimes cast the Crown in a bad light.

That, however, should not be an excuse to claim that the whole system is rotten. If it wasn't for the Queen, and the great work she has done, I'm not sure where this country would be today. She represents a monarchy which signifies stability in our country. I'm a great supporter of hers, and those who criticise her should get their facts right before opening their mouths. Not lowering the flag at Buckingham Palace to half-mast after Diana's death was a mistake, but that mistake was righted. No-one is perfect. A couple of mistakes in a reign of 45 years is a pretty good track record.

For instance, I was once one of many people who were invited aboard the Royal Yacht when it visited Glasgow. All the guests— and there seemed to be hundreds of them—were lined up on either side of this long, narrow top deck when the Queen and Prince Philip appeared out of a door at the far end.

For around an hour they made their way along, stopping to chat pleasantly with every group and showing an interest in each and every one of those people. Then when they had gone some folk near to where I was standing started having a go at Her Majesty.

"What does the Queen do, for God's sake?" one man said. "Ah hardly saw her."

And they all went on and on and on.

Because I knew one or two of the people in that group I felt compelled to challenge their ignorance. I said to them: "It's a real pity you lot didn't take time to stop thinking of yourselves and watch what that woman and her husband were doing. They were working from the minute they came out of that door until the minute they disappeared through the door at the other end. This was no social occasion for them. They were working the whole time, and they did a great job."

I made it quite clear how I felt, and those people shut up. One of them even sent me a letter of apology saying they had got carried away. But they were perfect examples of the type of folk I get annoyed with—blasting off on a subject they clearly know nothing about.

The Queen meets thousands of people she doesn't know every year, but somehow she manages to make each and every one of them feel special. That takes a special talent. I should know because it is what we in the theatre strive for every night when we are on stage. And I know it is not easy. Perhaps people wouldn't understand that unless they had tried it themselves.

13

NEW BEGINNINGS

A few weeks after moving into the lovely house in Hamilton Avenue I cast my eyes on the terrible wallpaper, the demolished kitchen and the lack of furniture. It was a shocking scene. I summed up my status in life thus; it was back to: "How much is a frying pan?" A nice gauge, I think, of one's position in the world.

But the main thing was that I once again had a house to call my own, a base from which to get myself and my career back on track. Both would take hard work, and a little bit of luck, but anyone who knows me well knows I've never shirked hard work in my puff. The luck would hopefully follow.

With the burden of the Metropole still firmly on my shoulders I knew it could potentially be a long time before I cleared the debts. Most of the money from shows I appeared in went straight to the bank to pay off those debts. As usual I appeared in the big Scottish pantomimes, and I also revived some of the Sam Cree comedy plays for successful tours, most notably *Run For Your Wife* which went exceptionally well.

In 1980 I asked my friend Bill Simpson to star with me on a tour with *Second Honeymoon*.

334

Bill had always been a ladies' favourite who could charm the birds off the trees.

He was catapulted to fame when he played Dr Finlay in that massively successful Sixties TV series. But Bill struggled when he came out of *Casebook* after eight successful years and 206 episodes. He appeared in plays and other TV shows, but a lot of things didn't work out and Bill suffered as a result.

He agreed to star in *Second Honeymoon*, but at the end of the tour I was amazed to read a big story in the *News of the World*.

We had had a great time on that tour but the story was all about how Bill had suffered badly. The article said his wife Tracy had insisted on renting the most expensive house at Kilconquhar Castle estate, and insisted on throwing big expensive parties for people like Jimmy Logan.

The whole story had Bill telling how Tracy had lived the high life with all his money. He said every penny was down the drain. I had been with Bill and Tracy throughout the tour, and I knew every word was nonsense. In fact, she had done a marvellous job for him on that tour, always there when he needed her. I was furious.

Later that day, Bill phoned me up and apologised. He said he was sorry but he had been offered cash, and made up the story to get the money.

I said: "I can't say I'm very thrilled about what you've said about Tracy after what she did for you."

"Well," he said. "She got some of the money, Jimmy. I didn't keep it all."

I was upset at that. He had presented a work of fiction to a newspaper just because he was struggling financially.

Bill was good at getting away with murder. If Tracy had walked into a room and Bill was in bed with a beautiful girl, Tracy would have come downstairs and said: "You'll never guess what has happened to poor Bill."

I always called him Poor Bill.

He was drinking more than he should have been, and, ignoring his doctor's advice, he went back to Spain, where he had previously owned a house and still had a lot of friends. Unfortunately the drink took its toll and Bill ended up in hospital.

He had planned to do the Immortal Memory at a Burns Supper with his friends in Spain, but he was suddenly called back to London. Bill recorded the Immortal Memory on cassette before leaving. He died shortly afterwards, and never saw those friends in Spain again.

Bill's recording was spoiled by a hum on the tape, and the quality was terrible. But listening to that recording made me realise what a beautiful toned voice Bill Simpson had. He was brought up in the same part of Ayrshire as Burns, and spoke about the bard with great authority. He was a kind of Scottish Richard Burton.

On the day of his funeral all his friends in Spain put their dining tables out in the sun, filled them with food and wine, and had the kind of party Bill would have enjoyed.

After his funeral in Ayr we went back to Bill's favourite hotel and drank a toast to his memory with his family. At the bar there was a chair known as Bill's Chair. And in that hotel Bill was always remembered by those who knew him.

At the next Burns Supper Bill's friends played his Immortal Memory, even though the quality was poor. And they have done the same every year since in his memory.

Years later I discovered his daughters had no recordings of Bill's in their possession, and were upset by this. I managed to persuade the BBC to give me three recordings of Bill in *Dr Finlay's Casebook*.

In the winter of 1980 I travelled up to Inverness where I was producing, directing and starring in the pantomime *Aladdin* at the

Eden Court Theatre, a beautiful new venue in the heart of the Highlands.

I played a lot at that theatre. On one occasion I put on the kilt to open a charity shop in Inverness, before heading off to the theatre for the matinee and evening performance of the panto- mime where I was playing dame. Afterwards, I got back into the kilt and raced down in the car to catch the Black Isle ferry.

I made it in the nick of time.

Back at the house I was staying in I always asked the landlady to leave the curtains open at night so I could look out at the tremendous view.

I poured a whisky, sat down and, with the fire roaring, soaked up the scene. I thought I looked like the Laird of Cockpen sitting in this smart kilt in this lovely setting in the heart of the High- lands.

Then I started laughing. I noticed I had forgotten to take my tights off after the pantomime.

The woman who handled the wardrobe on *Aladdin* was a strik- ing red-haired divorcee who, like me, seemed quite lonely. The best way to describe Pamela is to say that she had a twinkle in her eye, and a nice, dry sense of humour. We warmed to each other immediately, and I thought, as we were both in a similar situation, that there was no harm in asking her out. Some time later when I had arranged to visit some friends in the country, I phoned her to ask if she would like to come.

She said: "Yes, but I've got things to do."

"Oh?"

"You want me to come now, don't you?"

"Yes, I'd like that."

Over time we became closer until I eventually invited her down for a weekend at my house in Glasgow. As usual my father, who was living with me at the time, stole the show. I found myself in the kitchen cooking all the time while he entertained the guest non-stop in the lounge. He had someone to work on, and he was enjoying it.

When she was about to leave on the Sunday I asked her if she was hungry.

"Yes," she said.

"Would you like an omelette?"

"Oh, that would be nice."

So I whisked up some eggs, made an enormous omelette, put it on a plate and naturally assumed we would split it up the middle. Before I could say anything she was eating away. And she ate and ate and ate. Minutes later the plate was empty, and I said nothing, although I was thinking that this woman would never do me because I would spend the rest of my life cooking and cleaning while she sat back.

The next time I was speaking to her on the phone she suddenly said to me: "Did you enjoy the omelette?"

And as soon as she said it I realised she had been sending me up all along. "I like that," I thought. "That's what I call a sense of humour."

As the months progressed we became closer, and I believed we both thought we had something good together. It wasn't long before I asked her if she would like to come to live with me in Glasgow, and she accepted. That was in 1981, and it was a good arrangement, and over the next couple of years we lived together in a pretty happy relationship. It had problems like every relationship but, in general terms, we got on well together.

Around this time I also finally ridding myself of the nightmare that was the Metropole Theatre. It had sat derelict for years, a horrible blot on the landscape.

My shares in Scottish Television had acted as security for the bank loan to buy the Metropole.

In the late Sixties when my overdraft was gradually increasing, the bank insisted I sell my shares to reduce the burden of debt.

I told the bank that the shares were only going one way, and that was up. It would be far better to hold onto them, from their point of view as well as mine, if things should get worse at the theatre.

But they insisted.

Looking back, selling those shares was possibly the worst of all the disasters to beset me at that time.

If I had been allowed to hold on to them they would have later wiped out any debt, and I could have bought another few Metropoles with the money left over. Today they would have been worth a minimum of £500,000. But it wasn't to be.

After the Metropole closed a group of people took an active interest in the theatre—vandals. They nicked just about everything, no matter how big or small. In fact they spent so much time ripping out some things that if they had spent the same time doing an honest job they would have earned more money.

When they had presumably looted everything they could loot, they set the whole place on fire. The interior was destroyed, and firemen poured 66,000 gallons of water on those flames, flooding the basement.

I went once to see the damage. It was a wholly depressing experience. There before me was a dark, damp and twisted wreck of a place that had only a few years earlier been immaculately alive with the colour and joy of a Royal Performance and so many other great shows. Now it was dead and decaying. I can't put into words how upsetting it was to see my theatre in such a rotten state. It didn't seem like the same place. I was never able to go back.

That was in 1974. For the next ten years I fought a continuing battle with the corporation trying to get permission to demolish what was left of the Metropole so I could sell the ground for development.

The corporation, however, kept insisting that the front of the building was listed, and was of too great architectural importance to be bulldozed. It was an argument I couldn't understand because that building had become a dreadful blot on the landscape that anyone with any sense wanted rid of.

There could be no sense in preserving the Metropole if no-one was willing to put up the money to renovate and refurbish it. And no-one was.

I would have loved to have done so but the insurance money from the fire went straight to the bank. I even had to ask my bank manager for £1,000 to do the minimum work to secure the theatre, and make it safe.

In 1980 an accountant friend of mine, Gordon Avis, came up from London to meet with my bank with a view to finally ridding me of my responsibilities to the Metropole. After lengthy negotiations they hammered out a deal. If I sold the theatre I would take a percentage, and if I didn't sell it within three years the bank would take it over. In return I had to pay £12,500 back to the bank over the same period. After that the Metropole would no longer be my problem.

I never sold the Metropole and I paid back the £12,500. But the bank who I had been with for more than 30 years broke their side of the bargain by refusing to clear my overdrafts until they had sold the Metropole.

I went to another bank, explained the situation and asked if I could open an account.

"Sure," they said. "Would you like an overdraft?"

"No," I replied. "I want absolutely nothing to do with overdrafts."

Shortly afterwards I heard that my original bank were preparing to sell the theatre to a developer for £5,000, and such was my attachment to the theatre that I went to the bank and offered £5,000 which I didn't have.

I was desperate. I couldn't believe a theatre I had bought for

£80,000 twenty years earlier was now being sold for a fraction of that amount. And it stood on an enormous piece of ground. I felt the amount this developer was going to get it for was scandalous. So I put in an identical bid.

In the end that developer got his land for £7,000, and strangely enough he quickly got planning permission to demolish the Metropole and put up a block of flats. All of a sudden the listed nature of the building no longer seemed to matter.

For Jimmy Logan, it was the end of a long, nightmarish episode in my life.

I had looked at this beautiful building in 1964 and knew I couldn't walk away from it. I also came to the conclusion years later that maybe you shouldn't go into a business you love. It's better going into a business you can't stand the sight of. Then you don't make emotional decisions.

It's a bit like a family problem: the son is going wrong, and the mother and father make the wrong decision because they are too emotionally involved.

When you are emotionally involved you don't make a cold-hearted business decision. And in theatre terms I was emotionally involved.

I've said already that I don't regret buying the theatre. Thinking what might have been would have been far worse. And I did make a lot of mistakes running it that I wouldn't make now. But there is no doubt that there were people in Glasgow Corporation who were dead set on making sure Jimmy Logan never achieved his dreams in the Metropole.

There were two new arrivals in Hamilton Avenue in 1981—Pamela and her dog, Stanley. With my father and my own dog Benson all under the same roof it was suddenly hectic.

Benson was a white boxer with a black patch over one eye like a pirate, and black eyelashes on one eye and white eyelashes on the other. He was an adorable dog who had a little patch near his tail that he liked to have scratched.

Benson arrived in our household after he was given to the local vet George Leslie to be put down. But George wouldn't put an animal down if he kept it for more than 24 hours, and Benson won a reprieve.

George was a personal friend and when Annie, who was visiting, went into see him she immediately fell in love with this boxer.

"Aw, what's his name? Benson. I've got to have him."

"Sorry Annie, can't do," said George. "There's a lady coming this afternoon for him."

And she thought no more about it.

Benson, however, must have been destined to come to our house. He was sent back by four different owners before he came bounding into our living room one day when I was in the middle of a party of about 15 friends.

He picked me out, and before I knew what was happening I was covered in big, sloppy licks. Then he left me and, of all the people in the room, went straight over to my father, who was deep in conversation, and sat looking up at him.

My father took one look at the dog sitting at his feet, and said: "That's the stupidest dog I've ever seen."

And that was him. From then on Benson became part of the personality of the house. I had to have him.

Benson was like most boxers—very boisterous. His previous owners all seemed to be on the verge of nervous breakdowns but we hit it off. It wasn't long before he became the boss of the house. When we got a letter from the Scottish Boxers' Refuge asking us to become patrons he demanded we accept.

Benson had a number of traits, including the fact that he was what we called a "quick widdler". To make matters worse he always "widdled" in the middle of the night. It was so bad that I had to buy myself a tracksuit so I could get Benson out before he did some damage. I suspect that's one of the reasons he didn't get on too well in the other homes.

Benson also hated black dogs, which wasn't good news for Stanley, a black labrador. The day Benson met this black dog in the car he seemed none too happy. And Benson got the shock of his life when he charged into the house, ran up the stairs and turned round to see this black dog following him.

Benson didn't speak to me for two weeks. Dogs have a great way of falling out with people; Benson would sit staring at me, but if I looked away for a second that was it. When I looked back he would have his back to me, usually with one ear sticking up.

Then if I called his name he just ignored me. And this went on for two weeks after Stanley arrived.

The great thing about labradors, though, is that they are undoubtedly professional conmen. When I took Stanley and Benson out with a ball or a stick Stanley never got the ball, and he never got the stick.

Benson was the top dog, and he thought that was just fine. Then somewhere along the line, Benson decided: "Yeah, having this dog isn't too bad after all."

And from that moment on he never got the ball, and he never got the stick. Stanley just ran rings round him.

Despite all this K9 psychology, the two of them became very close. One night in my bed I was suddenly wakened by something thumping my side. It was Benson.

"He needs out," I thought. So I got up, staggered downstairs, opened the door and out rushed Stanley. Meanwhile, Benson was sitting quietly at the top of the stairs.

"Come on, Benson," I said. "You wanted out. What are you playing at?"

But Benson just sat there. And then I twigged. He didn't want out at all, but he knew Stanley wanted out and had woken me up to help out his pal.

One day Stanley stopped in his tracks, frozen to the spot. The vet discovered a tumour, and carried out a painful operation to remove it. Stanley returned to the house, but he was very weak.

Of course, Benson couldn't understand what was going on. He kept saying: "Aw, come on Stanley, let's go out and have a run."

When they went out Stanley walked very slowly while Benson ran up and down. But, gradually, Stanley got back to his old self and soon couldn't run far enough. Then, just as quickly as we had forgotten about it, the tumour returned with a vengeance.

George said to me: "I don't think there's anything I can do."

"Well," I said. "Operate. If there's nothing you can do just let him sleep on. If there's something let's try. Because he's got no other chance."

Sadly, there was absolutely nothing George could do. Saying goodbye to a dog like Stanley was like saying goodbye to a child, because he was a lovely dog. We buried him at the bottom of our garden and placed a stone on the ground with a simple inscription: "Stanley—A Good Dog."

That house holds many fine memories for me. One of my fondest is of "Old Bill", a marvellous pensioner who came along from time to time to do some handywork for us. He would say things like: "Come and see ma doors." They were never my doors, of course, they were his.

Although there was plenty to eat in the house, Bill always brought his own piece. And one of the dogs always got most of that.

Bill Rhodie was a lovely guy, part of the house. If he was away for a few weeks we would genuinely feel that the house seemed empty without him. Such was his presence.

Bill also took great pride in his work. He once told me the highest weekly wage he had ever earned was £27, and that involved working virtually round the clock to get the job done. In his day it was normal to be sacked just before Christmas only to be rehired after the New Year. This was done so his employers didn't have to pay him, and many like him, anything over Christmas and New Year.

I talked about Bill at a speech I made to the Institute of Directors in Glasgow. The speaker before me was the tycoon James Gulliver who talked brilliantly about his life in business, and the multi-million pound turnovers he was accustomed to. The assembled high-fliers were enthralled.

After a few opening gags, I said: "I want to tell you about Old Bill."

I told them of my warm feelings for Bill, and people like him, who worked their socks off often for only a token reward. Bill's pride in his work outweighed any reward, and recognition of that achievement mattered more to him.

I reminded these gentlemen that they were lucky to have people like Bill working for them, and even though they couldn't possibly get to know personally all the Bills on their workforce, recognising their achievements was absolutely vital. I think I struck a chord, because I noted most of these suits nodding in agreement.

Bill, sadly, enjoyed a good dram and I believe it became quite serious when he had two whisky bottles—one for each pocket. He had a bad fall, and died shortly afterwards. At his funeral the priest very kindly allowed me to speak from the altar about the gentleman Bill was.

The longer Pamela lived in our house, the more distant our relationship became. She became terribly unhappy with everything in her life. The warmth between us disappeared to the extent that it soon became obvious she wanted something quite different.

She had become so unsettled that one day she announced that she was moving out to live her own life in her own flat. But as she had been contributing to the running of my business affairs, she was still keen to work for me.

Pamela's problem was that she wanted to mix with younger people. Most of my friends had been friends for many years and came from every walk of life—painters, doctors, writers and so on. They were wonderful company, and certainly not dull.

But if Pamela was chasing youth she wasn't going to find it in my house. The age gap between us was not a problem for me. If anything she would have had a job keeping up with me. My life revolved 100 per cent around the theatre and I understood how that could be boring for someone who wasn't so keen.

She bought her flat in the West End of Glasgow, and I helped her with the furnishings. I helped her because I wanted her to be happy. And if she was going to be happy in her own flat then that was fine.

Just before she was due to move out I happened to mention that I had friends coming over for dinner on the Thursday night.

"You didn't tell me," she said.

She seemed shocked that I had no intention of living the life of a hermit or monk waiting around the house for her to come running. Just as I always had done, I had arranged a dinner party where I would cook the food, set the table and spend a pleasant evening with friends. It was one of my great loves.

I didn't tell Pamela about that dinner party, and she was not happy when she found out.

She remained as the hostess for the dinner party, and eventually decided not to move into her new home, preferring instead to stay with me after all. As Hitler said: "I thought I had won that battle."

At the end of 1981 I played pantomime at the King's Theatre in Edinburgh with Terry Scott, star of many *Carry On* movies and the TV comedy series *Terry and June*.

I had worked with Terry once before in the pantomime *Cinderella* in Newcastle in the winter of 1969. He was one of the ugly sisters and I was Buttons.

But I must be honest and say I never found him easy to deal with. He didn't turn up until the second day of rehearsals. So that was a bad start.

And as we went through the script on stage, he kept saying: "I'll change that, I'll change that, I'll change that." We waited for the changes but nothing happened.

Part of the production was the Balloon Ballet where I, as Buttons, would play Nureyev and the two ugly sisters would be the ballet dancers. I could tell he had never done the Balloon Ballet before so I explained to him how it was done.

I told him that the Balloon Ballet was a piece of pantomime material where you throw the balloon around the stage from one person to another while the music plays. The laughter comes when it goes underneath your legs, you drop it and generally make a mess of things.

About three days later the director Freddie Carpenter asked me if I thought I should be in the Balloon Ballet.

Given I had suggested it in the first place, I said:

"Why?"

"Oh, I just wondered."

"Well, look. If you tell me I shouldn't be in it because it is bad for the pantomime I will not be in it. But if you are telling me Terry doesn't think I should be in it, I will be in it because it is my material."

Little incidents like these were not helpful.

The following year Terry went to the London Palladium where he performed the Balloon Ballet. What a surprise.

Cinderella that year was one of the biggest ever successes at the Theatre Royal in Newcastle. It was a simply wonderful season. People couldn't get seats, and I kept getting stopped in the street by folk asking if I could get them a ticket. By that time I had been to Newcastle quite a few years running, and I was as well known there as I was in Glasgow.

One day the principal girl said to me: "Can you come up between shows and have a cup of tea?"

"Yeah, sure. What's wrong?"

"Well, Terry depresses me," she said. "All he can say is what a terrible pantomime this is. It's really annoying me."

So I went upstairs and took Terry to task.

I said to him: "Well, Terry, you may consider you are right about the quality of our pantomime but that is not important. What is important is that the place is packed and the public are fighting to get seats. I'm being asked all the time as a favour if I can get people tickets. When a pantomime is not going so well then I'll concentrate my energies on changing the pantomime to get it right. This, however, is not that pantomime."

So when Terry came to Edinburgh to appear with me in *Jack and the Beanstalk*, I knew what to expect.

We had a meeting in London with the director Clive Perry.

Clive said to me: "Jimmy, Terry would like his wife to do the choreography. Do you mind?"

And I said: "That's not my responsibility. You're the director. It's up to you to decide. I've never met Terry's wife and I don't know what she has done in choreography. So I couldn't give an opinion."

It turned out that quite a few of Terry's close relatives came up from England to take jobs on the production. I didn't say anything but I thought it was a pity because there were dozens of Scots who would have been far more deserving of that employment.

In the build-up to the panto we got a great deal of press coverage because Terry was a fresh face in Scotland. My lovely old Aunt Jean who lived in Gourock said to me: "Funny man that Terry Scott. I've heard him four times on the wireless talking about the pantomime and he's never mentioned that you're in it as well."

Then Clive Perry said he wanted me to come on stage in the opening scene with a cow.

"That'll be great," I said. "I can establish a rapport with the audience right away."

Well, it was great up until the first rehearsal. Afterwards Clive told me it wasn't right.

The problem was that Terry didn't want to be upstaged because he came on later with the cow.

I also noticed there were no understudies for Terry or myself so I went to see the manager.

"It's quite simple," he said. "If Terry's off we just carry on. If you're off we just close the show until you come back."

And that was out of order. If Terry was off I needed someone talking to me who knew what I was talking about. And if I was off I wasn't going to carry the can for letting down the punters and everyone involved in the show.

This was just one of a number of things that weren't right with that pantomime. Terry Scott was a difficult man to get on with, and if that affects the mood of the company it can affect the production. And that can be obvious to the audience.

The following year *Jack and the Beanstalk* was due to go on to Glasgow, and Glasgow always reserved the right to make changes because they were putting up a lot of the cash. One of the changes they made on that occasion was to say they didn't want Terry Scott.

And I know he wasn't pleased.

In 1984 I wanted to appear as Archie Rice in *The Entertainer*, a play by John Osborne about a failed music hall artiste. Although he was English and belonged to a theatre that did not exist in Scotland, I felt I knew Archie Rice.

I approached the Royal Lyceum in Edinburgh which was being run by a good actor and director, Leslie Lawton. But as a I sat in his office I saw on the walls at least half a dozen theatre bills saying: "Leslie Lawton in . . ." and I thought: "If it is a good part he would rather do it himself." And I was right.

In the same year I went to St Andrews to look at the Byre Theatre, a small theatre holding about 135 people that was being run by Adrian Reynolds.

I met his wife Marion, and in conversation told her about what happened at The Lyceum.

"Speak to Adrian," she said. "I know he'll be interested."

I did, and he said he wanted to direct me in the play. It was the beginning of a great personal friendship that has lasted over many years. I am now godfather to his daughter Kanchana.

In *The Entertainer* I played the part the way the part was meant to be played; as the English comedian with the English accent, and not at all what the audiences were expecting. Many might have thought I would have played the part as a Scot but the Archie Rice kind of comic never existed in Scotland. It would have been a cop out, and wouldn't have rung true.

Many of the audience who knew me from my music hall days were confused when they saw *The Entertainer* because the main object of this failed comedian was not to get laughs.

There were remarks like: "I've seen him funnier."

One night there was the incredible scene of some poor soul who loved me as a comic trying to laugh at the unfunny bits to give me support, and fading away as the evening went on.

Archie Rice hits the gin bottle quite a lot in the play, which prompted one woman to tell the manager as she was leaving: "I've spent a better night with toothache. And as for Jimmy Logan, he's obviously drunk."

However, we received wonderful notices from the critics, and as a play it was an undoubted success.

Before we opened I received a card from John Osborne to say how delighted he was that I was appearing in his play. We went on tour, and when I was at the King's Theatre in Glasgow, he flew up with his wife to see the play.

Afterwards, they came back to my house with all the other

actors for some supper. To be able to talk to John Osborne about his feelings when he wrote certain sections was a privilege not given to many others, and it gave me a new insight into the play.

When Osborne died the press spent a lot of time talking about his weddings, his outbursts of temper and his treatment of people. But there was little about his brilliance.

One woman wrote to say how *The Entertainer* had affected her when she saw it as an 18-year-old. She saw our production with her 18-year-old daughter, and said it had exactly the same effect on her daughter all those years later.

Death of a Salesman is another play that stands the test of time. But the actor has about "five mountains to climb" in the second half, and I found the energy of emotion required for that enormous.

One critic recently described *The Entertainer* as "dated".

This wouldn't apply to Adrian Reynolds' production. It still has meaning.

In fact, both of these plays are relevant today because they are about family relationships.

Adrian also directed me in *Uncle Vanya* at a lovely theatre in Basingstoke. Another challenge, and again the critics said we did a good job.

Another production of *Jack and the Beanstalk* followed *The Entertainer*, and that was when I got the invitation from Annie to see her opening in cabaret at The Algonquin Hotel in New York. I recalled the story of that magnificent trip—including my attempt to sing a Tony Bennett hit in front of Tony Bennett—at the beginning of the book.

When I returned, however, Pamela hit me with the biggest story anyone has ever told me.

"Jimmy," she said, "I think I'm pregnant and they think it's twins."

Her face lit up with joy.

"OK, let's wait until it's confirmed," I said to Pamela, trying to get over the shock. "They tell everybody that."

She was absolutely glowing when she told me. I had never seen her so happy. That in itself was perfectly natural. She was a woman who was on the wrong side of 30 and had been desperate to have children for some time. Now it finally looked like her dream was about to become a reality.

Later that week I went to Southampton for a surprise 80th birthday party for my friend, Commander Sid Glover. Afterwards his son told me: "Oh, thank God, Jimmy, those school fees are finished."

And I thought: "If everything goes according to plan my school fees are only just beginning."

I also went out for a drink with Heather Ewing's mum Irene Campbell who had moved to that part of the world. I told her about the possibility of the twins, and she was so delighted for me because she knew how much I loved children.

It was then that I phoned Pamela to find out if there had been any news.

"It's twins, confirmed," she told me.

And there was a pause.

She said to me: "What are you going to do?"

"I'm going to have a large whisky."

"And then what are you going to do?"

"I'm going to have another large whisky."

I sat down. Kids. At my age. How absolutely wonderful. I genuinely couldn't take in what I was hearing. I had always loved children. My pantomimes were testament to that. The idea of finally becoming a father seemed so fantastic.

Sponsoring the French kids in the Sixties was the closest I had come to becoming a parent, and provided me with a great joy, yet now here I was being told at the age of 58 that I was going to be a daddy.

I told Pamela that if we were to give these children a decent start in life we had to get married. My reasoning was simple; they should not be affected by the mistakes we had made in our lives. Our priorities had to centre on one thing, and one thing only—the twins. We had to do what was best for them, and raising them with a proper mum and dad was what was best for them.

She agreed, and almost immediately—when my divorce from Gina came through—we were married in a simple service at Spott, near Dunbar in East Lothian.

Then preparations started in earnest for the imminent entrance of those two little new arrivals. I had a nursery built in the house, and my great friend Lord Willis—the writer Ted Willis—gave us two wonderful antique cots. We received many other lovely gifts, and made up a video of a very pregnant Pamela, myself and the two dogs showing the children round their new home. It was along the lines of: "This is where you were born. This is the garden. These are the cars. By the time you see these they will be very old-fashioned. Come on upstairs. This is your nursery. Here's the bath," and so on. I always wondered what kind of home I lived in when I was born. That's why I made the video. We thought it would be nice for them to see when they were older.

Meanwhile, everyone I knew seemed to be just as delighted and excited as I was.

As the big day grew closer I was on tour with my own show. When I was in Inverness I got a phone call saying the doctor was taking my wife into hospital on the Sunday.

I thought: "Oh no he isn't."

So, with the help of my godchild Fiona Felgate, who was working in the theatre, we shared the driving down to Glasgow after the show on the Saturday night. I managed a couple of hours sleep before taking my wife into Stobhill Hospital at seven o'clock on the Sunday morning.

I stayed in the waiting room all day, and that evening the twins were born. During the labour I held her hand, waiting for the first glimpse of my own children.

And I remember her telling me: "It's so wonderful you're here because, although everyone here is nice, you are the only one I really know."

So I felt I was being useful.

My daughter was born first, a truly wonderful moment. She was so beautiful, just like a little flower. There was difficulty, however, when my son arrived a few minutes later. He looked slightly blue, wasn't breathing very well, and the paediatrician moved in there as quick as lightning. Their mum could sense something was wrong. "Is my baby all right?" she said.

I said to her: "He's fine, he's great."

But in my heart I thought we had lost him. The paediatrician worked on the little one for a while before putting him into an incubator. And our little boy pulled through.

Stobhill may have been an old hospital in desperate need of investment but the care and attention of the staff was just incredible. Each time a baby was put in an incubator a photograph was taken so the mother could see that her child was just fine.

Exhausted, elated and going through all the emotions possible, I returned home from this wonderful day to open "Uncle Willie's Bottle".

As you might expect, there's a story behind Uncle Willie's bottle. He was my father's older brother, and on his 90th birthday we took him for a celebration dinner at Dunblane Hydro.

"Invite up to 12 people," I said, so he invited 12 people all right. Twelve women to be precise.

When I went to pick him up he handed over this giant presentation "bell" of whisky that I'm sure someone had given him.

"Here, Jimmy," he said. "That's for you. Take it."

"I don't want that, Uncle Willie. Here, take it back, it's for you."

But there was no arguing with him, so I brought it back to my house and put it in a cupboard. Shortly afterwards my Uncle Willie died, and I mentioned that there would never be an occasion important enough to open "Uncle Willie's Bottle", as we called it.

However, I was wrong. This occasion was most definitely important enough, and when I arrived home I said nothing to our housekeeper Kath and my godchild Fiona until I had poured out the drinks.

"Well," I said, smiling. "First, a girl. Second, a boy."

A great cheer went up around the room. Although I'm an emotional man I then surprised myself by taking all of these momentous events very calmly.

I phoned up all my relatives—including Annie and Heather in America, and I felt so good. The following morning as I walked out the front door the reality of it all suddenly hit me, and I imagined the scene not too far off when I carried my own son and daughter into my home for the first time.

I stopped off at Carole Wilson's florist shop to get flowers, and noticed that the newspapers had the story already. As I walked into the shop a wee Glesca grannie with her flat feet and her messages came up to me, and just said: "Aw son."

Well that was me. There was no way of saying it, but I knew exactly what she meant and my eyes just filled up. Carole Wilson congratulated me when I finally got into the shop, but I was too overcome with emotion to talk. She asked if I wanted flowers, and I just nodded.

It's hard to describe the joy of my first meeting with the twins but having children is like dropping a pebble into a pool of water where the ripples go out and touch so many people.

The day the twins were supposed to come home I had a cold. I was so worried I might pass it on that I went into the hospital wearing a mask. The sister in Pamela's ward took one look at me, and said: "Mr Logan, don't be so daft. Get that off. If they're going to get a cold they will get the cold."

When they came home Pamela, of course, was absolutely exhausted and I must have changed about 12 nappies on that memorable first night. They screamed their little heads off all night, and about three a.m. Stanley just looked at me in a way that was saying: "What on earth have you brought home?" Benson burst through the door, walked round in a circle and went back out again. He was none too impressed.

Each time I changed the nappy the little ones would be crying like there was no tomorrow. But as soon as the new one was on . . . silence. And they were fast asleep. I thought it was just lovely.

And what can I say about giving them their first bath other than the fact that it was without doubt, no arguments on this one, the most frightening, nerve-racking experience I have ever had. I needed a couple of strong whiskies to calm down afterwards.

Those early experiences I had with the children must be universal. I never cease to be amazed how people always stop to look when they are passed in the street by a mother with her baby in a pram. Or at night how people always wake up wondering if they are OK, then creep into their room and put their hand on their little chest to check they are breathing properly.

Should anything happen to my wife, I was also determined to learn how to do everything for those children—from changing the nappies to getting the right formula for their milk.

I quickly found that being a father was the richest and most rewarding experience anyone can hope to have. As the years went past I had lost all hope that it would ever happen to me, but when it did I thought someone had truly smiled on my fortunes.

I'll never forget, for instance, the day I went out to buy their first birthday cards. Picking up cards that said "To My Son" and "To My Daughter" was an unbelievable sensation—even a year into this wonderful experience the thought of being a father still hadn't sunk in properly.

Watching the kids grow older was just great. There was nothing more exhilarating than a toddler stumbling towards you, arms outstretched shouting: "Daddy, Daddy." We showered them with presents, gave them lovely parties and made sure their every need was met, and more.

There was nothing more important in my life, and nor should there have been.

When my daughter was about two she was sitting in the arms of Kath—a lovely older lady who helped us look after the kids—contentedly watching television. She was dressed all in pink. I said to Pamela: "Now just tell me how I am supposed to say 'no' to that wee girl."

I was sitting on my chair trying to read the Sunday newspapers while my son—a typical wee boy—tried his best to stop me by clambering all over them. Finally, in desperation, I slipped away to one of the bedrooms for some peace and quiet. But no sooner had I done this than suddenly my little daughter started crying her heart out in the living room.

I rushed through to see what was wrong. "What happened? What happened?" I said.

Kath, who was more experienced in these matters, said: "We were watching the snowman and the snowman melted."

I went over, and tried to comfort my wee daughter: "Darling, what can your daddy do for you?" I said.

And the wee thing—who was talking like no-one's business by this stage—looked up through her tears and said: "Go and read your papers."

I laughed so hard I had to leave the room.

We all continued down this wonderful road until one day, when the twins were three, my wife announced she wanted to move house. She had been complaining about a number of things, and this seemed to be just another issue she wasn't happy with.

"What's wrong with this one?" I said. "We've made it beautiful and it's practically paid for."

"Yes, but I want one for the children that's all on the ground floor."

Well, needless to say she knew which strings to pull when it came to persuading me. If it was better for the children then that was the best reason possible to get a new house. We started looking around, and it wasn't long before I had done a deal with a fellow actor who owned a huge big house right next to the sea at Helensburgh.

We agreed that I would split this enormous place into two homes with us living in one, and his family in the other. It was a good deal for everyone because it still left us both with five bedrooms each.

However I hadn't counted on the sheer scale of the conversion work that needed to be done, and the whole thing cost me an absolute fortune. The new entrance had to match the style of the original features from the turn of the century, and I had plans drawn up to build a new kitchen, conservatory and bathroom. Then there was all the rewiring and redecorating that was necessary as well. It was one of the most beautiful houses I had owned, but the overheads were enormous.

After selling the house in Glasgow, and faced with the major renovations still to be done in Helensburgh, we decided it would be better for my wife and the kids to live temporarily at a flat in the basement of her parents' house in Inverness.

In the meantime I worked flat out getting the house ready for Christmas, and preparing for my pantomime. It was an exhausting few months, but by the time December came around the pantomime *Jack and the Beanstalk* with Una McLean had started, and the house was almost ready. When Pamela came down with the kids on the fourteenth of December the new kitchen wasn't quite finished and a carpet had still to be put down in the hall. The conservatory leading off from the kitchen had also not been built.

But although it wasn't perfect, it was shaping up, and it was more than habitable. Of that there is no doubt.

However, my wife wasn't impressed. The moment she saw the place, she announced: "There's no way I can cook a Christmas lunch here."

I tried to persuade her that we could cook Christmas lunch, but she steadfastly refused to change her mind. Instead we had Christmas lunch at the home of our next door neighbour Angela who saved the day by inviting us all round.

The subsequent festive period was pretty miserable, and I detected there was something up with my wife. I just couldn't quite work out what it was.

On the fifth of January I left for the theatre in Glasgow with my wife and the kids waving me off. "Bye, Daddy," they were shouting. "Bye, Daddy."

When I returned home that night I noticed the Volvo car I had bought Pamela wasn't in the driveway. My first thought was that there had maybe been some problem with the car.

The house was shrouded in darkness, and when I got in there wasn't a sound to be heard. That wasn't particularly unusual because sometimes they were all in bed when I got home. After pouring myself a whisky, I went to check on the kids.

Their beds were just wonderful. Before moving in people at the Scottish Society for the Mentally Handicapped had made two full-size beds for me—one shaped like a Cinderella-style coach and the other a double-decker bus which, when you lifted the top off, became two single beds. I put my number plate on the bus. Needless to say, the kids loved their beds.

When I walked into the room I felt as if I had suddenly been thumped by a sledgehammer; the coach was empty and the bus wasn't there at all. Most importantly, neither were the children.

As I walked back to the lounge there was an icy cold feeling at the base of my spine. I couldn't bring myself to comprehend the possibility that she could have taken the children. I repeatedly told myself there must be some other explanation.

In the kitchen, though, my worst fears were realised. There was a short letter from my wife on one of the worktops spelling out that she had decided she couldn't live with me any more, and had taken the children back to Inverness for good.

"I know you'll be upset about this but we'll talk about it," the letter said.

Upset wasn't the right word. In fact, there were no words to describe how I felt at that moment apart from, perhaps, a horrible, awful feeling at the bottom of my stomach that told me my whole world was collapsing all around me.

There could be nothing worse than someone having their children taken away from them, and here I was standing in this big new house facing up to exactly that reality. Yet none of it seemed real. I was so traumatised that I knew neither what was happening nor what to do about it. All at once I felt sick, dazed, depressed and utterly confused. After staggering around for a few minutes I phoned a dear friend, Jim Davidson, who came straight over to comfort me.

The next morning—after a sleepless night—I got up hoping it had all been a terrible nightmare. But of course it hadn't, and I sat at the breakfast table staring at my cornflakes unable to accept what had actually happened. There had been no alarm bells because I stupidly hadn't suspected a thing.

That morning at half past eleven I left for the day's pantomime performances at the theatre. My mind was mush, and I asked my dresser to keep an eye on me.

"I'm not feeling too great," I said. "There's a chance I might forget some things."

Just before the matinee performance was about to begin I stood at the side of the stage in my costume, wig and full make-up as the pantomime dame, and said to myself: "Logan, what on earth are you doing here?"

And all at a time when I could hear the anticipation of the audience and the children who were expecting me to make them roar with laughter, and inject some happiness into their lives. The show was more difficult than any I can ever remember. I think the auto-pilot clicked in and dragged me through at the other end.

How could I chuck it? How could I walk out of the theatre? The management had spent a fortune on the production. The artistes were all depending on me for their wages at the end of the week.

I had to do it. I had signed a contract. If I was in the middle of a big production and won the lottery, then of course I would be absolutely delighted, but I would never, ever just walk away. I would always keep to my word. In the theatre we have standards.

Actors are often the same. Their conscience tells them they have a job to do and the only way to do it is to the best of their abilities. You'll never be able to do that if you have been out on the bevvy.

The worst part was that I had to keep up the pretence that everything was OK twice a day for about five weeks after Pamela walked out. There was many a night when I just wanted to say: "Here, listen to this." But I didn't.

"How are the children, Jimmy?" people at the theatre would ask.

"Oh, great," I would say. "My wife's had to take them up to Inverness because her mother's not very well and she's the only daughter."

Each time I was asked I continued this ridiculous facade, while in reality the pain of the situation was tearing me to bits—an excruciating pain that ate away inside me day and night.

I phoned my sister Annie in America, and said: "I need you to be here for me."

She arrived on the next plane, and stayed for three months. Our next door neighbour Angela, despite her own problems, was also a wonderful support, and there is no doubt those two got me through that horrible period. If it wasn't for them I honestly don't know what I would have done. I may have got through it, but I would have been a complete wreck at the end.

Annie had seen me during my bad times in the past, but said that nothing compared to the traumatic effect losing my kids had on me. I was a mess for a long time, constantly tortured by the knowledge that the two most important parts of my world had been ripped away.

Each day was filled with pain. One morning, feeling not too bad, I put my dressing-gown on and wandered downstairs where Angela and Annie were preparing breakfast. I sat at the dining table and suddenly just burst into tears. I couldn't speak. Up until that moment I had seemed to be all right. I had held myself together, and I reckoned I was dealing with my problem, yet there I was just sobbing my eyes out. And there was nothing they could do to console me.

During this awful period it was agreed that I should go to Inverness because I was absolutely desperate to see my little ones. Annie came with me, and booked into a hotel, and when I got to my mother-in-law's house I was welcomed like a benevolent uncle who happened to be passing through.

"Oh, Jimmy," her mum said. "So nice to see you. Now how about a nice cup of tea?"

I stayed in the upstairs house that night, and my wee boy, who had toothache, insisted on sleeping with me. I comforted him when the pain woke him up.

Pamela and her mum couldn't have been more pleasant. "We've got some lovely lamb tonight, Jimmy, because we know how much you like lamb."

It was all so charming.

But their attitude was breathtaking; in fact it was breathtaking to the point that I genuinely don't believe they had any idea what they had done to me. When my wife took me downstairs to her flat she showed me how great it was looking for the kids, and told me how they had kitted it out with new carpets, flooring, units and so on. That was all very nice, but it was clear a tremendous amount of work had been done that would have taken a fair amount of time to do. In other words she was doing all this when I was spending a fortune getting the house in Helensburgh ready for the whole family.

When a woman leaves and takes the children it's awful. Take the house, but don't take the kids. I think there is an awful lot said about mothers and what they have to go through but people forget about the caring fathers, and there are a lot of them, who suffer terribly.

Angela saw that side of Jimmy Logan when she stood by her next door neighbour through those difficult times. I really got to know Angela over that traumatic period. I discovered what a caring, warm, generous woman she was, and she says she discovered what a lovely man I was. She had thought I would be just like a lot of the "plastic" people she had met in the theatre, but when my kids were whipped away from me she saw a man who was sensitive and in some ways strong, but able to cry at the same time. Some men think that is a sign of man's weakness, but I believe someone who is able to do that has a more gentle, yet stronger character.

I'm a very emotional person, and Angela was seeing Jimmy Logan, the man, as opposed to Jimmy Logan, the actor, for the first time. And she was impressed with that side of me. She saw a great many friends support me, and realised that that was partly because I would have done everything to support them had the boot been on someone else's foot.

363

Out of this awful situation I also got to know how wonderful Angela was. In my time of greatest need she, and Annie, were there for me. Angela told me if there was anything I needed done in the house just to let her know. She was absolutely marvellous, and the pair of them ran the house for me, relieving a great deal of potential strain.

Angela, at that time, also had few troubles to seek. Her marriage had yielded six children but was going through a hard time. At one point she actually left her husband, and then moved back in to give the marriage another try, but it wasn't working out.

Angela and her husband had decided their marriage was over, and were trying to sell their half of the house.

Soon I was trying to sell my half of the house too.

Although I never realised it at the time, I think the truth of the matter is that my wife was advised to move out of our house in Glasgow, and into a new home, before divorcing me. She would have had no claim on the family home in Hamilton Avenue because it was in my name, but she would have had a claim on the house in Helensburgh.

So the best thing for her was to get out of that beautiful house in Glasgow that was almost paid off, and move into that big place in Helensburgh that ended up having the kind of mortgage that would break the back of a horse. It was a beautiful home but so it should have been, given the amount of money I spent getting it right. In fact I spent too much money. I footed the bill for splitting the house in two, then built a new entrance hall in the original design and had the place rewired and redecorated. That was just the start. The conservatory alone cost about £26,000.

Pamela came down for just long enough to make it her home then zipped back up to her new life in Inverness.

The house had become a big empty mausoleum with too many bad memories and an enormous mortgage, so I didn't have too many qualms about selling it. I had to get out. But I would have had little choice anyway because my wife soon announced that she wanted half the proceeds.

For six months after the house was sold I stayed with an actress friend Pamela Kelly at her home in Helensburgh. I packed her dining room and the bedroom I was in with boxes, cases and parcels full of my belongings. I also put a lot of things into store until I found another home.

Pamela even allowed Stanley to be a house guest and found room for the children when they came to visit.

But it was all very hard to take.

Having finally got back to being in a very strong financial position in Glasgow, which had taken years of hard work to build up, I now felt as though I was once again back to square one. I was back to: "How much is a frying pan?"

At the time, I didn't realise what was being done to me. It all seemed so logical; if you get divorced she gets half the house. That's logical enough, so how could I complain? What a mug!

I had first met Angela years earlier when she was just seventeen.

John Mulvaney, a lovely comic actor who ended up in *Five Past Eight* with me, had a sister who was very friendly with Angela's mother Mary. One day John's sister phoned up and said: "John has been invited to Jimmy Logan's house and he's been asked to bring someone with him. Would Angela like to go? It might be a nice experience for her."

I met Angela again in 1977, very briefly, when her son Bruce was just 12 and came to see one of my pantomimes. He had just bought the record I did for the Lauder show and asked me to sign it.

I suppose we started "going out" towards the end of 1989, about eight or nine months after Pamela left.

Shortly afterwards the house was sold, and Angela moved into a flat in Helensburgh where she stayed for about eight months. I had bought another house in the town, and the guy who owned the adjoining house to mine was a builder. As Angela was looking for a new home, I asked if he was interested in selling it.

"I would be," he said.

"Great. I know someone who would be interested in buying."

So I phoned Angela up and she was very interested. She bought the house, and we moved into my house together while operating her home as a guest house. That side of things worked out well.

Meanwhile, we were both going through divorces.

Lawyers had become involved in mine, and Pamela set out her terms. She would offer me a divorce if I agreed to pay alimony. I, however, only wanted one thing—joint legal custody of our children. I insisted on this because they were both our kids. If a decision was being taken that could affect their upbringing I wanted to be in a position where I had a say. If she, for instance, wanted to change the school they went to I wanted her to at least discuss the issue with me.

Given the circumstances of our break-up I didn't think that was too much to ask. At no point did I ask for physical custody of the children but I was determined to try and get joint legal custody, where I would have a real say in how they were brought up. However, my lawyer John O'Donnell informed me to my horror of the difficulties involved in seeking that kind of joint custody.

The parent with possession of the child usually gets sole custody of the child, except in the most exceptional circumstances. In my mind this means that in the law's eyes fathers are a waste of time. They don't count. If a wife takes away the children she has complete and utter control immediately. The law virtually always presumes the mother is the natural choice to bring up the child, a stance which has resulted in some terrible injustices. There have been cases where the mother has walked out with her boyfriend leaving the father to bring the children up, and he has done the job wonderfully. Then when it has suited her, the mother has returned and the judge rules that the kids should return to their mother.

That scenario may not occur too often, but it is blatantly unjust and unfair.

I told Pamela I wanted joint legal custody but she refused to give me it. I decided to fight for what I thought were my rights as a father.

Firstly, I owed it to my children to do everything I possibly could to ensure what was best for them. And what was best for them was that I had a say in their futures. I was also angry at a legal system which tended to give great comfort to mothers, but not fathers.

By this time I knew about her male friend in Inverness, John. She had had her third child, to him, in 1990. I decided to file for divorce on the grounds of my wife's adultery and present the divorce courts with a case for joint legal custody of the children. It may have been against the odds, but I believed my children's futures were worth fighting for.

We had raised an action to go to court when my wife delivered the biggest possible bombshell. John O'Donnell arrived at the house one night with the kind of news he felt he could only deliver in person. He said to me: "Jimmy, I've been talking to your wife's lawyer and he is saying this could get very nasty."

At this point I was still paying her every month to look after the kids.

"What do you mean, 'very nasty'?" I said.

"Well, she wants to do a DNA test."

The moment he said it I knew exactly what had happened. All the past years had been a lie. I had held her hand as she gave birth to the children. Every day and every year I marvelled at the miracle and joy of this great gift that had been given to me. People stopped me in the street to say: "Hello Jimmy, how are the twins?"

I took them to America when they were still babies because my brother Bert was so ill in hospital in Florida. I had walked one night in Scotland under the stars praying he might live until he saw them. When he did, he said: "You know, you can hear about them, see their photographs and talk about them, but when you actually touch them . . ." I knew what he meant.

I wept that night when John said DNA. Not just for me, but for the children, for all the love I had to give them, the protection and caring they needed in their young lives, my plans for their future. And the horror of the situation was that the man now claiming to be their father had done nothing for them but hide what he knew from the day they were born. Then after six years, with pride he was about to say: "Yes, I am the father." But up until then . . . nothing. There was a strong and loving bond between the children and I which was to be taken away, not just from myself but from the children. And I wept.

The day the DNA results became known, Pamela sat these two young children down and told them: "John is now your daddy, and Jimmy is not your daddy. You can call him what you like, so what about Uncle Jimmy?"

It was blunt and to the point. Then came the phone call.

"Hello, Uncle Jimmy," said my daughter, giggling her head off.

"You're not my daddy," said my son. "You're my Uncle Jimmy. John is my daddy."

And he said it over and over again. He was like an old gramophone record. But that was just a child's way of handling the situation.

I felt as if someone had plunged a rusty knife into my stomach, then twisted it slowly. I said: "I don't care what you call me, as long as you know I love you."

But I did care very much.

There was the thrill of going out and buying birthday cards that said "Son" and "Daughter" on them and, as at least thirty videos show, we shared a loving and happy life. Yet it was all so brief. Now all that had been taken away from me in a phone call where they said: "Hello, Uncle Jimmy."

As usual I said nothing to the children and put on a front. Inside I was a wreck. I went to Inverness, took a room in a hotel to have some place to spend time with them, and said: "I don't care what you call me. You can call me Jimmy, you can call me daddy or you can call me anything you like. As long as you know I love you. I love you very much. What you call me is not important. Knowing I love you is very important."

Of course, what they called me *was* very important.

The divorce was a long, drawn out and messy process. Proceedings started shortly after Pamela left, but the hearing didn't go ahead at Inverness Sheriff Court until 1992, when I was preparing for three major plays at Pitlochry Theatre—Arthur Miller's classic play *Death of a Salesman, A Month of Sundays* and *Dominions of Fancy.*

There was a lot of press coverage between Pamela leaving me and the divorce case. I'm sure some people must have said: "There must be something wrong with him if his wife leaves him and takes the children."

Added to this were the regular discussions with my lawyer between rehearsals about the ins and outs of the case. It was such a stressful period that I developed a bad rash on one of my hands, and to this day I still have it.

In the run up to the divorce hearing itself I was trying to learn *Death of a Salesman* and *A Month of Sundays* at the same time, but I just couldn't retain the lines in my head. After four weeks, feeling very confident that I had finally cracked most of the lines in *A Month of Sundays*, I strode purposefully towards the rehearsal room. Five minutes after we started my mind went completely blank. I couldn't remember a single word of the play.

Instead of being sharp and clear, my head felt as though it was filled with cotton wool. Realising I had a serious problem, Joan Knight sent everyone home and sat with me. That afternoon I went to the theatre doctor, who listened to my description of what had happened and said: "Your mind is like a computer that is overloaded. You must give it a rest."

But I didn't have time to have a rest because of the two plays that were racing towards me.

The Pitlochry Festival director, Clive Perry, brought in a fine actor Martin James to take over my role in *Death of a Salesman*, and take some of the strain off me until I was ready. For a week I walked away from those plays, and tried to learn nothing. Then, very gently, I began picking up the lines of *A Month of Sundays* again.

Incidentally, the play is about two elderly men, one who is frightened of becoming incontinent and the other who is worried about losing his memory and mind. I played the man who was frightened of becoming incontinent. What casting. But it was a lovely play which worked.

After *A Month of Sundays* opened, I started to relearn *Death of a Salesman* in the full knowledge that I was facing a court case the week before I opened which would decide the children's future. I rehearsed in Pitlochry on the Monday that week. On the Tuesday, Wednesday and Thursday I was in Inverness for the divorce hearing. How did I do it? To be honest, I don't know.

At the divorce hearing itself I had only one witness, Fiona Clark, the daughter of Calum Kennedy. She was a woman in her thirties, very well groomed and a mother herself.

When she was asked: "When did you first meet Jimmy?" her answer was just wonderful.

She told the court that when she was about seven years old her mother took ill, and I took the family into my home until she was better.

"That was the nature of the man," said Fiona.

She said many wonderful things because she had seen me with

the children, and described the wonderful relationship I had with them. That was the only beautiful thing about the divorce—I had never dreamt that that lovely child from all those years ago would become such an elegant lady who spoke so well on my behalf at such a traumatic time.

At the end of the hearing the Sheriff said he would deliver his judgement later, so I went back to Pitlochry where I rehearsed on the Friday, Saturday and Sunday, before opening on the Monday night.

Somehow I managed to concentrate on *Salesman*, a play where it is said actors have five mountains to climb in the second half. Playing opposite Alice Fraser was a joy, and the wonderful cast were very supportive. I got probably the best crit I've ever had from John Linklater in *The Herald*. He described it as the performance of a lifetime, and *The Scotsman* seemed to agree. That was wonderful—a spark of brightness amid all the gloom.

The Sheriff took almost a year to publish his findings, and I couldn't get divorced because of it. John O'Donnell even lodged an official complaint over the amount of time the Sheriff had taken.

In the end I lost my case for legal custody. The Sheriff said the case was simply about divorce, the children and access. Nothing else. He left me with parental rights which, in practical terms, I don't feel amounts to very much.

I was given access to the kids for a week in the spring, two in the summer, a week in the autumn and either Christmas or New Year, depending on which was best.

But it was quite a tale.

The Sheriff considered the question of DNA unimportant. From the children's point of view, the important thing was who loved them, not what their DNA was. Under Scottish law children born in a marriage are deemed to be the children of the people who are married. Legally, the husband is the father and the wife is the mother.

The DNA aspect of the case threw up other questions entirely.

I have strong opinions on every aspect of this whole affair, but a lot of these opinions are best kept to myself. What was more important than anything was that when I fought that divorce I was faced with a choice. I could have accepted the situation and said nothing, but I wanted to be able to turn round to my children one day and say: "I fought that case because, win or lose, I was fighting it for you."

You bring up a child until that child is four or five years of age, and you adore them, and then someone suddenly turns round and says: "They are not yours."

No, that's not on. There is a strong bond there, an emotional link that no-one can take away and can never be broken.

The year after Pamela took the kids back up to Inverness I put a lot of my own money into setting up a theatre version of *Oor Wullie*, convinced that an on-stage version of the popular cartoon strip would be a big success on tour.

I wrote the show, assembled a young cast and got the whole tour organised. I, however, wasn't in the show. For this one, I wanted to stay behind the scenes.

Just after *Oor Wullie* started I was asked to star in the wonderful play *Sunsets and Glories* at the West Yorkshire Playhouse in Leeds, opposite Freddie Jones and other great actors like Marius Goring, Murray Melvin and Jeremy Sinden, son of Sir Donald Sinden.

I was suggested for the part by a wonderful choreographer Eleanor Fazan. She had convinced the director Stuart Burge, who thought I was just a Scottish comedian, that I would be perfect for the part.

Then she had to convince me.

Sunsets and Glories is the story of the only Pope to resign, Celestine V in 1294. I got the script on the Tuesday, read it the next day, talked to them about it that night, and they said they needed a "yes" or "no" right away because rehearsals started the following week. When Stuart phoned me asking me for an answer, I agreed to do it.

I went straight down to Yorkshire and shared digs with a great actor who has made an immense contribution to the British film industry, Marius Goring. I have to say I was a bit in awe when I met him.

We also shared the kitchen in our digs, and I not only did all the cooking for both of us but the washing up as well. Meanwhile, Marius, with a glass of wine in his hand, would sit at the table pontificating on every subject with great authority. His lovely wife Pru sent him back to our digs every Monday morning with a large box of food.

The play itself was challenging. Freddie Jones had prepared for his part for some time but I had the unenviable task of learning my lines as we went along. And because the play had been written by Peter Barnes, the London press arrived in full force. We received excellent notices, and I was particularly delighted with one crit which said: "Two performances are quite superb, Freddie Jones as Morrone [Celestine] and Jimmy Logan as his successor Boniface [Cardinal Gaetani], in two widely contrasting portrayals of absolute goodness on the one hand and cruel despotic intolerance on the other [That was me!]."

However, by going to *Sunsets and Glories*, which was a magnificent success, I left the *Oor Wullie* show to its own devices. And that wasn't a good move.

From day one the show didn't do the business it could and should have done. We opened in Dundee—Oor Wullie's home town—at the beginning of the Dundee Festival, but there just wasn't the interest in the show I thought there would have been. It stayed in Dundee for three weeks when it should have been there for one week at the most.

When the show reached Irvine we received a frantic phone call at our home in Helensburgh. The girl who was playing *Oor Wullie*—Ashley Jensen—had collapsed and was being taken to hospital.

We were in the process of getting ready to host a birthday party for my sister Annie, and a large number of friends and guests, including Rikki Fulton and his wife Kate, and John Cairney, Scotland's answer to Burns, were due to arrive at any moment.

So I asked Angela how she fancied playing Oor Wullie that night.

As John walked through our front door we ran out.

And I said: "John, there's the wine and there's the food. Can you look after everyone? We've got to go to the theatre."

And we disappeared in a cloud of smoke.

All the way to Irvine my face was white as a sheet. Beside me Angela was sitting with the script on her knee, and trying to learn it. She had had stage experience in the past, but I had never seen her performing in anything.

"It's all right," she said. "I'm sure I'll remember the words. Everything will be OK."

About eight weeks earlier Angela had looked at the script after I had suggested there should be an understudy. But I never dreamed Angela would actually be needed.

We arrived at the theatre, and the chap who was playing Fat Bob said to Angela: "Oh, you've got a marathon on your hands."

To be truthful, that wasn't the kind of statement she needed to hear.

Angela rushed in, had a quick run through, got dressed and made up, and the musical director said: "Just watch for the cues for the music."

And minutes later there she was at the age of 45 playing an 11-year-old Oor Wullie.

Her performance was wonderful, and she got through the whole thing without any problems. She did a great job.

When she first got in the cast were a bit funny with her, because they weren't sure if she was an Equity member. She had actually kept her membership going since she appeared in some episodes of *Dr Finlay's Casebook* years before, but no-one had the guts to ask her outright.

Eventually one of the cast brought the subject up in a roundabout way, and Angela dealt with it marvellously.

"What age are you?" she enquired of the suspicious younger colleague.

"Twenty-one," he said.

"Oh, goodness, I've been an Equity member longer than you've been alive."

So that was that problem out of the way.

From an early age Angela had always wanted to be in the theatre. Her husband was an actor, and she got some small parts in shows like *Dr Finlay's Casebook*. Mothering six children got in the way of her acting ambitions, but she joined drama groups and learned stage work.

Angela also quickly realised she had a photographic memory for scripts; an ability we would all love to possess. Thank God she had it that night.

Before the *Oor Wullie* incident she saved another play in a similar way—*Stage Door Canteen*, at the Dumbarton People's Theatre. This time the script arrived at half past seven one night, and the next day she went on and gave a powerful, faultless performance.

She gets a real kick out of the theatre, and tells me she loves watching me at a rehearsal because of the way I use my experience to hand on useful tips to other actors.

There were few bright moments with *Oor Wullie*, though. But, during a period when I was still trying to come to terms with the loss of my kids, the production just wasn't the big success I had hoped it would be. Its appeal in *The Sunday Post* failed to translate onto stage, and that was a big disappointment.

14

LOVELY BISCUITS

Had it not been for Angela I don't know how I would have coped with those terrible years leading up to the divorce case. I had walked down a very dark valley in my life, and you could say Angela was the silver lining that came out of the cloud which covered that valley.

During that whole period she was always there for me when I needed her. She gave me the strength to get through, and the loving care everyone requires in their worst moments.

When Angela told me she loved me I knew in my heart it was my dog she was after. My second black labrador—who also ended up being called Stanley—had her wrapped round his paw.

I think of myself as the luckiest man in the world to have found Angela, and as soon as my divorce came through I said to her: "Let's get married." We both knew the road we wanted to take.

Our wedding took place at the registry office in Hove of all places, a small seaside town in Sussex that was primarily chosen to avoid the attentions of the Great British Press, and because Aunt Mona lived there. She had long since forgiven me for that horrendous trip in my plane 30 years earlier, and was only too happy to play host to one of the happiest moments in my life.

We had told only a few people of our plans, so the day before the Big Day I went to the railway station and typed out little cards saying simply: "Angela and Jimmy are now Mr and Mrs Short or Mr and Mrs Logan, or 'You Two', on Friday 30th July at Hove. We hope to see you when we return to Scotland. With love."

I sent them to about 70 friends before we went off to Paris on honeymoon for a week.

The ceremony in Hove was lovely, and I smiled as I thought of those couples who spend a year preparing their wedding. I went into a florist's shop, and said: "I want a corsage of blue flowers for the bride and a white flower for the bridegroom."

And the florist said: "When is the wedding?"

"In half an hour," I replied. I was lying, of course. I had 45 minutes.

My best man was my nephew John Short, and among the 14 guests were Harry Gordon's daughter Bunty, and Jack Tripp, who was honoured with the MBE for his services as a pantomime dame. Angela, however, couldn't get over how nervous I was.

Afterwards, all I said was: "God, I need a drink."

Angela looked at me, and replied: "So do I."

When I was cutting the cake Mona was egging me on.

I said to her: "Don't worry, I'm well practised at this."

And the knife broke.

We went to a friend's wedding some time afterwards, and I said: "It's so nice to go to a wedding that isn't my own."

Everyone fell about, but I was deadly serious.

In the years leading up to our wedding in July 1993 I never had my problems to seek, and early that year the strains on my personal and professional lives finally took their toll on my health.

The first warning bells had sounded 10 years earlier after I organised the Royal Performance for the Prince and Princess of Wales. Anyone who has taken on that level of commitment knows just how much is involved. And to make matters worse, I had still to free myself from the shackles of the Metropole.

The alarm went off as I stepped out of a taxi in Glasgow a few weeks after that Royal Performance. My briefcase suddenly felt as if it was loaded with bricks, and I couldn't walk 50 yards up the road. It was a horrible feeling.

Standing there in Hope Street unable to lift my briefcase I decided it was time to see a doctor. He gave me a good check-up, and pronounced me perfectly healthy. A few days later a heart specialist delivered a clean bill of health too.

But deep down I knew something wasn't right. I insisted they do further tests, and after I was put on a treadmill, they discovered a problem.

"Jimmy," the consultant said. "We think you should have a heart-bypass operation."

I wasn't keen on such a drastic remedy. Eventually he suggested a drug which relieved the situation for a number of years afterwards.

However, the strain returned with a vengeance in 1992 when I was going through the divorce and preparing for those three major plays at Pitlochry. I found I could hardly walk up the hill to the house where I was staying in Dunkeld. There was a pain in my arms. It all seemed like *déjà vu*.

This time there was no debate. I was told I needed a quadruple heart-bypass operation.

It was only the third time I had been in hospital for anything worth shouting about. The previous occasion was when I banged my head in Perth, and the first time was for an operation to cure the "businessman's disease"—haemorrhoids.

On that occasion I had gone into a nursing home in Glasgow under a BUPA scheme expecting the best service that private health care had to offer.

The first thing I noticed was that the food was terrible.

But my spirits perked up a bit when, just before the operation, a wee man with an attaché case came down the corridor, and the nurse said to him: "There's a big star down there."

"Oh, I know, I know," he said.

When he came through the door, I said: "Hello, what do you do?"

"I'm the barber."

Good stuff, I thought. Private health care redeems itself. I reckoned this was like Hollywood, and that because I was a private patient I got a shave to make me feel better before the operation.

I got a shave all right. It just wasn't the kind of shave I was expecting.

Before I knew where I was, he had whipped off the bedclothes and started soaping me around the stomach area. I was petrified in case the nurse walked in looking for an autograph.

Then he took out one of those great big, massive open razors and started shaving me. As he stood there with my most valuable possessions in one hand, and the razor in the other hand, he asked: "Are you Kenneth McKellar?"

I was scared to say "yes" in case he gave me a Bobbit and said: "I don't like your programme anyway."

Years later I was rehearsing for the play *Brighton Beach Memoirs* at Perth Theatre in a room at the rear of the theatre. At the back of the room was what looked like a small single bed. During one tea break I sat down on that bed to collect my thoughts and get a few minutes peace and quiet.

But no-one had told me that bed wasn't actually a bed. Instead it was a set of drawers that had been covered over to look like a bed. When I sat down in the middle the whole thing collapsed around me, and one of the ends came up and whacked me on the side of the head. I was stunned for a few moments. Coffee was everywhere. Some people came in and sat me on a chair. There was blood streaming out of my ear.

I said: "Put something on it and let's carry on with the re-hearsal."

They said: "No, no, no, Jimmy, we think you should go up to the Infirmary."

I was taken to the small cottage infirmary at Perth where the doctors quickly diagnosed that I would have to go to Dundee to have the wound stitched or grafted.

I arrived there late in the afternoon, was put in a nice room with en suite toilet facilities and a television, and at eight o'clock I was lying on the operating table with a skin surgeon grafting skin onto my ear.

Before the operation I told him about a dear friend of mine, Jack Mastardi, a great plastic surgeon who came to my wedding to Gina in the Bahamas.

He said: "I'm not going to give you a present, but I will give you a gift of my hands. If ever you need any plastic surgery done I will do it for you."

And I said to this surgeon operating on me in Dundee: "You're going to get a terrible row from Jack when he hears about this."

The staff in that hospital were fantastic, a fine example of what is so good about the NHS. Three days later on the Monday morning I was allowed to leave, but before I left the surgeon told me: "You must take three weeks off."

And I said to him: "I've got news for you. Next Friday I'm opening in a play. I'm one of the leads so if I'm not there they won't open it. I've got to be there."

I think he thought I was a nut.

I went back that day to rehearsals with a big bandage covering my ear. They allowed me to take it easy, and I just slowly talked my part through. On the morning of the opening night I went to the small cottage hospital in Perth where they removed the big bandage and replaced it with another dressing that wasn't quite so obvious.

I opened in *Brighton Beach Memoirs* that night, and we ran it for a couple of weeks. Then we went up to Inverness. It went well.

The most painful time was when I returned to the hospital in Dundee to have the stitches taken out.

Oh boy, was that sensitive.

Before I was admitted to Ross Hall Hospital in Glasgow for my quadruple heart-bypass operation I was approached by the director of the Edinburgh International Festival, Brian McMaster. He asked if I was interested in producing and directing a show celebrating the heyday of variety and the music hall.

We had lengthy discussions about what could and would be done. I made it clear that the show had to recreate the joy of shows like *Five Past Eight* if it was to be done properly. Therefore, I had to have 12 Tiller Girls—not ten, eight or six. And there would have to be a 16-piece orchestra. Brian agreed.

I looked at the dates and noticed the opening night was in August—less than five months after my life-saving surgery. So I agreed to produce and direct this big show which we would call *The Fabulous Fifties*.

It was a brave decision. In order to meet the stiff targets I had set myself I had to get all the artistes I wanted signed up, and the programme finalised, before I went in for the operation that March.

The operation took place on St Patrick's Day—March 17—and this time I was in for a fortnight. Because of the intensity of the procedure I spent some time in intensive care with wires and tubes coming out of my arms and throat. When Angela and Annie saw me like that they were truly shocked. The rest of my time there was spent trying to regain my strength.

It's just as well I got *The Fabulous Fifties* ready before the surgery because, even though I knew the operation would tire me out for a while, I never realised quite how much. For the whole of March, April, May and June I had virtually no energy at all. One day I tried to take the dog out for a walk and barely got past the front gate.

When I returned from honeymoon in Paris, though, I felt rejuvenated.

And the four nights of *The Fabulous Fifties* were just wonderful. We used all the original Howard & Wyndham scenery and, by chance, I found four microphones designed just like the ones we used in the days of *Five Past Eight*. On either side of the stage there were boxes with changing numbers on them like they used to have in the old music hall, and we got special Fifties advertising slides and music for the interval.

I also arranged for two young ladies dressed like the tea ladies from The Ca' D'Oro to serve tea and biscuits to people in the audience at the interval. It was a throwback to what they did at the big Howard & Wyndham theatres.

And of course all the old gang were there; Johnny Beattie, Jack Milroy, Walter Carr, Mary Lee, Susan Maughan, The Platters, Karen Hunter, Adrian Fleming, Ann Fields. The director was Dougie Squires.

My pal Johnny Beattie did a marvellous warm-up dressed in a red suit he wore 30 years previously—and it still fitted him.

Johnny is a man of the theatre who has paid his dues, and knows the history of the theatre because he has been in it so long. He is one of the backbones in this country of the summer shows and pantomimes, and a real pro. His two lovely daughters, Maureen and Louise, have become wonderful actresses in their own right.

I was fascinated by the reactions of the audience when Johnny appeared later on in a sketch as an old man in a bed. It had been so long since a theatre audience had seen a sketch like that on the stage. To them it was an entirely novel approach and they loved it. In fact, *The Fabulous Fifties* was one of the hits of the Festival.

Then I got a call asking if I would appear the following month in a production of Neil Simon's *The Sunshine Boys* at the Royal Lyceum Theatre in Edinburgh, which was being directed by Maureen Lipman. They were under pressure to find someone, and I felt good, so I said yes.

I played Willie Clark, one half of a comedy double-act heading towards old age and the twilight of their careers. It was a touch ironic that I was soon having a harder time than my character Willie.

I may have felt good when I agreed to do *The Sunshine Boys*, but in hindsight I took too much on in the aftermath of the operation. For instance, I had no idea at that point that a general anaesthetic can affect a person months after it has been administered. Apparently it can affect the mind's learning capacity, and when the time came for me to learn the script I knew what they meant. "Ma heid wisnae right," as they would say in Glasgow, and I had a terrible job picking up the words.

Towards the end of the first week of performances I was feeling particularly strange. I found myself walking along corridors bumping into walls. When I got dressed at the theatre I had to hang on to the backs of chairs to stand up.

During the first half on the Friday night I came over all queasy when I was on stage. Picking the best moment, I walked into the kitchen which was part of the set, was as sick as a dog, and walked out again to carry on with the play.

As I've said before, there's nothing more important than the show. The audience never knew a thing.

However, everyone at the side of the stage saw how ill I was and immediately called a doctor. When I came off at the end of the first half he was standing there waiting for me.

"You can't go on, Jimmy," he said. "Go home to your bed immediately."

I discovered I had an acute infection of the inner ear; hence my confrontations with the walls earlier that day.

Luckily my understudy Bob Docherty was well versed and stepped in to do a wonderful job. Meanwhile, I was taken back to the house where I was staying and never moved from my bed for the next four days. I managed to return for the final few performances, but all in all it was an experience I never want to repeat.

All of this happened in 1993, the year I officially became a pensioner and qualified for a bus pass. A fine time to wind down and retire you may think. Many people were offering advice along the lines of: "It's about time you put your feet up." Not a bit of it.

The lifeblood of Jimmy Logan is, and always has been, the theatre, and I wasn't about to let the small matter of a life-saving quadruple heart-bypass operation take that away from me. As such, I'm pleased to report that there have been many great experiences since, both on and off the stage.

Had I decided to call it a day I would not, for instance, have had the opportunity the following year to work on one of the most exciting and emotional theatre performances ever to have taken place in Scotland. It was *The Big Picnic*, a giant play that was the brainchild of Bill Bryden, without doubt one of the most creative writers and directors around.

I first worked with him in 1990 on another magnificent play, *The Ship*. Both productions were epic not only in their stories, but through the sheer scale and innovation involved in putting them together.

The venue for these plays was The Shed in Govan, a huge old building that used to house engines for battleships. It was disused until Bill spotted it, and decided it would play the perfect host for his own unique brand of creative theatre.

For actors like me used to playing in traditional auditoriums it was a complete culture shock. There was no stage as such, and sometimes the audience followed the cast around. Many of the actors, including myself, couldn't get their heads around this concept when it was explained to them for the first time. But once we saw the set for *The Ship* being built we realised the imagination that had gone into it was truly innovative—and utterly brilliant.

Let me explain. In *The Ship* there were three tiers of seating on either side of The Shed, the lowest tier being about 30 feet off the ground. Those banks of seating were separated by a huge scaffolding structure that represented the last great liner being built on the Clyde. At one end of this huge structure the orchestra sat on a platform above a stage that could be wheeled in and out for different scenes.

And the audience looked down at this amazing scene, thinking they were peering inside this massive hulk of a ship. They could also see about 200 other members of the audience standing on the deck wondering what was going on.

When the music started these people suddenly saw a cast of about 30 people running towards them. They did the natural thing—and got out of the way. Then the cast start acting among those members of the audience. A truly remarkable concept.

At one stage the giant keel of the ship was lowered into a channel that opened up to reveal the activity of a ship being built; the noise of drills, the sparks of the welder's torch, dozens of men working away.

In the finale the audience members who had been standing were led to a lower platform where they looked up at the ship. Then they heard the Queen's voice launching the ship, and watched breathlessly as this huge structure slipped off into the darkness leaving only a bare centrepiece and the standing members of the audience between the banks of the seated audience on either side. Every night I, as the character who represented the famous Clydeside shipyard manager John Rannie, had the thrill of watching that ship being launched, and every night the audience cheered as it disappeared into the distance. When the music started off again the actors joined the audience and danced.

The whole thing was so realistic. Grandparents, mums, dads and the kids all came to that play and loved it. We often saw some of the older men in tears because they had worked all their lives in the shipyards, and it brought back so many memories.

The concept behind the staging of *The Big Picnic* in 1994 was equally impressive. The play started out at one end of The Shed with the audience on banks of seats around the opening wedding scene.

I arrived as the regimental Colour-Sergeant, a veteran of the Boer War, to announce the outbreak of the 1914-18 War. This was followed by short scenes of the men joining up and learning French before suddenly they all rushed back onto the acting area in their Army uniforms.

As the Colour-Sergeant of this battalion of the Highland Light Infantry (City of Glasgow Regiment), I stood in front of the men, and announced: "To France, slow march." Above us on a huge steel platform the orchestra played and, as we marched, huge white walls in front of us opened up to reveal No Man's Land, and the trenches. Meanwhile the audience followed the action, the banks of seating on one side of this amazing arena moving alongside the marching men. On the other side members of the audience walked alongside the men.

When the men went "over the top", and into this hail of enemy fire, the audience followed them for more than 200 yards on their perilous journey into No Man's Land. One astonishing moment came when a Scottish soldier got killed, and a trapeze artist representing an angel came down from above, picked the soldier up, and swooped back into the darkness. It depicted a true story from the Battle of Mons when many soldiers swore an angel came out the sky and helped to save their lives. The Angel of Mons became legend.

In the finale the regiment were wiped out before a young soldier rose to sing 'Abide With Me' in Gaelic. Then the dead soldiers rose and walked back across No Man's Land, with the audience following them, back to the spot where the wedding scene had taken place. Once there, they froze in different positions, representing all the monuments around the world in memory of the men who fell on those battlefields.

Standing before them was the minister and the wives, and while The Last Post played in the background, he read out the names of the men who died. In our final performance on Armistice Day 1994, a cloud of poppies was dropped onto this emotional scene.

It was truly remarkable theatre, the most exciting theatre I've been involved with. One day during a break in rehearsals I walked into Govan and saw the war monument there vandalised by graffiti. I was tremendously worried because it suddenly dawned on me that we were acting the parts of the actual boys named on that memorial who gave their lives all those years ago. I was engulfed by tremendous apprehensions that we were going to appear to be a bunch of actors with wee guns running up and down playing Cowboys and Indians; that we were not going to honour their memory by telling it like it was.

Thank God, I was very wrong. A strange magic happened. It happened to me when I gave the order to march to France with the pipes playing, and we were the boys. They were the young lads and I was the older fellow, and it felt right.

The audience reactions were fantastic. The play had a tremendous effect on people who came to see it. Women who would only have been children in the Second World War were telling me they wept because they thought of their own sons, and could see them going out into No Man's Land to be slaughtered.

One old soldier who had been in the Battle of the Somme was struck by the play's realism. And a group of veterans who had been in the actual Highland Light Infantry came along resplendent in their smart blazers, and all wearing the HLI tie. They had tears in their eyes because the images before them brought back so many memories.

The strange thing about *The Big Picnic* was the reaction of the Scottish press. Despite the standing ovations we received every night, and the obvious effect it was having on people who came to see it, the papers and media didn't like it.

I would say that sometimes, God bless them, critics just hate it when something indicates their criticism could be wrong.

One of the criticisms in the press was that the facilities for the cast weren't up to scratch. The dressing rooms were damp, and the Army clothes tended to remain damp from the night before. In fact, I became quite ill during *The Big Picnic* and had to cut back my part somewhat to get through.

The press went on and on about the conditions we were working in. Yes the dressing rooms were terrible, yes it was damp, yes the circumstances we were being asked to perform in were not what we were used to. But The Shed was never built to be a theatre, and the bottom line was that we didn't care.

What mattered was that we were taking part in the most exciting piece of theatre that we had ever worked in. *The Big Picnic* and *The Ship* were both rich in entirely different ways, but equally exciting.

The character I played in *The Big Picnic*, the hard-bitten Colour-Sergeant, was a leader of frightened men in a conflict that of course had so many ties to my own life.

My father was maimed in that War, and I'm still privileged to be the honorary president of Erskine Hospital, where he and many wounded soldiers like him were cared for in their greatest time of need.

I saw at first hand how my father suffered agony on a daily basis. When you lose a limb it still feels as though it is there—and the pain is terrible. I have looked at some of the video footage of the carnage in France and I always burst into tears watching it. My feelings on the subject run very deep.

My father was always reluctant to talk about the War but over the years I gleaned more and more from him. I remember watching a TV series about the War with him, and he never said a word. They came to Passchendaele and at the end he just said to me: "That's just what it was like. The shell holes were filled with water and if you went out to pick up a wounded man on a stretcher, and on the way back there was a barrage and he fell off into a shell hole, that was it. You didn't bother with him, you just left him to drown because he had fallen maybe 20 feet deep."

John Lauder's fiancee Mildred Thomson left more than £80,000 to Erskine Hospital when she died in 1975. If ever there was a love story that was it. Mildred never married. And at Erskine they have a ward named the Lauder-Thomson ward.

They gave me a suitcase of Miss Thomson's. It sat in a cupboard for long enough, then one night sitting at home on my own I brought it down and opened it up. Hoping she might hear me, I said: "Forgive me, it's not nosiness which causes me to do this, it's caring."

Inside I found 350 press cuttings about Captain Lauder's death and many personal things, messages and letters from his dad, Sir Harry, although all their love letters had been destroyed. There was also a book of tiny photographs, the size of cigarette cards. In one picture she is sitting on a chair with John Lauder sitting at her feet. She has her arms around his shoulders and he is holding her hands. They are sitting in front of the coal fire, gazing into the flames. For me, that image says everything about the women back home and says everything about the men who had to do a terrible job. It has love written all over it.

I had two enlargements made of that photo. One I keep in my own home, and the other hangs outside the ward at Erskine Hospital. Underneath are their names and dates, and the words I had inscribed: "Oh, there's somebody waiting for me", a line from a Harry Lauder song. It's very sentimental, I know, but that's me.

389

*   *   *

In theatre one of the most important rules is to have a good company. Each night when I arrived to perform in *The Ship* I said jokingly to the girl on reception: "Any calls from Hollywood for me?"

And she would laugh back: "No, Mr Logan, no calls from Hollywood."

That happened every night until one night there was a different girl on the phones.

"Any calls from Hollywood?" I said.

"No, Mr Logan," she said as I turned to go. "But the phones have been really busy."

A wonderful moment.

I was at the initiation ceremony when Bob Hope joined the Grand Order of Water Rats, an organisation of showbiz people which mainly raises money for charities. You have to be invited to join this great organisation, and I'm privileged to have been a member for many years.

For me, Bob Hope is one of the all-time great entertainers. Evidently he and his wife were staying at a big hotel when one of the organisers went to his room to discuss what would happen at the initiation ceremony. Hope was an elderly man by that stage, but when the guy from the Water Rats arrived Hope was in a dressing-gown making notes of his gags.

"Is he always like that?" the man asked Hope's wife.

"Since the day we married," she said. "If he has a show to do all his concentration goes on that."

Clearly he's a consummate professional and always has been. I saw his last appearance in Glasgow at the Concert Hall when he virtually shuffled on stage because he had been having leg trouble. During his act the music director would occasionally leave the orchestra to remind him of the things he should be talking about.

"Golf!"

"Oh yeah, when I was playing golf . . ." and he carried on into a familiar routine. He also showed clips from his films as part of the show. And what a dancer he was. He had danced with Jimmy Cagney, and Jimmy Cagney was an incredible dancer. Together they were just magnificent.

That was a few years ago, and I thought then that if ever a man should have been invited to have lunch at Buckingham Palace it should have been Bob Hope. Apart from anything else, during the War people like Hope and Bing Crosby provided the only glimpses of brightness in people's lives.

Newspapers were no fun; all they would tell you about was people being killed. But their films provided the light away from the blackout.

However, Bob Hope was never invited to Buckingham Palace. In 1998 he was finally knighted, and received his award in America, but I couldn't help feeling that as he was in his nineties it was a little too late.

It's a symptom, I suppose, of an honours system that has never been perfect. I've got as much idea as the next man how that system works, but I'm glad it has been widened recently to recognise ordinary people who are doing extraordinary things in their communities. That's absolutely great.

When I received my OBE in 1996, I was so thrilled and delighted that it was for my services to entertainment. Now that was an accolade.

I was at Pitlochry Theatre, up to my eyes learning lines for the role of the Devil, who returns to earth as a minister, in *Mr Bolfry*, when Angela phoned.

"Are you standing up or sitting down?" she said.

"Oh don't tell me," I said. "It's a bill we've forgotten about. The gas is going to be cut off."

"No," she said matter-of-factly. "I have a letter here from the

Prime Minister saying he has it in mind to recommend to Her Majesty The Queen that you be made an Officer of the most noble Order of the British Empire."

"I don't believe it," I said, sitting down. "You're kidding."

It was a wonderful moment, but also frustrating because at that stage I couldn't tell anyone.

I wrote back immediately, and said I would be honoured if the Prime Minister considered me. Then I just had to wait, desperately hoping no-one would change their mind.

When I say I told no-one of the OBE, I tell a small white lie. I told one person—Joan Knight, a director of hundreds of plays in her lifetime and a wonderful friend. She took over the running of Perth Theatre when it was in a very bad way and transformed it into a wonderful place. Joan was awarded the OBE.

When Angela phoned, Joan was rehearsing us in *Mr Bolfry*. But she was dying of cancer, and I noticed she was very down, exhausted and tired. Who wouldn't be in her situation? She was fully aware of her predicament, and what she was facing.

One day when we broke for lunch I said: "Joan, darling, come outside with me for a wee minute."

She was with a girl in the corner making notes. And she seemed lower than ever.

"Joan, I've got a secret I can't tell anyone but I'm going to tell you," I said to her when she came outside.

"I've had a letter from the Prime Minister."

She knew instantly what I was saying. It lifted her spirits. I could tell because her eyes sparkled.

"Oh Jimmy, I'm so thrilled."

There are other honours I am very proud of for my services to entertainment. In 1988 the Jimmy Logan who left school at 14 and received no education in drama whatsoever became a Fellow of the Royal Scottish Academy of Music and Drama. In 1993 I received the Gulliver Award for excellence in the theatre, and the following year Glasgow's Caledonian University conferred an honorary degree on me, and I became a Doctor of Letters.

Shortly before Joan died she was awarded a similar honour by Edinburgh's Queen Margaret College. She was very ill when the ceremony was held at Perth's City Chambers, but she was still telling me: "It's great, Jimmy, you're a doctor and so am I."

Unfortunately she wasn't able to finish the meal following the ceremony. But before she slipped off she pulled me aside and said: "Jimmy, remember we said we would go out to lunch together."

"Of course I do, Joan."

"Well, I'm allowed out next week for my last lunch at my favourite hotel."

It was an eerie journey when Angela and I drove to that lunch, making our way up the road behind Joan and a dear friend of hers who joined us.

"I can't believe this is happening," I said to Angela. "We're driving up the road after Joan fully aware there's a watch of time just ticking away."

We had a lovely meal, returned to her house and then Angela and I left. Two or three days later Joan passed away.

Her funeral was beautiful. As I sat in the church I knew the beautiful music emanating from the organ was being played by John Scrimger, a superb musician who had worked with Joan for many years who was paying his own rich tribute.

Afterwards there must have been around 60 car-loads of people who made their way out to her remote burial spot.

Joan was a great woman of the theatre who was a great director, and great at giving kids their first chance in the business. She was the woman who gave people like Ewan McGregor, one of Scotland's biggest stars today, his first acting break. The theatre could do with more Joan Knights because, like Clive Perry and Adrian Reynolds, she had her finger on the pulse of the audience. And that is a rare gift.

*   *   *

I patiently waited for the decision on the OBE. I knew when it would be announced, but not if it would be announced. The tension was unbearable because although the Prime Minister, Mr Major, may have had it in mind, if he changed his mind that was it. Or when it went to the Queen she might have said: "Oh no. Not him." If it got out beforehand they would definitely say: "Now wait a minute."

As happens with the honours, the list officially comes out on a Saturday but the press always find out on the Friday to give them time to prepare their stories.

That Friday during rehearsals for my next play, *Mr Bolfry*, my mobile phone started to go bananas. Every newspaper wanted to speak to me, and I was just over the moon at the news. It seemed like the start of a great journey.

The performance of *On Golden Pond* on Saturday night was something I will never forget. The theatre was like a piece of magic. When I walked on stage the applause from the audience lasted about three times longer than normal. There was a wonderful warm feeling in the auditorium.

It was magnificent to be received in such a nice way, but I still had a job to do. I had to make that audience think I was Norman Thayer, not Jimmy Logan. The night went like a dream, and at the end my co-star Edith Macarthur stepped forward to say how thrilled everyone was for me. It was a beautiful speech from one of Scotland's finest actresses who, amongst other qualities, brings dignity to the theatre.

We went on to a party afterwards where another actress friend, Clare Richards, who had worked with me previously, presented me with a photograph of my father. It sounds sentimental, but as I looked at the photo she put her hand on my shoulder, and for a moment I could swear it was my father's hand on my shoulder saying: "Not bad, son."

I phoned Heather in Florida, and said: "What are you doing on November 10."

And she said: "Nothing."

"Well, Heather, I'm sending you a ticket and you're coming with me to Buckingham Palace."

I could hear floods of tears at the other end of the phone. The people she told in America were more impressed and astounded than the people I told. But the Royal Family are held in more esteem across there than they are at home.

Heather and Annie both came over, and the first day we were all in London Heather kept saying to people: "This is my brother and he's going to the Palace tomorrow to get an OBE."

And I was saying: "If you do that again, you're not coming."

That night Annie threw a party for me with about 20 relatives in attendance. The next morning the car picked up Annie, brought her to the hotel where we were staying, we got in and went to the Palace. It was all due to start at 10.30, but I was advised to get there very early to get a good seat. We arrived with forty-five minutes to spare. I was taken to the picture gallery while Angela, Annie and Heather went to the ballroom in the Palace.

The ceremony at the Palace was incredible, memorable because the organisation and presentation could not be bettered, ensuring that the day would never be forgotten by those honoured and their guests.

As the Queen pinned a medal on my chest for my services to entertainment I could have pinched myself. We had a wee private conversation, and I told her I had been a long time in the theatre. We didn't chat for very long, however; she only had 140 medals to pin on in an hour and a half.

Afterwards we headed back to the hotel for a celebratory meal with relatives and dear friends. At one point I headed outside to buy some aspirin for my Aunt Mona and bumped into a woman who said to me: "Jimmy Short!"

I had no idea who she was.

"I was at school in Gourock with your sister Heather when we were six years old," she said.

I took her inside to meet her old school pal who just happened to be over from America for my biggest moment. What a coincidence.

That night Mona and her son Robert took us to a wonderful club in London, and we had another four-course meal and champagne. Then a piano was wheeled in, and we all sang.

The following day my agent, Susan Shaper, took us out for more champagne. And then that night we went to see Sir Cameron Mackintosh's show *Martin Guerre*. During the interval the manager sent for us and served us more champagne.

On the Friday we drove back to Scotland, and on the Saturday night we went through to Edinburgh for a cabaret I was doing for the charity Friends of the Edinburgh Festival. There was more champagne. On the Sunday Angela organised a party for Heather, and even more champagne was downed.

And then on the Monday Heather flew back to America. What a week!

In the end I got about 200 letters from people—from the Secretary of State for Scotland down to ordinary nice folk—saying how delighted they were for me. People were always stopping me in the street to offer their congratulations.

I got the OBE as a recognition of my services to entertainment. But just what did they mean by services to entertainment? Had I broken my career down at that stage I would have found that the vast majority of it was spent on the stages of great theatres and music halls playing everything from the dame in pantomime to Chekhov's Uncle Vanya.

Not so extensive, however, was my list of film and television acting appearances. In the great scheme of things they had been relatively infrequent. Yes, *Floodtide* provided my big break in 1949, but after that my screen appearances were few and far between. In film there was *The Wild Affair* with Bud Flanagan in 1963, the *Carry On* movies in the early Seventies, *Living Apart Together* with BA Robertson in 1983 and, in 1991, possibly my biggest movie hit *The Accidental Golfer*.

Well, I don't expect you to have heard of it. When I say it was my biggest hit, I mean in Sweden. Don't laugh.

The Accidental Golfer was a Swedish-made film about a street cleaner who bets his pal he can become an international golf star. I play the old Scottish golf professional who tries to teach him. The film opened in around a hundred Scandinavian cinemas, and was a huge success.

Of course no-one in Scotland has ever heard of it. But that doesn't mean I'm never reminded of it here.

Angela runs a guest house, and whenever any Swedish tourists arrive I say: "I've been to your country. It's wonderful. Here, I'll show you some pictures."

The moment they see me in the pictures they say: "Oh, *The Accidental Golfer*." And they rush out and bring the kids in, shouting: "*The Accidental Golfer, The Accidental Golfer*."

It's quite an experience. I wore a moustache in that film so they never recognise me in person. But the minute they see my photographs that's it.

My film appearances dried up after *Floodtide* in 1949, but since receiving the OBE a couple of years ago it feels like I've been in more films than I've watched. No less than four big movies in quick succession; starting alongside the director Hugh Hudson and the lovely actor Colin Firth in *My Life So Far*, and finishing in the summer of 1998 with Billy Connolly in *The Debt Collector*. Remember what I said about how great this business of ours is.

What great times I had on those film sets, each with their own little stories that made the experience worthwhile. Getting a role on *My Life So Far* was by no means easy. For a start they told me there wasn't a role for me. But I arranged to meet Hugh Hudson anyway because he had directed such great movies as *Chariots Of Fire*, and would be a hugely interesting person to meet.

The problem was that he could only meet me for breakfast in a Glasgow hotel—the morning after I did a show in Dundee. And I was saying to myself: "Should I really be trailing away through to Glasgow at that time in the morning when I know I won't get a part in this film. Yes, of course I should."

So I left the City of Discovery at the crack of dawn and found myself with Hugh talking about anything and everything at eight o'clock that morning.

I said to him: "Now I know there isn't a part for me in the film but I just wanted to meet you and it has been great."

And he looked at me, and said: "Now wait a minute. There could be a part."

He left me with the casting director and, about an hour later, Hugh phoned up on his mobile and said: "Don't let Jimmy go. We've found him a part."

And that early morning journey from Dundee had been worthwhile after all.

In the film, originally titled *The World of Moss*, the part I got was of Tom Skelly, the old retainer on a big estate, and the landowner was played by Colin Firth. During the 1914-18 War he discovers that moss packed in the wounds of injured men seems to have remarkable healing qualities. The film is a love story, and Firth, happily married with children, falls in love with a French woman who comes to his estate with his Uncle Morris, played by Malcolm McDowell. Colin Firth's mother is played by Rosemary Harris.

It really is a marvellous story, all seen through a child's eyes. It's just a pity that, like so many other British films recently, it hasn't been released.

The scenic effects were just incredible. We arrived on the set in the middle of spring to be confronted by the middle of winter. A big outdoor ice skating pond was built and covered in snow by a special machine. Or it looked like snow. In fact it was paper. The trees roundabout were also sprayed white. It looked absolutely wonderful.

It took them a while to get it right though. The ice pond collapsed the first time they tried to build it. Then it collapsed again because there was too much salt in the sand or something like that. And the 200 actors and extras were getting a bit fidgety because they had been told they would all have to skate on this thing at the same time.

Finally they built the pond using wood then covered it with a special wax that looked like ice, before covering the whole thing with snow. The ice-skaters ended up using rollerblades but no-one would ever have noticed.

My Life So Far was followed by another film appearance . . . in the big screen version of the opera *Lucia di Lammermoor*. But they wouldn't let me sing. To round things off they gave me the part of the priest in the wedding ceremony.

Before we began, the writer and director of *Lucia*, Don Boyd, announced to the artistes and extras that he was so thrilled to be working with the Jimmy Logan he had seen as a boy in pantomime and *Five Past Eight*.

He introduced me to a first-class audience that included a tenor who had flown in from Los Angeles, some incredible singers from the Scottish and Welsh national opera companies, and many other fine artistes who were at the very peak of their professions.

His wonderful build-up made me nervous. I sensed a feeling of relief when he also said I would not be singing.

The most memorable moment came about eleven o'clock at night when all these wonderful artistes sang inside this spectacular 15th-century church. Its stone walls and ceiling provided the perfect acoustics in which to appreciate the sheer beauty of the human voice. Try it in your bathroom, and if it has got lots of tiles you'll see what I mean.

Next up was *Captain Jack* with Bob Hoskins. Before filming started my agent Freddie Young said: "You're booked for two weeks."

And I said: "I've seen the script. I'll do it in two days."

We filmed on the very tip of the most northern point on Skye— a beautiful spot. I played the local policeman in what we refer to as a cameo role, but I was in that uniform long enough to give a few fishermen a bit of a fright. They looked shocked when I wandered into this old stone building that smelled of tar and fish to see them gathered round a bottle of malt.

For a moment there was a stunned silence. Then they realised who I really was, and piped up: "Come in, Jimmy, come in. Have a dram, man."

As I had finished work for the day, I did.

In the film itself, another which has yet to be released, I'm only on screen for a couple of minutes. But I have to say that the shoot was a magnificent experience. It was interesting to see the beautiful scenery of Skye, and the pier on the lovely bay where we would film, disrupted by a movie-set full of caravans for make-up, wardrobe and dressing-rooms of actors, all powered by one big generator.

I don't think the sheep had witnessed such activity for a long time.

There were a few familiar faces on the set. The wardrobe designer was none other than Alyson Ritchie, who used to be my wardrobe mistress at the Metropole Theatre; the same red-haired woman who was probably mistaken for Moira Anderson. Molly Weir, who starred in *Beneath The Wee Red Lums* at the Metropole in 1965, also had a part.

Bob Hoskins, a small man only in height, was a star on both sides of the Atlantic who was the most down-to-earth guy you could meet. Being in his company you get the feeling after a couple of minutes that you've known each other for years. He is also an actor who knows his craft inside out.

His description of how, at one press interview, his American co-star turned his back on the press leaving Bob to field all the questions was just hysterical.

We spoke for a long time, and I told him all about devolution and the new Scottish parliament. He was trying to understand a situation which people outside Scotland don't understand. Mind you, people inside Scotland don't understand it either.

In 1998 I was offered the role of Billy Connolly's father-in-law in *The Debt Collector*, a film which is said to be loosely based on the life of Jimmy Boyle.

Billy has been very successful at what he has done, and I admire and respect him greatly for it, but I wouldn't do, or want to do, his type of act. Billy has turned swearing into an art-form but I know he is just as funny if he cuts the swearing from his material.

My problem is that I'm old-fashioned. My swearing used to be "damn" and "hell". Say words like that and you were sure to get a clip round the ear.

However, swear words today have almost become part of the language. People who use them don't think there's anything wrong in doing so.

That aside, Billy stands up there amongst the great comedians our country has produced. I only realised just how good he was when I took over Jimmie Macgregor's radio programme on the BBC, and decided to include a section on the Scottish laughter makers past and present. In order to analyse his work, I listened to many hours of Billy on tape. His analysis of life and people was quite brilliant.

I saw another side of Billy in an American TV comedy series. I didn't think the series was right. Despite this, it was obvious to me that Billy was a fine actor simply because he made me believe in his character.

When the series came off early the Scottish press suggested he had been a failure. I wrote a letter to one of the newspapers pointing out that although the series was not successful, Billy Connolly most certainly was. His subsequent appearance in *Mrs Brown* with the wonderful Dame Judy Dench showed just how talented he is as an actor.

Incidentally, although she is acknowledged as one of our great actresses, Dame Judy handles comedy like a dream, and her work in that field should serve as an education to anyone who has ambitions to raise laughter.

Filming *The Debt Collector* was the first time I had been given the chance to work alongside Billy. It's strange how long that took given that he cited me as his inspiration for getting into comedy in the first place, and I once booked a folk act at the Metropole called the Humblebums, of which a virtually unknown Billy Connolly was a central part.

When he was there he suggested that I might be interested in a new production he was writing called *The Great Northern Welly Boot Show*. I remember looking at him and thinking: "This show will go down the drain and take every penny you have with it. I don't think you've got a lot of pennies and I don't want to be responsible for your financial ruin."

How wrong I was because that show was the springboard to his great career.

We filmed my scenes in *The Debt Collector* in May and June in Glasgow, and I spent a great deal of time off set having thoroughly enjoyable conversations with Billy. I can tell you he is just as funny off stage as he is on it, and tremendously popular with the cast and crew.

There was one magnificent moment when he was hanging around waiting to do a scene. He was approached by an extra on the film who said to him: "Aw Billy, how are you doin'? Someone told me Jimmy Logan is here."

"Aye, he's over there," Billy replied. "Why don't you go over and say 'hello'."

"Oh, ah couldnae dae that," she said.

Of course, Billy fell about in hysterics at the thought she could walk straight up to him, but she was too nervous to approach me.

"Y'know, Jimmy," Billy said to me afterwards. "If you and I were leaving a theatre, they would say to me 'Good night, Billy', and they would say to you 'Good night, Mr Logan'."

I also have great respect for Billy Connolly because he is absolutely fantastic with children. During filming, when he was with the kids he was just wonderful. He never spoke down to them, but spoke with them. And I thought the fact he could handle kids in that way said a lot about the man. It's an art to be able to do that, and I thought that was just great.

My life may have revolved more around the theatre but I was always aware of the immense power of television.

You only have to think of the great Tony Hancock. When he was good on television he was absolutely brilliant. Britain came to a halt when his show came on.

But television is a terribly fickle medium. He did one show which wasn't so good and suddenly people weren't so keen on him.

Television is a bit like having a dear friend coming to stay every weekend. The first few weeks it's just great, and then you start thinking it would be nice to have a weekend without him.

But it's unwise to forget the times when these television stars were great. Too often people only remember the poor episodes, and not the good ones. Years down the line they barely get a mention, and other people who were directly influenced by them get all the credit.

I've not quite disappeared from the TV, though. In 1998 I played the father-in-law of Rab C. Nesbitt's son Gash. *Rab C. Nesbitt* is a wonderful comedy, and quite different from anything else I've ever seen. For instance, those who like *Rab C.* think it is just marvellous, whereas those who don't can't stand it. I don't think there are any grey areas. There won't be many folk who say they can take or leave *Rab C.*—they either love it or hate it.

What is quite interesting is that when I appeared in *Rab C.*, these nice matronly ladies were coming up to me, and saying: "I saw you in that programme *Rab C. Nesbitt* last night. Of course, I don't really look at it but . . ."

My backside they don't really look at it. I reckon *Rab C. Nesbitt* must have a secret army of watchers who sit with the curtains closed lapping up every minute, then tell people they wouldn't watch such rubbish in a million years. They won't admit they have this terrible failing in their character.

I must be honest and say I've seen some scenes on *Rab C.* that I couldn't believe were on television. There seem to be no holds barred. Then again, I've seen many scenes that were just hysterical, and brilliant comedy. It's a complete mixture.

I think it's only right to point out that I believe Gregor Fisher, who plays Rab C., is a finer actor than many people give him credit for. A brilliant actor.

I won't try to describe in any kind of detail why I feel this, but perhaps I should quote Sir John Gielgud, who, when one posh interviewer asked him to name his favourite actor, replied in his oh so "terribly, terribly" dulcet tones: "John Wayne."

And the interviewer, almost disbelievingly, said: "John Wayne?"

"Yes," replied Sir John. "And if you don't think he is any good put on the understudy."

Sir John was saying that people would only realise how good Wayne was when he wasn't there, and someone else tried to perform the same role. And I think similar parallels can be drawn with Gregor Fisher in *Rab C. Nesbitt.* He is absolutely marvellous as Rab C. No-one else could possibly be Rab C. He has made the character his own, and if you don't think he is any good put on the understudy.

My appearances as a television actor are limited. They include roles in the early Eighties in *The Mad Death* and *The Nuclear Family*, and the one-hour special *One Man's Lauder* on the life of Sir Harry Lauder, and *Standing Room Only*, a one-hour tribute to the early days of music hall for STV.

The Mad Death was a major series from the BBC about a rabies outbreak in Scotland. It was tense, gripping and often frightening television. The series was shown in countries like France, Belgium and Holland where rabies is known to exist. The amazing thing was that people in these countries saw *The Mad Death* and said: "I'm not going to Scotland if that's what goes on there." Which was quite hysterical because we were trying to say: "This is what happens if we get what you've got."

The Nuclear Family was a fascinating piece of television that painted a nightmare picture of Britain around the year 2000 where everyone lived in underground tower blocks.

The nice thing about that series was that it was filmed in London where the cast, including myself, Ann Scott Jones and Gerard Kelly, were treated a bit differently than in Scotland. The presumption was that we were stars who knew what we were doing. In Scotland it tended to be more along the lines of: "These are the Scottish artistes. Let's wait for the stars from London to arrive."

I also played a retired major who was a bit of a con merchant in the popular soap opera *Take The High Road*.

These soap operas take a lot of stick, but in my opinion that's unfair. I was very lucky because I working alongside actresses like Edith Macarthur and Eileen McCallum, and all the wonderful people involved in that show.

It was a lovely experience because there was a real family atmosphere on set. The tight schedules mean the cast have to produce what I call "instant acting". They are usually thrown in at the deep end and just told to do it. There is never time to get things perfect, and as a result the cast protect and support each other. And I have tremendous admiration for that.

My character was killed off on the top of Ben Lomond. We were flown up by helicopter to the top of this barren hill, and while we were setting this death scene up, a silver-haired woman in her seventies stomped up to us.

"I walk up here at least twice a week," she said. "It's a good walk."

And she trudged off at a fair pace, disappearing into the distance.

Half an hour later a younger man appeared, exhausted.

"Have you seen a woman with silver hair?" he said. "I'm trying to catch her up."

And we had got there by helicopter.

I often remind my audiences that I was buried in the cemetery at Luss. My mother-in-law at the time told me it was a lovely funeral.

Of all my experiences in theatre, one of my most recent was one my most memorable. It was in July 1998, and Sir Cameron Mackintosh had put together an amazing production featuring excerpts from all his theatre hits over the years. It was hard to believe this was the same Cameron Mackintosh who had once worn thick black-rimmed glasses, and arrived in Glasgow as a young stage manager when *Hair* hit the Metropole all those years ago.

Hey Mr Producer included great moments from musicals like *Les Misérables*, *Cats*, *Oliver* and *My Fair Lady* to name just a few. Sir Cameron flew in Julie Andrews from New York, Tom Lehrer came over from LA and many other star names arrived from all over the globe.

Jimmy Logan was also invited down from Scotland to sing 'I Love A Lassie', from my musical *Lauder*.

There was a Royal Performance with the Queen and Prince Philip which was filmed for charity. It was magnificent just to be part of it.

Angela and I were flown down to London where we were met by a car that took us to the Lanesborough Hotel. I went in for a drink at the bar, and glanced at the snacks menu. It was the kind of place where you could have a small fish supper for £12.50, or caviar at three different prices—£55, £75 and £99. If you wanted to wash that down with champagne there was a nice bottle for £175. So I phoned up from the room and asked: "What terms are we are booked in under?"

And the girl at reception said: "Bed and breakfast, Mr Logan."

The bed was £300 a night.

So I said to Angela: "You are getting your breakfast, and that's it."

It was a wonderful hotel, with unique service. Each room had its own butler.

Sir Cameron also flew down a full pipe band—18 of them— for my performance. It went like a ball with the band and myself entering down through the stalls, and up onto the stage. The audience gave us a great reception, and seemed to love 'I Love A Lassie'. Mind you, it's such a great song that was hardly surprising.

However, there were so many people in the theatre that the pipe band were sent across to a lovely bar-cum-restaurant where they were able to relax between rehearsals and shows.

"Just enjoy yourselves," they were told.

We rehearsed for one night, then one afternoon, then we had a show on the Sunday and Monday. Well, on the last night near the end of the show one girl from Cameron's office said to me: "Here, your pipe band drank £750 worth of alcohol."

I fell about laughing. What do you expect from a good Scottish pipe band? They've got to be able to help sell the products of our country. And they certainly lived up to that reputation. Mind you, with the prices they charge in London for a malt whisky it wouldn't take long to add up to a sizeable amount.

A lot of people didn't know I had written and starred in *Lauder*. In fact most people these days, and certainly the younger ones, know me for those Hogmanay TV shows or, of course, all the pantomimes. At least they know who I am.

Someone once asked Danny La Rue how they should describe him in the programme of the production in which he was appearing. With anyone else, he told me, they would have to put things like: "Joe Bloggs—the doctor in *Eastenders*" or "John Smith—the porter in *Crossroads*."

"Just put Danny La Rue," he said.

And that's a nice way of putting it. I'm fortunate that when the name Jimmy Logan is mentioned most people have heard of me. They have their own perceptions of course, but at least they know who I am in the first place.

They may remember me for those Hogmanay TV shows, the pantomimes or even the *Carry On* movies, but I hope the pages of this book have provided a small insight into a life which has encompassed so many rich and wonderful experiences.

People are always coming up to me, and saying: "Ah didnae know you did that."

The most recent example is *The Celtic Story*, a great play telling the history of this great football club. Amongst other characters, I play Brother Walfrid, who helped to found the club. The play was produced by Eddie Crozier, who has my admiration for putting his money where his mouth is, something that always takes courage.

Ironically enough, the play was directed and co-written by Dave MacLennan, the son of my dear friend and former neighbour, Hector MacLennan. I first met Dave when he was about 13 and here he was directing me in this fine play. Hector's daughter became the actress Liz MacLennan, and his other son is the Liberal Democrat MP Robert MacLennan.

It has to be said there was a degree of surprise when it was announced I was going to be in *The Celtic Story*, because most folk think I'm a die-hard Rangers fan, which is nonsense. I think that perception comes from plays like *Wedding Fever* where I played a real bluenose, but the real Jimmy Logan, if the truth be told, knows virtually nothing about football and most certainly doesn't support a team.

I never knew for instance that there was the Premier League, the League Cup, a league tie, the Glasgow Cup, the Glasgow Charities Cup, the Scottish Cup, the European Cup and so on. And when I was appearing in *The Celtic Story*, trying to remember night after night which one they won when was more than a little difficult.

Given that I was surrounded by a talented company who know every detail of Celtic's history from that first game on the 25th of September 1888, it was most certainly not in my interests to get my facts wrong.

My father, who was a Rangers supporter, once took me to an Old Firm match at Parkhead. At that time he was nearly 80 but it didn't stop him standing up throughout the game shouting his head off: "Oh ya mugs, I could've scored that masel." With his one leg, of course.

When I was about 17 I went to Ibrox for a Rangers match and really enjoyed it. I thought: "I could really get to like this." But my business was more important, and the next time I went back was years later when I was invited to one of the corporate hospitality boxes.

As for religion, I've never yet liked a man for his religion, and I don't care what religion it is. I form opinions of people based solely on whether or not they are decent human beings.

I was born a Protestant. My sister Heather married a Catholic and became a Catholic, and her little boy Domenick was brought up a Catholic. But that doesn't matter to me. What matters to me is that they are doing well in life.

When Domenick was six years old I took him flying, and as we approached my plane Whisky Charlie he said: "I'm all right, Uncle Jim. I've brought these."

And from his pocket appeared a set of rosary beads.

And I said: "Well, son, as I'm piloting the plane let's hope they work for both of us."

One of my dear friends, Helen McBride, was what I call a good Catholic mum. She came every morning with her three lovely children to tidy my house. At 42 years of age she was struck down by a cancer. I took her a parcel in hospital, and in that parcel was a pail, a spade, a swimming costume, a towel and all the things she would need when she got out of the hospital to go on her holidays.

Included was a big blue scarf with the inscription "Up The Rangers" and a blue Rangers hat. And I took a photo of her in the bed wearing that scarf and hat. We shared great jokes about that.

I offered to take Helen and her husband to Lourdes. She smiled at me in her lovely way, and said: "No thanks, Mr Logan. I'm all right."

She sadly died not too long afterwards.

That was back in the early Seventies, but when I opened in *The Celtic Story* in August 1998 her daughter sent me that photograph with a note saying: "My mother would have laughed at you being in *The Celtic Story* and been delighted to know that photo was in your dressing room." And I kept it there all through our shows at the Pavilion Theatre in Glasgow and then the Gaiety Theatre in Dublin.

I also wound up the rest of the cast somewhat by putting a notice on my dressing room door that read: "Lodge Anima 1223— All men to roll up their trousers legs and bare the knee before entering."

As I've said I'm not particularly religious, but I've spent just about every day over the last two winters in Scotland's churches. As I write this in the summer of 1998, I'm planning to do the same again this winter.

My reasons for doing this started a couple of years ago when a friend of mine, Reverend Andrew Mitchell, and his wife Anne asked me to come to his church in Gartocharn to present an evening of family entertainment.

I said: "In the church?"

And he said: "Yes. My congregation are fed up with television. They don't like the language, the violence, the subjects and the crudity."

He told me they wanted a night like they used to get in the theatre where they could sit with their families without being apprehensive of being offended during the show.

I was about to go into pantomime at Kirkcaldy and between shows I thought: "What am I going to do in the church?"

I could see the altar, the cross and all the things that might inhibit an audience. As I looked through my family photo albums I realised they were full of images that told the story of Scotland's theatre. I also looked through my collection of music hall postcards.

After sifting through mountains of pictures I came up with about 180 photographs which my friend Bill Cousins, who worked on the technical side of theatre all his life, made into slides. I also managed to get some rare film of Harry Lauder on stage in 1931, Will Fyffe and other great music hall artistes.

Carefully going through the humour and songs I would use, I finished up with two hours of material that I thought would be the right kind of entertainment for a church audience.

The small church in Gartocharn held 200, and the night I was there it was packed. As I looked round I realised I had found my family audience. Mum, Dad, kids and Granny. This was an

411

audience that had been lost for many years except when the pantomimes came round. It was a remarkable discovery.

I set up a tour of churches with Bill and my stage manager at the Metropole, Sandy McFarlane. My show, *It's A Funny Life*, played to 63 churches, and the following winter *Laughter In The Aisles* went into the same number of churches again.

As I write I am preparing for another tour. With the kind permission of Ronnie Coburn, I am using his title *Look Back and Laugh* for those shows in November, December and January.

Then it's off to Kiev for a Burns Supper before I come back for another season at Pitlochry Festival Theatre.

And so, here I am in my 70th year still working as hard as ever.

The annoying thing is that I'm always planning ahead, a trait I think I inherited from my dad. Even in his eighties he was talking about what great plans he had for this and that. In many ways, I'm the same. I'm the type of person who, if I opened a hotel with six rooms, wouldn't be satisfied until there were twelve rooms. When I played the Palladium Theatre in Edinburgh, I would think: "Great, but what about the Palladium Theatre in London."

I'm never satisfied. I'm always striving for something else. Most people, I think, are like that. Forever spending their lives hoping that something perfect is waiting just around the corner. But it rarely is.

It's certainly my nature, but an unfortunate part of my nature. All I'm doing is opening up trouble for myself. When I wrote the musical *Lauder*, I wrote these words:

"Each man in his life wants his life to mean something, not just to be like a tiny grain of sand with millions of others, washed away by the tide of time. He wants his life at least to mean something for himself and those around him."

412

Harry Lauder was regarded as a successful man, yet was always trying to scale even greater heights. I'm regarded as a successful man with similar traits, yet sometimes I envy the man who has an "ordinary" job—a builder, plumber, or joiner perhaps—who has reached inner contentment. He is content with the life he has and he is content with what he has achieved. Anyone who achieves that level of contentment has undoubtedly achieved a successful state in their life.

In my personal life I have now achieved that inner contentment with a wonderful, wonderful wife Angela. We have both found what we want out of a relationship, and we are both terribly happy. I see my children growing into young adults, and want so much for them to get the best life can offer. They mean the world to me. The important thing in life, I have learned, is not work. It's people. And for me, the most important lesson you can learn in life is how to love.

Yet, in my professional life, I fear I will never find that inner contentment. And that is not necessarily a bad thing. I don't envisage Jimmy Logan winding down in the near future. I've got too much I want to do. In 1998 I did a TV series, a film, a wonderful play and I've written this book. Then I plan to spend the winter in those great churches with my one-man show.

What a wonderful existence.

Turning 70 is not a major consideration for me. There's many a man I'm so heartbroken to see who at 40 years of age has tried to get a job, but can't. And he gets into a rut because his mind is not being stimulated. The boredom eats away at him.

In my opinion, you've got to keep hitting back no matter how hard it gets. It's no good sitting at home, saying: "I'm 40 and I can't get a job."

I've had to start again. On a few occasions. The question "How much is a frying pan?" haunts me.

My problem is that I'm a gambler, and I gamble on instinct. I gambled on a theatre and it fell down around me. I didn't sit down and work out what would happen if it went wrong. Rightly or wrongly, that's not the way I work. And I don't regret it for a minute. If I hadn't bought the Metropole, I would have been tortured for years wondering what could have been.

I find that when disaster strikes I'm the kind of person who thinks about the situation, and takes a large whisky. I only need one large whisky because I know if I drink any more it's not going to solve my problems.

The next morning I wake up, and say: "Right, what am I going to do about this?" And I attack it.

The only difference is that maybe these days I take two nights. I wake up the first morning and say: "Oh dear."

Or I wake up in the middle of the night.

By the end of the second night I'm ready to enter the thick of battle again. Another trait I think I have inherited from my father—a man who succeeded in life despite the agonising pain of an amputated limb.

As for the future I have plenty of plans, none of which I will divulge at the moment in case they don't come off.

Retire? I can't afford to. And why should I? I would be lying if I said I felt old. I'm reminded of my age by others.

At one function recently this lovely young girl came over to me, and looking into my eyes said: "You're Jimmy Logan."

She was glowing. Her face was just radiant, armed with a smile that said she was so pleased to see me.

"Yes, I am," I said, feeling rather good about myself.

"Oh," she said. "My mother will be so thrilled when I tell her I've met you."

I composed myself and replied: "And what about your grandmother?"

Then there are the terrible pauses, which I hate. Taxi drivers are particularly good at terrible pauses.

I used to get into taxis and the driver would say: "Saw you on television last night."

If there's a pause in these situations, you know you are dead.

"I suppose they make you do things like that," he would eventually say.

On the other hand, if he said: "Saw you on television last night. No' bad."

That meant he thought I was good.

However these days it's more along the lines of: "Nice to meet you, Mr Logan. How are you . . . feeling? (Pause) And are you . . . (even bigger pause) . . . getting on with . . . (enormous pause) . . . things?"

And what he is really saying is: "How long have you been retired?" or "Are you out of work?"

It's a wonderful business I'm part of. The variety and rich experiences it provides help keep many of those within our business that bit younger in the mind. I always said laughter should be prescribed on the NHS. It's a wonderful tonic.

After playing the Empire Theatre in Greenock, a woman came up to me and said: "Y'know, Jimmy, I'm having terrible trouble just now. My husband has walked out on me, he's taken the kids, I've got no money and I'm behind with the rent.

"Everything was terrible until I was sitting in the gallery the other night and watched you and the family. I came out feeling as though I had had a fortnight's holiday because while I was in there I forgot all about my troubles and worries."

Laughter has tremendous value. I'm addicted to laughter. I love the sound of people laughing—it fills me full of joy and adrenaline. I love playing to family audiences, presenting good old-fashioned honest family entertainment. Seeing those people laugh, and enjoying what I'm telling them, gives me my biggest thrill.

I'm part of the greatest business in the world, and I hope I've been able to give a small flavour of that business on these pages. My only regret in writing this book is not being able to mention personally all the great and wonderful people I have worked with. And there have been so many.

Each one of them has contributed in their own way to a life of rich encounters that many people never experience. I am fortunate to have lived that life, and I'll always be grateful for it.

When I was filming *Captain Jack* with Bob Hoskins, I met a wonderful actress Helena McCarthy who had worked all her life on stage and film. We were filming outside a croft with a thatched roof and two Highland cattle in the yard. Helena was frozen stiff, and we went back to the hotel where I said: "I'll get you a drink to warm you up."

Then, doing the kind of stupid thing I can't stand people doing to me, I said: "So what have you been . . . (pause) . . . up to?"

And she trotted out a list of work the length of her arm.

"Well I was in an episode of *Casualty* and I have two other television programmes waiting to come out that everyone seems happy with. I also filmed a commercial in Morocco. My doctor has asked me to go in for a hip operation in November but I told him I have an audition coming up and if I get the part I won't be available until March. He said: 'Just let me know when you are free.'"

I said to her: "Helena, if you don't mind me asking, what age are you?"

She replied: "I'm eighty-eight."

Follow that, as we say in showbusiness.

It's the Helenas of this world that make me love the business I am in, and that's why, in 1999, I will be back at Pitlochry Festival Theatre.

I've enjoyed the last seventy years of this remarkable century. You could say its been a funny life.

But the new millennium is just round the corner and that's what

I'm looking forward to. Who knows, maybe I'll crop up on TV on the final Hogmanay of the 20th century. Or if I'm not in the Millennium Dome, I might even be the first Millennium Pantomime Dame.

Now follow that.

INDEX

K

L

M

P

Q

R